GARVEY

His Work and Impact

Editors:

Rupert Lewis and Patrick Bryan

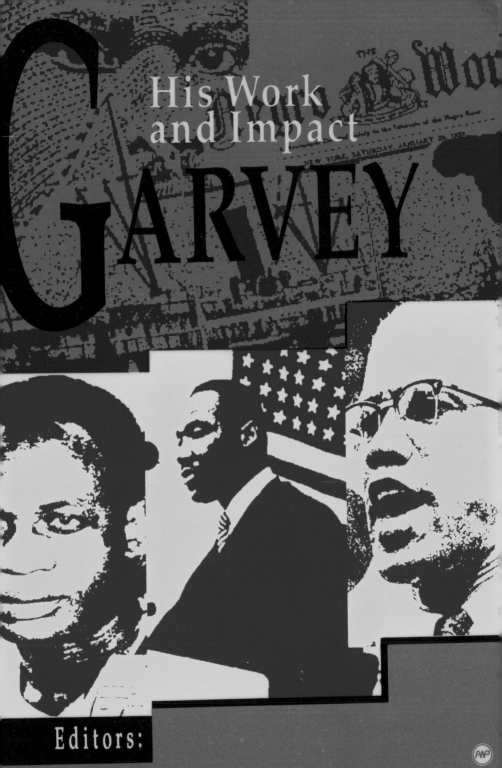

Garvey: His Work and Impact

Edited by Rupert Lewis and Patrick Bryan

Africa World Press, Inc.
P.O. Box 1892
Trenton, New Jersey 08607

Africa World Press, Inc.

P.O. Box 1892
Trenton, New Jersey 08607

First AWP edition, 1991

Cover design by Ife Nii-Owoo

Library of Congress Catalog Card Number: 91-70398

ISBN: 0-86543-225-2 Cloth
0-86543-224-4 Paper

Contents

Acknowledgements vii

Introduction 1

The Historical Background to Garvey and Garveyism

The Political Economy of Race in the Americas:
The Historical Context of Garveyism 11
Norman P. Girvan

The Development of a Black Ethnicity in Jamaica 23
Don Robotham

The Growth of Black Political Activity in Post-Emancipation Jamaica 39
Swithin Wilmot

Black Perspectives in Late Nineteenth-Century Jamaica:
The Case of Dr Theophilus E. S. Scholes 47
Patrick Bryan

Women and the Garvey Movement

Women in the Garvey Movement 67
Tony Martin

Women and the Garvey Movement in Jamaica 73
Honor Ford-Smith

Garvey and Cultural Expressions

Marcus Garvey and Cultural Development in Jamaica:
A Preliminary Survey 87
Beverly Hamilton

Unorthodox Prose: The Poetical Works of Marcus Garvey 113
Carolyn Cooper

Garvey Myths among the Jamaican People 123
Barry Chevannes

Garveyism and Religion

Garvey and Black Liberation Theology 135
Rev. Ernle P. Gordon

The Religious Thought of Marcus Garvey 145
Philip Potter

Pan-Africanism and other Ideological Issues in Garveyism

Garveyism, Pan-Africanism and
African Liberation in the Twentieth Century 167
Horace Campbell

Marcus Garvey and Nigeria 189
Adebowale Adefuye

The Ideology and Practice of Garveyism 199
Judith Stein

Garveyism: Organizing the Masses or Mass Organization? 215
William A. Edwards

Garveyism and Race in Jamaica and Cuba

Garvey's Perspective on Jamaica 229
Rupert Lewis

Race and Economic Power in Jamaica 243
Carl Stone

Race, Class and Social Mobility in Jamaica 265
Derek Gordon

The Left and the Question of Race in Jamaica 283
Trevor Munroe

Garvey and Cuba 299
Bernardo García Dominguez

Garvey's Legacy

Garvey's Legacy: Some Perspectives 309
Rex Nettleford

Select Bibliography 323

Index 331

Acknowledgements

The editors would like to thank Rex Nettleford, Director of the Department of Extra-Mural Studies, and Edward Greene, Director of the Institute of Social and Economic Studies, University of the West Indies, for their prompt agreement to jointly publish this book; Carl Campbell, head of the Department of History, and Carl Stone, head of the Department of Government, for their support. Thanks also to Janet Liu Terry, Publications Editor at the Institute of Social and Economic Studies, for her professional guidance; to Aubrey Botsford, of the UWI Publishers' Association, for editing, design and typsetting; and to Stephanie Harty for word processing. Alma Mock Yen, Christopher Cunningham and Conroy Julian, of the UWI Radio Unit, were always willing to assist us with the use of the conference tapes. Special thanks to Maxine Henry-Wilson and Judith Soares, who co-ordinated the conference, and finally to the Rev. Dr Philip Potter for his input.

Introduction

THIS IS A SELECTION of papers presented to the international conference ("Marcus Garvey: His Work and Impact") hosted by the University of the West Indies from 5 to 7 November 1987 to mark the centenary of the birth of Marcus Garvey. The objectives of the conference were: first, to assess and evaluate current scholarship on the life, work and impact of Marcus Garvey; second, to examine the issues of race, Garveyism and Pan-Africanism in light of contemporary reality; third, to enable scholars to meet and exchange ideas with a view to encouraging research and publications on the above; fourth, to be a stepping stone for the teaching of Garvey and Garveyism in schools.

The conference to a large extent successfully pursued these objectives. This publication, it is hoped, will further stimulate discussion on the wide range of issues which were raised by so many presenters and participants. The end-of-conference resolution stressed the importance of ensuring the early publication of the papers. Certainly, the availability of yet another publication on Garvey adds to the library of materials now available for the teaching of Garvey and Garveyism in the schools in the land of his birth and in which he was declared the first National Hero. Since Independence in 1962, Jamaican governments have mastered the art of recognizing key figures in the formation of the nation at the same time that the challenges they pose are either glossed over, ignored or re-interpreted to suit the interests of the ruling class. Nowhere is this more evident than in Garvey's case. It is therefore of great importance that the critical evaluation of the Garvey legacy not be lost in the sea of verbose tributes that were meant to bury the legacy with the body. This volume is also a homage to Garvey, in that it brought together black intellectuals and researchers on Garvey from Africa, the United States and the Caribbean who, together with surviving Garveyites, Rastafarians and others, engaged in a Pan-African discourse.

This was the second conference in Jamaica to reflect on Garvey's life, the mass movement he led and its impact. The first was sponsored by the African Studies Association of the West Indies and was held in 1973. This resulted in the publication *Marcus Garvey: Africa, Europe, the Americas,* by Rupert Lewis and Maureen Warner-Lewis (Mona, Jamaica: ISER, 1986). This second volume continues the tradition of bringing to readers recent scholarship on Garvey and Garveyism as well as current thinking on the issues of ethnicity and race in the New World.

The structure of this volume, with a few modifications, follows that of the conference. The first section, on the historical background to Garvey and Garveyism, opens with Norman Girvan's "The Political Economy of Race in the Americas: The Historical Context of Garveyism". The paper surveys the question of race in the

Americas, supplementing the traditional class/economic interpretation of the development of the region. Given that 1986 and 1988 marked the centenary of the abolition of slavery in Cuba and Brazil, respectively, the focus of this contribution is a timely one. Girvan argues that racist ideologies "became an integral and structurally 'necessary ' component of these societies, given the racial characteristics of the labour regimes which formed their base. Hence, ideologies of racial nationalism and race pride became equally necessary for the oppressed groups to defend and reclaim their sense of humanity, as well as to resist the most extreme and obvious forms of labour exploitation".

Don Robotham's paper is an overview entitled "The Development of a Black Ethnicity in Jamaica". It provides background material and raises important issues for historians and social scientists. Robotham argues that the development of a black ethnicity is probably the most "unrecognized and unstudied process in the history of people of African descent in the New World". He contends that this is the "central theme of the history of the people, right up to the present period...". Robotham's analysis provides a historical and analytical overview of the movement from ethnic particularism among slaves towards the formation of what nineteenth-century writers referred to as the "general Negro character". Robotham concludes by arguing that "there was a process by which a white ('backra') group was consolidated at the top; an entirely new group of Browns ('malatta') was established in the middle; and a black group ('nayga') was established at the bottom. This was the result of economic and political relationships ... which provided the foundation for the creation of new ethnic groupings".

The general studies by Girvan and Robotham lead into portraits and analyses of the contributions made by certain black politicians in the nineteenth century prior to the 1865 Morant Bay Rebellion and the career of a major black intellectual, Theophilus Scholes. Swithin Wilmot, in his paper on "The Growth of Black Political Activity in Post-Emancipation Jamaica", examines the political careers of Edward Vickars and Charles Price, who were elected to the Jamaican House of Assembly in the 1840s, and shows how they gained support among the free black population and helped to establish a tradition of black political activity which Garvey developed in the early twentieth century through the Universal Negro Improvement Association and the African Communities League, as well as through the Negro Political Union in the United States and the People's Political Party in Jamaica. Wilmot points out that Marcus Garvey Sr. was a speaker in August 1865 at a meeting in St Ann's Bay to protest conditions on the island.

Patrick Bryan's paper, "Black Perspectives in Late Nineteenth-Century Jamaica: The Case of Dr Theophilus E.S. Scholes", rescues a figure who has been lost to Caribbean scholarship. Scholes, a medical doctor, pastor and scholar, worked for several years in Africa and was an outstanding writer on topics of history and political economy. Bryan compares the work of Scholes with that of the Senegalese scholar Cheikh Anta Diop.[1] Scholes had argued that "the origins of European civilization go back to Africa through Egypt". He refuted the racist arguments that abounded in European academies, journalism, the church, and popular thought. Moreover, he had a profound grasp of nineteenth-century imperialism. In commenting on Bryan's paper, Locksley Edmondson recalled a discussion he had had with Ras Makonnen,[2] the pan-Africanist colleague of George Padmore. Ras Makonnen told him, "if you haven't read him [Scholes] or understood him you'll never understand pan-Africanism". Garvey would have known of T.E.S. Scholes, but more work needs to be done to establish whether there was a relationship, and if there was none, why. Scholes does merit, as does Robert Love,[3] a mentor of Garvey, a full-scale biographical study.

The importance of this section is twofold: first, the need to have a theoretical and historical understanding of the development of black ethnicity in the New World. Second, to understand the Afro-British intellectual and political tradition out of which Garvey came.

The section on women and the Garvey movement has two contributors: Tony Martin, the well-known Garvey scholar, and Honor Ford-Smith. This is an under-researched area in terms of biographies of leading Garveyite women, case studies of their role in the movement, and analysis of the treatment of gender issues within the UNIA. Martin, who has written a biography of Amy Ashwood Garvey – as yet unpublished – provides an overview of women in the Garvey movement. Ford-Smith critically examines the approach of the Garvey movement to this question from a feminist perspective. She argues that "the Jamaican feminist movement of the 1930s and 1940s was nurtured within the Garvey movement. Yet, strangely enough, the ideal image of womanhood upheld within the movement differed little from the ideal image upheld by the dominant colonial ideology in terms of the way it perceived women's position within the family, women's labour and sexuality. However, in practice, the movement was far more advanced. It offered black women a concrete experience in organization and leadership which was unrivalled in the island". She pointedly directs us not only to new areas for research but also offers new perspectives, without which historical analysis of the Garvey movement, in whatever part of the world we examine it, would be incomplete.

The relationship between the Garvey movement and the Harlem Renaissance has been commented upon by many writers,[4] but there is no comparable examination of the cultural work and impact of Marcus Garvey outside the United States. Cultural work was an integral part of the UNIA's agenda. Beverly Hamilton's "Marcus Garvey and Cultural Development in Jamaica: A Preliminary Survey" has diligently documented the range of Garvey's cultural initiatives in Jamaica as a playwright (as seen in his dramatic productions), as a cultural organizer at Edelweiss Park, and as a promoter. Garvey's cultural work utilized many of the forms of the 1920s and naturally reflected British influence, but the thrust of his efforts was towards black empowerment. Hamilton's contribution enables us critically to re-assess Garvey's work as an intellectual and to rethink Jamaica's cultural history in the 1920s and 1930s.

Garth White, an authority on Jamaican popular music, reminded conference participants that Garvey was a songwriter. Quoting from his popular song "Keep Cool", which had been choreographed by Patsy Ricketts in 1987 and performed by the L'Acadco dancers as part of their tribute to the centenary of Garvey's birth, White pointed out that the mood of "Keep Cool" is "deceptively quiescent and somewhat of a piece with the latter day 'Simmer Down' produced ... by Bob Marley and the Wailers, a group which continued the Garveyite tradition of pride in race and the use of cultural forms as implements of black liberation. Like 'Simmer Down', which advises a tactical holding of position by urban youth in the earlier sixties, 'Keep Cool' also brings attention to the fact that there is trouble, life can be awful, hard and dry, but be brave and true...".[5] White reminded us that the UNIA produced music in the gestatory period of the recording industry. As early as 1921, the Black Star Line did an instrumental recording of the Universal Ethiopian anthem. Moreover, in the Jamaican years the UNIA boasted the Universal Jazz Hounds. White provided many examples of Garveyite influence on popular Jamaican music, from the ska era to reggae, starting with the little-known Bongo Man Byfield, the famous Skatalites and Don Drummond through to Bob Marley and the Wailers and Burning Spear. Garvey is heard for the force he is among subsequent generations of creative artists.

Carolyn Cooper's "Unorthodox Prose: The Poetical Works of Marcus Garvey" offers textual criticism of Garvey's poetical works. Garvey wrote poetry, but he wasn't Claude McKay. His verses constitute an interesting source for any researcher, indicating that in Garvey's private moments as well as his public ones his preoccupation with his race was predominant. At least two generations of black radicals in the Caribbean since Garvey's time have ignored the cultural dimensions of liberation, obsessed by political and economic questions. Garveyism offers a timely corrective on the inter-relationship between politics, economics and culture.

Barry Chevannes's paper, "Garvey Myths Among the Jamaican People", explores the way in which Garvey survives among the people through certain ideas, prophecies and legends. A major source of these stories are the Rastafarians. A shortcoming of our conference was that we had no full-length analysis of the interconnection between Rastafarianism and Garveyism. While analysts of the Rastafarian movement have commented on the impact of Garvey on the emergence of Rastafarianism, there is no substantive historical analysis of the relationship between Garveyism and Rastafarianism.

The analysis by Chevannes covers popular culture and religion and leads directly into Ernle Gordon's evaluation of Garvey as an exponent of black liberation theology and Philip Potter's broad analysis of Garvey's religious thought. Work in this area represents an important effort to understand Garvey's world view. Gordon, in his presentation on "Garvey and Black Liberation Theology", argues that "religion for Garvey was neither mere philosophy nor ideology, but a relationship and an identity with the divine where the black man was not only an individual but a *person* made in the image of God, with dignity and self-esteem". Gordon links Garvey's politics with his religious ideas as part of his thrust towards liberation. He therefore sees Garvey as a forerunner of black liberation theology.

Potter, in "The Religious Thought of Marcus Garvey", comments on the originality of Garvey's interpretation of the Bible, pointing out that, for Garvey, "the Bible is a book which has to be read with discernment and discrimination from the core of its message about God, Christ and humanity. The Bible is a guide which obliges us to face our concrete situations in an existential way. And the concrete situation of the Blacks was the use of the Bible to denigrate them as children of Ham and 'hewers of wood and drawers of water', rather than as made in God's image and likeness and sharing the same blood relationship with all human beings. Garvey was in fact calling for a new hermeneutic, or interpretation, of the Bible.... The significance of Garvey's understanding of biblical interpretation is all the greater, because it is only in the last forty years or so that biblical scholars have been articulating this hermeneutical key". Potter differs with those who argue that Garvey was articulating a black theology, contending that he was preoccupied with developing a theology "which affirmed that humanity in all its racial variety finds its source and life in God".

There is a distinction between a political thinker who examines religion from the standpoint of political strategy and tactics and a political leader who is at the same time a religious person and thinker. Garvey belonged to the latter category. His thinking is more akin to that of Ernesto Cardenál and other religious figures in the Sandinista leadership of Nicaragua. The religious dimension of Garvey's legacy as presented by Gordon and Potter is an important piece in the predominantly secular scholarship on Garvey.

The section on Pan-Africanism and other ideological issues in Garveyism brings together four substantial papers. Horace Campbell's "Garveyism, Pan-Africanism and African Liberation in the Twentieth Century" argues that Garveyism laid the foundation for twentieth-century African liberation. As did so many other speakers, Campbell emphasized that "Garveyism was concerned with the fundamental principle of correcting the falsifications of the place of Africa, which is at the base of the intellectual culture of Europe.... Garveyism was one attempt by a section of literate Africans at the turn of the century to reverse the falsifications which have been presented in the history books". Campbell recognizes Garvey's contribution to a new intellectual culture and its importance in popular struggles. At the organizational level, Campbell points out that Garveyism was Pan-Africanism "at the level of popular mass organization to confront the ideology of racism". Important as the Pan-African initiatives of Du Bois were, there can be no doubt that the UNIA Conventions stood out for their international mass mobilization of representatives of black people in Africa and the diaspora. In his analysis, Campbell firmly links Garvey to the tradition of twentieth-century Pan-African struggle. He offers the conclusion that, "as long as capitalism exists, with its handmaiden, racism, the ideas which gave rise to Garveyism and Pan-Africanism will be part of the consciousness of Africans".

Adebowale Adefuye's paper, "Marcus Garvey, Pan-Africanism and Nigeria", examines Garvey's considerable impact on the Nigerian nationalists during the interwar years. Wearing both scholarly and diplomatic hats, as history professor and Nigerian High Commissioner to Jamaica, he argues that the "spirit and ideals of Garvey are strongly manifested in the activities of the present [Nigerian] government".

The session in which Campbell and Adefuye made their presentations also heard a stimulating comparative presentation by Locksley Edmondson entitled "From Garvey to Mandela: The Continuing Challenges of Black Liberation" and a challenging paper by the distinguished writer and historian John Henrik Clarke entitled "Marcus Garvey and the Concept of African Nation Formation in the Twentieth Century".

Among the more controversial papers at the conference was Judith Stein's "The Ideology and Practice of Garveyism", in which she contends that the strength of Garveyism "was its ability to incorporate ideas common among black elites and bring them to people who had been outside of political life". For Stein, Garvey was an elitist, and his models are seen as being rooted in British social-imperialism and American nationalism. The section concludes with William Edwards's "Garveyism: Organizing the Masses or Mass Organization?", which engages in a conceptual discussion of mass organization and of the masses in relation to the Garvey movement.

The final section, on Garveyism and race in Jamaica and Cuba, brings together Rupert Lewis's paper, "Garvey's Perspective on Jamaica", and Bernardo García Domínguez's, "The Garvey Movement in Cuba", along with a discussion of race in contemporary Jamaica. Lewis's paper examines Garvey's political ideas in the years after his deportation from the United States to show his importance to liberation struggles in the Caribbean and his relations with the Jamaican working class and the nationalist movement of the 1930s. Of importance also are Garvey's efforts to come to grips with the issues of race and class, which have been the concern of much social science writing in the region for nearly forty years.

Domínguez points out that the Garvey movement had support not only among West Indian migrants but among Cuban Blacks. The research being undertaken by Domínguez is of importance because of the dearth of studies on Blacks in Cuba during the early twentieth century. It enables us to understand the specific form of internationalist politics of the Garvey movement and the historic role of Blacks in the national liberation process in Cuba. Domínguez's paper originally formed part of a panel which heard interesting papers by Jennifer Ryan on Hubert Harrison, Régine Jasor on reactions to Garveyism in France, and Michael Case on Garvey and the general elections of 1930 in Jamaica.

Carl Stone offers a substantial analysis in his paper, "Race and Economic Power in Jamaica", documenting and analysing the patterns of ethnic economic power and assessing how far they have changed over the 150 years since the emancipation of the slaves. He concludes his overview of the ethnic economic division of labour in Jamaica since Emancipation with the statement that "there have been some important changes due to economic growth, economic crises, blackmarketeering, and sporadic political pressures which have opened up opportunities for black ex-slaves to move into professional, managerial and entrepreneurial roles in the Jamaican economy. These changes have enhanced black economic power, but it is the original intermediary ethnic minorities (Browns, Chinese, Jews, and Lebanese) that have benefitted most. A new urban-based capitalist class has emerged over the period, with Whites, Jews, Brown, Lebanese, and Chinese located in dominant positions of ascendancy". The issues raised by Stone are among the most sensitive in Jamaican political life. They are not frequently discussed; they are certainly not at the centre of Jamaican political discussion, though when raised as they were during the Garvey centenary considerable attention is paid to detouring them through charges of black racism. Of importance is that these charges of black racism are made not only by spokesmen from the propertied ethnic minorities but by a number of non-propertied black journalists and varied opinion makers who have thoroughly absorbed the mentality of opposing ethnic solidarity among Blacks whilst turning a blind eye to or ignoring ethnic bonding among the propertied ethnic minorities. Successful Blacks in the professions and struggling Blacks in business have also become major articulators of a false universalism which is not in their material interest. The changing of the old colonial order was too frequently seen narrowly in terms of political representative forms and insufficiently in terms of capital accumulation. Stone's conclusion goes into the significance of change for the development of productive forces. He concludes that "the powerful corporate controlling ethnic minorities are too numerically small as a class to provide the range and depth of economic leadership and private sector dynamism needed to move our economy forward to fuller employment, greater production and better living standards for the black masses. To expand the country's still narrow productive and economic base the inner circle of the corporate ruling class must be widened. Given the ethnic balance in the country this can only happen by promoting large-scale black entry into the corporate sector".

Trevor Munroe and Derek Gordon, writing from a Marxist standpoint, support Stone's arguments. Munroe argues for preferential treatment for Blacks vis-à-vis ethnic minorities in access to resources in the financial system, as well as the need for non-propertied Blacks to support propertied Blacks in this sphere.

Gordon's paper, "Race, Class and Social Mobility in Jamaica", examines the extent of changes in the position of the major racial groups in the post-World War Two period. Consistent with Stone's analysis, Gordon points out that "if the black majority is moving in the direction of expanding its middle class and capitalist class, it seems inescapable that this class development has not by any means exhausted its full potential, and is being held back by racial forces which operate directly in terms of economic power, as well as more indirectly through the medium of culture and ideology".

Munroe's paper, "The Left and the Question of Race in Jamaica", critically examines "the race perspective within that section of the left which traditionally assigns primacy to class contradictions". Examining the programmes of the PNP and the WPJ, Munroe reveals their gross inadequacies on the race question in contemporary Jamaica. Munroe states that there was an "absence of anything substantial on race in the classics, and a dogmatic approach encouraged the absence of anything substantial in our Marxism. What we should have sought, and did not, was a synthesis between our 'old' revolutionary nationalism and 'new' scientific socialism".

This final session was the most heated, controversial and political – in the broad sense of the term. The discussion saw a sharp interchange among Garveyites, black nationalists of varying persuasions, Rastafarians, Marxists, African nationalists, and Pan-Africanists. The discussion reflected differences not only in Jamaica but within Africa and the black diaspora among people who took the Garvey legacy seriously and some who were just waking up to its significance.

The concluding paper, Rex Nettleford's "Garvey's Legacy: Some Perspectives", provides a summation with a view to tackling the new challenges at the end of the twentieth century. Nettleford's focus is on cultural decolonization and the mastery of technology, especially communications technology, as well as "accessing power through the creative exercise of intellect and imagination". The cultural-technological focus is profoundly Garveyite, particularly as this relates to the reshaping of ourselves and our ability to transform our environment. His analysis was supported by the opening address, made by Marcus Garvey Jr., who spoke on the relevance of science and technology to black people.

Two areas not covered in this volume are oral testimonies and three papers discussing pedagogical problems in teaching Garveyism. Three Garveyites gave testimony: Mrs Ruth Prescott, Garvey's niece, provided a rare personal glimpse of Garvey the family man. Through her the audience shared what it meant to live with

Uncle Marcus. Mr Vivian Durham, former campaign manager of Garvey's People's Political Party, provided critical insights into the weaknesses of Garvey's 1930 electoral campaign. Durham, who published a book on Garvey in 1987,[6] died in mid-1988 and was one of the key links between the Garvey movement and Alexander Bustamante's Jamaica Labour Party. His death underscores the importance of oral testimony, as his departure has meant that valuable information on Jamaica's political history, especially in the 1930s and 1940s, has been lost. Mr Roy Carson acted in one of Garvey's plays put on at Edelweiss Park and worked with Garvey in the 1930s.

Papers of pedagogical interest, which could help to form the basis for another conference, were those by Dr E. Curtis Alexander ("The Pedagogical Implications of the Ideas of Marcus Garvey: Towards a Pan-African Studies Curriculum"), by Ms Barbara Sealy ("African Fundamentalism and Children"), and by Dr James Spady ("On Developing a Marcus Garvey Curriculum Module with the Marcus Garvey Memorial Foundation: The Philadelphia Public School Case").

While the 1973 conference focused on more-basic Garvey research, the 1987 emphasis was on the impact and implications of Garvey's life and work. Given that Garvey was essentially a political thinker and leader, he would have appreciated our concern to link analysis of Garveyism in history with the conditions of black people towards the end of the twentieth century.

Rupert Lewis
Mona, August 1988

NOTES

[1] Cheikh Anta Diop (1923–1986), Senegalese scholar and author of *Pre-colonial Africa, The African Origins of Civilization,* and *Civilization or Barbarism.*

[2] See *Ras Makonnen, Pan Africanism from Within,* as recorded and edited by Kenneth King (Oxford and London: Oxford University Press, 1973).

[3] See Joyce Lumsden, "Robert Love and Jamaican Politics" (Ph.D. thesis, history, University of the West Indies, 1988) for a substantial analysis.

[4] Tony Martin, *Literary Garveyism: Garvey, Black Arts and the Harlem Renaissance* (Massachusetts: The Majority Press, 1983).

[5] Garth White, "Music and Garveyism", paper presented to 1987 UWI Garvey Conference.

[6] Vivian Durham, *Marcus Garvey: Plights and Exploits* (Kingston: Golding Printing Service, 1987).

The Historical Background to Garvey and Garveyism

The Political Economy of Race in the Americas: The Historical Context of Garveyism

Norman P. Girvan
Consortium Graduate School of Social Sciences
University of the West Indies, Mona, Jamaica

Introduction

THIS PAPER SEEKS to locate Garveyism within the broader historical context of the political economy of race in the Americas. From the time of European conquest at the end of the fifteenth century, different racial groups were incorporated into the economy of the "New World" in different economic roles. These roles helped to define the character of the labour regimes which developed to service the European economic interest. The labour regime in any particular area lay at the base of the socio-economic structure which emerged from the colonial impact, with a corresponding ideology generated to bind the society together with a reduced resort to outright coercion. The characteristics of the labour regime also evolved through the different stages of capital accumulation in the capitalist centres – e.g., as commercial capitalism gave way to industrial capitalism.

Racist ideologies, it will be argued, became an integral and structurally "necessary" component of these societies, given the racial characteristics of the labour regimes which formed their base. Hence, ideologies of racial nationalism and race pride became equally necessary for the oppressed groups to defend and reclaim their sense of humanity, as well as to resist the most extreme and obvious forms of labour exploitation.

Colonial Labour Regimes or Racial Ideology

C.L.R. JAMES is said to have reminded us that "when Columbus landed in the New World, he praised God and enquired after gold". The initial interest of the Europeans was focused on the extraction and transfer of precious metals to the metropole: national wealth was held to be a function of the stock of specie. Hence, the colonial enterprise was concentrated on the indigenous societies covering the area of high plateau stretching generally from Mexico to Chile. These were relatively densely populated societies, with settled agriculture, onto which in large part centralized political systems (Inca, Aztec, etc.) had been superimposed, exacting tribute from the agricultural communities. It was these structures that the *conquistadores* sought to adapt to their extractive objectives. Indeed, the nature of the pre-colonial political order allowed for a relatively smooth replacement of the indigenous imperial class by the Spanish imperial class. But the fact that production had to be shifted both spatially and structurally to the requirements of gold and silver-mining meant that profound shocks were to be administered to the traditional forms of labour use.[1] Indian slavery and the institution of the *encomienda,* under which land, livestock and Indians were parcelled out to colonists by the Spanish Crown, became the characteristic forms of labour exploitation in this area.

The ideology required to cement and to legitimize a social order based on the absolute subordination of the native to the colonist was of necessity racist. It held the Indian to be an inferior form of animal life with an obligation to work for his masters and whose only hope for admission to the status of (subordinate) humanity lay in accepting the Christian faith, which meant recognizing the authority of Spanish rule and therefore accepting the legitimacy of his own enslavement and subordination. In this way and through the medium of religion, a regime of racial exploitation was transformed from the ideological status of a crime to one of a Christian virtue and responsibility. The Christian conscience of the Europeans was soothed while the Indian was conditioned to accept his enslavement as a sign of his good fortune.[2]

Outside of the high plateau, a second geo-cultural region was the lowland areas of the Americas within the tropical zone, thinly populated by peoples with simple socio-economic systems. This area stretches from the Brazilian Northeast through the Caribbean basin to the US South, and was destined for a different social economy of exploitation. Climatically suited for the large-scale production of tropical crops which could not be cultivated in Europe, it lacked a large indigenous population to provide cheap manpower. Thus, tropical lowland America required the large-scale organization of capital, imported labour and transport facilities to bring the area within the orbit of European capital accumulation.

The Portuguese, deprived by the Papal division of the main gold and silver-bearing areas, showed the way through the production of sugar in the Brazilian Northeast. However, it was the development of a dynamic mercantile capitalism within the northern European countries – originally motivated by the desire to secure through trade a share of the enormous treasure that Spain was plundering from highland America – which was to make this area the principal source of wealth and capital accumulation for Europe in the seventeenth and eighteenth centuries. At the heart of the system was the institution of the plantation, encompassing a relatively large land area, producing on a large scale a single tropical commodity for export to Europe, and utilizing a large quantity of African slave labour.

As in the early period of colonization of highland America, the social categories of race, caste and class were co-terminous in the long age of plantation slavery in the Americas. At the top were the white masters, in the middle the mulattoes, and at the bottom the black slaves. Indeed, by the time the plantation system began its full development in the Americas Indian slavery had ceased, and the terms "Negro" and "slave" became interchangeable to all intents and purposes. As in the case of Indian slavery, an ideology of racism was generated and systematically applied to legitimize the outright exploitation of one race by another. This ideology, however, depreciated not only the cultural attributes of the subject race. It was certainly the case that African speech, religion, mannerisms and indeed all institutional forms were systematically denigrated as constituting marks of savagery and cultural inferiority, in order to deprive black people of a sense of collective worth.[4] Nonetheless, the ideology of racism to legitimize African slavery was probably significantly broader in scope than that used to legitimize Indian slavery in that it extended systematically to the physical, genetic and biological attributes of black people. The very colour of the African's skin was held to be the first and the lasting badge of his inferiority; as were the characteristics of his mouth, nose and hair texture.

The desired consequence of extending the ideology of racism from cultural to physical attributes was to ensure that the African, whatever his degree of success in assimilating white culture, was permanently imprisoned in his status as a slave inasmuch as he was permanently imprisoned in his black skin. To be sure, assimilation of white culture amongst the Africans was considered desirable and indeed actively promoted by the Europeans. This internalized values of white superiority and their own inferiority amongst the Blacks, and therefore facilitated the task of maintaining their subjection and regulating their productive activities. To the Blacks, the incentive to attain cultural whiteness was the possibility of securing positions of relative privilege and comfort within the slave community, such as those of headman and house slave. But the Europeans were covered because by defining inferiority in physical as well as cultural terms, they ensured that no matter how culturally white an African might become he remained a "Negro" and consequently by definition a slave. This ensured that he remained permanently the subject of unmitigated exploitation and a source of primitive capital accumulation.

A third major geo-cultural region was formed by the lowland, thinly populated areas in the temperate zone, that is, the Brazilian centre-south, Argentina, Uruguay and Chile, and North America apart from the US South. Ecological factors meant that these areas were originally cast in the role of potential competitors with the mother countries. Thus, during the colonial period proper (fifteenth to eighteenth century) in South and North America the temperate lowland areas were in no way a principal focus of colonial activity, and were considered to be far less valuable than the gold- and silver-bearing areas and (subsequently) the plantation colonies. Indeed, those members of the pauperized and/or persecuted classes in Europe who managed to escape to become settlers in the "new countries" were able to secure foreign exchange only by selling their products to the principal colonial export economies. Structurally, therefore, these areas constituted the poor, underdeveloped peripheries of the major centres of colonial prosperity in the highlands and amongst the plantation colonies of the tropic lowlands. Hence, in the colonial period, Chile was a periphery of Peru, and the New England colonies a periphery of the American South and of the West Indies.

It was the transition from commercial capitalism to industrial capitalism in Western Europe in the nineteenth century that made necessary the massive and full-scale incorporation of these areas into the international capitalist order. This transition was itself fuelled by the dynamics of accumulation within commercial capitalism, anchored on slave-based production and trade; but having emerged within the womb of commercial capitalism the new industrial capitalism now required the dismantling of the mercantile system.[5] The process of proletarianization of the European peasantry which accompanied the industrial revolution at once created demands from the temperate areas for food to satisfy the growing urban populations and supplies of surplus migrant labour from Europe to provide the manpower for such production.

But the terms upon which labour was incorporated into the accumulation process in temperate lowland America were radically different from those applying to the areas based on Indian and African labour. In the first place it was free labour – more properly wage labour – rather than slave labour. In the second place it had a high degree of ethnic and cultural similarity with the employer class. This had important implications for the nature of the ideology was to be established. Ethnic-cultural similarity meant that it was not feasible to use a racist ideology as a means of social control; a regime of wage labour meant that this was in any case not necessary. Indeed, so far as the white community was concerned, the required ideology was precisely the opposite of one which taught that membership of the labouring group automatically condemned one to permanent underdog status. It was necessary to establish the ideology that any white worker, no matter how poor, illiterate and unskilled he might be, could by his own efforts achieve middle-class and big-capitalist status. For by promoting the belief in the possibilities for vertical mobility for the whites – of which the United States represents the fullest expression – class antagonisms could be dampened, and the European migrants could be persuaded to accept the consolidation of national bourgeoisies in these countries.

Whereas the terms upon which Indian and subsequently African labour were incorporated into the American colonial/capitalist economy were a predominantly racist ideology directed against the worker, for the European workers they were not. It followed that for the Indians and Africans the ideological aspects of the struggle against oppression had of necessity to contain a strong element of racial-cultural consciousness; i.e., an assertion of race pride, dignity and worth, both intrinsically and as opposed to the alleged superiority of European peoples and their cultures. So far as the attitude to European culture is concerned, the starting point must necessarily be a questioning of the alleged benefits of the European "civilizing" influence and a diagnosis of its truly brutal and exploitative nature.

Indeed, in the period of outright enslavement of the Indian and African, resistance was racial not only in terms of its ideological content but also in its concrete political objectives. When Indians and Africans took up arms against their oppressors – for violence was the only meaningful form of resistance available under the circumstances – their first concern was typically to kill as many white people as possible, or otherwise to remove them physically. For the Indians, this meant eliminating an alien people who had forcibly invaded and occupied their land, so that their previously independent communities could be re-established. The political objectives of African rebellions involved establishing new, independent black communities in the new world to which they had been brought. Where the rebellion was capable of capturing a whole country or large area, the Blacks sought to establish an independent state modeled along European lines. Haiti is the classic example of this, but there were several other notable attempts.[6] In other cases, the African armed resistance had the more limited objective of establishing autonomous village communities within an overall white-controlled territory; the Jamaican Maroons and the "Bush Negroes" of Suriname being two of the most successful of these.

The racial content of the struggle was also expressed in the form of instances of joint Indo-African operations against the whites. Juan Bosch records numerous instances of these in the Caribbean islands and on the mainland in the early years of Spanish colonization.[7] In this connection, he makes a number of crucial points:

> In fact, the Indians were enslaved in identical form as the blacks and Indian slavery was organized with the same methods as those used for African slavery.... On some occasions Indian rebellions were exclusively Indian, but in others black people participated; sometimes the opposite took place, i.e. black people rebelled and were joined by some Indians. Uprisings of some frequently stimulated or provoked those of others. The Indian and the Black understood each other well not only because both were under the same yoke, suffering the evils of slavery, but also because both had a social conscience of tribe and a very similar cultural level. Blacks and Indians were hunters, cultivators of communal lands, fishermen; their religions were animistic; their experiences of the white man were similar, as were their attitude towards him, either submission or hatred. The interbreeding of Blacks and Indians began at an early stage in the Caribbean, and children born of the mixture of the two races were known as "zambos" and were treated as slaves. The Indian and the Black influenced each other; they transculturated, as the anthropologists and sociologists say, and both had reasons to rebel against their owners.[8]

The Nineteenth Century: From Slavery to Caste

IT MIGHT BE THOUGHT that once Indian and then African slavery had been abolished and large numbers of European peasants began to flow into the Americas in the nineteenth century to become agricultural and industrial workers, the basis for a multiracial or non-racial proletarianization of the three major racial groups in the Americas would have been laid. In this scenario, social antagonisms would have been generated around property relations, e.g., peasant *vs.* landlord and industrial worker *vs.* capitalist. But this was not to be. A number of factors together conspired to ensure that racial categories continued to be an important component in the social economy of exploitation in the Americas and an important source of contradictions and antagonisms.

To begin with, the racist values and institutions that had become pervasive in these societies in order to justify the enslavement of the subject races could not be expected to be transformed overnight merely because of the passage of abolitionist legislation, or because Indians and Africans now worked for money-wages instead of receiving rations. Such transformations only take place in periods of revolutionary change, and this is exactly what the abolition of slavery was not: rather, it was a change in the basis of exploiting labour. One important result of this was that European immigrants entered societies in which racism was a way of life, and they naturally internalized such racist values and behaviour in the process of their assimilation into these societies. Nonetheless, the reasons for the persistence and reproduction of racism went far beyond mere cultural and institutional inertia. What it is crucial to recognize is that after the abolition of slavery proper, racism continued to serve an essential function in the overall growth and development of the international capitalist order in the Americas. That function was to maintain a large and, in some cases, virtually unlimited supply of unskilled, cheap and quiescent manpower for those sectors of the expanding economy which required it. To European workers, on the other hand, was assigned the role of supplying manpower that was to become both skilled and relatively high-income, thereby providing both the skills required by the dynamic sectors of the expanding economy and the market to consume its products and thereby permitting more accumulation. European migrants also supplied the individuals who would become big and small capitalists in their role as the principal agents in the development process. Hence, the racial segmentation of the labour force into what economists call "non-competing" groups was an essential characteristic of the process of economic development in the nineteenth and twentieth centuries. Correspondingly, racism had a contemporary ideological function to play in the process of accumulation in the Americas in this period.

Some clues as to what was taking place at this time are provided by the Brazilian sociologist Florestan Fernandes, in commenting on the virtually total non-participation of Blacks in the rapidly expanding economy of São Paulo after the Brazilian Abolition in 1888:

> The world of the whites was profoundly altered by the economic expansion and social development, linked at first to the production and export of coffee, and subsequently to urbanization and industrialization. The world of the blacks remained to all intents and purposes at the margin of these socio-economic processes, as if they were within the walls of the city but did not participate collectively in its economic, social and political life. Thus the [Abolition] did not signify modifications in the relative positions of the racial groups present in the social structure of the community. The caste system was abolished, but in practice the black and mulatto population continued to be reduced to a social condition analogous to what it had been before.[9]

He goes on to offer as one explanation that

> The "bourgeois revolution" effectively excluded the black man from the historical scene. It developed around two figures: the coffee planter, who perceived a growing social and economic role for himself resulting from economic expansion based on coffee; and the (European) immigrants, who tenaciously appropriated all the new opportunities, simultaneously eliminating the "negro" from the few relatively remunerative positions he had secured in artisan industry and small commerce. Thus the "negro" remained almost at the mar-

> gin of this revolution. He was negatively selected, having to be content with what now came to be known as "nigger work": unstable or difficult jobs, as miserable as they were underpaid.[10]

My view is that it was not so much that Blacks were excluded or did not participate in the São Paulo economy as that they were made to participate and thereby forced into selling their service cheaply to do the dirty work of the economy. And what Fernandes says about São Paulo bears an uncanny resemblance to the fate of Blacks in the United States after Emancipation: migrating to the northern cities in search of economic opportunities, which had been promised but never delivered. In the Reconstruction period in the South, American Blacks found that they came to be imprisoned in ghettos which were at once the physical and the symbolic counterparts of their being restricted to the dirty work of the urban economy.

Generally speaking, in the lowland temperate regions of the Americas into which large-scale European migration occurred, i.e., the Brazilian centre-south, Uruguay, Argentina, Chile, and North America apart from the US South, there were characteristic similarities in the racial pattern. White immigrants took the relatively highly-paid semi-skilled and skilled occupations in farming, industry and services, and benefited along with the owners of capital, in the tremendous growth and industrialization process taking place in these areas. Black people were maintained through a process of institutionalized racism in *minifundios* and share-cropping in the agricultural sector, and in the unskilled, low-paying and unstable occupations in the city. Indians were dispossessed through the expansion of the land frontier, and were either penned up on reservations or joined the Blacks in the cities as an institutionalized lumpenproletariat. Therefore, in these regions, while it is true to say that a process of proletarianization of all the races did occur, this process had a marked racial bias. It would be more true to say that the whites were proletarianized while the non-whites were lumpenproletarianized. This process was both reinforced by an ideology of racism, and in turn reinforced it. Since it benefited both white labour and white owners of capital it was characterized by a powerful alliance of attitudes and actions within the white community as a whole in relation to non-whites. Therefore it introduced a deep and abiding cleavage along racial lines so far as the development of a true "proletarian" consciousness, from the standpoint of relations of production, was concerned. Hence, it laid the basis for racially separate and independent strategies of mobilization amongst the black and Indian communities.

In the other regions of the hemisphere that were already densely populated by Indians (highland America) or Blacks (lowland tropical or plantation America) and into which European migration did not take place on a large scale, the non-white population remained in numerical majority. But economic and political power remained squarely in the hands of so-called creole elites, who were ethnically either of pure or mixed European stock and culturally of Euro-North American orientation, and who preyed upon the Indian and the black masses. The reproductive propensities of the socio-economic structure along racial lines are further confirmed by the pattern of immigration into these societies in the nineteenth and early twentieth centuries. Those European migrants who did end up in those societies tended to be rapidly absorbed into the warm embrace of the ruling classes, typically through the route of commercial and matrimonial activities. They thus came to occupy within a generation or so places of privilege and power in relation to non-whites who had been native to the habitat for centuries, sometimes millennia. On the other hand, non-white immigration to these societies, principally from Asia, came in at the bottom. It took the form of indentured labour to do low-paid, unskilled work on the plantations, which native Indian or black labour could not be induced to do.

We argue that in these areas both a racially biased labour regime and ideology were made to serve the objective requirements of "export-led" growth linked to the capitalist metropoles. In this period the industrializing world of the North Atlantic countries required cheap primary products to support its development, food for the urban masses, and raw materials for modern industry. From the techno-organizational point of view, there were two broad options open for the production of cheap primary products. On the one hand, productivity per man could be maximized; this required abundant natural resources, especially land in relation to population, skilled labour, and large supplies of capital. Conditions in lowland temperate America made this a feasible option: abundant natural resources were available in the area itself and Europe supplied the labour and the capital. In this option, although the incomes of farmers and workers were growing, the overall labour cost of production remained low because of growing productivity per man. Growing labour incomes also served to generate a dynamic domestic market, which could be used as the basis for a national industrialization.

The second techno-organizational option open for the production of cheap primary products was to maximize productivity per unit of capital and natural resources by using labour-intensive techniques. This option required that labour supplies be secured which were both plentiful and cheap. However, since a dense population also implies a high ratio of people to land, this option also requires that land should be secured easily against the competition of those already on it or with claims to it. This was only feasible where the social order permitted a sufficiently high concentration of politico-economic power to be mobilized to deprive the people of land and to secure their labour at permanently low wages.

These conditions were to a large extent met in the highland areas with large Indian populations, and the lowland tropical area where black "free" labour was available and Asian labour could be imported. Politico-economic power remained highly concentrated in these areas as a result of the heritage of the colonial order or (in the case of the Caribbean colonies) continuing colonial rule. Indeed it can be said that whether the constitutional status of these societies was that of independent state or European colony, the internal structure of all of them conformed to a situation of "domestic colonialism". To maintain the rigid stratification of these societies in the form of what was close to a pure "caste" system[12] and the continuing concentration of politico-economic power, the ethno-cultural differences which separated the creole elites from the masses could be made to serve an important ideological function. For they provided the ruling classes with a powerful instrument – especially in the historical context – to be used as an ideological justification of the miserable conditions, limited power and limited vertical mobility of the Indian and black masses. Thus, in the absence of the biological and cultural "purity" of the ruling class an individual was unfit to be a member of "society": by this means, the monopoly over politico-economic power was legitimized. The point here is that this racially characterized structure and ideology helped to legitimize the expropriation of non-white land and labour power at low cost in the service of the production of the cheap primary commodities required by capitalist industrialization in the North.

It can therefore be seen that the process of capitalist expansion in the Americas in the nineteenth and early twentieth centuries generated a new expression of the racial division of labour both within countries in the hemisphere and between them. Before, the categories white and non-white corresponded closely to those of master and slave or peon. Now, it became more complex. The white category comprised mainly *latifundistas,* industrialists, businessmen of medium-sized enterprises, and skilled and semi-skilled labour, while non-whites comprised mainly *minifundistas,* unskilled and low-paid rural and urban workers, underemployed and unemployed. Evidently, although the structure became more differentiated and the simple master–slave/white– non-white correspondence was broken, the relative ranking of the different racial groups remained the same, and ethno-cultural racism continued to be an important characteristic of intra-national and inter-national relations, and also an important instrument of exploitation.

It was therefore logical that resistance offered by Indians and Blacks to such exploitation would have a strong, if not predominant, racial content on the ideological level. In other words, in spite of the abolition of race slavery, Indian and black nationalism would remain not only "emotionally satisfying" but also objectively and ideologically relevant in the struggle against exploitation. The remarkable achievements of Marcus Garvey and his Universal Negro Improvement Association in the 1920s can be seen in this context. Garveyism captured the imagination of Blacks in the United States, the "Latin" republics of Central America and the Caribbean, and the Anglophone colonies in the Caribbean as well as some of the non-British colonies. In crossing the alleged "barriers" implied by language, metropolitan affiliation and constitutional status, the appeal of the movement demonstrated the structural similarity of the condition of black people all over the Americas over two generations after the abolition of negro slavery.[13] The *indigenismo* in the Mexican Revolution in the early twentieth century and also in Haya de la Torre's APRA movement, which emerged subsequently in Peru, can be seen in a similar light. In this context racial nationalism speaks to two distinct, though inter-related, conditions: first, the systematic denigration of the physical and cultural attributes of the subject race and, second, the objectively oppressed and exploited condition of the race, which the denigration of its attributes is designed to legitimize.

Naturally the Indian and black nationalism of the early twentieth century was different in its specific content from that which characterized the earlier rebellions against the condition of outright slavery. Garveyism, or Pan-African nationalism, was concerned with the subjugation and exploitation of peoples of African descent by white people in the Americas. It was also extended to a concern with the political and economic colonialism practised on the African continent by Europe. In relating the oppressed conditions of Africans in the Americas to those on the African continent, Garvey thus properly identified and spoke against the universal colonial condition of black people, and called for a Pan-African regeneration. The indigenismo of the Andean countries and particularly of Mexico and Peru was different in content and political objectives from black nationalism. In part it represented the assertions of the Indian peons in defence of their traditional communities against capitalist rural expansion, or their subjugated condition as an agricultural proletariat or semi-proletariat; in part it asserted their claims for participation in "national" – i.e. ruling-class – life. Culturally, *indigenismo* asserted the need to indigenize the "national" culture by removing its European bias and making it reflective of the indigenous culture.[14] Hence, Indian and black nationalism each responded both to the specific historical experiences and contemporary condition of the people who generated it.

On the other hand the struggles of white proletarians and other exploited white groups lacked the racial dimension. Whites had never had the experience of being a subjugated race, an ideology of racism was never utilized to systematically denigrate their physical and cultural attributes, nor were they restricted ascriptively to undesirable occupations considered at best miserable and at worst sub-human. The only sense in which an ideology of racial nationalism was important to the masses of white people was in the form of the ideology of white supremacy or superiority, which was the correlate of the ideology of non-white inferiority. In that sense white nationalism was used as an instrument for the subjugation and exploitation of non-white labour, ultimately in the service of the process of capital accumulation and with the white masses as its part material beneficiaries.

NOTES

[1] Celso Furtado, *The Economic Development of Latin America* (Cambridge, London: Cambridge University Press, 1971).

[2] Juan Bosch, *De Cristóbal Colón a Fidel Castro* (Madrid, 1970), p. 141.

[3] Lloyd Best, "A Model of Pure Plantation Economy", *Social and Economic Studies,* September 1968 and George Beckford, *Persistent Poverty* (London: Oxford University Press, 1971).

[4] Orlando Patterson, *The Sociology of Slavery* (London: MacGibbon & Kee Ltd., 1967), Chap. 4; Louis Lindsay, "Colonialism and the Myth of Resource Insufficiency in Jamaica", in Vaughan Lewis (ed.), *Size, Self-determination and International Relations: The Caribbean* (UWI, Mona: ISER, 1975), p 10.

[5] Eric Williams, *Capitalism and Slavery* (Chapel Hill: University of North Carolina Press, 1944).

[6] Juan Bosch, *De Cristóbal Colón*, pp. 138-156.

[7] Ibid., pp. 143-145.

[8] Ibid., pp. 138-139.

[9] Florestán Fernandes, "Relaciónes de Raza en Brasil: Realidad y Mito", in various authors, *Brasil Hoy* (México: Siglo XXI, 1968), pp. 124-125.

[10] Ibid., p. 128.

[11] Pablo González Casanova, "Sociedad Plural, Colonialismo Interno y Desarrollo", in F.H. Cardoso & F. Weffort, *América Latina: Ensayos de Interpretación Sociológico-Política* (Santiago: Editorial Universitaria, 1970).

[12] Rodolfo Stavenhagen, "La dinámica de las relaciónes interétnicas: Clases Colonialismo y aculturación" in F.H. Cardoso and F. Weffort, *América Latina*; and Beckford, *Persistent Poverty,* pp. 67-79.

[13] Marcus Garvey, *The Philosophy and Opinions of Marcus Garvey* (New York, 1969).

[14] Rodolfo Stavenhagen, "La dinámica", esp. pp. 194-5.

The Development of a Black Ethnicity in Jamaica

Don Robotham
Department of Sociology and Social Work
University of the West Indies, Mona, Jamaica

THE DEVELOPMENT OF a black ethnicity in Jamaica, or, for that matter, anywhere ı Afro-America, is probably the most unrecognized and unstudied process in the istory of people of African descent in the New World. The only notable exceptions re the early work of Frank Pitman, Sidney Mintz and Richard Price, and, to some xtent, the earlier work of Eugene Genovese. Yet that this is a central theme of the istory of the people, right up to the present period of the problems of nationhood, an hardly be doubted.

Today, this problem presents itself in the form of the characteristic problems of Third World country living in close proximity to the United States. Externally, the roblem is one of political and economic sovereignty. Internally, it appears as a cul- ıral and socio-political question: which are the classes (or alliance of classes) which an throw off the heritage of racism and cultural imperialism and promote the social, conomic and cultural emancipation of the people? What is the line of politics to be ursued, economically and politically, to secure these ends? What is the course of ıtellectual and cultural development to be pursued? In fact, as it is not difficult to ee, the external and internal issues are one.

Marcus Garvey and the nationalist movement he led and then inspired after 1938, ı which Bustamante and Norman Manley played central roles, represent the major ttempt in the colonial period to secure this emancipation. Michael Manley and the ocialist movement he led in the 1970s represents a further attempt, in the period ince Independence, to take up this challenge. The renewed elucidation and dissemi- ation of the ideas and work of Marcus Garvey, as well as the renewed study of the ntire national movement of 1938, marks a resumption of that process, after an in- erval of reaction, for the late 1980s and the 1990s.

And lest it be thought that this is a matter of purely Jamaican or Afro-American ıterest, it should be pointed out that the process of ethnic consolidation and the reation of a black culture has gone further in the Caribbean and Afro-America than nywhere on the African continent. Even in South Africa, where the process of eth- ic unification is most advanced, it is apparent that important and deeply felt subjec- ve and objective cultural contradictions still obtain and will continue to obtain for considerable period of time. What has taken place in the Caribbean and Afro-America therefore, with all its peculiarities and weaknesses, is a historic developmen whose international significance is yet to be appreciated and acted upon.

None of this is to imply any absurdly exaggerated, indeed ridiculous, claim tha the Caribbean and Afro-America are holding up to Africa the mirror of its future Nor is it to suggest that cultural unification processes in Africa will or should follov any particular uniform path. On the contrary, the difference in the historical politico-economic and cultural situations of Africa and the Caribbean make it in evitable that the continent will traverse an infinitely richer, more world-historica and, for that reason, more complex and difficult path. What we have in the Carib bean and Afro-America is simply one, historically very specific, case of unificatio from which some useful general perspectives can be derived.

The question is thus posed: what is there about our historical development whicl has produced this development and compells us to return to this national issue agai and again? This paper is an attempt to analyse the historical basis for the significanc of this issue during the period of slavery.

Ethnic Particularism Among Slaves

THE QUESTION that is being posed is probably difficult for many to grasp in its ful historical depth. This is certainly not through any failure of intelligence. Indeed, thi is simply itself proof of, on the one hand, how deep and thorough-going aspects o this historical process really have been and, on the other, of its persisting incomplete ness as a whole. Perhaps the best way to introduce this problem is by pointing to th contrast between the situation that obtained during the early period of the estab lishment of the plantation system in Jamaica in the closing years of the seventeent century and the early years of the eighteenth, and that which existed at the end of th slave trade in 1807.

At the beginning of the enslavement under the English planters, the most salien feature of the situation among the people was the depth of division between th various ethnic groups brought over from Africa. Writer after writer (the most loqua cious probably being Charles Leslie, in his dubious account of life in Jamaica at tha period), commented on this fact. The people captured and enslaved were fron various ethnic groups. They spoke different languages, had different family and kin ship systems, had separate folklores and religious systems and varied and differin economic and political systems. There is an underlying unity to the broad Niger Congo grouping (especially in its Bantu branch) from which the people in the mai originated. But this is at the broad historical level. This unity did not prevent th emergence of separate ethnic groups with their separate identities in Africa, just a it did not in Asia or Europe.

But there is an additional factor contributed by the slave trade and the particula state of relations between the different ethnic communities in Africa at the time This is the well-known fact that many of these groups were in a state of chronic war fare and enmity with each other. Whether and to what degree this enmity and war fare was due to the slave trade is not being discussed here, simply the fact of th existence of intense mutual hostilities. Thus, the problem which people faced o being enslaved in the Caribbean was not simply the problem of an abstract isolation and ethnocentrism of one group to another. It was also the fact of conscious and quite concrete traditions of "insularity" and even enmity between many groups from which the people came, stretching back in some cases to time immemorial.

Not much imagination is needed to realize that, whatever the historical roots of these hostilities, the fact of being sold into slavery, sometimes by members of the selfsame group now confronted in the Caribbean as fellow slaves, could only have intensified the ill will which had emerged between traditional ethnic groups. Recrimination and individualism rather than solidarity and co-operation was thus what characterized the initial phase of enslavement in the Caribbean. Hence, no doubt, the invention and elaboration of *obeah* at this period, as Donald Hogg suggested in 1955. The historical enmities from Africa were not only carried over but intensified by the initial phase of enslavement.

Contrast this with the period of the end of the slave trade leading into emancipation. The most marked feature here was the almost total subordination, if not absence, of any separate mother tongues, any of the traditional separate ethnic identities dividing the people. Other ethnic and social divisions there were, born of slavery and the slave trade. Of the traditional "tribalism", "Kromantsi" or otherwise, there was little sign.

Putting together his work on Jamaica (possibly copied from other historians of Barbados, I am informed by Dr Hilary Beckles), Leslie wrote in 1739 of the various peoples enslaved by the English in Jamaica:

> They are far superior in number to the whites, that one should think it would be unsafe, considering all circumstances, to live amongst them. The reasons of the Planter's security are these: the slave are brought from several parts in Guiney, which are different from one another in language, and consequently they can't converse freely; or, if they could, they hate one another so mortally, that some of them would rather die by the hands of the English than join with other Africans in an attempt to shake off their yoke.[1]

A point of similar significance was made by Edward Long, in the latter part of the eighteenth century:

> The Africans speak their respective dialects, with some mixture of broken English. The language of the Creoles is bad English, larded with the Guiney dialects, owing to their adopting the African words, in order to make themselves understood by the imported slaves; which they find much easier than teaching these strangers English.[2]

Writing during apprenticeship, on the other hand, the stipendiary magistrate Dr R.R. Madden struck an entirely different note:

> The distinctive marks of the several tribes have almost faded away since the abolition of the slave-trade, or merged into the general negro character, such as it is to be found at the present time all over the island.[3]

Sad to say, historians have had precious little to say about this "general negro character", apparently failing to notice in the twentieth century that which did not escape the eye of the expatriate observer of the nineteenth. To what this blindness has been due is an interesting subject, fit for a conference all by itself. What constituted this character? How was it formed? Against what obstacles and with what consequences? And, most critical of all, with what strengths, contradictions and weaknesses and *with what future*? Of these issues, hardly a word has been written, at least for the Caribbean. It is the issue of the basis for the formation of this black character during the period of slavery that I wish to try and address here.

Formation of the Black Character

WITHOUT ANY QUESTION, the single most important factor affecting the ethnic unification process of the people during slavery was the economic system of plantation slavery. Here one is referring to the system of organizing labour in gangs and the entire labour regime of the plantation, best elucidated in Barry Higman's classic book. The first thing to realize in this regard is that the policy of the planters on the association of labour from different ethnic backgrounds was the polar opposite of what it came to be in the colonial period of imperialism, when the various labour regimes were being established in Africa, in particular those associated with mining.

In Africa, during that later period, the substance of this policy was *apartheid*: each ethnic group was housed separately in separate compounds and even placed in separate occupational categories. Elaborate systems of headmen, usually selected by the colonial authorities and/or the employers, were established over each ethnic group in the workforce, thereby artificially fragmenting the workers into as many "tribal" contingents as possible.

Such a policy implicitly assumed that, left to themselves, economic and social processes would overcome traditional ethnic divisions and thus pose a serious threat to the power and economic strength of the colonizers. Hence the need to intervene in these processes and to divert them along a definite direction.

During slavery this was not the policy. Then the assumption was, with reason, quite the opposite: namely, that to keep too large a number of any single ethnic group together on a single plantation was to court disaster. On the contrary, the correct policy was to scatter people from the same ethnic background far and wide among a number of different estates so as to reduce the security danger.

This policy probably sprang from the practical imperatives of "supply" as much as from the political situation obtaining in Africa during the period of the slave trade. This was a situation of warring polities, the Asante, Denkyira, Akyem, Akwamu, and Fante in present-day Ghana, for example. These peoples not only had strong military traditions but also were familiar with forms of military organization in the *asafo* companies and the traditional Akan military organization, strategy and tactics; most of all, they had recent military experience combined with a fierce tradition of independence. To pursue a policy of concentrating groups of people of that background recently enslaved on relatively isolated plantations in Jamaica in the absence of any decisive technical-military superiority, and with a small white population, would have been suicidal. Indeed, where the exigencies of the slave trade did compel planters to accept such concentrations they were frequently confronted with revolts.

On the other hand, to scatter people of the same ethnicity was not only a sensible defensive policy, but brought positive advantages of its own, because, as Leslie pointed out, the ill will thus stimulated between members of the different ethnicities contributed in its own right to the security of the slave masters.

For these reasons, then, people were mixed into the labour force of the estate. Having been mixed, the principles which governed their distribution in the labour force and the various positions which they came to hold had nothing at all to do with traditional ethnicities or with the traditional economic culture. As Higman's work made clear, positions in the slave labour force were allocated on the basis of age and sex. Labour began at age five, when one went into the "piccanniny" gang until about 13, irrespective of sex. Thereafter, one was promoted to the "second" gang, which had a dual composition: young people of both sexes between the ages of 14 and 18, and "older" people beyond the age of 30 who had been partly worn out by toil in the "great" gang and had been retired to the second – already started on their bitter downward march out of the labour force into death or desolation. Then there was the "great" gang itself, made up of the sturdiest people, and in many cases, as both Higman and Lucille Mair have shown, more female than male.

Such was the composition of the labour force in the main. Other duties and positions existed, especially for men, in the field, in trades and in the household, but these were the main "posts" during slavery. These labour gangs were between twenty and forty in size and were under the supervision of foremen, the notorious "drivers". For the youngest gang, the supervisor was frequently a female, a so-called "driveress". For the other gangs, usually the supervisor was male. There is some indication of a tendency to select drivers from persons born in Africa, with the idea that this would ensure the severity of the supervision over supposedly Jamaican-born people. But firm evidence of this as a widespread practice has yet to be adduced.

In any event, that is somewhat beside the point here. More to the point is the change in the basis of leadership among black people now enslaved in Jamaica. The fact is that traditional ethnicity now no longer played a role in the establishment of that most revered and authoritative of African statuses – that of *elder* or leader. The leaders now were the drivers and other seniors selected on a basis related to the occupational and socio-ethnic hierarchy of the plantation system. The values of "success" and respect articulated by such a system of leadership were radically different from the basis on which the *abusua panyin* (lineage elder) and other village elders were chosen in Africa. Thus the aspirations of the people and their sense of themselves were transformed accordingly.

Equally to the point is the hours of work of the labour gangs mentioned above: outside of crop, the work day could last 12 to 14 hours. During crop at least 15 to 16 hours was normal, running into over 24 hours on some occasions as the "spell" from the field was brought straight into the boiling house without any break. Such a regime, was, of course, completely different from anything which had been known to the people in Africa. There, work took place in small kin-based groups with a domestic slave possibly also involved in the process. And, most critical from our viewpoint, these work groups in Africa were ethnically uniform and knew nothing of the harsh continuous toil under brutal supervision and "discipline" that was part of the labour routine of slavery.

Now in Jamaica, the situation was fundamentally different. The work groups were ethnically mixed, relatively large and laboured long and hard, continuously. Few things can break down stereotypes more thoroughly than being compelled to work together over long periods of time with groups of others with whom one is subject to a common punishment and misery and on whom one is dependent as a matter of everyday life and death. This process eroded traditional ethnicities, built up new social and kinship relations, and consolidated ties in the labour force on a single estate.

In short, the entire economic culture of the plantation system brought forth a new ethnicity among the slaves.

It was particularly effective, given the residential arrangements on the typical estate. Again there was no segregation by tribe in daily living on the estate. Apart from the house slaves, who lived near the Great House, and mulatto tradesmen, who to some degree may have lived apart, slaves of varying ethnicities were thrown together in the same slave village. Thus, the layout of the slave village was in complete contrast to the situation in the typical African village, where to this day people live beside others of the same ethnic background and the same language and customs. There, people of different backgrounds lived side by side, socialized with each other, had provision grounds beside each other, went to market together, and, most vital of all, formed family and kinship ties with each other. Religious beliefs and practices too, often a critical area of ethnic conservatism, were subject to this pressure from mixing and, consequently, so was the socialization, upbringing and culture of the next generations.

Within this sphere of everyday life, the issue of the socialization of children obviously occupies a special place. For it is not difficult to see that how this developed must have had a decisive bearing on the issue being discussed here. Again, general statements based on solid fact are not possible at this moment.

There is some evidence of a practice of upbringing in which children before the age of five would be brought together while their mothers were in the field and allocated to the supervision of an old Nana of the estate. If this is so, then it would mean that the erosion of traditional ethnicities among such "Creole" children would be particularly effective: between two (after the traditional long period before weaning) and four, they would be under a common, again collective, regime. Then, over the next seven years, they would again toil together in a probably uniformly "creole" "piccanniny" gang. No doubt important peer group relations would form during these years which would further intensify the process of the erosion of traditional ethnicity. But again, not much, if anything, is factually known of adolescence during slavery. All we can safely conclude is that the process of living and upbringing during slavery, whatever its details, did not run contrary to the tendencies which arose out of work but on the contrary reinforced and intensified those processes.

So far, the effects of economic processes have been confined to a discussion of factors operating on a single estate. But it would be a mistake to think that these were the only economic forces eroding traditional ethnicities during slavery. For contrary to the impression of slavery which many have – of a system composed of isolated plantations or so-called "total" institutions in which people lived sealed off each group from the other – the reality, at least in Jamaica, was quite different.

There were in fact many and varied ties between slaves on different estates. One is not referring to illegal and surreptitious ties, although these must have been legion. What is being referred to are perfectly legal and legitimate social ties which arose out of the system of everyday plantation labour and life.

Let us take some of the less obvious ties first. It was a fairly common situation in Jamaica for a single slave master to own more than one property, on each of which stood a labour force. A number of examples of this are given in Higman's book and especially in the thesis from which the book derived. For example, Bodles pen, then in the parish of St Dorothy and at present a government agricultural station, belonged to the same owner as Danks in Upper Clarendon: the well-known Beckford family. It was common practice for the workforce at Bodles to be walked up to Danks to work after they had finished their work in St Dorothy.

Other examples of this are given concerning another pen called Hope, near Porus, which I take to be the area of the present housing estate of Hope Village at the top of Melrose Hill in the parish of Manchester. Slaves from this property were also taken to work on another estate in the Pratville area which belonged to the same owner.

Even more intriguing examples come from lower Trelawny. These cases arise out of absenteeism as well as from ownership of multiple properties. Many of the estates in this area were operated by an attorney, who was also an owner, by the name of Tharp. Tharp on occasion consolidated the labour force from various estates, took slaves from estates of absentees for which he was responsible and utilized them according to his own imperatives. How widespread such practices were and how they operated precisely and with what network of ties arising, one is not able to say at present, although again, Higman's work contains many fascinating clues. But again it is fairly clear that such practices must have brought groups of people from different estates into regular contact with each other, as a result of the orders and actions of the slave masters, regardless of what they themselves did or wished.

Indeed, we now have even greater support for these ideas in the very important work done by Verene Shepherd at the University of Cambridge. She points out in her recent, seminal thesis that movement of slaves was an integral and inherent part of the operation of pens, which could not have functioned at all without slaves to carry cattle and products from pen to estate. In an extended personal note to the author commenting on an earlier draft of this paper, she made the following telling observations, which deepen, document and extend my basic thesis:

> The main role of pens was to produce commodities to sell to sugar and coffee estates among other properties and places. Pen slaves also jobbed on other units. In jobbing, working on the roads and in marketing the products of the pens, slaves were bound to come in frequent contact with those not in the same tribe....
>
> Even if planters tried to scatter tribes, because Jamaica was not a classical plantation [system] which operated as an enclave with little or no inter-property links, slaves were bound to come in contact. In

> fact, in 1834, out of 227 marriages between apprentices conducted in St Ann by the Anglicans, 30 involved couples from different pens within the same parish. 22 were "mixed" marriages, i.e. they involved [people] from pens and estates....
>
> In Jamaica, about one-third of the pens were owned by sugar planters who [tried] to integrate their economic activities, lessen their dependence on independent penkeepers and provide plantation inputs locally. Such pens were also used for seasoning fresh arrivals, a sure case for inter-tribe mixing, as pens were generally located in healthier parts of the island, for siphoning old estate slaves (who would then go to the pen to do light work), as well as provided jobbers for the estate when needed. Hence, Bodles slaves going up to Danks.... It was not only pens owned by the same planter which had links with estates. The independent pens also forged links with various other units....
>
> Tharp owned 9 contiguous properties. Two were pens, but he also owned a pen in St Ann, miles away from his estates. But this pen – Chippenham Park – provided some of his Trelawny estates with working stock. Both the internal marketing system and the internal commodity (plantation) trade are crucial for this.

We will return to these extremely important observations at a later point.

Another aspect to recall is that when properties went bankrupt or when through legacies or other reasons ownership changed, it could also result in the transfer of one body of people from one area of the island to another. Certainly this is what happened in the case of some of the people from Seaford, St Thomas, whom Lord Seaford transferred to his property at Montpelier, according to Higman. Transference of entire bodies of people was also possibly an occurrence of some importance during the coffee boom at the end of the eighteenth century and the collapse which followed it.

We also have to consider, as an important source of movement of people, the fact that roads had to be built and maintained, that sugar and molasses had to be transported to the docks, and that, above all, people had to go to their provision grounds on the so-called "mountain" of the estate. The well-known, pioneering paper on this subject by Mintz and Hall notwithstanding, a careful study of the entirety of the ground-provision economy during slavery has yet to be made. And yet it is of critical importance in understanding not only ethnicity but property ownership, inheritance, kinship and family ties, and the position and role of women, all of which, it is now established, varied during slavery. All of these processes stimulated movement, even if within limited areas, and would have played an important role in broadening the ethnic and social ties of the people outside the boundary of a single plantation. In the absence of concrete studies, one can only point to them as areas urgently in need of deeper investigation from a variety of angles.

The most important source of movement and another arena of ethnic erosion due to economic factors has been left to the last. This is the internal marketing system and what Shepherd refers to above as "the internal commodity (plantation) trade". The former, as Mintz and Hall long ago established, went back at least into the early eighteenth century, if not before. And the significance of the latter trade, involving airly extensive food producing and marketing operations by some estates, is not new, Higman and Shepherd having devoted a whole chapter to it in their theses.

But it is certainly hitherto an unexplored and hardly evaluated dimension of amaican socio-economic life during slavery, as far as the published material is con- erned, and enters not at all into the received academic conceptions of the planta- ion system. It involved the sale of fresh meat from pens to coffee and sugar roperties for the consumption of the white population, as well as the sale of plan- ains and other ground provisions to supplement the diet of the slaves. In return, the offee and sugar properties would supply the pens with rum and other produce, some- imes on a cash, sometimes on a direct barter basis. There was also the matter of the upply of meat and other produce to slaves in the towns and to the town population nore generally. All of these operations obviously required extensive movements of laves over a prolonged period of time and on a frequent basis. The scale, character nd significance of this entire, hitherto "hidden", antagonistic and dependent sub- ystem (a concept used by both Shepherd and myself independently of each other) s unknown to the present author. But it is clear that its existence, not to be confused vith the "peasant-slave" internal marketing system, adds yet more reinforcement to he basic argument.

Again, from our point of view, it is critical to appreciate that this was a perfectly egal means of association between groups of slaves. These key market places, such s Linstead market or Brown's Town market, Savanna-la-Mar or Lucea, were cul- ural centres of erosion and assimilation of the first order, just as they are today. Just s today, they must have been centres by means of which new items of material cul- ure were distributed and popularized. They must have also been centres of religious ctivity and dance and song. Just as today, these must have been important political entres for revolts to be planned. And many a friendship and family tie traced itself ack to the joys and vagaries of the marketplace. From this point of view, the inter- al marketing system and the pen and commodity trade, because of their economic ignificance during slavery, possibly played an equally important role in undermin- ng the old and encouraging the new during the period of slavery, as did the labour egime and the gang system.

Taken as a whole, then, one can conclude that the economic system which ob- ained during slavery, including the totality of operations connected to pens, provi- ion grounds, commodity trade and marketing, played a decisive role in undermining ne old ethnicities and laying the foundation for new and broader ethnic identities.

But the question naturally arises: if the economic system undermined old eth- icities, what did it create? After all, it is only for analytical purposes that the proces- es of destruction and creation can be separated. In real life it is nearly one and the ame process, the manner and context of the destruction to a great extent and at the ame time determining the character, form, content, process, contradictions, and osition of the creation of the new ethnicities which arose. We will return to this cru- ial question after the political experiences and other subjective processes which avoured the destruction of the old ethnicities are discussed.

Processes Creating the New Ethnicity

IN THIS SECTION, I propose to outline some of the subjective processes which contributed to the undermining of the old ethnicities and the erection of the new. In this connection, it is necessary to point out that while economic processes provide the basis for the experiences which undermined the old divisions, they are not to be identified as by themselves producing a change in the outlook and attitude of black people enslaved in Jamaica. It may seem obvious, but it is still necessary to emphasize that changes in outlook and attitude are subjective changes and can never occur until and to the degree that subjective processes initiate them. It is from this point of view that a full understanding of the operation of these subjective factors in and of themselves is indispensable for understanding the processes being discussed.

The most important of these was the political experiences of the people. First in importance was the experience of the cycle of revolt and repression and once again revolt. If one examines the entire history of our enslavement under the English, it is possible to discern three broad phases of revolt and, corresponding to these, three broad phases of our subjective development.

The first phase, up to the early years of the eighteenth century, is characterized above all by individual acts of resistance. No one should think that such a characterization is a confession of ignorance of the well-known facts of organized slave revolts going back to the seventeenth century. Such revolts did occur, but they were not the typical form of resistance of the period, whereas later they did become so. In the first phase of enslavement what we have are individual acts of heroism amidst a sea of demoralization and passivity. A person would run away, or malinger on the job, or destroy tools or stock or crops or buildings. Another would resist without any hope of support, or commit suicide in bitter-sweet release, and, to use the idiom of a later period, "fly away home". What was common to these acts was their spontaneity and desperation. Hence their lack of attention to organization, to mobilization, to ideology, to strategy and tactics and all the other necessary paraphernalia of politics.

Are they to be classified as "political" at all? Is it going too far to dignify them with the term "resistance"? Were they not as much confessions of impotence and defeat, the ultimate in selfish surrender? These are questions which are sorely in need of sober, but not abstract, evaluation. That is to say, such an evaluation must place itself squarely within the context of the time and of the options which were realistically available then. It must try to avoid the temptation to declare every malingerer a hero or denounce every suicide as spineless. Out of such a process of evaluation should come the realization that, while this state of affairs more reflected the chaos of the initial phase of enslavement, individual acts of resistance, when they really were acts of *resistance,* served at least two critical purposes.

In the first place they served to inspire. Out of this inspiration came the first traditions of indigenous folklore which were handed on from generation to generation to motivate others. In the second place, because they failed, they served as lessons: i became clear over a period of time that a more organized and purposeful approach to resistance was required.

This was the more so, as a terrible vengeance was wreaked on all resisters who were caught, to encourage others. The hanging and quartering and gibbeting and slow burning and burial alive and many other "cruel and inhuman punishments" which were routinely administered can never be forgotten nor forgiven. These are in crying need of study by our own historians and social scientists.

At the same time more careful consideration needs to be given as to the likely effect of this *White Terror* on the unification process. On the one hand, there is every reason to believe that when, after the crushing of Tacky's revolt in Jamaica in 1760, the head of the slain leader was severed and placed on a pike and marched on the long journey into Spanish Town Square to be once again displayed before the assembled people as a lesson never to be forgotten, the intention to terrorize was only too well achieved. Techniques such as these were critical for instilling deep within the breast of the then emerging new black ethnicity a sense of fear, inferiority and awe before the ruling white power; likewise, the peculiarly planter method used of combining this terror with tangible material reward for those who were willing to betray their people.

For example, at Worthy Park estate there existed the practice of freeing a single slave each Christmas out of the over 300 people enslaved. The slave who "behaved", who betrayed plans of revolt, could depend on the word of the planters: he or she would most definitely be freed. What is more, clear evidence exists to show that within the body of field slaves, who were overwhelmingly black, social strata existed. Drivers, for example, in some cases controlled the distribution of flour and mackerel and the allowances of "osnaburgh" the people were given to wear. They could also, on occasion, determine who did field work and of what intensity and who was punished and to what degree. They had power over the allocation of women to various jobs in the field and did not shrink from using such powers to their advantage. Where polygamy existed, it is quite possible that this was also a privilege accorded to drivers.

Some also had larger provision grounds than the others and were permitted routinely to utilize the slave labour force "on the side" on their own grounds. Some had stone houses, with flooring and proper roofing and wooden beds and tables and did not sleep on grass on the ground in thatched huts made of wattle, like the mass of the people. Others owned cattle and, let it be said, there were slaves who owned slaves during slavery, albeit a small minority.

One can safely say that the hallmark of this "planter method" of control during slavery was not simply the use of terror alone or of bribery alone. It was in the peculiar combination of calculated doses of terror and bribery that its effectiveness lay. It cannot be repeated too often that it is not possible to understand and appreciate the achievement of any of our national heroes, Marcus Garvey in particular, or of our failures as a people, if the insidious nature of the opponent they faced continues to be ignored. Yet the effect was in its very nature temporary and the policy a self-defeating one. Terror and bribery had existed before Tacky, yet they did not stop him. Both existed after Tacky, but did not stop Bogle. Terror and bribery were used by Eyre in 1865, as he so boldly declared, but did not stop Garvey and 1938. Of course, there is no need to relate the methods used against Garvey.

Paradoxically, what the policy of terror and bribery ultimately achieved was to elevate Tacky and anyone who revolted knowing the terrible retribution which faced them to a legendary and justly heroic status. In the long run, terror and bribery built up a tradition of cross-ethnic heroes and so played a vital role in creating that very sense of unity which it was its aim to shatter. At the same time, it compelled the people to develop their approach to the task of revolt on a broader basis.

This brings us to the second phase of the revolts. What characterizes this phase, corresponding roughly to the first half of the eighteenth century, was the organized nature of the revolts. Here we are dealing with true premeditated acts of revolt which involved groups of people, usually from a group of adjoining estates in the same parish. The Maroon revolts and Tacky's revolt are typical.

These revolts do not merely represent a political advance, but are themselves the expression of an ethnic and cultural advance along the road to unification. Their very possibility derived from the fact that a broader sense of unity had to some extent developed. They usually lasted longer because they were more organized, and in the case of the Maroons of course ultimately ended in victory for them. In this case, notwithstanding the price paid for this victory in collaboration with the slave masters, the basic effect of these revolts was to strengthen even further the traditions of struggle, even when the revolts failed.

At the same time they had their limitations, the chief being narrow-mindedness and an orientation to the past. These features derived from the fact that many of these revolts had an ethnic core, frequently "Kromantsi" (Akan). This traditional ethnicity provided the leadership and the basis to some degree for the intensity of the loyalties generated and so contributed materially to their success. But therein also lay the source of their failure. For this narrowness also acted to partly shut out others of a different ethnicity and so limited the scale of the revolt and its prospects.

Strictly speaking, these were not revolts against the system of slavery as such. They were attempts of one group of people to extract themselves from slavery while leaving the system intact for the others. The political aims thereby followed: Monica Schuler and others tell us that the aim of Tacky was to establish a chiefdom in one area of Jamaica along the lines of the Akan states in Ghana, not too differently from the Maroons. How people of other ethnicities may have greeted such a prospect one can only speculate. But it is not difficult to imagine that some who were traditional rivals of the particular Akan peoples involved may well have hesitated before that not necessarily very inviting prospect. The result of this narrowness was thus frequently failure.

The point to grasp however, is that this narrowness, the classic example of which is the Maroon–British Treaty of 1739, was no accident. It was an expression of the point which ethnic unity had and had not reached. This is why in evaluating the role of the Maroons and Tacky in this period one cannot be ahistorical. Absolute and abstract moral judgments are of no value here. It should be more than enough that, in the context of their time and the unity and consciousness it was then possible to achieve, they sought the maximum.

But compared to the third phase of revolt, the approach of the Maroons and Tacky really pales in significance. Again, it would be the height of naïvety to think that this was some personal failing and lack of foresight on the part of those movements. The truth is more complex: the broader historical scope of the last phase of revolt was not the doing of Sam Sharpe, Dove and Gardner. On the contrary, it was the broader and deeper unity – the new political culture that had evolved independently – which created them.

The central feature of this revolt was that its scope was unprecedentedly broad. It was not the traditional Maroon-type revolt, looking to the past and seeking to extract the particular group of rebels from the system while leaving it intact. This was a frontal attack on the very system of slavery itself. Its aim was a different system for all: freedom. It not only drew in people organized on the basis of traditional ethnicity but also included people who were already free who opposed slavery. Its ideological outlook and political culture did not derive from traditionalism but was heavily influenced by Christianity. It aimed not to go back to the past but to build a new social system which pointed to the future. These qualities and not so much the geographical spread and the duration of the revolt are what give it its historical significance.

These qualities were not the creation of Sam Sharpe and the others, but of the historical circumstances which had evolved to that point. In keeping with this situation, there is no mention of any traditional ethnicity having a significant role in the events. The ethnic and cultural situation had decisively changed. Very significantly, it was also the first revolt to attract a truly international dimension of support.

A very major role was played in this process by religious and linguistic changes as well as by the growth of an indigenous folklore, music and art. Mervyn Alleyne and Beverly Hall-Alleyne have done important work in this area in the field of linguistics which needs pursuing, and for religion there is the much-neglected work of Donald Hogg and Mary Turner.

Looking at the aspect of religion, a number of things become apparent. In the first place there is a rough correspondence in religious evolution to that which took place in politics, where, as is well known, religion played an important role. There was an initial phase dominated by *obeah*. Then came Myal in the middle of the eighteenth century, creating an ideology around which organization and broader (but still narrow) ties could be built. The really critical development, however, was the coming of the Black Baptists George Lisle, Gibb, and Baker towards the end of the eighteenth century and the broader and varied movement of "Native" Baptists, "Native" Methodists and other religious and cultural tendencies which were stimulated.

Judging from the work of Hogg and Turner, this movement really played a decisive role at the subjective level in constructing the synthesis for consciousness in which traditional ethnicities were dissolved. Its peculiarity lay in this: it established a new ethical code for the people not only in the religious but in the *cultural* sense. Or, to put it more accurately: in order for such an effective and transforming revolution of values to occur in the context of the time, precisely such deep religious underpinnings were required.

Among other things, this new outlook regarded each black man, woman and child as morally and culturally (but, alas, not socially) equal. It had no room for traditional ethnicity and did not recognize it. At the same time it was a *national* Christianity for black people and for all people and not for "European" Baptist or "European" Methodist or whomever. In the context of the time, this was, next to language, the clearest expression of the new ethnicity of which Madden wrote.

That is why this religious tradition – in the period of the "Baptist War" in 1831 and right after emancipation, when the hollowness of "freedom" without land and power became apparent, in the period of Bogle and Gordon and down to the end of the nineteenth century and the first decade of the twentieth under Bedward – constituted the main ideological and even organizational vehicle for the interests of black people. Prior to Garvey and the modern national movement, this Revivalist outlook was not just the leading ideological force among the people; it was second only to ethnicity as a fundamental structure of the culture as well.

Thus we had a process by which objective and subjective processes led, on the one hand, to the erosion of the basis of the old ethnicities and, on the other, to the creation of new ones, not mechanically and simply, but with difficulty, contradiction and discontinuity. Of course, demographic factors, such as the growth and distribution by region and by age of Jamaican-born versus African-born slaves were also important. But not by themselves. This, therefore, brings us to the issue of the character of these new ethnicities which were created.

Summary and Conclusions

IT CANNOT BE DOUBTED that in general this was a process by which a white ("backra") group was consolidated at the top, an entirely new group of Browns ("malatta") was established in the middle, and a black group ("nayga") was established at the bottom. This was the result most of all of economic and political relationships which provided the foundation for the creation of the new ethnic groupings.

The general position of all Whites derived from their economic and political position as the slave masters and the only group able to attain full civil and political rights. As a result of these common economic and political circumstances a notoriously, profligate and racist creole plantation culture evolved among them which has left its terrible stain on the country to this day and remains a chief feature of the heritage of the existing ruling classes and a major obstacle to the progress of the country.

The formation of a brown group likewise derived from economic and political relations. As Higman demonstrated, most of the relatively privileged domestic and trade work during slavery was a preserve of Browns who were slaves, especially brown males. Browns who were free, on the other hand (about half at emancipation), clearly enjoyed many caste privileges and owned property, including land and slaves. The majority were oriented for much of the period to privately petition the Jamaica House of Assembly to declare them "honorary Whites" in some legal respect or the other rather than to come together to challenge the system of slavery and privilege as a group, as Gad Heuman has shown.

Finally, the black group was consolidated as a group because economic and political relations made them in the main slaves – and, among slaves, the most oppressed and brutalized group in the field, with no rights whatsoever. Where black people were free, political and economic, as well as cultural, factors placed them in the lowliest position among the so-called free Coloureds and Blacks.

Thus, a critical feature of the dissolution of the old ethnicities and the consolidation of the new was that these new groups were not established side by side on an equal footing. On the contrary, as everyone knows, the White dominated the Brown who dominated the Black. All groups were required to accept the hegemony of the ruling group among the Whites.

As inevitably happens in such situations, the culture and outlook of the dominated groups found itself penetrated by that of the ruling group, which was itself stratified, against which the culture of each struggled to develop. And this struggle to develop and to throw off the racist hegemony was not only one against an external enemy but, of course, also against an enemy within.

Thus, an absolutely critical feature of the situation derived from the fact that *all the ethnicities which evolved were socially stratified*, as has been pointed out above; and strata within each subordinated group were found whose social position and material and status interests to a greater or lesser degree and in various situations led them to make common cause with the oppressor, who identified themselves as far as this was allowed with the dominant ruling white group, and who actively assisted in the subordination of their own and of others and in maintaining the overall system of oppression. Equally, other strata among the oppressed were driven to seek another destiny: to struggle to throw off the system of oppression. Thus the *class* basis of the new ethnicities is undeniable and, indeed, their class foundations and divisions gave a particular timbre to their sense of ethnic identity and cultural, social and political outlooks and activity.

Depending on which social strata from among the oppressed led the process of struggle, the process and outcome varied. Given the stake which some strata among the oppressed had come to have in the system of oppression, disunity, compromise and renewed subordination were often the result.

The most momentous of the occasions on which these divisions revealed themselves was in the "War" of 1831, when a division opened between the Sam Sharpe trend, which favoured strike action to end slavery, and those, like Dove and Gardner, who favoured armed struggle. Implicit in these divisions are differing views on a fundamental historical, socio-ethnic, economic and political issue: what the character of post-emancipation economy, society and culture would be like and on what basis the transition to capitalist wage-labour should be made. At stake was whether the transition would be on the basis of transforming slaves into wage-labourers on the selfsame estates on which they had previously worked, or on the basis of transforming them into a class of free "yeomen farmers" as the foundation on which socio-economic differentiation and market relationships would again lead to the emergence of capitalist wage-labour. The Sam Sharpe trend tended implicitly to the former outcome, while the Dove and Gardner trend tended to the latter. Clearly, these class issues carried with them very different consequences for ethnic and national development. And we know how the "debate" was resolved on that particular occasion and with what lasting results. Class and ethnic issues have thus always been inextricably intertwined. Whatever the outcome, all classes were compelled to confront the national and racial question and, indeed, represented different vehicles for solutions to the cultural, racial and national question, once the new ethnicities had evolved as the historical reality.

Therein, then, lay our historical peculiarity: a distinct new black ethnic group had evolved but within a system of racial and national oppression and on the basis of a definite system of property relations. *From this point on* a new historical dialectic and driving force was necessarily imparted to our development: either the full flowering, emancipation and triumph of this nationality or its destruction. Any socio-political movement, class, alliance of classes, or ideology which seeks to be relevant must address this as a central issue in the life of the people and the country.

ACKNOWLEDGEMENTS – In lieu of a bibliography, which is not appropriate here, I wish to acknowledge the work of Jack Alexander, Barry Chevannes, Michael Craton, Nancy Foner, Eugene Genovese, Derek Gordon, Douglas Hall, Barry Higman, Donald Hogg, Rupert Lewis, Lucille Mathurin-Mair, Sidney Mintz, Frank Pitman, Richard Price, Maureen Warner-Lewis, Verene Shepherd, Monica Schuler, Raymond Smith, Mary Turner, and many others whose work has, perhaps to their dismay, influenced me in arriving at some of the above analysis.

NOTES

[1] Charles Leslie, *A New and Exact Account of Jamaica* (Edinburgh: R. Fleming, 1739), p. 310.

[2] Edward Long, *The History of Jamaica* (London: T. Lowndes, 1774), Vol. 2, p. 426. See also pp. 403-475.

[3] R.R. Madden, *A Twelvemonth's Residence in the West Indies* (Philadelphia: Carey, Lea and Blanchard, 1835), Vol. 1, p. 135. See also pp. 126-135 for a brief account of tribal stereotyping during slavery.

The Growth of Black Political Activity in Post-Emancipation Jamaica

Swithin Wilmot
Department of History
University of the West Indies, Mona, Jamaica

I

THIS PAPER INVESTIGATES the role of Blacks in the politics of Jamaica in the first three decades after the abolition of slavery in 1834. The traditional focus in the literature on Jamaican politics in this period stresses the challenge mounted by the coloured professionals and merchants against the dominance of the white planter class. Only passing reference is made to the Blacks who held office and scant attention is paid to the Blacks who had sufficient property to vote.[1] Moreover, general assumptions about apathy and disinterest among the Blacks in the island's political institutions are held by scholars who have concentrated on the office holders and not the electors.[2]

Undoubtedly, the property qualifications for office and to vote at elections excluded the mass of people from the formal politics of the island. To contest a seat for the Assembly an individual had to be male and had to have an annual income of £180 from land, or landed property worth £1,800, or real and personal property worth £3,000. A voter had to be male and could vote on a freehold with an annual income of £6, or if he paid or received a rent of £30 per annum, or paid direct taxes of £3 per annum.[3] Nevertheless, Blacks in free Jamaica were determined to participate in the politics that governed their lives. It will be demonstrated that they were eager to represent themselves rather than to depend on Whites and Coloureds to do so. As far as the Blacks were concerned, this political voice in the island's affairs was crucial to the enjoyment of the new era of freedom and civil equality.[4]

Only two black men, Edward Vickars and Charles Price, were elected to the Jamaican House of Assembly before its dissolution after the Morant Bay rebellion in 1865. Research in progress indicates that they were strongly supported by black and coloured artisans and small farmers, some of whom were ex-slaves who had purchased land after Emancipation. Through the efforts of Vickars and Price and the support they galvanized among the free black population, the tradition of black political activity was laid in this formative period of free Jamaica.

II

EDWARD VICKARS was a Kingston landlord who learned his politics in the 1830s, when the black and coloured groups in Kingston first challenged the hegemony of the white mercantile community in that parish. The Blacks and Coloureds tried to establish a common political force; but this was frequently undermined by old racial and class divisions as well as by the political cunning of the white group. The old aristocracy of skin, nurtured in slave society, continued to weaken the attempts of the Blacks and Coloureds to develop joint positions, and Vickars was among the many Blacks who, in 1836, elected Daniel Hart, a Jewish provisions and dry goods shopkeeper, instead of John Samuel Brown, a wealthy coloured merchant.[5] By 1839 Vickars was one of three Blacks who had seats in the Kingston Common Council which administered the local affairs of the island's chief commercial centre.[6]

Once he had established himself in local government, Vickars turned his attention to the important task of winning a seat to the Assembly. In the general election of 1844 he unsuccessfully contested three seats, even though he had the strong support of the Baptist ministers, who had been mobilizing the small settler vote against taxation and the new immigration schemes and were urging the disestablishment of the Anglican Church. Indeed, it was the growing strength of the Baptist campaign that prompted the governor, Earl Elgin, to call a snap election a year early. Since the electoral law stipulated that claims to vote had to be recorded in the Island Secretary's Office in Spanish Town at least twelve months before, and in the Parochial Vestry Books six months before voters could exercise the franchise, the Baptist voters failed to make a great impression in the polls.[7]

Vickars's next opportunity came the following year, in a Kingston by-election. That parish had three representatives in the Assembly, and the tradition had been established whereby two seats were held by a white protestant and a Jew, who together protected the interests of the large and influential mercantile community, and the third was occupied by Edward Jordon, the leader of the coloured community, who also claimed to represent the interests of the Blacks.[8] Vickars and his Black supporters were intent on ending this tradition when one of the incumbents, George Orrett, a white merchant, died in 1845. The Kingston Blacks felt that the time had come for them to have one of their own to defend their interests, especially as the increasingly conservative Jordon had failed to support Blacks for local offices in Kingston in the 1830s and early 1840s.[9] Despite the firm support of Blacks and support from some Coloureds, Vickars failed to defeat Richard Hitchins, a white merchant.

An analysis of the respective voters underlines the race and class dimensions of Jamaican politics in this period. It is clear that Vickars's supporters were primarily black artisans who had purchased home lots in Kingston, while Hitchins' support was essentially based on the white mercantile community, Christian and Jew. Of the 168 votes for Vickars, the occupation of 82 has so far been ascertained. Fifty-nine, or 72 per cent, were artisans – shoemakers, bricklayers, carpenters, cabinetmakers, tailors, etc.; eleven were small shopkeepers and liquor retailers; six were professionals – ministers of religion, teachers, and solicitors; four were draymen; and two were fishermen. Of Hitchins's 213 voters, the occupation of 88 are known so far. Sixty, or 68 per cent, were merchants and wholesale/retail shopkeepers; 14 were artisans; and eight were professionals.[10]

Two years later, in 1847, Vickars finally won a seat to the Jamaican Assembly when he captured one of the three seats for the parish of St Catherine in a by-election. Vickars defeated Archibald Palmer, a white physician, who had the support of the white and coloured professional and planter class in St Catherine. Vickars polled 99 to Palmer's 43 votes. As was the case in Kingston, Vickars's support came primarily from the black artisan class in Spanish Town.[11] However, unlike Kingston, the St Catherine constituency included rural areas, and many of the artisans had been able to purchase small lots of land after 1834 as absentees and local planters sold off marginal land on pens and estates surrounding Spanish Town. Thus, 47 of Vickars's 99 supporters had purchased land since 1834; two bought under one acre; 19 between one and three acres; 15 between four and six acres; four between seven and ten acres; and seven between 11 and 15 acres. Twelve of these voters had bought lots on Patten Park, four had purchased lots on Glade Pen, and three had bought land on Kensington; all three properties were located in the hills two to three miles north of Spanish Town.[12] Thus, black artisans in St Catherine had more opportunity to acquire the freehold franchise than the Blacks in Kingston. This was the basis of Vickars's significant victory. The St Catherine Blacks rejoiced. When Vickars returned to Kingston by train from Spanish Town he was greeted by over a thousand supporters who carried him aloft through the streets of Kingston, the parish where he had been defeated in 1844 and 1845.[13]

Vickars's career in the House of Assembly reflected his commitment to improve the quality of life for Jamaican Blacks, who demanded fundamental changes in the new era of freedom. Along with other liberal members of the Assembly, Vickars strongly supported larger grants for popular education.[14] He urged the reform of the penal code as he opposed the reintroduction of whipping and pioneered measures to rehabilitate young offenders against the law.[15] He vigorously opposed increased taxation on the food imports of the poorer classes, while some of the luxuries of the rich were left at old rates.[16] He supported the imposition of a special tax on exports to defray the cost of immigration rather than have the cost fall on the general revenue.[17]

Moreover, rather than join the panic which spread throughout the planter class once England adopted free trade after 1846, Vickars argued that the decline of the plantations provided an opportunity to diversify the economy away from the traditional staple exports, thereby encouraging greater self-sufficiency and local food production. Jamaica, he argued, could no longer depend on "imperial bounty" and had to utilize her own "energy, enterprise and the adoption of rigidly economic habits" and had to rely on "our great natural resources". Then, he continued, Jamaica would be a beacon for the development of Africa, to which Jamaica was bound by "ties of consanguinity scarcely less strong than those moral and political affinities which hold us strongly to our allegiance to the Crown of England".[18] Such progressive views had very little support among the Jamaican ruling classes in this period.

Furthermore, Vickars was the only Jamaican politician who called for the introduction of universal male suffrage to replace the restrictive property qualifications for the franchise. This formed part of his campaign to broaden the base of representation in the Assembly and to give more Jamaicans a say in the political system in their country.[19] Neither the Whites nor the Coloureds were about to adopt such a measure, which was sure to strengthen the hands of the Blacks in the island's politics. Indeed, Vickars's call for universal manhood suffrage came twenty years before the United States adopted it, temporarily altering the political structures in the former slave-holding states where the Blacks enjoyed a majority.[20] His commitment to broaden the suffrage was not only political opportunism which would alter the colour of the Jamaican electorate. His principled approach was clear for all to see when he refused to scrutinize voter lists for elections he was involved in on the grounds that all adult males should have the vote.[21] It was part of his programme to safeguard the new civil liberties of the mass of Jamaicans and he was therefore consistently critical of measures to restrict the already narrow franchise,[22] or to limit the powers of the elected vestrymen vis-à-vis the nominated magistrates.[23] In free Jamaica, Vickars stands out as one of the few who consistently and unrepentantly demanded equal representation for Blacks, and for this he was accused of being raciSt[24]

Charles Price, a builder, was the only other black man to win a seat in the Jamaican Assembly. He achieved this during the general elections in 1849 by defeating a white solicitor, Francis Lynch, the son-in-law of Dr Turner, the Senior Magistrate of St Catherine and a member of the Legislative Council. Despite strong support from the professional and planter groups in St Catherine and St John and the public endorsement of the governor, Lynch failed to defeat Price, who had canvassed for some period before the election and attracted the firm support of black artisan and small farmers in the parish.[25]

III

THE STEEP PROPERTY qualifications for office ensured that no other black Jamaican entered the Assembly in this period. However, other liberal white and coloured politicians benefited from the support of black electors at various stages. In the 1844 general election, small freeholders, many of them black, helped to defeat planters in three parishes, Vere, St Mary and St Thomas-in-the-Vale.[26] By the early 1850s, black freeholders had profoundly influenced election results in other rural parishes, St James, Portland, Metcalfe and Trelawny. In the last-named parish in 1852, George Lyons, a Jewish shopkeeper with close business ties to the peasantry and political links with the Baptist communities in Trelawny, defeated Henry Shirley, one of the island's largest proprietors and later Custos of the parish.[27] An analysis of this election reveals that Lyons's 95 voters owned between them 3,645 acres, while Shirley's 43 supporters represented property totalling 64,763 acres. Thirty-one of Lyons's voters owned land in three Baptist free villages in the parish, Kettering, New Birmingham and Hoby Town. Twenty others owned between one and three acres of land elsewhere in Trelawny. Moreover, Lyons's voters paid £468.6.3 in taxes in 1851 while Shirley's 43 voters had paid £4,555.7.7 in that same year.[28] This victory underlined the electoral strength of the black freehold class once they were mobilized by black politicians or coloured and white liberals.

At the level of local government, the Vestry, lower property qualifications for office enabled Blacks to win seats as vestrymen. In the parish of Metcalfe, five of the ten vestrymen in 1853 were Blacks, and Donald Ball, a black tailor in Annotto Bay, provided leadership.[29] In the parish of St David in 1857, nine of the ten vestrymen were black and the mostly black freehold class dominated the politics of the parish.[30]

Furthermore, the broad mass of Blacks, excluded from the franchise and formal political participation, also demonstrated a keen interest in the politics of the island. Men and women, ex-slaves who were determined to consolidate their freedom, associated with black, coloured and white candidates for office who espoused progressive causes. When they challenged the planters in rural areas and the merchants in urban constituencies, hundreds of ordinary labourers and town dwellers gathered at the hustings to watch the proceedings. Election riots broke out whenever the people believed that the conservatives had used underhand schemes to defeat the liberal candidates.[31] When the "people's" candidates were victorious, as was the case with Vickars's victory in St Catherine in 1847, joyous celebrations in the streets of Spanish Town and Kingston reflected the broader masses' perceptions of the formal politics from which they were excluded.[32]

IV

THE GROWING INFLUENCE of the black small farmers and artisans quickly became a matter of great concern for the Colonial Office, absentee planters and conservative local white and coloured politicians. As early as 1839, Sir Henry Taylor, a senior official in the Colonial Office, had urged the imposition of Crown Colony government as the surest way to prevent a "future black ascendance" in Jamaica's politics. A decade later, Earl Grey, the colonial Secretary, returned to that theme and urged administrative reform before the Assembly became a "black parliament".[33]

In the 1850s the Jamaican Assembly considered a variety of measures that addressed the hysteria about black political influence in free Jamaica. More stringent registration procedures were adopted, and although the freehold qualification was unaltered a special tax of twenty shillings was imposed on claims to vote in 1858. Importantly, the pool of voters was increased so as to include clerks and overseers, who could be relied upon to strengthen the political base of merchants and planters.[34]

Both Vickars and Price felt the impact of this measure. Vickars decided not to seek re-election for St Catherine in 1860, as it was certain that Charles Hamilton Jackson, a prominent coloured politician, would defeat him.[35] In 1863 Vickars tried again in Portland, only to be narrowly defeated by two other coloured politicians.[36] In 1864 he made his last bid for the Assembly at a by-election to fill two of the three seats for Kingston. On this occasion he was defeated by two white merchants, as the altered franchise had clearly changed the composition of the Kingston constituency.[37] Price lost his seat for St John in the 1863 general election, as his black supporters had no vote.[38]

Nevertheless, the voice of black Jamaica could not be silenced even though it had been gradually diminished in the formal electoral process. The 1860s was a time of growing hardship for ordinary Jamaicans beset by low wages, growing unemployment and natural disasters – droughts and floods which destroyed provisions and drove up the price of food.[39] Blacks participated in island-wide meetings which complained of the apathy of the governor and the Assembly in the face of these hardships. Marcus Garvey's father, a mason, spoke at one such meeting, held in St Ann's Bay in August 1865.[40]

V

THE LEADERSHIP of the Blacks throughout the island was drawn from the ranks of black ministers of religion, teachers, artisans, and shopkeepers. The following is an extract from the speech of the Rev. Edwin Palmer, a black Baptist clergyman, at a meeting of Kingston Blacks in May 1865, and it summarizes the mood of black Jamaica in that crucial year in the island's history:

> The people are wretchedly poor and destitute as the authorities oppress them with the burden of taxation. The government only employs white and coloured men in public offices and the black man is neglected. The planters oppress and rob the negro and trample him under foot. Look at the merchants of Kingston, who do they employ?; only white and coloured young men; but the time will come when they will be compelled to do it. The time is come for the negro to throw off the yoke; it is time for him to arise and seek justice; he is the only beast of burden and trampled on all sides.... Let us be like men. Let us show our rights. I can tell these men who oppress us that we won't long submit to it. The Government forgets that the negro pays the largest amount of taxes yet they get no return. It is a wicked and oppressive government only for the poor negro. We form the greater portion of the community and yet there is nothing done for us, but we will show all these great big men what we will do in seeking our rights.[41]

Paul Bogle's march to Morant Bay in October 1865 climaxed this widespread agitation among black Jamaicans who, thirty years after Emancipation, were still demanding their rightful place in free Jamaica. Bogle's methods were unique but his passion for black justice was not. Blacks before him had tried to influence the political process to make it more responsive to their needs. However, the suppression after Morant Bay and the introduction of Crown Colony government shut them out of the political process. The struggles of Robert Love and Marcus Garvey renewed the black involvement in Jamaican politics and built on the traditions laid in the post-Emancipation period.

NOTES

[1] Gad Heuman, *Between Black and White* (Westport, Connecticut, 1981); Mavis Campbell, *The Dynamics of Change in a Slave Society* (Rutherford, New Jersey, 1976).

[2] William Green, *British Slave Emancipation* (Oxford: Oxford University Press, 1976), p. 321.

[3] Philip Curtin, *Two Jamaicas* (New York: Greenwood Press, 1970), p. 180.

[4] *Morning Journal,* 3 November 1847.

[5] C.O. 137/211, Sligo to Glenelg (Private), 18 June 1836; *Jamaica Despatch*, 13 January 1840, House of Assembly Poll-Book, Kingston election, 1836.

[6] *Watchman,* 11 June 1838.

[7] "The Elections – the Franchise", *The Jamaica Magazine,* 1, pp. 481-492.

[8] *Falmouth Post,* 30 September 1845.

[9] *Jamaica Despatch,* 13 January 1840.

[10] *Falmouth Post,* 14 October 1845; House of Assembly Poll Book, Kingston election, 1845; Island Record Office, Land Deeds; Jury Lists, Kingston; Jamaica Almanacs.

[11] *Morning Journal,* 17 and 18 July 1849; *Falmouth Post,* 14 September 1849.

[12] Island Record Office, Land Deeds; Jury Lists.

[13] *Morning Journal,* 3 November 1847.

[14] *Daily Advertiser,* 26 February 1855.

[15] *Morning Journal,* 4 December 1848; *Falmouth Post,* 5 December 1856; *Daily Advertiser,* 12 July 1854.

[16] *Daily Advertiser,* 14 March, 1855.

[17] *Falmouth Post,* 12 February 1852.

[18] *Morning Journal,* 5 September 1849.

[19] Ibid., 17 and 18 July 1849.

[20] Eric Foner, *Nothing But Freedom* (Louisiana, 1983), p. 46.

[21] *Morning Journal,* 3 November 1847.

[22] *Falmouth Post,* 22 February 1856.

[23] Ibid., 5 January 1852.

[24] *Jamaica Guardian,* 12 November 1864.

[25] *Falmouth Post,* 12 March 1850 and 28 June 1849; *Morning Journal,* 6 September, 1849; The former parish of St John is today's West Central St Catherine.

[26] "The Elections – the Franchise", *The Jamaica Magazine,* 1, pp. 481-492.

[27] C.O. 137/322, Berkeley to Newcastle, 26 May 1854; *Falmouth Post,* 16 and 17 September 1852.

[28] Swithin Wilmot, "Race, Electoral Violence and Constitutional Reform in Jamaica, 1830-1854", *Journal of Caribbean History*, Vol. 17, 1982, pp. 1-13.

[29] *Falmouth Post*, 26 January 1854; the former parish of Metcalfe is now South-East St Mary.

[30] C.O. 137/334, Report of Stipendiary Magistrate Ewart, 24 March 1857. The former parish of St David is now Western St Thomas.

[31] C.O. 137/309, Sir Charles Grey to Earl Grey, No. 17, 27 February 1851; *Colonial Standard*, 30 January 1851.

[32] *Morning Journal*, 3 November 1847.

[33] Wilmot, "Race, Electoral Violence...".

[34] Curtin, *Two Jamaicas*, p. 188.

[35] *Jamaica Tribune*, 9 July 1860; *Morning Journal*, 27 July 1860.

[36] *Morning Journal*, 17 March 1863.

[37] *Jamaica Guardian*, 12 November 1864.

[38] *Jamaica Guardian*, 19 February 1863.

[39] Douglas Hall, *Free Jamaica* (London: Caribbean Universities Press, 1969), pp. 239-243.

[40] *Jamaica Watchman*, 7 August 1865.

[41] Parliamentary Papers 1866, XXX, p. 107.

Black Perspectives in Late Nineteenth-Century Jamaica: The Case of Dr Theophilus E. S. Scholes

Patrick Bryan
Department of History
University of the West Indies, Mona, Jamaica

Longa tibi exsilia et vastum maris aequor arandum. (Virgil, Aeneid II)

I
Scholes in his Jamaican Context

IN 1875, AT THE AGE of nineteen, Theophilus Scholes left Jamaica for the Isthmus of Panama. He had been born in Trelawny, in Stewart Town, where he probably received his education at elementary school level from the Baptist community. As his religious admirers admitted ten years later when he returned to Jamaica, for a brief stop prior to his first visit to Africa, he left Jamaica

> A christian lad, hardly knowing whither [you] would go, actuated by a laudable desire to develop the faculties of [your] mind, whereby [you] might be of greater service to [your] fellowmen in the service of God.[1]

A few months' stay in Panama was followed by a decision to join one of Her Majesty's (Queen Victoria's) ships of war. For three years the islander feasted on the world outside Jamaica – the coasts of Central and North America: he landed at San Francisco and Vancouver Island, visited the Sandwich Islands, northern Chilean and Peruvian ports, Montevideo, and sailed through the Straits of Magellan.

The hope for an increasing number of Jamaicans and West Indians in the latter half of the nineteenth century was emigration. From then through to the 1930s, Jamaicans and other West Indians were to migrate to Central America labouring on railway and banana enterprises, to Ecuador, Brazil, and Panama for the Isthmian Railroad, and then to the Panama Canal itself. Among the emigrants were people described as "in the middle walks of life", sons of the small settler families, and a large number of artisans, whose earnings in Panama, albeit paid in silver, were substantially higher than in Jamaica. Tradesmen in 1888 in Jamaica earned between 2/6 and 6/- per day. In 1886 they could earn £2.75 per day if they reported directly to the Compagnie Universelle, or between £4 and £5 per day if they were employed by contracting firms.[2] The policy of importation of East Indian labour drove wages for workers down, and much of the migration sprung directly from desperation. The planters had their way: boats lined up in harbour with East Indian labour beside boats in the same harbour with black workers on their way to Central America. It is instructive to note that most East Indians worked eventually not on sugar but on banana plantations, since planters always preferred "creole" labour for the sugar plantations. East Indian labour was for a long time subsidized by general revenue, most of which came from the pockets of the small settlers.

The land Scholes left behind him in 1875 had been severely dislocated by the decline in the sugar industry, starved of capital, competing unsuccessfully against cheap beet sugar, which Britain chose to import over the more expensive cane sugar. The white planter class was much alarmed at the callousness of the metropolitan power, which ignored their pleas for a protected market in Britain. After all, they were loyal subjects of the Crown. The planter class had been partly rescued by the opening of the US market, where prices for sugar were marginally better. Later, especially in the 1880s, professionals and merchants linked themselves through the banana market in the United States to the system of commercial agricultural production. One consequence had been the reduction of land available to small settlers, who had in effect pioneered the banana industry. Banana ceased to be "nigger business";[3] small-scale producers of subsistence crops, coffee, and bananas were squeezed out of land ownership, and even more out of land leases, as big banana producers relentlessly pushed them back into the interior. The establishment of the railroad in the 1880s or, more specifically, the extension of the railroad to Montego Bay and Port Antonio provided some labour for the hard-pressed peasantry, but when the railroad was completed, by 1895, small farmers also resorted to migration.

Occupations for black people in Jamaica were limited to manual occupations, the artisan trades, the Constabulary (established in 1867 in the wake of the Morant Bay Rebellion of 1865), the teaching profession, and preaching. The bureaucracy was dominated by metropolitan servants; the competitive examinations for entry into the civil service could be nullified at the governor's "discretion".

Levels of taxation were high. As far as land was concerned the smaller acreages were taxed at a higher level than large acreages; huts were taxed at a higher level than mansions. Admissions to the lunatic asylum increased, though the rate of recuperation improved. The incidence of crime – praedial larceny, cutting and wounding, disorderly behaviour, obscene language – increased. The masses sometimes resorted to revivalism, for example in 1883-84 and again during Bedward's long stewardship at August Town. The rural and urban masses resorted to begging, pimping, stealing, prostitution in the spreading slums of Fletcher's Land and elsewhere. Urban deprivation was aggravated by rural–urban migration. The determination of the elite to hold on to their land at all costs and their subsequent reluctance to sell land in small lots and the government's own reluctance to sell land at competitive prices to small farmers – not until the mid-1890s anyway – created the anomalous situation where extensive acreages of land were underutilized and atomized pieces of land were intensely cultivated.[4] The Board of Supervision itself expressed some surprise at the low level of charity relief, given what was obviously the cancerous spread of poverty. But then, to qualify for poor relief in Jamaica, a prospective candidate had to prove complete destitution, and that he was starving.

In this system, it was the victim who was blamed. Blacks, so the view went, were poor because they were lazy and reluctant to do agricultural labour. Class and racial prejudice can never serve as a sound background to good or accurate judgement.

It was the churches more than anyone else who attempted to come to terms with the situation, though their limited resources could not achieve all they would have wished by way of providing educational facilities, for example. As the nineteenth century drew to a close under the umbrella of the Pax Britannica (peace at home and just war abroad against the savages of Africa, India, Australia) the small settler class found it more and more difficult to support their churches, and spoke of "owing the parson money". The ruthless system of credit in the countryside, whereby small settlers mortgaged their crops and lands to Christian and Jewish merchants and lost their crops and land in the process, must have been an important factor pushing the working class out of the colony for opportunities elsewhere.

Yet the British Empire had been designed to uplift "subject peoples". No doubt there were ardent workers who sought to civilize the masses as a means of ensuring social control, for it was ever assumed that the Jamaican masses were combustible, and liable to explosion when "led away" by the vitriolic language which the middle and upper classes of Jamaica were often inclined to employ. The cloud of Morant Bay never lifted, up to the end of the nineteenth century, and the outburst at Montego Bay in 1902, when the police and the Court House were attacked with sticks and stones, was a grim reminder of the danger of mass violence. Mass anger was directed against sugar estates in 1884 (in St Ann in particular), and dockworkers sat down in 1895. The solution again was more East Indians, or more Chinese labour. But the East Indians and Chinese also exploded into violent riots, in 1884 and again in 1902.

The civilizers saw the solution as devising an educational system which taught Blacks to obey and recognize their position – divinely ordained in society – and to achieve levels of education which would not drive them away from the collapsing plantation system. Yet planters and their allies, in face of the massive abuse of workers on sugar plantations – for example, paying in dead beef, or in rum, or sexually abusing children (daughters) of workers – insisted that civilization for Blacks would be derived from their continuous contact with whites on sugar estates, that is to say from lecherous bookkeepers who were not generally allowed to marry, or headmen who acted as pimps.[5]

It is true that attitudes to Blacks were not always hostile. It was recognized, not only in the statistics of government but also through the observation of those the corridors of whose minds were not snarled by prejudice, that contrary to the myth of laziness the black yeomanry carried the burden of taxation, produced the food which they ate, and marketed it through the internal marketing system – an alliance of small settler and higgler. While marriages were not popular among the mass of Jamaicans, concubinage was not endowed with the instability and absence of family that the "uplifters of the subject people" assumed. When a female migrant declared that she had gone to the "Republic" with "God as her compass" she was probably enunciating the feeling of many migrants who left the island to improve themselves. Many improved themselves, others died. The death rate of the migrants who went to Panama was 15 per cent of the total who went, and this figure appears, it is confessed, an underestimate. The age group which lost this number of workers was the

15 to 40 age group. Thirty per cent of the children died. The death rate in the Canal Zone between 1881 and 1888 ranged from a low of 43.5 per thousand to 66.8 per thousand.[6] Malaria and yellow fever were major scourges. Back in Jamaica, the malarial mosquito, tuberculosis, diseases of the intestinal tract also took their toll of the poorer segments of the population.

So, then, many of Jamaica's lazy Blacks went to Panama, and elsewhere, to die.

The black Jamaican middle class, far from turning their backs on such problems as these, addressed themselves to the problems of the majority classes. They did so especially through the columns of *The Jamaica Advocate,* but from time to time employed the columns of *The Daily Gleaner* as well. A few, such as the Rev. C.A. Wilson,[7] wrote accounts of late nineteenth- and early twentieth-century Jamaica which demonstrate some sensitivity to the black situation. So too did the Rev. R. Dingwall, despite his obsession with sexual immorality. In 1887, five Blacks produced a work in celebration of Jamaica's Jubilee, which was an attempt to assess the progress of Blacks since Emancipation.

This in brief is the Jamaica in which Scholes grew up in part. While he remained away from Jamaica for most of his life, it would be untrue to suggest that he was unaware of conditions in Jamaica. On the contrary, partly because of his travels he was able to bring a perspective on Jamaican affairs which traced the problems of the island to one thing, imperial rule, and its ideological buttress, racism. The decision of Scholes to go to Africa was inspired by the urge of West Indians – the Jamaican was described as "emphatically" a colonizer, or the Anglo-Saxon of the Far West – to bring the peoples of Africa into "Western civilization". These Jamaicans or West Indians were to promote the idea that black men could live like Christians. But the "civilization" of "Africans" was not good enough, as Scholes and other members of the black educated class recognized. What was needed above all, Scholes came to realize later, was a monumental effort to demonstrate scientifically (using the very instrument of the Europeans) that all men are equal before God, and that racism has no place in human society.

One of the few biographical sketches of Scholes suggests that he was inspired to undertake missionary work in Africa by the example of the missionary explorer, David Livingstone (of "Dr Livingstone, I presume?" fame). Livingstone could hardly have been the only influence, however, since as early as 1843 there were 20 Jamaicans among 24 who helped to found the Basel Mission (later the Gold Coast Presbyterian Church).[8] In any event Scholes entered Missionary College in London, the college founded by Dr H. Grattan Guinness, and stayed there for two years. Going north to Scotland, Scholes entered the University of Edinburgh, where he completed, so runs the account of John Bruce, a five-year course in medicine in four years at the Royal College of Surgeons and Physicians. About eight years later he took the M.D. degree at the University of Brussels.[9]

The Stewart Town community gave him a warm address of welcome in 1885, following his return from Edinburgh, congratulating him above all else for his decision to "bring glad tidings of salvation to the benighted millions of Africa". For "this above all other considerations we bless God for you.... Evangelise the fatherland under the auspices of the lately organised Missionary Society of the Western Churches of our coloured brethren".[10]

Scholes, who was a pastor of the church (Baptist, presumably), as well as a highly qualified medical practitioner, left for the Congo River in 1886, where he served for five years. He returned to New Calabar, this time, in 1894 where for two years he superintended an industrial mission. He himself refers to "two years [spent] on the coast of Guinea".[11] The circumstances under which Scholes decided to cease his mission work are not explained, only that there were circumstances over which he had no control, and that after his experience in Africa he dedicated himself more to the Brotherhood of Man and less to the Fatherhood of God; in short, a broader humanitarian missionary field.[12]

Scholes, except for occasional brief visits, never returned to Jamaica. He is almost entirely unknown in Jamaica. We know from Herbert Thomas's account that he was a "sambo" of enormous physical size, and from John Bruce that he was a "huge Negro ... proud of his African blood". Inspector Thomas, the abrasive imperialist, condemned him as one of those black men who, having been civilized by the white man, endeavoured to stir up racial hatred among his black brethren. A pity it was, lamented Thomas (who had been a victim of Scholes's sharp tongue during a patronizing speech in London) that Theophilus Scholes was not more like Sir Conrad Reeves, Solicitor General of Barbados, who had enjoyed – if that is possible – the distinction of a public funeral.[13]

Most of what we know of Scholes comes from his own writings. In 1897 he wrote a pamphlet, "The Sugar Question of the West Indies", and then in 1899 a larger work, *The British Empire and Alliances, or Britain's Duty to Her Colonies and Subject Races.* In 1905, perhaps responding to the intensification of British imperialism under Joseph Chamberlain, he published "Chamberlain and Chamberlainism". His work *Glimpses of the Ages, or the Superior and Inferior Races So-Called, Discussed in the Light of Science and History,* published in two volumes (1905 and 1907), brings together much of what he had written in his earlier work. This enormous "glimpse" of history reveals Scholes as a man of tremendous irony and biting sarcasm, and as a scholar capable of employing the tools of history, anthropology, archaeology, anatomy and linguistics to refute the idea of the inferiority of coloured people and the superiority of the "colourless" race. It is also an acerbic criticism of the hypocritical nature of Western civilization. The work is at once scholarly and polemical, and truly he could have said with Aeneas *vestigia retro observata sequor per noctem et lumine lustro.* Scholes's work is clearly a consequence of his experiences in London, Africa and the British West Indies.

Before proceeding to a discussion of Scholes's ideas we need to clarify what may seem to be a mere assumption that there were black perspectives, especially when, as in the case of Scholes, black thinkers were very obviously alienated from the folk tradition and were among the most skilled manipulators of European culture in Jamaica. Secondly, the outlook of educated Blacks on the mass of uneducated Blacks did not differ substantially from the attitude of the more generous-spirited members of liberal white society. Scholes was quite specific about the cultural gaps between educated and non-educated Blacks. Referring to the West Indies in particular, Scholes states:

> Inasmuch as some of these people, from a desire to emulate have, by means of sustained industry and its results, the acquisition of property, education, and other accomplishments qualified and are qualifying themselves for the larger sphere, or larger responsibility, the entire division ought to be considered as consisting of two distinct classes – civilized and uncivilized – occupying separate and precise spheres. Hence, the practice of referring to and of treating Ethiopian communities – British, American, and others – as though they all belong to the uncivilized class is arbitrary and unjust.[14]

This view of Scholes's was not unique to him. It was also a view shared by educated black Americans of the same period who, accepting the belief in progress among the bourgeoisie, were hostile to the tendency to lump them with the "meaner" sort of the race.[15] Social mobility was supposed to be the consequence of their burnished image of Western culture. It was not unusual for educated Blacks (especially teachers) to speak of "civilizing" their black brethren in Jamaica, or in Africa for that matter.

The black perspective arose precisely because intellectual competence or lofty cultural attainment or membership in the most prestigious professions did not lead to social acceptance, because of racism. For the black intellectuals' claim to be civilized to be validated Blacks generally needed to be "civilized". The redoubtable editor of *The Jamaica Advocate,* Dr J. Robert Love, expressed great annoyance at the discrimination experienced by the Rev. P. F. Schoburgh aboard a coastal steamer, a man who, according to Love, was "one of the foremost black men in the Colony, in education, character, social standing. A denial of his rights not only awakes but startles us all. If he is treated with indignity, what must be the lot of the many unfortunates of his race who travel on these boats?"

The growing feathers of the wings of educated Blacks were plucked by racism to ensure that Blacks flew at an ordinary pitch. The content of the education received by the black middle class was consciously formulated to steer them away from "folk-culture", to Anglicize them and thereby remove them from the cultural, intellectual, even spiritual world of the Jamaican masses. On the one hand, therefore, personal progress demanded distance between them and the Afro-Jamaican masses. On the other hand, their own merits were assessed not only in terms of their ability to manipulate European culture, manners, religion, but in terms of their membership of a race which was viewed negatively.

Racism in Jamaica (where a black worker could lose his employment at the Public Works Department because he refused to address the young child of a white doctor as Mister[16]) enforced upon its victims a consciousness of race, so that cultural "progress" or lack of it became synonymous with racial progress or lack of it. The achievement or lack of achievement of one became the achievement or lack of achievement of all.

Not surprisingly, educated black Jamaicans, in spite of the distance between themselves and the uneducated majority, were acutely conscious of the formidable obstacles placed in the way of the progress of members of the black race of all classes. J.H. Reid lamented the fact that black farmers had access only to the slopes, and that they received "standing room" only. W.F. Bailey observed that the plantations monopolized land in order to reduce the access of the Jamaican coloured masses to land ownership. Sugar estates kept Blacks in serfdom. Robert Love spoke strongly against the abuse of the system of land lease, which gave tenants extremely insecure leases, and condemned the system of taxation, which discriminated against the majority classes. The Rev. Dingwall discussed the tendency for planters to discriminate against black labourers in favour of East Indian labourers. The Rev. Wilson condemned the manner in which the "privileged caste" exploited the ill fortune and ignorance of poorer men, by superior knowledge of the law. Several black spokesmen challenged the adverse conditions under which labourers worked on sugar plantations – inadequate housing, low wages, the competition with contracted East Indian labour. Robert Love and others called attention to the abuse of black women by the white book-keepers on sugar plantations, and to the need to educate black women, since the black race would rise by families, not by the successes of individual black men. Robert Love, from the columns of *The Jamaica Advocate,* attacked "class legislation", and made little or no distinction between class and race in this context. Black spokesmen of the period, then, addressed themselves to issues of class and race in Jamaican society, to the local system of exploitation, which hindered the progress of the race. Also recognizing that the main avenue for black progress as a whole rested in education, they showed themselves thoroughly dedicated to the cause of furthering the educational progress of the majority classes. Claude McKay in his early works showed an acute awareness of the tragedy of Blacks:

> You [Jamaica] hab all t'ings fe mek life bles'
> But buccra 'poil de whole
> Wid gove'mint an' all de res'
> Fe worry naygur soul.

As a constable he was concerned about the brutal application of the law ("Strokes of the Tamarind Switch") and with the plight of prostitutes driven to their trade by poverty and bad example. But yet, the tone of the poem "Cudjoe Fresh from the Lecture" pays some tribute to the "civilizing" influence of British culture and accepts Africa as "uncivilized".

> Yes, Cous' Jarge, slabery hot fe dem dat gone befo';
> We gettin' better times, for these days we no know;
> But I t'ink it do good, tek we from Africa
> An' lan' us in blessed place as dis a ya.

For McKay England is home, but so is Jamaica:

> Jamaica is de nigger's place,
> No mind whe' some declare;
> An' though dem call we "no land race"
> I know we home is here.[17]

II
Concept of Africa

IT IS CLEAR, however, that personal esteem and black pride rested in Africa's redemption, an Africa which had been carved up by the European powers. But from the point of view of black intellectuals, Africa had not progressed significantly since the first days of civilization and was, relative to Europe, backward, politically divided, and weak.[18] But the black thinkers, much influenced by the Christian tradition and more prone to live up to the demands of that tradition in their personal conduct took their cue from the Acts of the Apostles: God "hath made of one blood all nations of men for to dwell on all the face of the earth". The Rev. Dingwall saw the hope of the black man in Psalm 68: "Princes shall come out of Egypt; Ethiopia shall soon stretch out her hands to God".[19]

The redemption of Africa by Blacks in the diaspora was analogous to the redemption of Joseph's people by Joseph, who had been held captive in Egypt. Practical steps were taken to organize Africa's redemption. Dr Albert Thorne, who had settled in Jamaica during the 1890s in St Ann (where he built an industrial school) organized a resettlement scheme for Blacks, pointing to Nyasaland as the venue for that settlement. The purpose of Thorne's "African Colonial Enterprise", as set out by Thorne, was to:

> 1. Assist enterprising members of the African race now resident in the Western hemisphere to return and settle down in their fatherland, Nyasaland, British Central Africa, being the site selected.
>
> 2. To develope agricultural, commercial and other available resources of the country.
>
> 3. To give the natives a suitable and profitable education.
>
> 4. To extend the Kingdom of God in those vast regions, by leading such as are in darkness and error or superstition to Jesus Christ.
>
> 5. To improve the status of the African race.
>
> 6. To foster and cement the bonds of friendship and brotherhood between all races of mankind, without respect to colour or creed.

The irony is that the advocates of African redemption – whether the pragmatic programme of Dr Thorne or the idealistic or visionary perspective of the Rev. Dingwall – used much of the language of the paternal imperialists, such as Archbishop Nuttall, who aimed for a universal Christendom linked to Anglo-Saxon cultural domination. African redemption was linked to growth of the dominant world civilization in Africa itself. British imperialism became linked with African redemption through Christianity with its message of universal brotherhood.

Theophilus Scholes shared some but not all of these views. His experience in Africa itself, however, added a dimension to his thought which was absent from that f his Jamaican colleagues even though he persisted in viewing the progress of the world in light of basic Christian humanism – "Love thy neighbour as thyself", "Do unto others as ye would that they should do unto you" – and in light of a "law of goodness as the highest and most important law". Whatever his views about African religious beliefs prior to his sojourn on the African continent, Scholes attempted to come to terms with those beliefs; and attempted to discuss man's innate capacity for belief in God. In the Lower Congo, Scholes informs us, God was called Nzumbi or Nzambi Ampungo; in Lower Nigeria (New Calabar), Tamuno. He noted that in reply to his suggestion that Africans did not "love" God, the reply was "*Nzambi, tuavanga, outo keba, outa vana dia, tuno ozolele, wevi?*" ("God who made us, who keeps us, who gives us food, why should we not love him?")

He dismissed the notion that the belief by Africans in a supreme being came from foreign influences. He discusses, further, Congolese theology and the particular relationship between polytheism and the belief in a supreme being:

> In a manner no doubt crude and rude, yet these idols in the aggregate of their functions took the place of the Mediator – excluding, however, His sacrificial work, for certain of the idols were themselves recipients of spiritual offerings.[21]

Of course, Scholes's work endeavoured to establish that the dominance of the "colourless" race over the coloured races was based not only upon violence but also upon deliberate distortion and misrepresentation. "Hence, the principle by which the alleged superiority of the white race, and inferiority of the coloured races, founded upon their supposed physical and mental differences, have been established is essentially Procrustean".[22]

Scholes's refutation of the concept of coloured inferiority was elaborate. He endeavoured to establish that Egyptian civilization was founded by Blacks. Like Cheikh Anta Diop more recently, he utilized fully the works of the Greek historian Herodotus to establish the origins of Egyptian civilization. Calling upon archaeology and linguistics he established a relationship between Egyptian civilization and the civilization of the Greeks. Thus, just as Egypt passed its civilization on to the Greeks, the Greeks passed it on to the Romans, and the Romans on to Europe. Thus, the origins of European civilization go back to Africa through Egypt. Of all civilizations, the most imitative was Europe's, which relied on other civilizations – e.g., the Mexicans, Incas, Egyptians – whose growth was spontaneous. As far as the claim goes that Africans were barbarians, an examination of Mandingo society, with their use of iron, their standard of housing, their social relations, demonstrates that the "barbarism" of the Mandingoes was closer to "civilization" than the "societies" of the English and Germans when Julius Caesar found them. Emulation is the basis of the spread of civilization, and through that process civilization will return to Africa from modern Europe. The Egyptians were the founders of mathematics, along with the people of India, and the mathematics, astronomy, trigonometry, and geometry upon which modern European science was based came originally from the much-maligned black race of Egypt. The Greek gods were born in Egypt. "In religion, according to Herodotus, the tenet of the immortality of the soul was borrowed by the Greeks from the Egyptians". The spring of European art, no less than of European science, is

Egypt and not Greece. In short, "there exists no evidence in support of the assertion that between the Negro and the Caucasian there are mental differences of a racial character".[23] The claim that Caucasians have larger skulls and presumably "bigger brains" metaphorically and empirically is also false. Finally, the capacity of formerly enslaved Blacks in the Americas to adjust to the demands of "European civilization" – in all its aspects: journalism, art, theatre and so on – is final proof that people of African descent are intellectually and morally the equals of the Caucasian race.

III
Racism and Empire

SCHOLES, IN HIS strong criticism of the functioning of the British Empire as it af- fected coloured people, sees racism as an important mechanism to ensure the domination of the white property owners over their labourers. There is no doubt in Scholes's mind that racial domination supplemented class domination. He refers sar- castically to Chamberlain's comment that the British Empire consisted of 54 million people – ignoring completely the existence of several more million coloured people in the same empire: Chamberlain's imperialism was aimed at securing the interest of these 54 million Whites. In 1865 the British government had committed itself to the protection of the subject people but towards the end of the century had broken that pledge and resorted to open oppression. "The reasons which Englishmen give for having broken their pledges to coloured subjects of the British Empire are that these races cannot govern themselves, and this fact is the result of lower mental and moral capacity".[24] Racism was converted by Chamberlain, then, into an ideology which facilitated the exploitation of the coloured race by the colourless race.

> It was Chamberlain who as Secretary of State for the Colonies advised Parliament against carrying out the unanimous and urgent recommendation of the Royal Sugar Commission which was to the effect that the only means of restoring prosperity to the British West Indies was settlement of the peasantry upon the land.... It was Chamberlain who sanctioned closing of schools to one half of the children of Jamaica's tax-paying peasantry, on the pretext of an empty treasury, whilst at the same time granting from the same empty treasury £20,000 to the non-tax-paying sugar planters.[25]

The broken pledges of Great Britain, argued Scholes, had come about because of the presence of powerful industrial rivals which made it necessary for England to increase the exploitation of coloured communities. British pledges of 1858 and 186 would have led logically to the "social recognition of the inhabitants of those [the coloured] states".[26] The British Empire therefore came to define more sharply the differences between the members of the hegemonic state and the members of the coloured daughter states, in order to realize "the policy of exploitation". To achieve this new and intense level of exploitation the hegemonic state resorted, in allianc with white minorities, to "misrepresentation, defamation, exaggeration, insults, abuse".[27]

The Empire, then, lived a contradiction – a contradiction between what Scholes calls the "foreground" and the "background". The foreground consisted of the elaborate institutions of government and bureaucracy – from Poor Law Commissions and Audit Offices to Public Works Departments and other "appliances of modern civilized government". The background consisted of the ignorant masses of the coloured population, subject to poverty, oppression, degradation, vilification, and humiliation. Generally, the purpose of this abandonment was: first, to exploit more effectively the coloured races; second, to assure the support of the white colonies and colonists; and third, to secure the friendship of the Euro-Americans, in the form of an Anglo-Saxon alliance or partnership. The latter was a concession by Britain to American "injustice".

> So in noticing Britain's change of policy towards the coloured races of the Empire, their exclusion from the land, their limited educational facilities, etc., we fail to see the relation which these parts bear to one another and to the whole British policy until we gain the summit of the mountain exploitation.... In other words exploitation is achieved by absolutism, absolutism is achieved by separation, and separation by those political, social, and economic tactics of exclusion, limitation, and imposition that we are now considering.[28]

Scholes was also bitterly aware of the various rationalizations employed to justify exploitation, including peculiarly and hypocritically humanitarian motives. In reference to Chinese labour in South Africa, for example, Scholes noted the contemporary protests against Chinese slave labour, and how similar protests were not raised against identical systems of labour exploitation among the Kaffirs. He argues, however, that the protests against Chinese slave labour did not arise because of any sentiments of humanitarianism for Chinese labourers, but because Chinese labour competed with white labour.

Scholes's attack was not confined to the British Empire. He commented extensively on the ruthless exploitation of black labourers in the Belgian Congo, where he vividly describes experiences of rapine, murder, dismemberment, the use of wives as hostages for the rubber tax and food tributes, and mutilation. "But at the head of this banquet of corpses and blood, in the Independent State of the Congo, sits Leopold II in regal magnificence", and "these aspects of forced labour are the gloomy chambers of abuse and wantonness, into which the great halls of the monopolist Companies give access".[29]

In Scholes's view the imperialist structure is maintained by a system of unstable alliances, by force, and by a system of tribute in the form of pensions and salaries paid to the hegemonic state which dumped its surplus manufactures on a captive market. The empires, and the British Empire in particular, violated the utilitarian principle of the greatest good for the greatest number, in its urge to use the coloured sections of the Empire as a safe field for speculative ventures. The coloured states were little more than coaling stations, dockyards, which were paid for by the colonized people. They received in return instruction in the Christian faith, protection of life and property, and education. Scholes concludes:

> I am constrained to believe that either war or revolution, or the two combined, will be the means employed to renew the movement of the world forward. And the increase of arms being regarded as the putting on by war, of its armour, the increase of socialism must similarly be regarded as the putting on by revolution of its armour".[30]

The disillusioned Scholes saw the "long pent up but just anger [of the oppressed coloured races] like tongues of fire, shall light up the Empire with an appalling rebellion". The British Empire would collapse like those of Egypt, Babylon, the Empire of the Medes, Persians, Greeks and Romans, especially since the situation of the coloureds in the British Empire was ignored for other less important considerations.[31] The Empire had an economic system which drained the resources of the tropical areas of Empire, very much as a giant sponge applied to a "pail of water".

Theophilus Scholes continuously referred to the example of the British West Indies, but in the generalized context of imperialism. The Jamaican or British West Indian case could not be isolated from the situation in the Belgian Congo, from Nigeria, or from South Africa. In Jamaica the peasantry were the main taxpayers. The less land owned, the higher the tax. Exploited Africans were in the identical position. The control of administration, supported by the Colonial Office, made it possible for white minorities to exempt themselves from taxes, and to impose the hut tax on Africans. The imperial system was an elaborate arrangement whereby the land resources of the colonies were appropriated by white minorities for their own profit. Peasants in Jamaica were limited in their access to land, in the same sense in which the Kaffirs or Congolese were deprived of their land. In spite of the fact that the sugar industry was a paralytic industry, which required the support of the tax-paying peasantry for survival, the imperial arrangement was one which supported a parasitic planter class.

IV
Christianity and the Black Experience

IN JAMAICA, as we have noted, the various churches had been active in the evangelizing of Blacks, and like the Catholic Church of the sixteenth century proved to be an important agency to secure European control of the Americas. In fact, men such as Scholes were caught in the difficult position of being men who were avid pursuers of the Christian faith and being victims of the prejudices which existed within churches as organizations. The Protestant churches, in Scholes's view, were the major buttress of the contemporary views which Europeans cherished about black people. Of course, membership of Christian churches can and does coexist with malignant prejudice and the practice of discrimination, precisely because members of a church are more closely associated with the prejudices of their societies than with the churches' message of brotherhood. Scholes commented on the contradiction between the preaching of brotherhood and the practice of racism:

> Spurned by politics and hounded by literature, surely in the all-embracing arm of the church of Christ, the Ethiopian may wipe his tears away, assuage his grief and rejoice in his full welcome as a man and a brother! In theory, the Ethiopian does receive Christian protection. But the Church fails to carry her theory into practice.... And this is especially true of the Protestant section of the Church. If the Church had fully recognized the Ethiopian as a "man and a brother" Politics and Literature would have done likewise, for in this respect at least they would reflect the action of the Church.

Scholes then turned to the "frenzied hatred" of the Southern (US) church towards Blacks; but side by side with that frenzied hatred was the anomalous effort by the same Southern churches in the US to send missionaries "to teach Negroes in Africa that God is no respecter of persons". The attack by Scholes on the Protestant missions coincided with a period in which there was a more pronounced tendency for leadership in the mission stations of Africa to be white, as the new imperialism became associated with the "white man's burden."

Claude McKay had also grown up in the Baptist faith, but later rejected the Baptist fundamentalism of his parents and described himself as a "free thinker" who found religious fundamentalism too inhibiting. Later McKay returned to the church – the Catholic Church – genuinely believing, like Scholes and Blyden, that the Catholic Church placed greater emphasis on the brotherhood of all men. This folly may be excused on the grounds that there were no imperial Catholic powers, with the exception of the senile empires of Spain and Portugal.

In many respects black intellectuals of the period were comparable to their Haitian counterparts; and the similarity is not purely coincidental. The fact is that they were all responding to the same stimulus; the emergence of quasi-scientific racism, which sought to establish that abilities were genetically inherited, from generation to generation. Haiti's political instability (varied with extensive periods of dictatorship) and the continued practice of African-derived voodoo was used by racists to argue that the black man was innately savage. The outlook of the Haitian intellectual was very similar to that of the Jamaican intellectual: the rejection of African culture, the expectation that Africa would emerge when European civilization was transferred to Africa, the view that slavery was a means of mobilizing Blacks in the diaspora to spread civilization. Hannibal Price argued, for example, that "in working for the white man the Negro received from him the light. This was not the intention of the slave owner, it was the will of God". Like Scholes, Firmin of Haiti "insisted that Egyptian civilization is the fountainhead from which sprang the Greek and Latin cultures, and that the development of the arts and sciences among white people of the West rested upon an African foundation". Caucasian presumption, he observed, could not abide the idea that "the whole development of human civilization originated with a race which they considered to be radically inferior to themselves. The Egyptians were Negroes".[23]

V
Black Organizations

SCHOLES BELIEVED that exploitation is "limited by its own inherent injustice", and generally hoped that the leadership of the Empire would correct injustice and return to the paternalist spirit of the 1860s. Failing that, a massive explosion would destroy the Empire. He did not preach against Empire, and emphasized that his criticism was intended in a patriotic spirit. Even Dr Robert Love seems to have adopted a similar position. His critique of the colonial system as it existed in Jamaica was couched often enough in terms of the rights of Jamaicans as "British subjects". Since Scholes did not reside in Jamaica he can hardly be accused of hiding away from proposing solutions or the necessary tactics to correct the situation. Robert Love, on the other hand, agitated for membership in the Jamaican Legislative Council of black men or of men who showed some sensitivity to the miserable condition of the majority classes in Jamaica. The huge dock workers' strike in Kingston in 1895 was taken by Dr Love to mark a "new departure" in the social history of the island, and he proposed the formation of labour clubs all over the colony which could mobilize Blacks politically to achieve objectives which were consonant with their own aspirations. J.H. Reid saw the strike and the formation of the Jamaica Union of Teachers as predecessors of a movement for black unity, across class.

The ominous-sounding "People's Convention" founded at the end of the century was intended to enable Blacks to "enjoy without any distinction the full political manhood embraced in British citizenship". At the same time, it would link itself with "forces and influences outside of Jamaica", presumably the Pan-African Association.

In the People's Convention, whose activities were programmed to coincide with Emancipation Day (August 1), was an aggressive and promising political association where "Negro" became synonymous with "the people", and where every encouragement was to be given to the consideration of "the history of our Fathers, and to contemplate the destinies of our children". In any event Emancipation was given not by "Act of Parliament only but in reality". The Convention discussed women's rights, the abuse of Jamaican migrant workers, the use of flogging as an instrument for the elimination of praedial larceny. The Convention was concerned not just with "local issues": there were no strictly local issues, not for Blacks. The Rev. C.A. Wilson was to point out that the "mix-up of races" did not "make for patriotism"; J.H. Reid had pointed out that Jamaican Whites identified with the soil and not with the Jamaican people. Black national consciousness was coming to be moulded around a response to the situation of Blacks the world over. The view of the educated Black was perhaps amply summarized in the statement of the "black doctor" mentioned by Henderson, a visitor to the island: The black doctor described himself as an "imperialist, a protectionist [who] believed in God, and Jamaica and the Negro race".[3]

The People's Convention, emerging at the end of the nineteenth century, was significant not for its permanence, or even for its long-term effectiveness, but rather for the transition which it sought to make between protest and critique to organization and action by black Jamaicans. It is significant, too, because it demonstrated a black nationalism which was both centred on the progress of the colony and on the history and future of the black man internationally.

VI
Conclusion

CONSCIOUSNESS IS SHAPED, and at the same time circumscribed, by the sum total of social and cultural experience; so that the consciousness of 1900 reflected the environment of that period. The black intellectuals, among whom we include Scholes, bestriding the dual cultural world of Europe and Africa, sought to bridge the gap by asserting the principle of human brotherhood. Christianity had been used by Sam Sharpe to assert the moral unacceptability of slavery; Scholes used it precisely to seek to reassert the viability and vitality of those beliefs in a world in which, as the Rev. Dingwall had expressed it, "internal righteousness shall rule the world".

Scholes's contribution rested in part on his recognition that the schizophrenic colonial universe of Jamaica was nothing more than a microcosm of an external reality that preached but never believed that "God was no respecter of persons". Scholes, to a significant extent a pioneer of black history so defined, was relentless in his determination to establish that Blacks had a history of distinction. But he went further, to establish that that history was the root, if not the branch, of all that was assumed to be civilized in 1900. And all this was done with an irony and intellectual aggression which we can hardly miss in his acerbic dismissal of racism:

> So then, unless it can be proved that when these Egyptians were the greatest civilized power in the world they were white, and when the white races of today were barbarians they were black or brown, the theory that the white skin only is associated with progress and greatness cannot be sustained; neither can the obverse, that the dark skin is associated with littleness, be maintained.[35]

Dr Theophilus Scholes is virtually unknown in his native Jamaica, but happily his contribution to the Pan-African movement was not unknown to Jomo Kenyatta or Ras Makonnen, who called on him in London (where he had been a freelance writer) in the 1930s, to give him thanks for the "great stimulus they had derived from reading his books".[36] The old man, then past three score and ten, was much moved by the tribute. That he was consulted over the proofs of Sal Plaatje's (founder of the ANC) book, published in London in 1916 as *Native Life in South Africa,* was indication enough that Scholes's intellectual worth was recognized. Scholes figures also as a member of the African Society as of September 1903. He was also linked with Dusé Mohammed (a Garveyite in the 1920s and a Nigerian nationalist in the 1940s). Scholes may have exercised, according to Immanuel Geiss, an "indirect influence upon Padmore's group" and "after Blyden he was the first West Indian author to make an important contribution to the emergence of Pan-Africanism".[37]

It is not known whether or not Garvey met Scholes, but it is difficult not to as sume that the aggressive political organizer from nearby St Ann was acquainted wit the work of the formidable Baptist from Stewart Town.

NOTES

1 The biographical information comes from Herbert Thomas, *The Story of a West Indian Policema* (Kingston: Gleaner Co., 1927), and from John Edward Bruce, "Dr Theophilus E.S. Scholes, M.D" in *The Voice of the Negro,* Vol. IV, No. 7, March 1907, pp. 114-115.

2 CO 137/532, 1887, Enclosure to Governor Norman's Despatch No. 364, 25 Oct. 1887. Dr Gayleard' Report on Conditions in Panama.

3 See Ansell Hart, "The Banana in Jamaica", *Social and Economic Studies* (Vol. 3, No. 2, Sept. 1954)

4 Veront Satchell, "Rural Land Transactions in Jamaica, 1866-1900", M.Phil. (History), UWI, Mona 1986, especially Chaps. 5 & 6.

5 *Jamaica Advocate,* "Confessions of a Planter" (Felix Holt), Sept. 6, 1902.

6 Velma Newton, *The Silver Men: West Indian Labour Migration to Panama, 1850-1914* (Kingston ISER, 1984), pp. 125-6.

7 Rev. C.A. Wilson, *Men With Backbone and Other Pleas for Progress* (Kingston: Educational Suppl Co., 1913) and *Men of Vision: Biographical Sketches of Men Who Have Made Their Mark* (Kingston Gleaner Co., 1929).

8 Rev. Koramora, *Centenary Report re the West Indian Assistant Founders of the Erstwhile Basel Mis sion Church Which Is Now Known by the Name Gold Coast Presbyterian Church, 1843-1943* (Ghana 1943).

9 John Bruce, "Dr Theophilus E. Scholes".

10 *Daily Gleaner,* 21 August 1885, "Address to Revd. Dr Theophilus Scholes", Stewart Town (10 Augus 1885).

11 T.E.S. Scholes, *Glimpses of the Ages, or the "Superior" and "Inferior" Races So-Called, Discussed i the Light of Science and History,* 2 Vols. (London: John Long, 1905 & 1907), Vol. 1, p. 211.

12 John Bruce, "Dr Theophilus Scholes".

13 Herbert Thomas, *Story of a West Indian Policeman,* p. 368.

14 T.E.S. Scholes, *Glimpses of the Ages,* Vol. 1, p. 355.

15 Walter Weare, "The Idea of Progress in Afro-American Thought, 1890-1915", in Ralph Atterman *The Question of Social Justice* (Madison, Wisconsin, 1983), p. 53.

16 *Jamaica Advocate,* May 16, 1896.

17 Claude McKay, *Songs of Jamaica* (Florida, 1969).

18 Rev. R. Dingwall, "Outlook for the Jamaican People" in *Jamaica's Jubilee, or What We Are and Wha We Hope to Become, by Five of Us* (London: S.W. Partridge & Co., 1888).

19 Ibid., pp. 122-8

20 Scholes, *Glimpses* (Vol. 1), p. 127.

[21] Ibid., p. 155.

[22] Ibid., p. 219.

[23] Ibid., Vol. 2, p. 282.

[24] Ibid., Vol. 2, p. 481.

[25] Ibid., p. 468.

[26] Ibid., p. 333.

[27] Ibid., p. 318.

[28] Ibid., p. 284.

[29] Ibid., pp. 216-8.

[30] Scholes, Vol. 1, p. 111.

[31] Ibid., Vol. 2, p. 331.

[32] Scholes, *The British Empire and Alliances, or Britain's Duty to Her Colonies and Subject Races* (London: Elliot Stock, Paternoster Row, 1899), pp. 288-89.

[33] David Nicholls, *From Dessalines to Duvalier: Race, Colour and National Independence in Haiti* (Cambridge and London: Cambridge University Press, 1979), p. 130.

[34] John Henderson, *Jamaica* (London: Adam & Charles Black, 1906), p. 103.

[35] Scholes, *The British Empire,* p. 399.

[36] Immanuel Geiss, *The Pan-African Movement* (translated by Ann Keep) (London: Methuen & Co. Ltd., 1974), p. 110.

[37] Ibid., p. 110.

Women and the Garvey Movement

Women in the Garvey Movement

Tony Martin
Wellesley College, Massachusetts, USA

FOR THE NEXT twenty minutes* I will outline Garvey's associations with women in and around the Universal Negro Improvement Association and the role that women played in the UNIA.

Garvey's organization was, of course, the largest pan-African movement, the largest international mass movement that our people have produced. It is my feeling that black radical movements have tended to give a greater role to women than other comparable movements. The UNIA was no exception to this pattern. Women, it seems to me, were fairly well integrated at all levels of the UNIA.

I do not think there was a specific feminist rhetoric in a modern sense. We must, therefore, draw our conclusions from the practice of the UNIA, which, in terms of the roles that women played, stands up very well against contemporary and more recent organizations.

Garvey himself had enjoyed close relations with women in his own family, long before he founded the UNIA. He considered his father stern, but he seems to have been particularly close to his mother, whom he described as a saintly woman, too good for the time in which she lived. When Garvey moved to Kingston in his late teenage years he sent for his mother and brought her to Kingston from St Ann to stay with him. She later died in Kingston. Garvey had one sister, Indiana. All his other siblings died in infancy, I believe. He seems to have had a reasonably good relationship with his sister. Indiana, who had preceded Garvey to England, helped to facilitate Garvey's own voyage to England around 1912. In the 1920s, Indiana lived in the Garvey household in New York City. So Garvey, one might possibly argue, brought to the UNIA this sort of personal relationship with the major women in the immediate family circle.

The first member of the UNIA, founded in the summer of 1914, shortly after Garvey returned from England, was a woman, a very young woman, Amy Ashwood, who would in due course become Amy Ashwood Garvey, the first wife of Marcus Garvey. She was then only 17 years old. Since she had actually met Garvey only a few days before the UNIA was founded, she may possibly have been exaggerating somewhat

* EDITORS' NOTE: This article is a verbatim transcript of Professor Martin's presentation at the conference "Garvey: His Work and Impact".

her own role as co-founder of the association. But she *was,* apparently, the first *member* of the UNIA. Ashwood's mother, interestingly enough, also became involved with the work of the UNIA during that early period in Kingston, August 1914 to March 1916. Quite a few other women played an active role in the association in that initial period prior to Garvey's departure for the United States. A list of the original UNIA executive in Kingston reveals that almost half the members were women. One of them was Garvey's sister, Indiana, who was involved at the very beginning. From the very beginning, too, the UNIA had a practice of having lady secretaries in each division. Later on there would be lady presidents as well.

Even though various positions were set aside specifically for women, this did not preclude the appointment of women to regular positions at the very highest levels of the organization at the same time.

For the first year or two, the UNIA here in Jamaica was very much in the tradition of Caribbean social welfare organizations. I am fascinated by the kinds of activities that the association indulged in here in 1914, 1915 and 1916. Those activities were, in many ways, indistinguishable from the types of activities that so many of our social organizations have indulged in. They held concerts and fund-raising events; they fed the poor, they visited hospitals, they talked to the sick, and they had a treat for the poor at Christmas time. They tried to set up a school – an industrial school. They tried to run a labour bureau, finding jobs for unemployed persons.

Occasionally at their weekly meetings they discussed topics pertaining to women. One of the prime activities of the group in this early period was holding debates: to some extent the UNIA, apart from everything else, was a debating society. One of the earliest debates was on the topic: "Is the intellect of woman as highly developed as that of man?" Marcus Garvey himself participated in this debate, and I am happy to say that he argued in the affirmative – that is, that the intellect of woman *was* as highly developed as that of man. On another occasion, and again this is very early, here in Kingston, the debate was: "Women or men: Whose influence is more felt in the world?" I did not make a note of the outcome of this particular debate, but it does show a certain kind of concern for this kind of question, even though, as I mentioned earlier, I am not aware of any specific feminist rhetoric in the modern sense.

Once the UNIA relocated to New York in 1916 and Garvey settled down to organize we find once more that women tended to play a fairly well-integrated role in the movement. Some of the highest positions in the UNIA were held by women. The best known of these women is Henrietta Vinton Davis, a woman who had been an associate of Frederick Douglass, the great Afro-American leader. She was an orator, a Shakespearean actress. She had toured Jamaica some years earlier, though it is not clear if she had made contact with Garvey. The UNIA had a series of vice-presidencies, and in her very long career in the association she served as vice-president on various occasions. For quite a while she was an international organizer, one of the highest positions within the UNIA. Significantly enough, later on another woman held that same post of international organizer, Madame de Mena. Several of the high-ranking members in the other departments of the UNIA were women. In the early 1920s, for example, one of the main people in what Garvey called the Negro Factories Corporation was a woman. The Negro Factories Corporation ran a string of businesses – because one of Garvey's main ideas was that of self-reliance. Garvey sought to demonstrate that black people could do things for themselves, successfully. And so one of the businesses that the UNIA ran in Harlem was a printing press, and a very young woman was actually the head of that printing press. Her name was Lillian Galloway. I am not sure what her background was. I have seen photographs of her taken around 1922, and judging from the photographs she could not have been more than about thirty or so – a very young woman to be holding such a responsible position in this great organization.

Garvey had international conventions on an annual basis. For his first convention, in 1920, something like 25,000 people turned out at Madison Square Garden in New York City. Sometimes at these conventions there would be special emphasis placed on the accomplishments of women of the black race. Art work and literature produced by women would sometimes be displayed, and famous women would make appearances. For example, the famous Afro-American contralto, Marian Anderson, sang at one of these UNIA conventions, in 1921 or 1922.

Many of Garvey's concerns – his ships, his universities, his schools – were named after famous members of the race. One of his ships, the *Phyllis Wheatley*, was named after one of Afro-America's major figures: Phyllis Wheatley, Afro-America's second poet, Afro-America's first woman poet, and, I believe, America's second poet, white or black.

Garvey also came into contact, in an intimate way, with some fairly well-known women who were not in the UNIA *per se*. In 1918, for example, as Garvey was still moving around the country, building the infrastructure of the organization and establishing contact with Afro-American leaders, one of the leaders he came in contact with was Ida Wells Barnett, a very important name in Afro-American history for all kinds of reasons. She was a pioneer in the women's club movement among Afro-Americans. She was a pioneer member of the National Association for the Advancement of Colored People, although she did not remain in it very long. She was disenchanted with it. But she was perhaps best known for being a major figure in the campaign against lynching, one of the most heinous crimes that any civilized society has ever had to deal with. Black people in the United States were killed in the streets almost daily, and Barnett, for many years, was a major campaigner in the crusade against lynching. In 1918 she came into Garvey's Liberty Hall, his meeting place in Harlem, and delivered a speech there, so he must have had some reasonably close contact with her. She lived in Chicago, so coming to New York meant a fairly major undertaking on her part, in those days when one would have had to travel by train.

Garvey also came into close contact with Madame C.J. Walker, another major figure in Afro-American history. Walker was a cosmetologist. She is normally considered to be Afro-America's first millionaire, at least Afro-America's first female millionaire. She seemed a somewhat unlikely person to be friendly with Garvey, but the fact is that Madame Walker, despite her riches, never lost her race consciousness. She was involved in one or two radical organizations herself, and she had no hesitation in funding organizations for racial uplift. She was somebody Garvey admired, and she invited him to a meeting she held in 1919 when she was trying to found an organization, a pan African-type organization, which among other things wanted to send black delegates to the peace conference coming up in Versailles after the First World War.

There was one occasion when Garvey allowed, very unusually perhaps, a white communist woman, Rose Pastor Stokes, to address the UNIA convention. There was a communist cadre within the UNIA who wanted Stokes to speak and Garvey allowed her to do so, explaining that, given the democratic organization of the UNIA she was free to say what she wanted. He was not, however, prepared to surrender his race-first organization to communist control.

The UNIA had a variety of auxiliaries. There were auxiliaries for youth, auxiliaries for women, auxiliaries for military factions within the organization. One of the most powerful and popular and best known of the auxiliaries was the Black Cross Nurses, an all women's organization. There is a lovely photograph showing Black Cross Nurses on parade, probably taken during one of Garvey's international conventions. These conventions were preceded by a lengthy parade: in 1920 the parade was ten miles long. One might perhaps expect a women's auxiliary for nurses; that is a traditional female occupation, you might say. More surprising, perhaps, and a sure indication of Garvey's attitude to the whole question, is the fact that Garvey also had a paramilitary auxiliary for women. There were two paramilitary organizations in Garvey's movement: one was the Universal African Legion, which was male; the other was the Universal African Motor Corps, which was female. So here we have women obtaining military training, dressed in military uniform. All this has to be highly in advance of anything in Garvey's time or since, because I know of no other major organization or mass movement in the United States, black or white, that has had a female paramilitary group. In fact, in recent times, some feminists have been talking about or insisting on being conscripted into the army.

Now, Garvey was a black nationalist. He preached a doctrine of race first, self-reliance and nationhood, and the woman question was intimately involved in the race first question. Race first meant that black folk would have to put their racial self-interest first. Garvey argued that all races did it and that black people might as well do it, too. Garvey told black people, among other things, to take down the white "pin-ups" from their walls. He was opposed to the gross advertisements for skin lighteners that used to adorn the newspapers of that generation. He encouraged, in fact he established, through his organization, a factory that made black dolls, so that young black children would not have to deal with the question of beauty being seen through the eyes of white folk all the time.

And so Garvey was to some extent against inter-marriage. He was against miscegenation. Now, he wasn't against light-skinned people, as some might have argued. Racial mixture had taken place during slavery. There was nothing to be done about that now, but with slavery over the practice of miscegenation should not be encouraged. Garvey was very upset by what he called "rich black men marrying poor white women". He argued, in an early article, that in Jamaica black men were very often poor. Their parents sacrificed and sent them away to study. They became doctors or what have you; they returned to Jamaica and brought a white wife with them. Then they died, and the money they had accumulated through the hard work of the race went back to Scotland, or Wales, or wherever she came from. Garvey actually promoted and provided an alternative to the white "pin-ups" he denounced by placing in his newspaper, *The Negro World,* photographs of beautiful black women.

I think it is instructive to contrast the situation of black women in Garvey's movement, where women were being exalted in positions of eminence, with the situation of black women in the Communist Party of the United States. Claudia Jones, a famous woman in the Communist Party in the 1940s and early 1950s, once wrote an article in *Political Affairs,* the theoretical journal of the Communist Party of the United States, in which she lamented the position of black women in the party. She pointed out that white men in the party, once the revolution was over and the time came to socialize, didn't have a problem because they could socialize with the white women in the party. She claimed that the white women in the party didn't have a problem because they had the white men in the party to socialize with, and the black men as well. The black men didn't have a problem, she claimed, because when the revolution was over, after a hard day's revolution, when they got back to party headquarters, they could socialize with the white women. The black women in the party, she said, were the only ones left out. There was nobody for them to deal with. The situation described by Claudia Jones would have been unthinkable in Garvey's movement.

Garvey himself waxed poetic on more than one occasion on the question of black women. His famous poem on a black woman begins, "Black Queen of Beauty, thou hast given color to the world". The same poem refers to the times when the black woman was the Queen of Nations; to the times when people such as Caesar and Antony – he is referring to the Cleopatra story here – and other figures in antiquity paid deference to the black woman. According to Garvey, the race became weak, slavery ensued, and the black woman involuntarily became the mother of the world. But he looked forward to the time when the race would rise again and the black woman would again be able to enjoy dignity and respect.

From very early the question of the dignity of women was very dear to Garvey. For example, at the founding of the UNIA in Jamaica in 1914, the following clause appeared in the aims and objectives of the UNIA: "To rescue the fallen women of the island from the pit of infamy and vice". In truth, this provision was not especially unusual, since other conscious individuals elsewhere in the Caribbean were addressing that problem at the time. Apparently prostitution was a fairly widespread problem, at least in the larger towns and cities in the Caribbean. I've seen similar references in the press in Trinidad for around this period. So Garvey was very much in the tradition of reformers at the time who were upset at the rampant prostitution of black women in the country. When Garvey returned to Jamaica in the 1920s and early 1930s, there was at least one occasion on which he had cause to protest against what he called the ragged and half-naked condition of the female banana carriers on the wharfs. He said that very often tourists would delight in taking photographs of these half-naked women as they loaded bananas on the ships. Garvey protested against this.

Garvey, among other things, tried to build a nation. The UNIA was a nation in microcosm, and it addressed itself to every aspect that a nation should. It had its parliament, it had its ambassadors in a very literal sense, it had its paramilitary arm, it had its economic base. It also had its cultural expressions. And so Garvey indulged to a very great extent in the whole question of cultural and literary criticism. And I'm not sure why this should be, but many of the poets of the Garvey movement tended to be women. The most prolific poet of all was Ethel Trew Dunlap of Chicago and, later on, Los Angeles. The themes discussed by these poets, men and women, very often included subjects dealing with women. The black-is-beautiful theme, for example, was very common. There were themes of the "new" negro woman standing up against white oppression, and so on. One of Afro-America's greatest sculptors was a woman, Augusta Savage, who was a member of Garvey's organization and participated in the artistic work. In fact, she did some bronze busts of Garvey.

I'll end by mentioning briefly Garvey's own two wives who were both very powerful persons in their own right. At the age of 17 the precocious Amy Ashwood was a sufficiently powerful speaker to impress Garvey by her participation in a debate at the East Queen Street Baptist Literary Union. It was not only her physical beauty but also her ability as a public speaker that attracted Garvey to her. She accompanied Garvey around Jamaica, later on around the USA as well. She was one of the officers of the Black Star Line and in the Negro Factories Corporation. She was a high officer in every aspect of Garvey's movement. She spoke from the public platform the way he did. When she broke with Garvey three months after their marriage she continued as a major pan-African figure. She organized women's movements and race movements in a variety of areas including West Africa, Barbados and England.

His second wife, Amy Jacques Garvey, was an amazing woman in her own right, as Maureen and Rupert Lewis[1] have demonstrated. I remember hearing her speak when she was about 76 years old at a worker's meeting in Kingston in 1972 or 1973. She was even then a powerful speaker. She, too, spoke from Garvey's platform. She also ran the organization almost single-handedly when Garvey was either imprisoned or otherwise unavailable....

NOTE

[1] Rupert Lewis and Maureen Warner-Lewis, "Amy Jacques Garvey", *Jamaica Journal,* Vol. 20, No. 3, August–October 1987, pp. 39-43.

rom certain tasks which violated the female ideal. By paying lower wages for the asks women did at the workplace and none for the work done in the home, it jusified male privilege at the workplace and at home. It excluded middle-class women rom the professions and imprisoned them in the home, the darling dependents of he leisure classes, and offered them social work as a fitting "hobby".

In Jamaica, the main promoters of this ideology were the church, upper-class women and the forces of the market itself. However, here, as almost everywhere else, the arguments underlying the ideology were so persuasive, based as they were on the extension of biological properties into the social arena, that those interested in social change tried to manipulate the arguments in favour of the problems they sought to change rather than to directly confront it. The domesticated homemaker was seen as progressive. It was good for all well-thinking and virtuous women to aspire to become like this image.

Within the UNIA, the image of women promoted did not challenge the dominant ideology of woman as both housewife and mother. Rather, it applied and adapted it to the needs of black nationalism. The sacred role of woman as Black Madonna and mother of the race was promoted in Garvey's poetry, speeches and other writings. In Garvey's view (in Love's also), black women needed to be uplifted. This meant relieved of certain onerous tasks in the public sphere (for example, those requiring great physical strength), and put on a kind of pedestal. The following poem by Garvey himself illustrates these notions:

THE BLACK WOMAN

Black Queen of beauty, thou hast given colour to the world!
Among other women thou art royal and the fairest!
Like the brightest of jewels in the regal diadem,
Shin'st thou, Goddess of Africa, Nature's purest emblem!
Black men worship thy virginal shrine in truest Love,
Because in thine eyes are virtue's steady and holy mark,
As we see in no other, clothed in silk or fine linen,
From ancient Venus, the Goddess to mythical Helen.
Superior Angels look like you in heaven above,
For thou art fairest, queen of the seasons, queen of our love:
No condition shall make us ever in life desert thee,
Sweet Goddess of the ever green land and placid blue sea.[6]

In the first place, the poem challenged the notion of a white religious pantheon and demolished Euro-centric notions of beauty. In this sense, this poem reflects the strong tendency in the UNIA to give black women a weapon against the inferiority enforced by white colonial standards of beauty – which upheld thin lips, straight hair and pale skin.

At another level, the poem idealizes the black woman, by placing her above the base, but active, nature of the male. Women are "nature's purest emblem" – passive. They are also to be seen as things of beauty to be surrounded by the wealth of African civilization. Woman is to be seen as a queen. She is to be the final arbiter on questions of morality and she is to be worshipped. There is an obvious contradiction between what is described here and the actual state of the majority of women in Jamaica. While Garvey was clearly attempting to inspire in women a vision of themselves as heiresses to more than the drudgery of the canefield, the danger here is that the standard he proposes reflects that of the class who put them in the canefields in the first place. The hierarchy of so-called civilization – in this case royalty – remains, as does the concept of woman as the personification of "the finer things of life".

In "The Black Mother", another poem by Garvey, he pays tribute to the "love that never changes", the mother's love, which at home shields the child/man from the "fierce tempest" of the outside world.[7] The mother is personified as "the rock that ne'er rifts asunder". This love has been given to man to provide a centre for him wherever he may roam. The poem reflects the view of women as a superior civilizing force, a pure force which perpetuates the best of culture, provides a haven from the competitiveness of the market place.

In "Song of the Negro Maid", Garvey discusses the issue of chastity. The poem is narrated from the point of view of a young, black woman. She says:

> I look at man in grim dismay;
> He tried my virtue all to steal.

The young woman is relieved because in spite of the fact that "The white man forced my head to bow, / My chastity to treat with scorn...",[8] she did not give in and takes pride in the respect she has for both her race and her own morality. The poem, therefore, suggests that in matters requiring sexual control, the onus is on the woman. It is woman who upholds standards of chastity and who must exert self-control. Women's sexual nature, then, must be more rigidly controlled than that of men. This again, is a view which is typical of the age.

The difference between Garvey's vision of womanhood and that of the colonizers is that it applied what was essentially a vision of upper-class white women to black women of all classes. The women the European ideology glorified and idealized were upper middle class and white – since only they could attain the attribute of delicacy and "refinement". For the colonizer, the black woman was doubly defined into nature: as women, they were closer to the innocent primitive intuitive, and as Blacks, they were more animal and sexually promiscuous.[9] Because of this closeness to savagery, there was little hope of refinement. Garveyism refuted the racism of the colonizers' vision, but upheld with reverence the notion of the woman as the homemaker, culture bearer and as someone who intrinsically carried the memory of the race.

The Garveyite woman, like the middle-class woman, was expected to participate in voluntary service to the race/class. Garvey unapologetically saw the man as head of the patriarchal family and spoke out against illegitimacy and female-headed households.[10]

Women's Leadership of and Participation in the UNIA

N ACTUAL PRACTICE, women in the Garvey movement created their own image of ne black woman, and this differed from both the nineteenth-century ideal and from ne vision of womanhood upheld by Garvey himself.

First, the participation of women in the leadership of the organization is one of he most striking features of the association. Female leadership in most organizaions of the time was rare. The UNIA both insisted on it as a principle and in pracice produced many dynamic women in leadership. The style of the Garveyite female eadership was varied. Garvey's two wives, for instance, had two very different styles, ut both were powerful leaders in their own right.

It is often forgotten that Amy Ashwood, later to become Garvey's first wife, was o-founder of the UNIA in Kingston in 1914. She was both secretary of the associaion and an activist in her own right. As a young woman she supported the notion of ocial work as a solution to the problems of black people and as suitable work for vomen. She described herself as a social worker and in the early days of the UNIA nitiated social work activities. In 1914, for example, the ladies of the UNIA sold arificial flowers and bouquets to raise money for a Christmas treat for the poor and lanned an Industrial Farm and Industrial Fund.[11] This school was apparently enisioned as being mainly for men, as in 1915 a statement of the objectives of the organization pledged to train "our men to a better knowledge and appreciation of griculture and the soil".

Agriculture, in spite of the West African experience to the contrary, was then lefined as men's work. Working class women were to be trained to "be good and eficient domestics".[12]

However, Ashwood influenced the organization, especially in its early days, to ay serious attention to the issue of the equality of women. In 1914, for example, the rganization debated the question, "Is the intellect of a woman as highly developed s that of a man?"[13] She also organized the ladies division (not auxiliary), which ormed part of the UNIA from its inception. Later on, this division was developed nto the Black Cross Nurses' Women's Arm. After the headquarters of the organizaion moved to the USA, Ashwood continued her work there, working as an editor for he UNIA paper, *The Negro World,* until the end of her marriage to Garvey.

The way in which their marriage ended itself raised questions about the rights of vomen within the UNIA. Although all the facts are not clear, some of the things conributing to the break-up of the marriage included Ashwood's relationships with ther men and drinking in public.[14] The controversial divorce raised for discussion vithin the movement questions about monogamy, the right of wives to have the male riends they chose, fidelity in marriage, appropriate conduct for women in public, and the ethics of friendship between women. This arose because of her friendship with Amy Jacques, who allegedly created a situation in which Garvey would find his wife vith another man.

Later on in England, where she lived after leaving the USA, Ashwood remained an important activist for the Pan-African cause, becoming an associate of Sylvia Pankhurst, the socialist feminist. Pankhurst, in fact, wrote the introduction to Ashwood's book on Liberia.[15]

Garvey's second wife, Amy Jacques Garvey, was also an important activist and one of the most important organizers for the UNIA. She worked as an editor of *The Negro World* and, during Garvey's imprisonment, worked tirelessly to keep the organization going. She published both his books and her own *Garvey and Garveyism,* which was the earliest documentation of the movement. In many ways, she typified the ideal image of the woman in the Garvey movement as it developed in the USA. Although her literary and intellectual skills account for much of the documentation of the movement, she did not question her role as wife or mother, combining these duties with her responsibility as a tireless supporter of Garvey. The ambivalence of her position on the situation of women can be seen in the quote below from a discussion on women in black liberation struggles:

> Black women are not traitors, they are not cowards, they are truly the better half of black men. The masses need intelligent, dedicated leadership from women. Women don't want to jostle men for jobs. They want what they merit, and to which they can contribute their God-given qualities in trying to liberate this civilization from greed and hate.[16]

Apart from Garvey's wives, there were many other women active in the leadership of the movement, both at the local level and at the level of the executive. Henrietta Vinton Davis, for example, was at one time President General and International Organizer and was part of a delegation to Liberia while Garvey was imprisoned. The UNIA was unique in that it always kept a place on the executive for a Lady President and Lady Vice-President.

In addition to women's involvement in the leadership, large numbers of women participated in all the activities of the organization. The UNIA placed far more emphasis on women's organizing in their own groupings than any other nationalist organization at the time. The Black Cross Nurses carried out social work activities and learned health care. There was also a girl guide grouping and motor corps. A Women's Day was part of the UNIA Convention of 1922, with Marian Anderson, the black contralto, featured as a major attraction.[17] In *The Negro World,* a women's page often examined women's contribution to the black liberation movement.

An important part of Garvey's philosophy was the emphasis placed on the development of black self-reliance through the growth of small business. A women's manufacturing department and bazaar which made Black Cross Nurses' uniforms, Panama hats and other clothes was established in the United States as a means of achieving this objective.18

In reality, Garveyite women both participated in and led a movement which drew women out of the home and immersed them in public life. It created in practice the image of a woman as intellectual, policy maker, manager and activist. It also created an image of woman as someone who had the right to demand and depend on her own organizational groupings and leadership.

Garveyites and the Women's Movement in Jamaica after 1927

IN 1927, GARVEY RETURNED to Jamaica after being deported from the USA and set up his headquarters at Edelweiss Park in Kingston. In 1926, Jamaica had only had eleven UNIA branches to Cuba's 52 and Trinidad's 30, but the establishment of the headquarters of the organization in Jamaica was to increase the influence of Garveyism. With its stage shows, concerts, parades and public debates, Edelweiss Park became an important cultural centre and a place for stimulating consciousness at both lower and middle class and working class levels.

In 1929, the sixth International Congress of the UNIA took place in Jamaica, and a debate took place between Garvey and Otto Huiswood (a brown Surinamese Communist from the American Negro Labour Congress). The two men debated the question of race and class. Huiswood argued that the "negro problem" could only be solved by co-operation between black and white labour and that Garvey's failure to recognize this and to confront class struggle was a grave weakness in his programme.[19]

In the same year, Garvey launched his People's Political Party and began his attempts to enter Jamaican electoral politics. What is most striking about the aims and objectives of this party, as compared to earlier aims and objectives, is that there is no mention of women. This may indicate that in the later years of the organization the earlier emphasis on women lessened.

Debates like Garvey's and Huiswood's on the question of the relationship between race and class, coupled with the contradictory theory and practice on women and the apparent lack of emphasis on the position of and specific interest in women, may be some of the factors that influenced women like Satira Earle and Adina Spencer to speak out against capitalism and the exploitation of women. These two women were to become working-class activists in the struggles of 1938. Earle is described by Ken Post as one of the most active members of the UNIA, and was also the Lady President of the St Andrew Division of the UNIA. In 1935, after Garvey left Jamaica, she was one of those who attempted to organize a labour union among his supporters. She was on the platform at the inaugural meeting of the union and revealed her frustration with the cautiousness of the middle-class male leadership in the movement in the following words:

> Wake up men, if you are afraid to carry on, I will organize a committee of women and launch out against capitalists in this island and leave you drowsy men behind.[20]

Adina Spencer, whose *nom de plume* was "Woman of the Masses", was a frequent contributor to *Plain Talk*, a Garveyite paper. She was an outspoken critic of female unemployment:

> We the women of the masses have been suffering day and night with poverty and actual wants, due chiefly to lack of employment and conditions brought about through the depression confronting Jamaica as

well as other parts of the world. There is no work for us to do nor other economic opportunities enabling us to rise to a higher standard of life, thus uplifting our womanhood.

As coloured women, we are calling on government to aid us. It is appalling to see the thousands of women willing to earn an honest living, walking in the streets, trying to get employment."[21]

Spencer was an active figure in the strikes of 1938. Like Aggie Bernard, she was active both in the labour organization and in the supportive activities which kept the male strikers going.

There was another trend of feminism which grew out of the Garvey movement and became dominant. It was the liberal feminism of black middle-strata women such as Una Marson, Amy Bailey and Madame de Mena. The latter two were deeply involved as feminist activists and organizers. On the other hand, Una Marson, the little recognized writer, was the main exponent of the literary side. She made her earliest contributions in concerts at Edelweiss Park. She was also first reviewed in *The Black Man.*[22] It was probably due to experiences such as these within the movement that Marson continued to insist on the importance of an organizational forum for writers and to search for ways in which to link her political and artistic talents. Hence it is that she was among the first to insist on the importance of creole as a legitimate language of literary expression. Her attempts to understand the complex problems facing young black women led her to write in her newspaper articles some of the clearest records of women's experience of the 1930s. She also wrote poetry and drama which made visible the experience of the black woman while exploring the contradictions of sexuality, religion and identity that faced her in Caribbean society. With Amy Bailey, she co-founded the Jamaica Save the Children Fund in 1938 and also testified before the Moyne Commission of 1938 after the riots — recommending a tax on bachelors as a solution to the problems of child support by men.

Amy Bailey was particularly influenced by Garvey's ideas on self-reliance and upliftment. A visitor to Edelweiss Park in her youth, Bailey later combined her particular type of Garveyism with her feminism in her work in Jamaica in the 1930s and 1940s. In the 1930s, she led a major campaign against business places in the press, in an effort to widen employment opportunities for black women. She fought for the rights of women teachers to hold jobs normally reserved for men, for the right of married women to work in the civil service and for banks and stores to hire the daughters of the upcoming black middle strata who had been trained in clerical work.

It was Bailey who later on founded the Housecraft Training Centre for working-class women interested in becoming trained household helpers. In so doing, she brought into being Ashwood's 1914 ideas for the training of working-class women.

In 1937, Bailey, de Mena and a few others, formed the Women's Liberal Club, an organization which aimed at the building of Jamaican national identity and the question of women's place within that. The club's main objectives were to:

(1) Foster and develop a national spirit among the women of Jamaica.

(2) Encourage women to take an active and intelligent interest in local and world events.

(3) Study negro history.

(4) Study social and economic conditions at home and abroad.

(5) Advance the status of Jamaican women, socially and politically.[23]

The Women's Liberal Club was to become the feminist organization which had the most impact on the lives of black women of the middle strata. It could not have done so without the organizational experience of the UNIA and the activism of working class women like Adina Spencer. Madame de Mena's experience as an orator and as an elegant, well-known example of the gracious, beautiful Garveyite woman was an essential element in attracting to the women's movement the approval of those who had supported the work of the UNIA. The demands of women like Adina Spencer also gave credibility to their assertion that women had an employment problem.

From this basis the members of the Women's Liberal Club were able to challenge the legitimacy of the groupings of upper-class and white women which at the time provided female organizational leadership and push for gains for black women. After the 1938 uprising, in her testimony before the Moyne Commission, Mary Morris Knibb condemned the racism among these upper class women and criticized them for inhibiting the leadership potential of black women. The first women's conference of 1939 then pressed the demands of women for wider jobs in education, the police force and the civil service and the judiciary. It demanded political rights for women on the same terms as men, called for the registration of fathers and the enforced contribution of men to their children's financial maintenance. It called on the government to encourage birth control propaganda and to permit medical officers of the government to be allowed to spread birth control propaganda and to include birth control in their services for women.

The delegation of women who waited on the governor was made up of one woman from the plantocracy and another from a British suffragette organization, but its leadership came from the Women's Liberal Club, the Bailey sisters and Madame de Mena. The government granted the women's demands for political rights soon after, against the background of reform which followed on the uprising of the year before. The Club then organized the campaign of Mary Morris Knibb for election to the Kingston and St Andrew Parish Council. Knibb won.

What is important to note about all this is that nowhere in the feminist organization of the 1930s or in the UNIA itself was the image of woman as home-maker or mother or social worker challenged or replaced in theory. A great deal more research needs to be done, but so far it appears that the image as an ideal, a model, remained intact. The closest it came to being challenged was by the working-class women whose insistence on more jobs for working-class women in varied fields with fair pay challenged the established division of labour, the divide between factory and home. Their daily lives showed that women remained human, strong, lively and capable of struggle even when they did not conform to the dominant image of the time. It was not these women who made the gains of 1938. The gains went first and foremost to the middle strata, whose strategy had been to struggle quietly for paid work in areas of the economy where female control could be justifiably extended, given the dominant ideology – areas like child care, teaching and professional domestic service. They also justified women's participation in politics on the basis of their nurturing instincts. The practical strategies of women of all classes enabled middle-strata women to make small political gains by manipulating the contradictions of the time without confronting the ideology or the material relations that determined the contrasting daily lives of the women of different classes. The women who reaped the gains of the struggles of the earlier organizations of Garveyite women did not evaluate the relationship between their struggles and those of working class women. Amy Bailey, for example, voted against universal adult suffrage. She felt that government should be the privilege of intelligent, educated women.

The absence of a theory of women's subordination that transcended the ideology and class relations of the time resulted later on in great limitations being placed on the gains women made. The great danger of the approach used was that sometimes the reforms simply resulted in women's subordination recomposing in a new way. Instead of eliminating discrimination against women, they backfired; the old contradictions re-emerged and placed women in a possibly weaker position. For example, the emphasis on the image of the domesticated home-maker was taken up and used by the colonial state after 1944 as a justification for female unemployment in the 1940s and 1950s.

Nevertheless, whatever the assessment of their gains, the UNIA was clearly the training ground for black feminists of the 1930s. From its ranks came both the liberals and the women of the working class who helped to organize the early labour movement. It is an example of how political practice sometimes outstrips the theoretical limits of stated philosophy and how study of that practice ultimately leads to a wider analysis of the problem under study.

ACKNOWLEDGEMENTS – This article is based on research conducted with Joan French as part of a larger study, "Women, Work and Organization in Jamaica 1900–1944". I am indebted to Joy Lumsden for assistance with details on the life of Catherine McKenzie.

NOTES

1 *Jamaica Advocate,* Aug. 10, 1901.

2 Rhoda Reddock, "Women, Labour and Struggle in Twentieth-Century Trinidad and Tobago, 1898-1960", unpublished Ph.D thesis, University of Amsterdam, 1984, p. 342.

3 Kumari Jayawardena, *Feminism and Nationalism in the Third World in the Nineteenth and Early Twentieth Century,* (London: Zed, 1986); and Rhoda Reddock, "Women, Labour and Struggle."

4 B. Ehrenreich and D. English, *For Her Own Good: 150 Years of Experts' Advice to Women* (New York: Anchor Press/Doubleday, 1979), p. 10.

5 Jayawardena, *Feminism and Nationalism,* p. 9.

[6] Tony Martin (ed.), *The Poetical Works of Marcus Garvey* (Massachusetts: The Majority Press, 1983), p. 44.

[7] Ibid., p. 59.

[8] Ibid., p. 69

[9] Rhoda Reddock, "Women, Labour and Struggle", p. 68.

[10] Interview with Mariamne Samad (UNIA member), April 1984.

[11] The source of this information is an undated clipping in the Garvey file at the National Library of Jamaica.

[12] *Daily Chronicle,* August 26, 1915.

[13] *Daily Chronicle,* December 4, 1914.

[14] Interview, Mariamne Samad, May 1985.

[15] Rhoda Reddock, "Women, Labour and Struggle," p. 346.

[16] *Massachusetts Review,* 1982.

[17] Tony Martin, *Race First: The Ideological and Organizational Struggles of Marcus Garvey and the Universal Negro Improvement Association* (Connecticut: Greenwood Press, 1976), p. 27.

[18] Ibid., p. 34.

[19] Ken Post, *Arise Ye Starvelings* (The Hague: Martinus Nijhoff, 1978), p. 3

[20] Quoted in Ibid., p. 241.

[21] *Plain Talk,* August 24, 1935.

[22] Beverly Hamilton, "Marcus Garvey: Cultural Activist," *Jamaica Journal,* Vol. 20, No. 3, August-October 1987, p. 28.

[23] Joan French and Honor Ford-Smith, "Women, Work and Organization in Jamaica, 1900-1944," unpublished research study for the Institute of Social Studies, The Hague, Netherlands, 1985, p. 246.

INTERVIEWS

Rupert Lewis, Garvey scholar, 1985.

Amy Bailey, Jamaican Feminist, January and February 1985.

Mariamne Samad, UNIA member, May 1985.

Garvey and Cultural Expressions

Marcus Garvey and Cultural Development in Jamaica: A Preliminary Survey

Beverly Hamilton
Freelance Journalist
Kingston, Jamaica

The company (Edelweiss Park Amusement Company) has established the Park as a Centre for training, development and presentation of local talent, but only a small fraction of the citizens of the Corporate area have taken advantage of the opportunity to see these artists perform from time to time. It must be said without contradiction that no foreign companies appearing abroad or that have appeared in Jamaica can acquit themselves with better satisfaction to the public than the different units at Edelweiss. (Editorial, New Jamaican, *9 July 1932)*

Ran Williams, the latest natural original comedian in Jamaica has been given the chance to develop his skill at Edelweiss Park.... That he has been getting on by leaps and bounds goes without saying ... and if he should obtain the heights of CUPIDON or becomes a local Harry Lander he will have to thank Marcus Garvey (as many of us are thanking him now) for giving him the chance to "make good". ("The Spectator", writing in Blackman, *13 August 1929)*

Nothing promotes the unity and respect of any people to a greater degree than Art, and so Mr. Cupidon is niched into the scene of Drama called the Progress of the Race. His success then is of more than personal or even communal interest. It has Racial Significance. We bespeak for Mr. Cupidon the brightest success. (John Coleman Beecher in Blackman, *23 April 1929)*

GARVEY'S CONTRIBUTION to Jamaica's cultural development is yet to be com-
'ehensively documented; hence this paper is offered as a preliminary survey. The aterial has been gathered from two primary sources: Garvey's newspapers and oral stimonies from actors in that cultural arena. It seeks to describe the activities which ıme about directly from the Garvey movement in Jamaica and to a lesser extent condary activities such as those inspired by the Garvey message. Areas such as the cial and historical development of individual art forms have been omitted.

At the outset, one might be tempted to assume that Garvey's contribution to th arts was mainly at the surface level, but on delving deeper into the cultural history Jamaica, the truth sooner or later becomes self-evident: that the Garvey era, pa ticularly between 1927 and 1935, can be regarded as a special cultural period with i own distinctive style, drawing from the folk and religious traditions of the countr while at the same time being influenced by Broadway, with the greatest emphas being placed on the creative muse, the original piece, whether in music, poetry drama. And so it had to be, for the man who founded an international organizatio which preached racial self-help, self-reliance and black pride, who sought to thro off the shackles of mental slavery would naturally see the importance of the arts this process.

Even before he launched into his lifelong, monumental task of trying to libera an entire race, the arts held an attraction for the young Marcus Garvey. Born just years after the abolition of slavery, the young Garvey was to suffer some of the soci consequences of the slave legacy, like most other black youths: limited education opportunities and a stultifying cultural atmosphere. But the young Garvey sought remedy these through a self-conscious effort of self education. He was more fo tunate than most others in that he had his father's extensive library at his dispos and so early in life developed a love of reading, a love which was to remain througho his entire life. In addition to his father's library he had access to that of his godfathe Mr Alfred Burrowes, a printer to whom he was apprenticed from the age of 14.

Garvey, like many other rural youths, went to Kingston, the nation's capital, search of brighter prospects and to broaden his horizons. He arrived there arou 1905, after working with Mr Burrowes in both St Ann's Bay and Port Maria. At th latter place he is said to have met the noted Pan-Africanist, J. Albert Thorne, at th home of a bookseller and businessman, Richard Elias Scarlett, who would later be come one of the founding members of the UNIA.[1]

Garvey quickly became immersed in the intellectual life of Kingston. He joine the National Club, a nascent political group, and worked on its paper, *Our Own*. Lat he was to start his own paper, *Garvey's Watchman*, thus beginning a lifelong care in journalism.

He also became interested in elocution and debate. The story is told that whe he first tried to enter discussions held in barber shops and on park benches, he wa rudely rebuked and told, "Country boy, shut you mouth!"[2] The young Garvey wa hurt by this stinging retort and set about learning the art of public speaking. H visited different churches every Sunday "to get points in platform deportment an oratory" from the ministers. Alone in his room he practised aloud what he ha learned, reciting passages and poems as well as imitating appropriate body gestures

The lessons seem to have paid off early. In 1910 he entered an all-island eloc tion contest, representing the parish of St Ann, and came third overall. So serious did he take this venture that he successfully took a heckler to court, whom he accuse of unnerving him during one of the presentations.[4] Around this time, too, he bega to organize public speaking contests among youths in West Kingston.

This early period of Garvey's life was followed by a period of extensive trave throughout Central America, where he saw at close range the hardships suffered b West Indian workers on plantations. After this he travelled to Britain and Europ where he was to learn first hand of the effects of European colonialism in Africa. He was to come in contact with the Egyptian nationalist Dusé Mohammed Ali, on whose paper he worked. Here again he had the opportunity to deepen his cultural knowledge by reading widely about the cultural history of Africa. Dusé Mohammed Ali was an eminent historian among other things. All these experiences led him to found the Universal Negro Improvement Association in 1914 on his return to Jamaica, with the broad aims of seeking to redress the disabilities of black people through co-operative effort and self reliance.

Garvey struggled with his fledgling organization for two years in Jamaica with limited success. But even from the beginning one could see that cultural concerns formed a part of regular activities. Weekly meetings then included debates, as indicated in the following:

> A debate on the Press or the Platform, which has the greater influence? followed a finely read dialogue between Miss A. Ashwood and Mr A. Daily entitled "Sixteen". Mr Marcus Garvey led for the Press supported by Mr Daily and Miss Ashwood, whilst Mr L. Small led for the Platform supported by Mr L. Fraser and members of the audience. When the issue was put to the vote, Mr Small's side won with a large majority. Next Tuesday (6th Oct.) at 7:30 the association holds its next general weekly of musical and literary evenings to which members and the public are cordially invited.[5]

As indicated at the end of that report, literary and musical activities were carried out on a regular basis. One early report even stated that "the object of the association is to improve the elocutionary and literary tastes of the youth of the community".[6] At another meeting a unanimous resolution was passed calling on the UNIA to establish "a city band for discoursing free music to the people of Kingston, and especially playing in the Victoria Gardens three times a week and at such places as the citizens of Kingston might request for the benefit of one and all".[7]

The early UNIA was asked to submit names of outstanding black men in Jamaica for inclusion in the historical work of Dr William Ferris, M.A., of Yale University,[8] entitled *The African Abroad or His Evolution in Western Civilization*. Among the names submitted were Dr Robert Love, to represent literature and oratory, and Mr B. de C. Reid,[9] for music.[10]

The early UNIA also staged fundraising concerts and there were regular lectures at meetings, such as the one given by Mr H.A.L. Simpson[11] on "The Abuse of the Jamaican Dialect"; it held elocution contests (Garvey won one of these) and it ran a library and reading room.

Garvey left Jamaica in 1916 for the United States, in order to do some fundraising for his young organization. Mrs Garvey tells us that he hoped to return to Jamaica to establish a trade centre and black cultural centre.[12] However, what was planned originally as a five-month speaking tour was extended into an eleven-year stay during which time the UNIA grew into the largest Pan-African movement ever, with over 1,200 branches in over 40 countries at its height. International conventions brought thousands of people together to hear at first hand the grievances of their fellowmen. The UNIA was also radicalized ideologically, preaching "Africa for the Africans", directly to the masses, demanding an end to colonial rule in Africa and encouraging blacks to practise an assertive nationalism.

Culture and the arts were to be an integral part of this assertiveness. During the American period, there was an extensive debate carried on, primarily in Garvey's newspaper, *The Negro World*, about the functions of culture. One of Mrs Amy Jacques Garvey's editorials sums up the ideal promulgated by the UNIA: "Let the canvas come to life with dark faces; let poetry charm the muses with the hopes and aspirations of our race; let the musicians drown our sorrows with the merry jazz; while a race is in the making and steadily moving on to nationhood and to power".[13]

The Negro World fostered the arts, in particular literature. It ran book reviews, short stories, articles on literature, culture, plays, films, and art exhibitions. For years it ran a full page of poems sent in by members from all over the world. The Garvey movement coincided with the Harlem Renaissance, influencing it as a catalyst but also promoting some of its major figures.

Culture was integrated in the administration of the UNIA in America, which had choirs, bands and dramatic clubs attached to different divisions. At the executive level there was a musical director in the person of Rabbi Arnold Ford, and the revised UNIA constitution called on each division to maintain a band where possible.

In other words, when Garvey returned to Jamaica in 1927 he brought with him a tradition of promoting the arts via the UNIA. He was to continue this tradition in Jamaica, extending it, perhaps because he himself was to participate as artist, in a more involved way than previously and to act as promoter. "Marcus Garvey had been one of the first people in the 1920's to consider the public recreation and entertainment of the poorer people in the Kingston and St Andrew area. Edelweiss Park was the locale for dances and the projection of new stage talent", wrote the noted Jamaican dancer Ivy Baxter.[14]

Dances, dramatic presentations, musical revues, vaudevilles, comedies, variety concerts, choral renditions, elocution, singing and dancing contests, films, picnics, fairs – all these activities were fostered at Edelweiss Park, the headquarters of the St Andrew division, under the direct sponsorship of the UNIA, earning for this venue the title "the mecca of entertainment, especially for the poorer classes".

"As much as we are trying to develop ourselves in business, religion, politics and so on, we have to build ourselves up in Art", Garvey told the 1934 UNIA Convention, held in Kingston,[15] one which conducted art, music, and literature sessions. Another idea was that black people must develop their own cultural norms, and their own aesthetic, their own body of literature, music, art, poetry, painting, sculpture, etc. Another prevalent idea was that the black artist had a duty to his race and should create works which were for the most part if not overtly uplifting then certainly not degrading. Predictably, this aspect was cause for debate even within his own organization. Garvey criticized the writer Claude McKay and Paul Robeson on this score. He called McKay's novel *Home to Harlem* a "damnable libel against the Negro".[16] Of Paul Robeson he wrote: "Paul Robeson is a good actor. There is no doubt he is one of the frontliners of the profession, but featured as he is as a negro, he is doing his race a great deal of harm. The Producers have been using Paul Robeson from *Emperor Jones* to *Stevedore* to put over a vile and vicious propaganda against the Negro".[17]

On the other hand he praised Ernest Cupidon, Jamaica's most famous elocutionist and impersonator in his day (some say the greatest ever) for his devotion to his people. After Cupidon's performance at a mass meeting at Edelweiss Park one Sunday night, Garvey commented: "As they all know, Mr Cupidon is an accomplished artiste – one of the stars of the island of Jamaica, and we are proud of it. We know this about him, that as high as Mr Cupidon climbs, he goes with his people; we cannot say that of some stars in other lines because they on the contrary get away from their people".[18]

But if the artist had a duty to his people, the reverse was also true: the people had a duty to support their own artists. It was therefore a symbiotic relationship. "We must encourage our own black authors who have character, who are loyal to their race, who feel proud to be black and in every way let them feel that we appreciate their efforts to advance our race through healthy and decent literature"[19] was the comment in a *Negro World* editorial.

Writing of a specific Jamaican situation, a souvenir concert in support of Cupidon, Garvey reiterated this idea:

> The Cupidon concert at the Ward Theatre last Saturday night was a success. We are pleased of it. It shows that our people have at last learned to appreciate their own. Once upon a time, the patronage for anything like a concert where our people are starred would be poor, because our people were taught to see no good in their own. It is pleasing to know that we are having race consciousness that leads us to see good in ourselves and always to lend a helping hand to our own.[20]

Garvey also believed in state support for the arts. He ran for the general elections in 1930 under the banner of the People's Political Party (PPP), the first modern political party in Jamaica. The ninth plank of the party manifesto stated that, if elected, the PPP would seek to establish: "A National Opera House with an Academy of Music and Art". One should interpret the National Opera House to mean some kind of performing arts centre. To understand the foresight of this policy it must be pointed out that the Jamaica School of Art was not established until 1950 and the Jamaica School of Music not until 1962.

Edelweiss Park

BUT GARVEY WAS NOT a mere visionary or one who made promises and dreamed dreams; he was an activist, one who got things done. What he promised to do if elected to the state apparatus, he set out to demonstrate within his own organization; for during his time at Edelweiss Park that venue became a major cultural centre, offering training to artists, showcasing talent and hosting several kinds of cultural events. It also maintained its own cultural units: two choirs, one sacred, the other secular; a dance troupe known as the Follies; two orchestras and a band. There was a director of entertainment on staff in the person of Gerardo Leon (whose real name was Gerald Lyon), a multi-talented artist who came to Edelweiss with a wealth of experience in show business developed locally and overseas.

Cultural activities were institutionalized and formalized when the Edelweiss Park Amusement Company was established in 1931. This was capitalized at $30,000 with shares offered to the public at $2 each.[21] The company had the task of managing the cultural units, presenting high-class productions and seeking out local talent. It also had the task of managing certain recreational facilities, such as restaurants, rest rooms and games rooms. In addition the venue was a place which could be rented to other groups for rehearsal.

A secretary of the company, Daisy Whyte, gives an idea of the layout in this promotional letter sent to prospective patrons in 1931:

> We hereby inform you that the Edelweiss Amusement Co. Ltd. has been organized for the purpose of supplying high class and healthy amusements and sports for the people of Jamaica and the residents and citizens of the Corporate area of Kingston and St Andrew in particular.
>
> We have realized that as a country we are very much lacking in variety entertainment and amusements which are necessary to every civilized community. Our community has for the past three months retained competent masters in music, dramatics, singing and comedy to train different troupes and individuals for use by the Company of Edelweiss Park and different centres of the island....
>
> Edelweiss Park covers an area of one and a half acres of land, and has an open air theatre well laid out with a capacity to accommodate 8,000 people seated. The grounds are also fitted out for other amusements which will be opened to the public on the 21st instant with apparatuses and devices that we have just brought down from Europe. You can always ring up Edelweiss Park and book your tickets for any of the affairs to be staged there or get them at the gates.[22]

This letter was written two years after the historic 1929 UNIA Convention, an event which caused extensive refurbishing and expansion to be done to the physical facilities to accommodate the thousands of delegates expected to attend. Garvey appealed for voluntary labour and the people responded with activities going on from 8 a.m. to 11 p.m., according to one eyewitness.[23] An advertisement for the official opening at the end stated: "The stadium and pavillion have been constructed to seat 15,000 persons for the great International Convention of the Negro Peoples of the World that will take place from 1st to 31st August".[24]

The Park was again refurbished in 1932, following a policy decision to introduce new and different types of entertainment. A promotional piece appearing the day before the official opening described the policy and physical setting in this way:

> Tomorrow night the Edelweiss Amusement Company will open up Edelweiss Park as Jamaica's centre of permanent amusements of every variety and attraction. The company at its inception, over a year ago, intended to carry out this plan of making the Park a centre for the people of the two parishes of Kingston and St Andrew and visitors to

the city for obtaining all that they may want in line of healthy amusements.

The Park is being nicely fitted out to accommodate every class of patron. The variety that will be introduced will cover every range of modern sport. There will be radio programmes, orchestral music, popular entertainers, side-shows, games and dancing. There will be a variety of stalls, restaurants, lunch rooms and refreshment parlours. The ambitious plans of the promoters aim at giving the people just what the citizens of the cities of the world get during their hours of leisure.[25]

Although Edelweiss Park was the main venue for major UNIA cultural events, it certainly was not the only venue. Liberty Hall, situated at 76 King Street, the headquarters of the Kingston Division, had its own sphere of activities on somewhat similar lines. There was a Kingston Amusement Company,[26] established to promote cultural activities there. Liberty Hall also maintained its own cultural units: an adult choir, a children's choir and a band.

Perhaps the most regular of the cultural activities was the weekly Sunday night meetings at Edelweiss Park. During Garvey's stay in Jamaica, this represented a major attraction for the populace and thousands turned up weekly to attend. The meeting represented a combination of religious services, cultural activity and a political forum. It would start with a procession of uniformed groups during which the UNIA choir would open with the hymn "From Greenland's Icy Mountain". Then would follow the religious part of the programme – readings from the Scriptures and the *UNIA Ritual* followed by a sermon based on the text but often interwoven with UNIA philosophical projections of racial upliftment. The chaplain general or some other minister of religion might take this section.

The second section would be the cultural part, and here the Edelweiss Park sacred choir generally took part, as well as the band. But in addition there would be solo items, whether voice or instrumental, recitations, dramatic monologues, poetry reading, as well as performances from the orchestra. The meeting would then end with a major speech by Marcus Garvey or some main UNIA official; sometimes there would be guest speakers from outside the UNIA. Garvey's topics often served as a second sermon, as they were frequently philosophical in tone, but often were political. A description of a typical Sunday night meeting illustrates the point:

> The meeting was called to order by Mr Simeon E. McKenzie, first vice president and commenced with the singing of the opening ode "From Greenland's Icy Mountains" followed by the prayers and the hymn "God of the Right Our Battles Fight". Mr Bellamy then read a lesson from the Scriptures, 2nd Corinthians chpt. 5:1-11, after which the band treated the audience to a selection of *Ernauir* and led off the musical programme with an overture *Fraternity*. The choir followed with an anthem "How Lovely is Zion". Again the band treated the audience to a selection of *Ernauir* and Miss Daisy Greenidge who was next on the programme for the recitation of "David's Lament for Absalom" made a wonderful impression upon her hearers.[27] The interpretation

> was so perfect that the President General commented on it in glowing terms and congratulated Miss Greenidge. Miss L. Hewie who rendered "The Holy City" completely captivated the audience and Mr and Mrs George McCormack followed with a duet. Mr Cecil Moore recited a panegyric on the Hon. Marcus Garvey and was vociferously applauded. *Cavalleria Rusticana* by the band, an anthem by the choir – "I was glad" – was followed by another selection – "Home Songs" – ended the musical programme".[28]

Other Edelweiss Park cultural units found an outlet in the regular variety concerts and musical revues, vaudevilles and dramatic presentations staged there. The variety concert seemed to have been the most popular event and a report of one of these can give an idea of the range of presentations:

> The chairman of the afternoon was the Hon. Marcus Garvey and in his opening address he promised all an enjoyable evening.
>
> Our comedian Cupidon was in his best form. Surely it can be said that his presence on the stage is humour enough so original and plain that everyone may understand him and still so full of wit and sense while Racca and Sandy in the same sphere of comedy, filled the house with laughter.
>
> It must be universally admitted the *Zingarella* as recited by Lady Henrietta Vinton Davis was unparalleled for its delivery. The pathos was such that sent a shudder through the bones of very individual in the audience. To hear her is to hear perfect elocution....
>
> The Farce – *A Night in Paris* – was a specimen of which special mention must be made. Mr Roosevelt Williams who played the role of Duke Wilson – a perfect crook....[29]

At other times, presentations would feature individual cultural units. For example the sacred choir might perform an oratorio or cantata; the Follies would perform in regular musical revues or cabaret shows or there might be full-length dramatic presentations.

From time to time certain days of the week were set for certain presentations or activities. According to a veteran Garveyite, Z. Munroe Scarlett, at one time the schedule was Mondays for dance, Wednesdays for drama, while Sundays saw the regular mass meetings.[30] Sometimes there would be "Gala Weeks", with a different activity every night. An advertisement for one such from 21 to 26 October 1929 gives an idea of the kinds of events staged there. On Monday night there was a big treasure hunt and vaudeville show; on Tuesday there was a big concert extravaganza with "classical and jazz music unending". Performers included the Jamaica Military Band and other artists such as comedians Ranny Williams and Racca and Sandy[31] and dancers Pearl Campbell, Agnes Hinds and Maria Kelly. On Wednesday night there was a mass meeting addressed by the UNIA's first assistant president-general, Mr E.B. Knox.[32] On Thursday there was a picnic and treasure hunt; on Friday night there was a big political meeting with top PPP personnel as the main speakers.[33] On Saturday night there was another show and treasure hunt. And of course on Sunday there was the regular Sunday night meeting.

Some of the cultural events were openly political. The best example of this was the programme planned to welcome Garvey's release from prison, which was originally scheduled for Christmas Eve 1929. The programme included the combined choirs of Edelweiss Park and Liberty Hall and both orchestras of Edelweiss Park. Garvey, referred to in the promotional pieces as "The Chief", was to deliver a new message to the negroes of the world, "The Negro and His Cause".[34] In addition, a grand procession with bands and regalia was planned to accompany Garvey from jail. The colonial authorities got wind of it and let him out unannounced a few days earlier.[35]

Other special concerts were of a more religious nature, such as the harvest festival, which combined religious services with concerts. At Easter there would often be a sacred cantata, while at Christmas there would be Christmas morning concerts.

From the foregoing it will be seen that a variety of cultural activities was promoted by the Garvey movement. We will now look at the individual art forms promoted.

Elocution

OF ALL THE ART FORMS, Garvey loved that of oratory and elocution best. It is the one in which he excelled, a fact attested to by friend and foe alike. A reporter of the *Panamanian American* newspaper once wrote:

> He would probably pass unnoticed in a crowd – until he speaks. He has the most precious of all bounties, the gift of eloquence. His speech is smooth and unctuous without any touch of the American twang despite his long residence in the United States. His English is that of an Oxford scholar and when he speaks – his hearers listen.[36]

Garvey himself was to concur with the reporter's assessment of the art of elocution. "To be a good speaker or elocutionist is to hold a grand prize among men", he stated in one of his lessons to students attending the School of African Philosophy.[37] And a veteran Garveyite, Vivian Durham, himself an accomplished orator, agrees with the reporter's assessment of Garvey's skills. He has described Garvey as "the Demosthenes of the Negro people".[38]

In Jamaica the UNIA sponsored annual elocution contests on an all-island basis. It would appear that these contests were open to both men and women, competing against each other at first. In 1929 the winner was George Bowen, second was Iris Patterson and third Miss S.C. Lee.[39] However, according to veteran Garveyites, there was later a men's section separate from the women's section in this competition. One person remembers Una Marson, the noted playwright and journalist, winning the women's section one year while Cupidon won the men's section.[40] Cupidon did win the competition in the years 1931 and 1932, but *The New Jamaican* only gives a report on the men's section for the 1932 competition:

> Mr E.M. Cupidon was able to retain his championship which he won for himself last year in a graphic presentation of *The Blacksmith's Story* and certainly deserves the place given him by the judges. Mr H.O.B. Harriott who recited *Mark Anthony's Oration* was awarded second place whilst Mr A.J. Greenidge, St Catherine representative who presented *Chatham on the American War* was awarded third position. Mr Archie Lindo was heard to great advantage in his wonderful rendition of *The Shooting of Dan McGrew*. His delivery was of a very high standard, and it might be said that he painted the whole picture in his enunciation and excellent dramatizing. He was given fourth position. *The Impeachment of Warren Hastings* was recited by Mr P.N. Blake who represented St Andrew and this won for him the fifth position.[41]

In addition to these contests, elocutionists were given the opportunity to demonstrate their skills at the weekly Sunday night meetings, where persons such as Iris Patterson, dubbed the "poet laureate" of the UNIA, would recite her own poems, and others, like Ernest Cupidon, George Bowen, S.C. Lee, and Henrietta Vinton Davis of the United States would participate. Elocutionists also appeared on variety concerts where a range of presentations from comic to tragic might be performed. By far the greatest exponent of this form was Garvey himself in his weekly speeches, a major drawing card for large audiences.

Special UNIA events would be the occasion for outstanding speech presentations, the most outstanding in Jamaica being the 1929 UNIA Convention. An editorial in *Blackman* stated then that "the high standard of oratory to which Edelweiss has grown accustomed tended to a higher than usual excellence inspired by the grandeur of the occasion".[42]

The convention also featured a Women's Night where oratory was the main skill demonstrated. "Who would attempt to describe the impassioned language and magnetic power with which Madame de Mena made her great deliverance or the quiet dignity and elegance of the speech of Lady Davis or the energy and fervour with which Mrs Robertson recorded her travels, through the States in the interests of the UNIA. All these brought the fire of oratory to bear on the situation".[43]

Debates were also fostered by the UNIA, and the 1929 Convention again provided the opportunity for these. One such pitted Jamaican representatives against some American delegates. The topic was "Resolved that the Negroes of the West Indies had made more progress since Emancipation than those of the U.S.A." The Americans won hands down, according to Vivian Durham, one of the contestants.[44] By far the most dramatic debate took place between two giants – Marcus Garvey, leader of the UNIA, and Otto Huiswood, of the American Negro Labour Congress and a communist. Here was an occasion to present arguments based on separate ideological approaches to real-life problems. The topic was "Resolved that the Negro problem can only be solved by international labour cooperation between black and white labour". Huiswood supported it while Garvey opposed. Naturally Garvey won – he was on his home territory. *The Gleaner* described the event as "an oratorical feast".[45]

Garvey's Plays

DRAMA WAS PROBABLY the art form that benefited most from the Garvey movement in Jamaica. Garvey himself wrote plays, some seven of which have so far been identified: *Roaming Jamaicans*, *Slavery from Hut to Mansion*, *Coronation of an African King*,[46] *Let My People Go*,[47] *Ethiopia at the Bar of Justice*,[48] *A Night in Havana*,[49] and *Wine, Women and Song*.[50]

Roaming Jamaicans depicts the life of Jamaicans in the USA, Central American countries, Cuba, and Haiti, "their life abroad and return to Jamaica".[51] *Slavery from Hut to Mansions* is described in its blurb as "a revelation of the horrors of slavery",[52] while the *Coronation of an African King* is said to be a dramatization of the work of the UNIA. The plot centres on attempts by European leaders to destroy a worldwide black organization. They fail and eventually an African king is crowned.

These plays could be called pageants, in that they had extremely large casts. There were 120 characters in *Slavery from Hut to Mansion*, and 80 in *Roaming Jamaicans*. Garvey seems to have used the classical tradition of battles taking place offstage in his plays. Mr A.W.A. Atherton, chief reporter for *Blackman*, wrote of *Coronation of an African King*:

> The audience's knowledge of the terrific conflict which was being waged was secured from the many soldiers who were brought wounded and dying into the hospital near the battlefront. In the distance sounded the din and roar of the tremendous battle, guns belching flames, thunder and sudden death, the voices of black orators sounding above the thunder of the guns inspiring their countrymen on to victory over the dead bodies of their comrades and the screaming voices of women and children as the bleeding bodies of the relatives passed them on the bloodstained streets".[53]

Besides these plays, Garvey is credited with writing at least three mock trials – one a murder trial, another a divorce case, and a third a trial based on his own trial in Jamaica.[54]

Garvey also directed his own plays and, according to one informant, "he drilled you day and night".[55] Garvey also played the role of actor, appearing as a judge in a mock trial written by Ernest Cupidon and performed at Edelweiss Park.[56]

Other persons wrote and staged plays at Edelweiss Park, chief among them Ranny Williams. Indeed Garvey's greatest contribution to the development of drama in Jamaica was the encouragement and development of Ranny Williams, who was to emerge later as Jamaica's leading male comedian for decades. Williams himself always credited Garvey for developing his early career. He describes how he got into drama:

> I was first a hoofer [back line dancer]. Soon I was a frontliner and then a feature dancer with partners in front of the frontline. A large UNIA conference was being held and Mr Garvey gave me permission to sit

> in on sessions. My observations later formed the basis of successful monologues I performed imitating some of the more eccentric and popular delegates".[57]

From these monologues Williams was to go on to stage several plays at Edelweiss Park. *Say It Singing*, a musical comedy, was staged in October 1929 to help raise funds to defray Garvey's legal costs.[58] Garvey was in the Spanish Town prison at the time on a charge of contempt of court arising from a plank of his political manifesto. This play depicted a "cabaret show given in a salon for the benefit of hotel guests".[59] It allowed many of the Edelweiss Park artistes, such as the comedy team Racca and Sandy (who played a husband-and-wife team), to show off their skills: Lurline Hewie, the noted soprano, Kid Harold, the tap dancer, and Arthur Bennett, also a dancer.

Several other plays by Williams followed. *Blacks Gone Wild* (originally *Niggers Gone Wild*) appeared a month later. This was described as "the last word in music, comedy and tragedy".[60] Other plays by Williams at Edelweiss Park were *Landing the Landlord* (described as a comedy farce), *Old Black Joe*, *King Balshazzar*, and *She's A Sheba*. There are several references to other untitled pieces, farces and monologues which he performed, usually as part of variety concerts. One advertisement for an Easter concert promoted five different farces by Williams, each one presenting a different idea – comedy, pathos, tragedy, pantomime, and minstrelsy.[61]

The great impersonator and comedian Ernest Cupidon staged at least one play at Edelweiss Park, a mock trial called *Uncle Fixam's Trial* (from his conviction on the charge of practising *obeah*). The cast line included Marcus Garvey, Dr E.C. Da Costa and Mr T.R. McMillan as judges of the High Court. Cupidon himself acted as the prisoner, while Ken Hill appeared as the attorney for the defence.[62]

Plays were also performed at Liberty Hall by UNIA members. Mr Sidney Grey, an officer of the UNIA in Cuba and later in Kingston, wrote several plays which were performed at Liberty Hall. One was *The Slave Ship*, which dealt with the Middle Passage. He recalled that during one of the scenes when slaves were unceremoniously tossed overboard, Madame N.L.T. de Mena, the UNIA international organizer, fainted. Grey said he was associated with the comedy team Bim and Bam[63] and helped to write *A Gun Court Affair* in the 1970s, thus providing another link between Garvey's work and popular Jamaican theatre.

The comments of the noted Caribbean dramatist Errol Hill about the Garvey era are instructive:

> A significant first step in the establishment of popular Jamaican theatre was made under the aegis of the Marcus Garvey movement in the 1920s.... This movement ... unleashed within the Jamaican society ... large, untapped energies among the masses of black people. These energies, directed mainly towards social and political advancement, were at the same time necessary to create the kind of national consciousness out of which a viable indigenous drama can emerge....
>
> In 1921 the first Liberty Hall in Jamaica was established. From that date to 1935 when Garvey left Jamaica for England, the Kingston and St Andrew Liberty Halls became the arena where the mass of the population could view a continuous, almost nightly spectacle of bur-

geoning local talent. The St Andrew Liberty Hall, situated just below the main concourse of city and suburban traffic at Cross Roads, sponsored everything from popular dances and balls to debating, choral concerts and dramatic presentations, the last named taking essentially the form of epic pageantry.[64]

Perhaps the one limitation to the dramatic form which the Garvey enterprise abetted was the exaggerated emphasis on elocutionary skill. Garvey's stage encouraged the known penchant among the folk for elaborate, declamatory speech, a practice which left its mark in the speechifying tendency so noticeable in the indigenous theatre. However, what may be considered a temporary disservice to the Jamaican theatre was of positive value to the Garvey movement.[65]

Dance

THE UNIA ALSO FOSTERED the art of dance. At Edelweiss Park there was a troupe of dancers known as the Follies under the direction of Gerardo Leon. Leon had spent years in show business in New York, Cuba, Belize, and Paris before coming to Edelweiss Park.[66] At one time there were two companies of Follies consisting of sixteen dancing girls and eight comedians. However, there were many more girls under training. Leon's son, who was a child during this period but who used to be around Edelweiss Park regularly, remembers some 200 girls and 100 men under training. They had to go through a rigid programme and had to be up by 5 a.m. to run a mile around Race Course,[67] then jog back to Edelweiss Park. At other times they would be taken to view the latest films, often several times to see one film, in order to learn some of the latest steps. The Edelweiss Park Amusement Company secretary, Daisy Whyte, more or less concurs with some of these observations: "We have 250 chorus girls and men under a comedy master who has given them three months of hard training", she stated in a promotional letter of 1931.

The Follies were definitely one of the most popular groups at Edelweiss Park. They performed in cabaret shows and musical revues, as well as at other concerts under non-UNIA sponsorship, and were often part of Ranny Williams's plays. It would appear that they did a variety of steps, from Broadway-type dances to more folkloric movements. Singing often accompanied their dancing, and in the revues they had to act as well.

Some of Jamaica's top show dancers were associated with Edelweiss Park. Kid Harold[68] (who died in 1985), of the duo Harold and Trim, was personally recruited by Garvey and Gerardo Leon. According to him,

> Garvey called me into his office one Sunday. Mr Garvey said, "Harold, how long have you been in show business?" I said, "Just a couple of years". He said, "You are very good. We are going to run shows here you know. I want you to help me. I want you to help Gerardo. We would like to get yourself and your partner Trim on the big occasion nights".

> I have never met a man in my life like Mr Garvey. He was embedded in the people of Jamaica and that is something.... He helped quite a few boys and girls to get a leeway until they start to appear at different places in show business.[69]

Kid Harold could not take up the offer immediately, because he was contracted to another promoter, but he started to judge dance competitions Saturday nights; later he was one of the regular artists at concerts there and appeared with his partner Trim in many of Ranny Williams's plays at Edelweiss Park. He said that Garvey's legacy in this field was to provide some of the best professional dancers on the entertainment circuit.

Dancing competitions were a regular feature at Edelweiss Park. In 1930 there was a special marathon contest lasting a whole week. Twenty couples were selected each night with 100 dancing couples competing on the final night. Dancers competed in the categories classical, rustic, tap, apache (including the old-time jig), quadrille, waltzing, tango, and lindy hop.[70]

Both Edelweiss Park and Liberty Hall, on King Street, were the venues for public dances, places where the general public could go for an evening of social dancing. It was not unusual to see ads like these: "Extraordinary vaudeville – Follies and Musical Programme at Edelweiss Park – 7:30 to midnight. Dancing after musical programme".[71] Impromptu dancing often took place at other UNIA events, such as fairs and garden parties. At one such, it is said that "dance-mad youths" were led to engage in "frenzied demonstrations of the very latest steps".[72]

Music

MUSIC FORMED an important part of UNIA activities in Jamaica. Indeed there were few occasions or functions sponsored by the UNIA which did not have some kind of musical presentation. Music was fostered by the maintenance of musical groups, through the many concerts held at UNIA venues, the Sunday night meetings and parades, by the training of musicians, and by encouraging the writing of music.

At Edelweiss Park there were two choirs, two orchestras (a concert orchestra and a jazz orchestra), and a band, making five musical units at that location alone. Liberty Hall also had a choir for adults, a children's choir and a band. The choir at Edelweiss was under the direction of the noted tenor Granville Campbell, and this one performed weekly at Sunday night meetings. According to one member, the training was rigid. Members had to attend any five practice sessions out of a total of ten per week before being allowed to perform on Sunday nights. For each appearance they would be paid two guineas.[73] The other choir performed at concerts and specialized in more popular songs and spirituals.

Edelweiss Park was able to attract some of the best singers in Jamaica from time to time, more so on special occasions. Among them were Johnny Lyon, male soprano; William Spooner, a baritone; Mrs Steadman, a soprano who joined with the UNIA regulars; Granville Campbell; Lurline Hewie, dubbed "the nightingale of the UNIA"; Iris Patterson, contralto; and the McCormacks, among others.

There were singing contests at Edelweiss Park run on an all-island basis with sections for sopranos, contraltos, tenors, and basses. The 1932 contest was won by Myrtle Bennett, second was Blanche Savage and third was Miss C. Fletcher. In the baritone section George Bowen was first, M.U. Porter second, and George McCormack third.

On the more popular side, the Follies performed songs. Some were Broadway hits, but others were original pieces written by Gerardo Leon, their director. Leon was a prolific writer who staged several revues at Edelweiss, among them *Smiles and Kisses, Finding a Wife, Pep and Ginger, From Smith Village to Constant Spring, The Girl from Linstead, Good Gracious Annabelle, Good Morning Satan,* and *Fifty Thousand Pounds.* Leon provided one direct link with the development of popular Jamaican music, as he was later to write the mento songs for his brother Rupert Lyon, who performed as Lord Fly in the 1950s and 1960s. Mento, the first popular Jamaican musical idiom, would later give way to ska, rock-steady and reggae.

The troubadour team of Slim and Sam[74] also performed at Edelweiss.[75] Slim and Sam wrote a special song in tribute to the Garvey movement, "The Marcus Garvey Melody".[76]

Garvey himself composed songs, the most famous being *Keep Cool*, written while he was in jail in Atlanta. This song was aired regularly at Sunday night meetings and seems to have been a specialty of Lurline Hewie. Garvey received endorsement from one of Jamaica's most famous musicians and musicologists of the era, Astley Clerk. One promotional piece for the song stated:

> Mr Astley Clerk is one of Kingston's most humane and respectable characters – when he says anything it is worthwhile listening to if it concerns music. Mr Clerk says the words of the song *Keep Cool* by Marcus Garvey is inspiring and the music is superb".[77]

The song is exhortative in tone, though not overbearingly so; the first verse goes:

> Suns have set and suns will rise
> Upon many gloomy lives;
> Those who sit around and say
> "Nothing good comes down our way",
> Some say: "What's the use to try?
> Life is awful hard and dry".
> If they'd bring such news to you
> This is what you ought to do.
>
> (*Chorus*) Let no trouble worry you:
> Keep cool, keep cool!
> Don't get hot like some folk do,
> Keep cool, keep cool!

Garvey also published in 1934 his *Universal Negro Improvement Association Convention Hymnal*, containing songs by both himself and Arnold Ford and some traditional numbers. One of these, "Jubilee", was written in tribute to the Centenary of the abolition of slavery:

Jubilee has come today
Praise to God the only King;
Centuries have passed away,
And good freedom's rights begin.

Chains and blocks are gone to hell
Souls of men and women too:
Saintly prophets did all tell
Slavers, hardy, story true.

Come what may I'm free to dwell
Where the sun and stars do shine;
Never more can slavers sell
This triumphant soul of mine.

Garvey held a concert at the Ward Theatre in 1934 at which he presented his songs with music written by Mr B. de C. Reid, one-time director of the Jamaica Military Band. In introducing the programme, Garvey said he had written "several poems and other articles which had been set to music by Mr Reid" for the purpose of "encouraging every Jamaican to exercise whatever creative gifts they possessed in the realms of poetry and music".[78] He heavily criticized the practice of copying other people's taste and norms in music and poetry.

Rally songs formed a part of the regular training received by the juveniles of the UNIA as well as the adults. In Jamaica there was a book with compositions by some of the top UNIA personnel along with standard UNIA songs from the United States. Composers included Charles Johnson, President of the Kingston Division; The Rev. S.M. Jones, an AME minister; and Madame de Mena, UNIA International Organizer. The themes vary from racial pride and upliftment to African redemption, from praises to the UNIA leader to standard religious themes. The imagery of black people rallying behind the flag of the UNIA stands out. In "All Around the World", written by Madame de Mena and sung to the tune of "Old Black Joe", this theme is apparent:

All around the world our Negro Leader's been
All around the world he called to Negro men
All around the world now he's back here again
The Red, the Black and Green is waving
All around the world.

(*Chorus*) Keep waving, keep waving
Keep Afric's flag unfurled
The Red, the Black and Green is waving
All round the world.

Another, by S.M. Jones, echoes a similar theme:

> Listen to the voice of Garvey, the Negroes friend
> Hear him telling the people everywhere to unite
> Sing the song of New Negroes till we obtain our land
> Garvey comes to lead his people home again.

The preface to this book of songs sums up quite clearly its intention:

> In presenting this little book for your use, I desire to state that the intention is to get you to make the best use of these songs. As you are aware, songs are very catching and songs have been used at all times and in all ages to keep our minds in certain direction.
>
> The direction in which the Hon. Marcus Garvey is seeking to place your mind today is Racial Pride, Racial Unity and the Redemption of Africa. The constant singing of these songs will have that effect on your minds and will also help to bring some of the minds of those opposed to our cause in line with ours.

From time to time, articles on music would appear in the Garvey papers. These included an article on jazz by the noted historian J.A. Rogers.[79] The director of Liberty Hall's choir once had a series in *Blackman* called "Musical Echoes".

Plastic Arts

GARVEY WAS a lover of the plastic arts – painting, sculptures, ceramic pieces and antiques. He was known as an avid art collector, especially of African-oriented pieces. Amy Jacques Garvey gives us an insight into this side of her husband:

> He had no recreation, as it was dangerous to go to the theatre so his idea of relaxation was to go around to antique shops and buy these old pieces. When he brought them home he would spend time and patience placing them in the right setting, colour scheme and effective lighting. Sometimes other objects had to be removed and new positions found for them. He enjoyed sitting in an easy chair and contemplating the beauty of the setting he had created, or the exquisite workmanship of a "Satsuma" from Japan, a "Delph" vase from Holland or the delicacy of an egg-shell goblet.[80]

It is significant that when he was leaving for Jamaica one of his first instructions to his wife was to crate two large paintings, including an oil painting of himself.

Somali Court, his home at Lady Musgrave Road, as well as his offices at Edelweiss Park were decorated with art pieces. Outside his home was the statue of an African girl. One day this statue was stolen by some men who drove up the driveway and snatched it. Later it was found broken in pieces in Greenwich Pen. According to Mrs Garvey it was felt that the statue was a fetish used by Garvey to practise *obeah* and so its destruction would break Garvey's spell over the Jamaican people.

Inside the Garvey home were to be found different art works. His niece, Ruth Prescott, then a child, remembers some of the decor:

> There were lovely velvet cushions and a wall to wall carpet with a border and pattern. There were beautiful statues and pictures – paintings, vases, Spanish jars some of them of porcelain and some painted.[81]

Art was one of the topics for discussion at the 1934 UNIA Convention in Jamaica. Garvey himself chaired the session and said:

> Art was a very important subject but this was probably not realized by a large number of people, particularly of his group because it was a subject of culture rather than a subject of everyday occupation. One's civilization is not complete without its Art, the highest form of expression of human intelligence. That is my interpretation. Art is the highest form of genius.[82]

Garvey encouraged the delegates at that conference to become more appreciative of art. He noted that while black civilization in the past had created monumental works such as the pyramids of Egypt or the statues of Benin, it was not enough for the present generation to rest on these laurels; they had to create their own artistic works of merit.

Garvey's newspapers carried articles of general discussion on art as well as reviews of exhibitions both local and overseas. *The New Jamaican* once carried an article on art restoration.[83] One issue of *Blackman* carried a review of an art show in London by Ghanaian art students curated by their tutor, one Mr G.A. Stevens, a former art master at the Prince of Wales College in Achimota. His object in teaching the students was "to wean them away from the apathy of an imposed European tradition in art to the enthusiasm and colour of their native style".[84]

Moreover, Garvey used his regular column, "The World As It Is" to encourage his readers to develop a taste in art. He wrote in 1932 in support of an art exhibition at the Jamaican Mutual Assurance Society's Building:

> Even though most of us haven't any artistic taste, we ought to seize the opportunity of seeing the Exhibition before it comes to a close. In other parts of the world, the cultural and intelligent class would be very much attracted to an Exhibition of this kind. If some of us can do nothing more, we ought to imitate those who have good taste to see the Exhibition. In that case, we may become lovers of art afterwards. Nearly everyone must have a first time in everything. It wouldn't be bad for some of us to have a first time in seeing the Exhibition of works of art.[85]

Alvin Marriott, the well-known Jamaican sculptor, was inspired by Garvey. An article in *Blackman* encouraged him in his work and described him as "the Michael Angelo [*sic*] of not only Jamaica but of the West Indies" who had been "showing his talent as a polished sculptor and finished artist by his numerous works of art that have been gaining the praise and approbation of even the fierce critics".[86]

Marriott himself was an admirer of Garvey and attended some of his meetings. He once visited his home in order to do a sketch. Garvey, he reported, had a very busy schedule and so could not sit for too long but he did manage to get "a nice profile of him".[87] Marriott was later to do more than one bust and statue of Garvey, including the one at his shrine in National Heroes Park and the life-size statue in St Ann's Bay. "Garvey was a cultured man. He had brilliant ideas.... As an artist I am dedicated to Garvey as I am to no other", he has stated.[88]

Another mainstream artist who was directly influenced by Garvey is Jamaica's most famous intuitive painter and sculptor, Mallica "Kapo" Reynolds, who was once a member of the UNIA.

The Garvey movement indirectly influenced other popular art forms. The banners carried on parades, the regalia, the uniforms, and the pageantry of some of the dramatic productions encouraged artistic expression.

Literature

THE GARVEY NEWSPAPERS published poems sent in by readers from all over the world. Among the most prolific was Iris Lucille Patterson, frequently dubbed the "poet laureate of the UNIA", and J.N. Preston, a writer from Cuba. Patterson's poems are largely exhortative:

> Awake Jamaica! How long will thy lethargic slumber last?
> How oft review the gloomy nightmare of thy past?
> Behold! Now is the acceptable time
> Awake! Put on thy strength and fall in line.[89]

Other poems were religious and some could be humorous, as this one in praise of the inestimable Cupidon:

> In ages when the stage of life
> Was full of internecine strife
> The gods to blunt the hateful knife
> Sent Cupid on.[90]

Although no major Jamaican author published in the Garvey papers, nevertheless Garvey gave strong support to mainstream writers. He believed in the development of a Jamaican literature, and many editorials in his newspapers addressed the subject. One such, which took the form of a review of the anthology *Voices From Summerland*, edited by J.E. Clare McFarlane, later poet laureate of Jamaica, stated in part:

> This Anthology of Jamaica Poetry as the phrase implies is indeed a collection of the flower of our Jamaican verse literature in mild but penetrating fragrance emanating from every source. One turns the leaves and pages of a new book as if desiring from its mere contents to anticipate the final impression of the study. Even this preliminary exercise at once reveals the wide sources of origin of the Anthology, the

variety of their contribution; and makes of this little work a true and useful repository of the best in our poetical literature.

Mr J.E. Clare McFarlane has otherwise made large contributions to Jamaica poetry. He is engaged in ceaseless activity to promote the love of literature in this country. This his latest effort in the collecting into one volume the choicest specimens of our island poetry is apart from the merits and usefulness of the work, a labour of love, an expression of patriotism, strong, fervent and aggressive, for which we congratulate him.[91]

One of the features of the Garvey newspapers was the front-page editorial which appeared once a week, often taking the form of quotes from important poets or prose writers. Words from Shakespeare, Shelley, Mirabeau, Ella Wheeler Wilcox, Walt Whitman, Thomas Jefferson, Lloyd George, and Confucius were to be found on these pages.

Strong support was given to Nancy Cunard, a well-known white radical, described as "a renegade member of a wealthy shipping family who became involved in a variety of black causes".[92] A special reception was held for her at Edelweiss Park when she visited Jamaica to collect material for a book.[93]

One surprising article appeared in *Blackman* welcoming the visit of Rudyard Kipling to Jamaica to recuperate from a recent illness in 1930. "Many of us have been charmed by the beauty and wisdom of his work and our appreciation of this immortal can be best expressed in wishing him a speedy recovery, and a pleasant stay in 'the land of springs'...".[94] This is a far cry from the *Negro World* column which said of Kipling that he was "the poet laureate of British imperialism ... the only great artist in the history of humanity who has proved capable of misusing his art for dark purposes and destructive ends".[95]

Articles of general discussion on literature were to be found in the newspapers as well. *Blackman* carried a series, "Chats on Literature", which did a survey of English literature from Elizabethan times to the nineteenth century. Articles on black writers such as Paul Lawrence Dunbar and Alexandre Dumas were also highlighted.

Associated with a love of literature was a love of reading. Garvey kept an extensive library, and this was used by outsiders from time to time to do research. They would make appointments with his secretary, and his wife would be informed and would accommodate them. His library showed a wide interest in different topics — art, religion, politics, science, and history, among others.[96] *The New Jamaican* once ran a full-page article on the "Techniques of Reading" and encouraged readers to read widely. In the *Message to the People* he told prospective UNIA leaders "One must never stop reading".

There were several entertainment programmes at Edelweiss, such as fairs, garden parties, Coney islands, indoor sports, dress promenades. Later there were films and "radio programmes", the latter it would appear being no more than the use of the microphone to amplify songs and speeches. Garvey endorsed a policy of constructive and healthy recreation. A *New Jamaican* editorial stated:

> The people here want more recreation, they want to go out more, they want to come in contact with each other to exchange views and to develop the true spirit of friendship.[97]

Of interest is the fact that the Edelweiss Park activities received endorsement from no less a person than Mr Josef von Sternberg, the director of Marlene Dietrich, who visited the park with a party of Hollywood luminaries shortly after the inauguration of the "Night Life" programme in 1932 and who was "loud in his praise of Edelweiss Park".[98]

The Garvey era in Jamaica formed an important link in the cultural history of the nation. The movement encouraged local talent and set up professional artistic groups (one of the earliest to do so). Edelweiss Park operated as a cultural training centre and it allowed several major artists from the performing arts to showcase their talent. Above all, the inspiration provided by Garvey's message encouraged artists to do things for themselves and create their own works.

NOTES

[1] Interview with Z. Munroe Scarlett by Beverly Hamilton, 1977, and Kevin Sinclair, 1984 (private collection). Richard Scarlett was his father.

[2] Amy Jacques Garvey, *Garvey and Garveyism* (Published by A. Jacques Garvey, 1963), p. 6.

[3] Ibid.

[4] J.J. Mills, *His Own Account of His Life and Times* (Kingston: Collins and Sangster, 1969), p. 109.

[5] *Daily Gleaner*, 3 October 1914.

[6] *Daily Gleaner*, 14 September 1914.

[7] *Daily Gleaner*, 8 October 1914.

[8] William Ferris would later join the Garvey Movement in the US and work on the editorial staff of *The Negro World*.

[9] B. de C. Reid was a bandmaster of the Jamaica Military Band. Years later he set some of Garvey's songs to music.

[10] *Daily Gleaner*, 14 January 1915.

[11] H.A.L. Simpson later contested the 1930 general elections in Jamaica under the banner of Garvey's People's Political Party.

[12] Amy Jacques Garvey, *Garvey and Garveyism*, p. 14.

[13] *Negro World*, 10 July 1926.

[14] Ivy Baxter, *The Arts of an Island* (New Jersey: Scarecrow Press, 1970), p. 296.

[15] *Daily Gleaner*, 18 August 1934.

[16] *Negro World*, 29 September 1928.

[17] *The Black Man*, June 1935.

[18] *Blackman*, 18 May 1929.

[19] *Negro World*, 29 September 1928.

[20] *Blackman*, 6 May 1929.

[21] *Commercial Advocate*, 25 April 1931.

[22] Letter to prospective patrons dated December 1931 from Daisy Whyte, secretary, Edelweiss Park Amusement Co. Ltd. (National Library of Jamaica).

[23] Interview with Roy Carson by Beverly Hamilton, 1984 (private collection).

[24] *Blackman*, 25 July 1929.

[25] *New Jamaican*, 3 October 1932.

[26] *Blackman*, 13 July 1929; also interview with Cyril Stewart by Beverly Hamilton, 1987 (private collection).

[27] According to Miss Greenidge, this piece was a favourite of Garvey's which he frequently asked her to perform. Interview with Daisy Greenidge by Nettie Campbell: Bronx Regional and Community History Studies Project at the Bronx Institute at Lehman College, New York, 1982.

[28] *Blackman*, 27 April 1929.

[29] *Blackman*, 6 June 1929.

[30] Interview with Z. Munroe Scarlett by Kevin Sinclair, 1984.

[31] Stage names for Ivan Joseph (Racca) and Felix Lawrence (Sandy).

[32] Garvey was then serving time in the Spanish Town prison for contempt of court.

[33] This gala week took place before the by-election to the KSAC which Garvey was contesting from prison. The speakers were J. Coleman Beecher, T.A. Aikman and L.P. Waison.

[34] *Blackman*, 14 December 1929.

[35] Tony Martin, *The Pan African Connection* (Cambridge, Massachusetts: Schenkman Publishing Company, 1983), p. 121.

[36] Tony Martin, *Race First: The Ideological and Organizational Struggles of Marcus Garvey and the Universal Negro Improvement Association* (Westport, Connecticut: Greenwood Press, 1976), p. 101.

[37] Tony Martin (ed.), *Message to the People: The Course of African Philosophy* (Dover, Massachusetts: The Majority Press, 1986), p. 44.

[38] Interview with Vivian Durham by B. Hamilton, 1984 (private collection).

[39] *Blackman*, 28 September 1929.

[40] Interview with Cyril Stewart by Beverly Hamilton, 1987 (private collection) .

[41] *New Jamaican*, 25 August 1932.

[42] *Blackman*, 3 August 1929.

[43] *Blackman*, 10 August 1929.

[44] Interview with Vivian Durham by Beverly Hamilton, 1984.

[45] *Daily Gleaner*, 9 August 1929.

[46] *Blackman*, 16 August 1930.

[47] Interview with Z. Munroe Scarlett by Kevin Sinclair, 1984.

48 Interviews with Daisy Greenidge by Nettie Campbell, 1982; Roy Carson by Beverly Hamilton, 1984; also see Iris Patterson "Marcus Garvey as I Knew Him" in booklet *Look For Me in the Whirlwind* (Quebec: Bilongo Publishers, 1978).

49 Interview with Vivian Durham by Beverly Hamilton, 1984; Daisy Greenidge by Nettie Campbell, 1982; and Roy Carson by Beverly Hamilton.

50 Interview with Daisy Greenidge by Nettie Campbell; Roy Carson by Beverly Hamilton.

51 *Blackman*, 16 August 1930.

52 Ibid.

53 *Blackman*, 21 June 1930.

54 Interview with Roy Carson by Beverly Hamilton.

55 Ibid.

56 *New Jamaican*, 5 September 1932.

57 Ranny Williams, "My Life in Theatre", Ranny Williams Collection, National Library of Jamaica.

58 *Blackman*, 1 October 1929.

59 *Blackman*, 11 October 1929.

60 Blackman, 10 November 1929.

61 *Blackman*, 19 April 1930.

62 *New Jamaican*, 5 September 1932.

63 Ed "Bim" Lewis and Aston "Bam" Wynter.

64 This I think refers mainly to the plays written by Garvey himself and not to his associates.

65 Errol Hill, "Marcus Garvey and West Indian Drama", May 1971 (unpublished paper).

66 Interview with Sammy Lyon by Beverly Hamilton, 1987 (private collection).

67 Now National Heroes Park.

68 Kid Harold was the stage name for Harold Smith. At the time of his death in 1985 he was the oldest entertainer in Jamaica.

69 Interview with Kid Harold by Kevin Sinclair, 1984 (private collection).

70 *Blackman*, 17 May 1930.

71 *Blackman*, 8 June 1929.

72 *Blackman*, 3 April 1929.

73 Interview with Z. Munroe Scarlett by Beverly Hamilton, 1980, and Kevin Sinclair, 1984.

74 Slim Beckford and Sam Lawrence.

75 Interview with Roy Carson by Beverly Hamilton.

76 African Caribbean Institute of Jamaica (ACIJ) Living History Seminar series, September 1897: "Garvey and Culture".

77 *Blackman*, 18 May 1929.

78 *Daily Gleaner*, 24 July 1934.

79 *Blackman*, 7 February 1931.

80 Amy Jacques Garvey, *Garvey and Garveyism*, p. 179.

81 Beverly Hamilton, "Ruth Prescott Remembers", *Flair Magazine (Daily Gleaner),* 19 August 1984.

82 *Daily Gleaner*, 18 August 1934.

83 *New Jamaican*, 25 March 1933.

84 *Blackman*, 5 April 1929.

85 *New Jamaican*, 25 March 1933.

86 *Blackman*, 26 September 1929.

87 Interview with Alvin Marriott by Beverly Hamilton, 1986.

88 Ibid.

89 *Blackman*, 1 June 1929.

90 *Blackman*, 14 June 1929.

91 *Blackman*, 3 May 1920.

92 Tony Martin, *Race First*, p. 31.

93 *New Jamaican*, 29 July 1933.

94 *Blackman*, 22 February 1930.

95 *Negro World*, 7 October 1922.

96 Interview with Roy Carson by Beverly Hamilton.

97 *New Jamaican*, 8 October 1932.

98 *New Jamaican*, 17 October 1932.

NOTES ON INFORMANTS/INTERVIEWEES

Z. Munroe Scarlett (1902–1984) was a vice president of the Kingston division of the UNIA and a co-founder and executive secretary of the Whitefield division of the UNIA. His father, Richard Elias Scarlett, was a bookseller from Port Maria at the turn of the century and was one of the founding members of the UNIA in 1914. Munroe knew Garvey before he started public life. He said that Mr Cotterel, with whom Garvey worked in Port Maria, boarded with his father. The elder Scarlett's house was apparently a meeting place for Pan Africanists, as it was said that Garvey met J. Albert Thorne there. During Garvey's time, Z. Munroe Scarlett was a member of the sacred choir attached to Edelweiss Park. He also helped in the political campaign of 1930, when Garvey sought a seat in the Legislature. Later he wrote for *Blackman*, sending in divisional reports as well as personal poems which were published from time to time. After Garvey's departure from Jamaica, he was involved in labour activities and played a major role in the waterfront strike of 1938, encouraging workers not to break their strike and to agitate for the release of Bustamante and St William Grant. He later went on to form the Afro-West Indian Welfare League and two newspapers, *The Negro Voice* and *The Jamaica Advocate*. He also co-founded a short-lived political party, the Jamaica Liberal Party, which contested the 1946 general elections. Z. Munroe Scarlett is commonly referred to as one of Jamaica's "unsung heroes". He remained a fervent advocate of repatriation until his death in 1984.

Roy Carson (1911–) worked for seven years as a mail clerk at Edelweiss Park during Garvey's stay in Jamaica. He also performed weekly duties at Garvey's private residence. He also participated in the cultural activities within the UNIA, acting in two of Garvey's plays and entering elocution contests. After Garvey's departure he himself engaged in cultural promotion. He also worked in organizing small farmers, influenced, he said, by the experience gained in the PPP campaigns of 1929 and 1930.

Daisy Greenidge worked as a secretary at Edelweiss Park and later as manager of *Blackman* printery. She was a regular performer in elocution at Edelweiss Park. She acted in two of Garvey's plays. She later became a founding member of the PNP.

Vivian Durham (1909–1988) was associated with the Kingston division of the UNIA in Garvey's time. He was very active in citizens' associations, debating clubs, journalism, and labour unions. He acted as Garvey's campaign manager for the KSAC elections; however, he did not support Garvey in his bid for a seat to the Legislative Council. Durham also participated in the cultural activities promoted by the UNIA, mainly debating contests. After Garvey's departure, he became a founding member of the BITU and later joined the Jamaica Labour Party. He worked as secretary to Isaac Barrant in the late 1940s in Bustamante's first cabinet.

Iris Lucille Patterson (1900–) was an elocutionist and contralto who performed regularly at Edelweiss Park. She was dubbed "the poet laureate of the UNIA" in Jamaica, as she frequently penned some verse for events as they occurred. Her poems were regularly published in *Blackman* and, later, *The New Jamaican*. Her uncle, Adrian Daily, was one of the founding members of the UNIA and was associate secretary of the first executive.

Sammy Lyon (1917–): Son of Gerardo Leon (whose real name was Gerald Lyon), the director of entertainment at Edelweiss Park. As a child, he was present with his father at many of the activities at Edelweiss Park.

Harold ("Kid Harold") Smith (1911–1985) was known in entertainment circles for his tap dancing. He was a part of the comedy team known as Harold and Trim and leader of a dancing group known as the Butterfly Troupe. He was associated with Edelweiss Park for many years, working as a judge for dancing contests and later helped in training artists. He appeared regularly in the plays written and produced by Ranny Williams and staged at Edelweiss Park.

Ruth Prescott (1920–): Niece of Marcus Garvey and daughter of his sister Indiana Garvey, who along with her husband Alfred Peart were founding members of the UNIA. As a child she and her mother lived at 2 Trafalgar Road (now the site of the Small Business Association), which was owned by Garvey and which was across the road from his personal residence at 38 Lady Musgrave Road.

Alvin Marriott (1902–) is one of Jamaica's foremost sculptors. He met Garvey more than once during his lifetime and said he did more than one portrait. Marriott sculpted the bust of Garvey which is now placed in National Heroes Park above the grave, and also the life-sized statue of Garvey which now adorns Lawrence Park in St Ann's Bay. Garvey's paper *Blackman* gave encouragement to Marriott in the 1920s and 1930s.

Cyril Stewart (1916–) was a member of the juveniles attached to the Kingston division of the UNIA. As such he attended the 31 days of the historic 1929 UNIA convention at Edelweiss Park. Later he became a full member of the Kingston division. After Garvey's departure he became involved in trade union activities and has been honoured by the movement for his contribution to the TUC.

Unorthodox Prose: The Poetical Works of Marcus Garvey

Carolyn Cooper
Department of English
University of the West Indies, Mona, Jamaica

THE VALUE of Marcus Garvey's "poetical works" is largely archival.[1] We read his verse today not because of its intrinsic merit but primarily because it constitutes a part, however negligible, of the corpus of writing of a remarkable man. Garvey himself acknowledged the limitations of his modest verse. In the foreword to the 1935 edition of his experimental 1927 composition, "The Tragedy of White Injustice", Garvey pre-empts his critics:

> It must be remembered that this is not an attempt at poetry: it is just a peculiar style of using facts as they impress me as I go through the pages of history and as I look at and note the conduct of the white race.[2]

Analysis of Garvey's "peculiar style" is, in part, the subject of this study. But I wish as well to demonstrate that, though much of Garvey's verse ought to be allowed to slip quietly into oblivion, there are a few poems, several stanzas and the odd line that altogether suggest Garvey's literary sensibility, his control of rhythm, tone and image. Ironically, Garvey's poetic skill is much more fully developed in his prose than in his verse, unfettered there by narrow metric constraints.

In the 1935 foreword, Garvey draws attention to the stylistic deficiencies of his verse and also to its uncertainty of genre. He classifies "The Tragedy of White Injustice" as "... not verse, neither is it orthodox prose, but it is a kind of mean adopted for the purpose of conveying the desired thought".[3] This generic ambiguity characterizes much of the work produced after "The Tragedy of White Injustice" and unambiguously labelled "poetry". "The City Storm", from the 1927 *Poetic Meditations*, is an excellent case in point. On the page, the piece is divided in lines, arranged in stanzas and visually disposed to poetry. But this is mere poetic licence, for in structure "The City Storm" is essentially a prose passage in which Garvey reflects on the philosophical implications of natural disaster. His rhetorical sentences do achieve an eloquence that is not often accomplished in the more laboured verse, but the structure of the piece is nevertheless prose at base:

> I wondered to myself when I saw the weakness of my brother

In the moment of apparent danger and infinite distress,
How is it he finds heart to enslave the rest of his fellowmen
When conscience must tell him withal, we are in reality one?[4]

This uncertainty of poetic structure is not peculiar to Marcus Garvey. Tony Martin, in the chapter "Garvey the Poet", in *Literary Garveyism,* attempts to illustrate the "poetic quality of Garvey's prose"[5] by simply rearranging on the page an extract from Garvey's "If I Die in Atlanta" speech:

After my enemies are satisfied,
In life or death
I shall come back to you
To serve
Even as I have served before.
In life I shall be the same:
In death I shall be a terror
To the foes of Negro liberty.
If death has power,
Then count on me in death
To be the real Marcus Garvey
I would like to be.[6]

What Martin calls "free verse"[7] is not simply prose, however eloquent, cut up into lines. Poetry is essentially metaphorical, not literal discourse.

For literary critics, it is the form of Garvey's verse that immediately poses aesthetic problems. The lofty themes of personal integrity, race pride and revolt against ubiquitous injustice, for example, are often rendered in pedestrian style. There is thus an ironic disparity between the ideological radicalism of Garvey's themes and the conventional, prosaic form of the worst of his verse. There is a turn of phrase from "The Tragedy of White Injustice" which, quoted out of context, aptly summarizes the problem of form in Garvey's verse: "a bloody mix-up everywhere" (p. 7).

The "mix-up" is evident in recurring structural problems such as forced rhymes, awkward rhythms, odd metaphors and even lines without apparent rhyme or reason. Examples abound in the 70 stanzas of "The Tragedy of White Injustice". For example, in verse 4, the surprisingly simplistic image of "American Indian tribes", "Asia's hordes" and "Africa's millions" is underscored by the flippant rhythm of the lines:

American Indian tribes were free,
Sporting, dancing, and happy as could be;
Asia's hordes lived then a life their own;
To civilization they would have grown;
Africa's millions laughed with the sun,
In the cycle of man a course run;
In stepped the white man, bloody and grim,
The light of these people freedom to dim. *(p. 4)*

In verse 10, the problem of plodding feet and anti-climactic rhyme is compounded by a strained metaphor: "Thus, they claim the name of our country, all / of us they make then their real foot-ball" (p. 5). Similarly, in verse 19, the ungainly rhythm of the lines and the awkward rhyme undercut the noble sentiment: "So down the line of history we come, / Black, courtly, courageous and handsome" (p. 8).

There is, as well, the distortion of meaning to accommodate the need for rhyme:

> Centuries of wonder and achievements
> Were cast before him in God's compliments;
> But, like the rest, he has now fallen flat,
> And must in the Lord's cycle yield for that. *(p. 9)*

My final example of awkward rhythm and forced rhyme is nicely ironic:

> Under the canopy of Nature's law
> We shall unitedly and bravely draw
> On the plains of God's green Amphitheater,
> Swords, in rhythm with Divine Meter. *(p. 12)*

Though Garvey's verse is not often "in rhythm with Divine Meter", it is not altogether execrable. There is a declarative line from verse 21 of "The Tragedy of White Injustice" which in both cadence and under-statement exemplifies the strength of Garvey's better verse: "This is no shallow song of hate to sing" (p. 8). Indeed, there is a generosity of spirit and a largeness of vision in some of the poems that encourage reflective analysis. For example, the final verse of "The Bearers", from the 1937 *Poetic Meditations,* is uplifting:

> 'Tis true the world is reckless, vile and tough;
>   But there is always room for doing good:
> There never can of goodness be enough,
>   In blessing Nature's wanton brotherhood;
> Will you now join the faithful, sturdy band,
>   To make a better home for man to live?
> Will you now stretch to me the other hand,
>   And state – "As freely I receive, I give?" *(p. 36)*

The exhortative poem, "Get Up And Do", condemns fatal passivity in appropriately brisk rhythms:

> You sit and quarrel all your life,
> And blame the moving world at large:
> You fail to enter in the strife,
> To sail in fortune's happy barge.
> Get up my man and do the stuff
> That leads to blazing glory's fame:
> Hold on, and be like good Macduff,
> And damn the man who'd foil you' name. *(p. 82)*

Similarly, "Get Up And Work" is tersely epigrammatic:

The Negro sits and pines all day:
His opportunities slip away;
Get up and work your mind my Lord,
And grasp the good the days afford. *(p. 72)*

There are several memorable lines in *The Poetical Works of Marcus Garvey* that assume the authority of aphorism. Note the following examples: "If you must strike to live, strike hard and sure" (p. 66); "To live is of superior wit, / To fail is thus to feel" (p. 76); "When blacks fight blacks in white men's war / They're fools for all their valiant pain" (p. 87); "All men should have the freedom of all rights, / For nature made no sovereign but the soul" (p. 103); and finally:

All life must be a useful plan
That calls for daily, serious work –
The work that wrings the best from man –
The work that cowards often shirk. *(p. 90)*

The insistent end-stopped and internal rhyme work/shirk is effective, the similarity of sound of the words underscoring, ironically, dissonance of meaning.

There are also those poems in which Garvey's irreverent wit is evident: "George S. Schuyler Again" is a satirical piece in which the use of flippant rhythms and facile rhymes – the very essence of doggerel – is entirely appropriate, reinforcing the contemptuous tone of Garvey's derogatory observations:

George S. Schuyler is a joke;
His brain must be like sausage pork
Or he must be a "nutty" ass
To bray at those he cannot pass. *(p. 72)*

"Wanting to Desert" is similarly satirical, the rhythm of the lines supporting the tone of mockery:

A negro who got rich did stray
    To claim he was not of the race.
But all the world could only say
    He was a fool and sore disgrace.
You cannot change your skin, my man,
    For nature made you as you are;
Your wish to break your father's clan
    Is ignorance that goes too far.
The woman of another race
    You choose to share your fortune with
And have her take your mother's place
    May slay you as in Siren's myth.

And when you find the deed unwise
    It will be late, too late to mend,
For then the race you did despise
    Will count you out with traitor's end. *(pp. 104-105)*

In "The White Man – Spirit of Mussolini", one of a number of poems in which he vilified Mussolini is the object of Garvey's righteous indignation, the satirical tone s much more sombre. In verse two, for example, the grim shopping-list account of European cupidity is chilling in its very casualness:

To India he goes with glee
For stores of shining, precious stones;
And off to China for his tea,
And Africa for ivory-bones. *(p. 91)*

n the opening stanza, there is an ironic reversal whereby animal imagery is applied o the predatory European, not to the "native":

The white man stands with murd'rous gaze,
And looks with envy at all wealth;
For gold he has a burning craze
That crowns him with his bloody stealth.
From shore to shore he roams at large,
With maxim guns and poisoned darts:
He sails aboard his nimble barge
To rip and bleed his victims' hearts. *(pp. 90-91)*

Similarly, in "The Devil in Mussolini", the stereotype of black bestiality is inverted:

This Mussolini – devil – man –
Has come from out the darkest cave,
And savage-like, in looks and deeds,
He seeks to take the life God gave. *(p. 99)*

The literal and moral savagery of Europe is sardonically imaged in the paradox of a errible beauty wrought of human suffering:

And Cecil Rhodes, in Kimberly,
Did flog the mining natives, too,
That ladies might, at "Wemberly",
Wear diamonds with the shades of blue. *(p. 91)*

The complicity of the Church in the imperial enterprise gives weight to Garvey's imprecations:

The blacks were kept in clanking chain
Two hundred years, and little more:
The Bishops spurned the hellish pain,

And blessed the trips from Afric's shore. *(pp. 91-92)*

Garvey's ironic vision juxtaposes the religious and the political in language tha approximates contemporary liberation theology. For example, in verses 9 and 10 c "The Tragedy of White Injustice", there is muted ironic humour in the disparity be tween the glib rhetoric of the proselytizing Christian colonizers and the evasiv silence of their practical greed:

They say to us: "You, sirs, are the heathen,
"We your brethren – Christian fellowmen,
"We come to tell the story of our God";
When we believe, they give to us the rod.
After our confidence they have thus won,
From our dear land and treasure we must run;
Story of the Bible no more they tell,
For our souls redeemed we could go to hell. *(p. 5)*

In verse 16, Garvey's ironic reference to "tribal gods" underscores a chauvinist dis tortion of Christianity to accommodate racist/tribalist ideology: "No other race sha kill the sturdy Blacks / If on their gods we turn our backs" (p. 7). In verse 13, th theological absurdity of a "Jim Crow God" is the focus of Garvey's wit:

Their churches lines of demarcation draw;
In the name of Christ there is no such law,
Yet Black and White they have separated,
A Jim Crow God the preachers operated,
Then to Heaven they think they will all go,
When their consciences ought to tell them NO. *(p. 6)*

In the hymn, "For He Is God", from the 1934 collection *UNIA Convention Hymns* Garvey affirms, in paradox, his optimistic vision that the plural gods of white racisn will finally bow to the one "Almighty God ... Master over all" (p. 119): "For He i God, and God is God, / And no more gods shall e'er be God" (p. 119).

There are a few poems in *The Poetical Works of Marcus Garvey* the theme of whic is black womanhood. In most, women are idealized in sentimental language. For ex ample, "The Black Woman", from the 1927 *Poetic Meditations,* is pure hyperbole:

Black queen of beauty, thou hast given color to the World!
Among other women thou art royal and the fairest!
Like the brightest of jewels in the regal diadem,
Shin'st thou, Goddess of Africa, Nature's purest emblem!
Black men worship at thy virginal shrine of truest love,
Because in thine eyes are virtue's steady and holy mark,
As we see in no other, clothed in silk or fine linen,
From ancient Venus, the Goddess, to mythical Helen. *(p. 44)*

The opulent religious imagery, the classical allusions, the expansive rhythm of th lines, the archaic *thee*s and *thou*s engender Garvey's new mythology. The redeeme lack woman, no longer servile, becomes a metaphor for the race restored to its riginal nobility.

By contrast, "The Song of the Negro Maid" is a poignant evocation of the actual ondition of the lives of poor black women in America. Structurally, the poem is efective. Garvey assumes the persona of the woman and attempts to illuminate her nterior consciousness. The first line of the poem, the heart of the woman's lament, resents a perspective on man that sounds remarkably contemporary: "I look at man n grim dismay" (p. 69). To be fair to the spirit of the times, this line, read in context, efers to the predatory white man, not the black. For indeed, the woman, "queen of elf" (p. 69), affirms loyalty to her racial group:

> With firm respect I love my race:
> No one shall lead me thus astray,
> Of kin to lose the ancient trace
> That makes me what I am today. *(p. 69)*

From the foregoing analysis it is evident that it is at the level of theme rather than oetic technique that Marcus Garvey's verse yields its most fruitful rewards to the ympathetic critic. Since Garvey's rich ironic wit so poorly masquerades in the illitting garb of poetry, one must attempt to provide some explanation for the fascinaion that poetry held for Garvey and his followers. Tony Martin observes in the hapter "Poetry for the People", in *Literary Garveyism,* that doing poetry was very nuch a Garveyite thing:

> The writing of poetry was little short of an obsession with Garveyites. Everybody did it. Rank and file members of the organisation did it. The editors and columnists of the *Negro World* did it. High-ranking UNIA officials did it. Garvey did it.[8]

t is this popularity of poetry, its mass appeal, that seems to explain Garvey's reference for that "mean", neither verse, nor orthodox prose, with which he experinented first in the 1927 "The Tragedy of White Injustice".

Garvey recognized that the compelling power of his political message could be eightened if it was presented in the emotive language of poetry. In the 1935 oreword, Garvey elaborated on his method:

> All good psychologists realize that if you set a man thinking you are likely to produce, through him, results that never would have been possible otherwise. The object I have in view is to get the Negro to accomplish much for himself out of his own thoughtfulness. To arouse that thoughtfulness, he must be shocked or otherwise he must be driven to see the unusual that is operating against him, and so this little pamphlet was written during a time of leisure in jail in 1927, in the peculiar form in which it appears.[9]

Garvey's ideological commitment to functionalist art as a primary aesthetic priniple makes him akin to contemporary black nationalist cultural activists. Rex Nettleford, in his recent essay "The Spirit of Garvey: Lessons of the Legacy", traces th genealogy of Garvey's ideas:

> Among the heirs of Garvey are the popular poets of utterance – the Bob Marleys, Jimmy Cliffs, Peter Toshes and Mutabarukas – thrown up by a generation of Jamaicans who find in the tangible emblems of political sovereignty no real solution to their people's continuing degradation which is the result of Western civilization's unrelenting efforts to humiliate Africa and all that springs therefrom.[10]

The line of descent is perhaps most direct to the performance/dub poets who ar generally, politically committed, and favour poetry as a powerful medium for a ticulating their vision of the transformed lives of alienated black people. To inte sify the affective appeal of their work, performance poets like Linton Kwesi Johnso Jean Breeze and the late Mikey Smith often employ other art forms, drama and musi – whether a lone drummer or a full-scale reggae band.[11] In technique as well a theme, there are parallels between Garvey's unorthodox prose and the experime tal, multi-media work of contemporary performance poets. The strong oral/messag element in dub/performance poetry at times overshadows rigorous attention to pur ly aesthetic techniques associated with the scribal poetic tradition. Some of the pe formance poetry of even the best of these practitioners can appear "flat" when simp read on the page. The themes may seem trite and the rhythm of the lines flawe But when these same poems are performed sensitively, to a responsive audience wh support the poet's communal craft, it is then that the work is actualized.

I do not wish to suggest, however, that dub/performance poetry is essentially ba verse, redeemed by the transforming power of the word become flesh. For there such a thing as bad performance poetry. We hear it all the time in the work of aspi ing amateur artists who, like Garvey, have caught the poetic spirit but have not be come engaged in the rigorous process of discipleship.

Marcus Garvey's unorthodox prose was a means to an end, not an end in itsel And, indeed, it is the rare poem, the rare stanza, the rare line that resonates wit poetic authority. Verse 22 of "The Tragedy of White Injustice" achieves a fine equ librium of message and music, especially if one transposes it from English metri into a dub idiom:

> Man will bear so much of imposition,
> Till he starts a righteous inquisition.
> History teaches this as a true fact,
> Upon this premise all men do act.
> Sooner or later each people take their stand
> To fight against the strong, oppressive hand;
> This is God's plan, raising man to power,
> As over sin and greed He makes him tower. *(p. 9)*

Marcus Garvey's verse does not often tower above the limitations of its shaky fo mal foundations, but it does have its fleeting moments of rhetorical power. Let Ga vey have the final word. An injunction from "The Tragedy of White Injustice" widened beyond its immediate context, suggests an appropriate way of reading Marcus Garvey's unorthodox prose: "If you were wise you'd read between the lines" (p. 3).

NOTES

[1] Tony Martin's useful anthology, *The Poetical Works of Marcus Garvey,* is the text on which I base this preliminary study. Martin's choice of the somewhat precious term "poetical works", not simple "poetry", suggests the archaic quality of the verse.

[2] Marcus Garvey, *The Tragedy of White Injustice,* London, 1935; rpt. 1986 (Baltimore, Maryland: Black Classic Press).

[3] In his Preface to *The Poetical Works of Marcus Garvey* (Dover, Massachusetts: The Majority Press, 1983), p. viii, Martin emends "mean" to "mean(s)", missing, I think, the subtlety of Garvey's meaning – "mean" as intermediate form between poetry and prose.

[4] Tony Martin (ed.), *The Poetical Works of Marcus Garvey,* p. 47. Subsequent references cited parenthetically in the text.

[5] Tony Martin, *Literary Garveyism* (Dover, Massachusetts: The Majority Press, 1983), p. 141.

[6] Ibid. The prose original appears in John Henrik Clarke (ed.), *Marcus Garvey and the Vision of Africa,* (New York: Vintage, 1974), p. 169.

[7] Ibid.

[8] Ibid., p. 43

[9] Garvey's "luxury" may not be entirely ironic. For, as George Lamming observes in *The Pleasures of Exile,* (London: Michael Joseph, 1960; rpt. 1984, London: Allison & Busby), p. 114, "Temporary imprisonment is the greatest service an imperialist can do a nationalist leader. It is in the solitude of the cell that he gets a chance, free from the indulgence of his followers, to think things out".

[10] Rex Nettleford, "The Spirit of Garvey: Lessons of the Legacy", *Jamaica Journal,* Vol. 20, No. 3, Aug.-Oct. 1987, p. 3.

11 Pamela O'Gorman, in the essay "On Reggae and Rastafarianism – and a Garvey Prophecy", notes the "dissolution of the ancient unity of music, song and dance" in Western culture, and its reintegration in contemporary black culture. *Jamaica Journal,* Vol. 20, No. 3. Aug.-Oct. 1987, p. 87.

Garvey Myths among the Jamaican People

Barry Chevannes
Department of Sociology
University of the West Indies, Mona, Jamaica

IN A COUNTRY where recollection of history is largely dominated by oral rather than written tradition, mythology plays an important role in the development of national consciousness. The world of reality becomes transformed into the world of symbols, and mortal men acquire the divine characteristics of heroes. In this sense Marcus Garvey was already one of the heroes long before he was accorded that title by an official act of government.[1]

It is fairly certain that most of the prophecies and feats attributed to Garvey nowhere originated with him. Garvey, whatever his shortcomings, did not regard himself as divine or visionary. Nevertheless, the people regarded him as such, and that is surely a remarkable fact. To the Bedwardites in the 1910s and 1920s, Garvey was the reincarnation of Moses, as Bedward was the reincarnation of Aaron – the two brothers, one a prophet, the other a high priest, on whom God had bestowed the responsibility of leading his chosen people out of bondage.[2] Garvey was not yet dead before the people were making divine claims for him. The significance, therefore, of what I have called the Garvey myths does not lie in what they tell us about the man himself, but what they tell us about the Jamaican people, about ourselves.

In the Rastafari movement, there are many myths, some of them dealing with ganja, some dealing with Haile Selassie, but most dealing with Garvey. Those dealing with Garvey are perhaps not confined to the Rastafari as such, but as the largest and most influential nationalist movement to derive inspiration from his work, the Rastafari are their main transmitters. I have found seventeen different myths, twelve of which keep recurring, and the other five heard only once. This is to indicate the strength of their influence throughout the movement. I have grouped all but one of them into four broad categories:

(a) Those which attribute heroic or divine characteristics to Marcus Garvey himself;

(b) Those which confirm the messianic role of Haile Selassie;

(c) Those which are addressed to the struggles of the people; and

(d) Those which are curses.

In the first category there are four myths. The first deals with Garvey's role a John the Baptist — that is, his own conception of himself. None of my informant who counted this myth claimed to have actually heard Garvey himself say this abou himself, but the myth is nevertheless widely believed:

> "I never hear him speak, but people tol' me who listen to him that there was a man coming after Marcus Garvey that he was not worthy to loose the shoelace at his feet. And we consider Marcus Garvey a very high man, in other words the highest man on this land. And if he tell us that word, how, the man must be very much higher than him."

Others are even clearer in their insistence that there is no need to have heard Gar vey say it or to have read it in his *Philosophy and Opinions,* for by reading the Bibl one can see that it was the same work John did. "It was only a rehearsal". The rea question, therefore, was to find the worthier one. Rastafari stated that in the lat 1930s they at first thought it might have been Bustamante, but decided against it sinc Bustamante was not a black man but a mulatto, a fact which apparently made it neces sary for St William Grant to introduce him to the port workers in 1938. Moreove Bustamante's outlook was not anti-colonial.

> "Well, when this man Bustamante come we wanted was to lay hold of the man, saying it was him. But when we look at the man eye, and see them red, white and blue at his office, we say, 'No, this couldn't be the man!' Then we turn away from him and we seek it on the saying of the Honourable Marcus Garvey, saying 'Africa by Africans, those at home and those abroad' ".

The "red, white and blue" colours hanging in the office of Bustamante was an in dication that Bustamante's political leanings were towards the defence of the Britis Empire. This, coupled with the racial factor and the recollection of Garvey's slogan "Africa for the Africans, at home and abroad", prompted their rejection of Bus tamante.

Every hero must at some time face some kind of trial. Nor could he be a hero i he did not overcome it. Garvey did both. In 1933 he was sentenced to the Spanis Town prison for publishing a campaign manifesto judged to be seditious.[3] Accord ing to one version of a myth, he placed a seal on the door of the cell he occupied, an to this day it has neither been opened nor inhabited by another man. Others ad more to it.

> "I was told that Marcus Garvey was a kind of mysterious man. You couldn't do him anything. He was a mysterious man like a superman. They set up all kind of various different traps to destroy him because them didn't want him to preach and turn the people heart back to Africa. But dem couldn't catch him. One time they sent him to Spanish Town, so I learnt, and they set him a bath, but they poison the bath to let him go in there and bathe and to kill him. And when him go, him say, 'No, not this one!' ".

A "mysterious" man is one whose movements are mysterious, unfathomable, a superman. The traps laid for Garvey were laid by the enemies of the black man, those who saw the danger of his nationalism.

An identical story is related by another informant, but this time the hero was Leonard Howell, thought of as being the original propagator of the divinity of Rastafari.[4] The recurrence of this same motif leads to the suggestion that it has wide currency in Jamaican folk beliefs. We know that ritual baths are a form of healing employed by folk healers and other religious practitioners in Jamaica. Naturally, if baths can heal, so also can they destroy.

The third in this category and undoubtedly the most widely current of the entire body of myths is one which says that Marcus Garvey is alive, that he did not die. It became all the more popular when in collaboration with the British government the Jamaican government had his remains brought to Jamaica and entombed in the National Heroes Park in 1964.

> "I was at the send-off preaching for him. And him say that him have some friends in Jamaica, but him not coming back. And you will hear him dead and him ashes will be coming to Jamaica to rest, but when the ashes come, test it to see if it is an animal ashes or a mortal ashes. And him preach the farewell sermon and him go away".

The event being described in the excerpt was Garvey's departure for England on his self-imposed exile. According to this account, he did not feel that everybody was against him but that he still had friends in Jamaica. Nevertheless he was not coming back, not even his ashes. Embellished a bit, the myth relates that his enemies shall three times present ashes as his. Some informants go as far as to name the animals, such as the cow, whose remains the Jamaican establishment will try to pass for Garvey's.

Garvey, then, cannot die, so where is he? When President Tubman of Liberia paid an official visit to Jamaica in 1954, he was thought of by many to be Garvey himself. To those who remembered Garvey's aborted attempt to set up a colony of Blacks in Africa, the visit by an African head of state, a first in Jamaica's history, would evoke a special sentiment. At any rate, Tubman was, if not stocky, certainly short and black.

Sister Missis remembers seeing a picture of Marcus Garvey printed in *The Daily Gleaner* in 1953, so how, she asks herself, could he have died in 1940?

> "On the front page of the Gleaner one part, I see Marcus Garvey, the half of him as usual, for him never take the full photograph, only the half of him with his big stout, hefty felt hat on top of his head, stick around his hand like this, black tie, white shirt, and I see mark under him, 'Marcus Garvey'. Marcus Garvey in Congo, civilizing the Congolese them!. In nineteen fifty and three and I saw that! Under no heavens and earth I could never let go that! You see this country here? Whatever effects that is in this country is very bitter. I must need tell you the truth. They are very bitter".

For her the belief in Garvey's continued existence, albeit in the Congo, is linked to the suffering of his people in Jamaica. The "effects is very bitter".

The last in this group is one which attributes to Garvey the saying that he will return riding on the winds of a storm. According to one informant this was fulfilled in 1951, the year Hurricane Charles struck Jamaica. It is the only myth which places Garvey in a mass destructive role, but as we have seen he left Jamaica apparently feeling a sense of being let down by his people. The storm was punishment for betrayal.

In the second grouping we find three myths which seek to establish the messianic role of Selassie. In 1930, Garvey staged a play entitled *The Coronation of the King and Queen of Africa,*[5] which some took to be the enactment of a real event, especially as one of Garvey's aims was to establish an African empire, the equal of the British or any other. The idea, therefore, of an African king was one which many took to.

> "He always pass sentiments informing us that there shall be a coronation of an African King, but he never gave the full details. He spoke at Edelweiss Park with an open speech that there's a prince in Africa to be crowned king for the black people of the world, and when such a king is crowned then he Garvey's work will be finished. He said so. He said, 'When the King is crowned my work will be finished'. So every equipped character knows that he's the forerunner to the king, while he was on the international subject of negroes' equality and the redemption of Africa, of 468 million negroes from the western world".

Selassie was the only prince to be crowned king, therefore it was of him that Garvey had prophesied. A simple deduction. Some even pinpointed the year when, and the place where, Garvey foretold the divinity of Selassie.

> "It was 1928 by George VI Park, and him look at the elements and say, 'Unu say the elements blue, but let I tell unu: as black as the elements! As black as God himself!' ".

The reference could easily have been to the Fascist aggression against Ethiopia which most would have understood. To some, however, Garvey was saying that Selassie was the Messiah, but they did not know it at that time.

The third category represents the single largest grouping of the Garvey myths. I have collected seven in all. They foretell doom, hardship, redemption, all relating to struggle. What binds them together is the fact that they are addressed to the people. For example, one of the very first told to me by informants, Rastafari and non-Rastafari, was that, according to Garvey, anyone who passed through the 1970s could pass through anything. I have heard this many times, but without finding out why the 1970s. Undoubtedly, conditions were extremely bad, and the country was just beginning to feel the full impact of the world capitalist crisis with a dramatic rise in the cost of fuel early in 1974. As 1977 approached, it took the form of doom – "when the sevens clash" – and was even popularized in pop songs. Then, as July 1977 approached it became "the three sevens clash". Naturally, for some, 7 July (7-7-77) was a day of particular significance, and some politicians even tried to secure mileage out of it.

Another myth tells of Garvey's attitude to migration:

> "Marcus Garvey told the people, 'Black people, don't go to the white

> man country. Look for Africa and go in your own country. The white going fight you, people, don't you hear? In 1954, President Tubman come to this country and when he go back to write and he said he had seen the infirmities in Jamaica, so a lot of skilled men is to come to Liberia and find life, because life is there. He said he don't prefer brown; black people he wanted. More skilled men. And you will get a house to live in for three months furnished, until you build your own. And I have seen a lot of people sell their cultivation, sell their mule and sell whatever they had and going to book for Liberia'. A man, the name of Seaga said now, 'Gentlemen, £57 to go to Britain'. Them want a lot of workers in Britain. And the people them go and take back them passport from going to Liberia and book for Britain. Some of them man them said, 'Man, you don't hear? The prophet Marcus Garvey said that black man must not fight to go in the white man country. Keep out and look for your own country!' Marcus Garvey said".

The occasion was the massive exodus to Britain, which began in the very late 1940s and continued up to about 1960.[6] During this time thousands of Jamaicans sold their belongings and trekked to the United Kingdom, crossing the Atlantic in cheap banana boats. Many travel agencies sprang up and, according to this informant, inveigled the migrants away from going to Liberia, where they were invited to come by Tubman, with the enticement of a low fare. As they booked their passage Rastafari reminded them of the instructions of Garvey. The interpretation this informant gave me for the mass migration movement was therefore a condemnation of the migrants, who in rejecting a black country in favour of a white country provided another instance, if you will, of betrayal by a people still not yet conscious of their destiny.

The theme of insufficient race consciousness appears in another saying attributed to Garvey, heard rather frequently when Rastafari expound on the infidelity of the people to his ideals. "Black people, you are not going to know yourself until your back is against the wall, because you fight against one another, and when it is too late that time you will find your back up against the wall". "Yes", added sister M.B., "everything against the poor man! Ho! Because everything gone against the black man, everything!"

Two other prophecies, or perhaps two versions of the same, have war as their themes, with that graphic symbol of blood. The first is one told by Sister Missis that I have heard nowhere else.

> "Him said, King Street, blood shall reach the bridle upon the horse neck, because if you steal the black man, him laugh; if you beat him, him laugh; if you kick him, him laugh; but he wouldn't like to be in this country to turn a flea when the black man them get vex. That's what he said".

This tells why there shall be bloodshed, and who will shed it.

A more difficult one is the second, which says simply that "Swallowed-field shall be a battlefield". Who the contending sides will be, when, and with what outcome are questions the prophecy does not attempt to answer. It is up to anyone to interpret. Some regard it as a confrontation between the army and the police, based o the presence of a police depot alongside Swallowfield Road and the presence behin it of the northwestern section of the military camp, and the occasional animosity be- tween members of both forces. Others offer that it refers to an event to take plac at the National Stadium nearby. Still others are content to leave it as is and to awai its fulfillment. This reggae superstar Bob Marley has done in one of his songs.

The next two relate to redemption. According to one Rastafari, Garvey prophe- sied that a set of people will rise up from the Dungle and overthrow the government Garvey, he believes, was referring to the Rastafari, for it can be said that the Dungl and other slums of the West End, which housed many a peasant youth, were the stron- gholds of the Rastafari.

But the most widely heard prophecy is that which interprets the growth of the cit of Kingston to the very borders of St Catherine as a sign that redemption is near Garvey is credited with saying that when you see Kingston and Spanish Town joine together into one, then you will know that your redemption is at hand. Because i implies divine intervention, this prophecy is one of the more apocalyptic.

In the fourth and final group we have two curses. The first was the curse agains "Bag-a-wire". Bag-a-wire was a mad derelict who used to walk the streets o Kingston dressed in crocus or burlap. The name was probably Bag-an'-wire, t describe perhaps the burlap bags sewn with wire. According to the myth he was Garveyite who had betrayed Garvey and was condemned by him to wander throug the streets, loathsome and contemptible, dressed in sackcloth. Every child knew Bag- a-wire and many used to stone him. He died many years ago, but the Burning Spea revived the myth when he originated the Garvey trend in Jamaican popular music o the seventies:

> Marcus Garvey words come to pass,
> Marcus Garvey words come to pass,
> Where is Bag-a-wire?
> He's nowhere around
> He cannot be found.
> Marcus Garvey words come to pass,
> Marcus Garvey words come to pass.

A different sort of curse was that placed on Norman Manley, founder and for 3 years leader of the People's National Party. The legend is based upon a case in court in which Manley found himself as legal advocate for one of Garvey's enemies. Thi was the period prior to Manley's entry into politics.

> "The case at King Street. The judge ask Garvey if him don't sail a flag, and him say yes. And him ask him if is him emblem there, and him say yes. And I think the judge ask Manley if him see a flag, and him say he see a piece of dirty cloth. And Mr. Garvey said, 'That same piece of cloth, you shall use it when you roll up your shirt sleeve and fight for the same people you are fighting against. But you shall be ten years late!' ".

In 1937, after a period of soul-searching, Manley entered politics and threw the weight of his prestige as a famous barrister behind the nationalists from the middle strata. The People's National Party (PNP) was formed on a platform of broad national unity in the struggle for independence. With backing from Bustamante, who by the end of the upheavals in 1938 had established himself as the leader and organizer of labour, the party was about to move forward into internal self-government under adult suffrage, when Bustamante suddenly defected and formed the Jamaica Labour Party (JLP) to contest the 1944 elections. Bustamante won a landslide victory. Not until 1955 did the PNP, under Manley's leadership, finally come to power, "ten years late".

But the curse was even made to extend to his son, Michael, who assumed leadership of the party following his father's retirement. Independence from Britain came in 1962 under Bustamante and the JLP. In 1972, Michael Manley came to power, again, say some interpreters of the myth, ten years late.

There is, finally, one last: a prophecy of Garvey foretelling the coming to Jamaica of the Ethiopian Orthodox Church. It does not easily fall into any of the above groupings. Many Rastafarians feel that one should not join any organization, for whatever "join can bruk" – that is, whatever is joined together can be broken – and this they are against. When the Orthodox Church was first set up, in the 1960s, they further denounced its practice of baptism. Baptism was one of the practices rejected by young Rastafari during the 1950s as being too close to the Christian and Revival traditions. Also there was the very sensitive question of the divinity of the Emperor, on which the Orthodox Church maintained diplomatic silence. Those who were received into the Church found themselves on the defensive.

Many of the foregoing are really prophecies. However, if they are taken and understood not piece by piece but in their totality as pronouncements of a man who has joined the ranks of "heroes", in the original sense of that word, then they should be treated as part of the mythology of the Jamaican people. A myth is not necessarily completely the creation of fertile imagination, as are the Anansi folk tales, in which animals and insects speak and act like human beings. We must allow for the fact that myths have a basis in real life. Indeed, Garvey may have said some of the things he is believed by Rastafarians to have said. There is no good reason not to believe that he did not look up in the sky and say God is black. After all, he not only was not an atheist but actively envisaged the establishment of a black church replete with black bishops and clergy.

But Garvey is alleged to have said things which clearly did not become the subject of a myth. Moreover, not everyone who heard him speak was disposed to construe what he might have said as evidence either of his own or of another's divinity. The focus of our attention, therefore, inevitably turns from what he may or may not have said to the manner in which what he said was interpreted by some of those to whom he said it. Whereas some valued his teachings in a political way, others valued them in a religious way. Bedwardites and Rastafari were among the latter.

An important difference between the Bedwardites and the Rastafari, where Garvey was concerned, was that the Rastafari abandoned the view which identified Bedward as the reincarnation of Aaron and placed him alongside Garvey, the reincarnation of Moses (Garvey's middle name was Mosiah): to both these figures, the one high priest in charge of religious life, the other prophet in charge of secular life, God entrusted the leadership of Israel out of bondage into the promised land. Instead, Rastafari compare Garvey to Selassie, as Moses (or John the Baptist) is compared to Jesus. Jesus, it is pointed out, came to fulfill the works of, therefore to supersede the former.

Ideologically speaking, then, it is the advent of Garvey which provided the break with the Revival concept of nationalism, though not with the religious form it took. The Bedwardites, while calling for the black "followers of Christ" to crush the white "Pharisees, Scribes and Sadducees", retained the view that white was superior to black; so that the end of white oppression would at the same time be the transformation of black into the status of white.[8] This contradiction, discredited by Garvey's teachings, was resolved by the proclamation of a black God.

For a man who died only 47 years ago, whose wife was an ardent defender of his cause up to 1973, it is significant that there are so many things said about Garvey in a manner that clearly clothes him with divine qualities. These are in one way or another the tales of people in the search for nationhood. They are expressions of hope formulated against a background of failure, the most recent of which was Bedward's. It is necessary to believe that Garvey is not dead, because sometime soon he will reappear from somewhere to complete and fulfill what he had undertaken.

But a noticeable feature of some of these myths and prophecies is their historical and contextual derivation. I do not recall hearing about the clash of the sevens until the period of the 1970s, and not before 1976. Similarly, the coming of the Ethiopian Orthodox Church was said to have been prophesied only as the event itself came near. There is a way that myth-making is an ongoing creative process.

Myths about Garvey are therefore part of the national consciousness of the Jamaican poor, dispossessed Blacks, once the object of enslavement, still the object of oppression in a society which only now is beginning to demonstrate that it values Blacks as much as it values whites. It is no accident that the main bearers of the oral tradition about Garvey, the magical works he performed, the prophetic things he said, are at the same time foremost exponents of black nationalism, the Rastafari.

NOTES

[1] This paper is an edited version of an excerpt from a larger study of the Rastafari movement conducted in 1974 and 1975 while I was a Research Fellow at the Institute of Social and Economic Research. The study is unpublished.

[2] An example of mythology playing a role in the development of a national consciousness is the Kimbango movement in the group. See Effraim Anderson, *Messianic Popular Movements in the Lower Congo,* Studia Ethnographica Upsaliensia 14 (Uppsala: Abmguist and Wicksells Boktrycheri, 1958); also G. Ballandier, "Messianismes et Nationalisme en Afrique", *Cahiers Internationaux de Sociologie,* Vol. 14, 1953. Alexander Bedward was a Revival prophet and healer who between 1895 and 1921 led a following numbering thousands of Jamaicans in both Jamaica and parts of Central America. Until Garvey's UNIA, his was the largest movement of black people in Jamaica. Bedward was once arrested and tried for sedition. He issued a call for "the black wall" to rise and

crush "the white wall" that was surrounding and oppressing it. Please see the present writer's "Religion and the Black Struggle", *Savacou,* No. 3, 1972.

[3] See Rupert Lewis, *Marcus Garvey: Anti-colonial Champion* (London: Karia Press, 1987).

[4] M.G. Smith, Roy Augier, and Rex Nettleford, *The Rastafari Movement in Kingston, Jamaica* (Kingston: ISER, 1961).

[5] As is widely known, Garvey's activities in Jamaica included the promotion of arts and culture.

[6] George W. Roberts and D.O. Mills, "Studies of External Migration Affecting Jamaica", *Social and Economic Studies,* Vol. 7, No. 2, 1958.

Garveyism and Religion

Garvey and Black Liberation Theology

Rev. Ernle P. Gordon
Rector, Church of St Mary the Virgin (Anglican)
Kingston, Jamaica

MARCUS GARVEY WAS NOT the first person to articulate a black theology, but he vas special in the sense that his theological ideas inspired many black churches to be tarted in Africa and he tried to concretize his ideas within a religious structure in he African Orthodox Church. Garvey's black liberation theology is important for he Caribbean religious structures today as they seek to liberate themselves from the mported ideological notions of Western Christianity, which domesticate rather than iberate.

Gayraud S. Wilmore claimed that before black nationalism was explicitly articu-ated in the resolutions of the Pan-African Congresses and the philosophy of Marcus Garvey,

> Black preachers and laymen had drawn cultural and political implications for African colonization and black self-determination in the United States – not from egalitarian ideologies flowing from Moscow, Paris or Washington, but from the *Bible,* and *black theology* as interpreted by men who believed the gospel and found in it the most penetrating and moving justification for racial solidarity and elevation. At the centre of the theology of liberation was the mission of the descendants of Africa to return.[1]

herefore, it is important that we remember the excellent work of Bishop Henry Mc-Neal Turner of the A.M.E. Church (1834-1915), who according to Edwin S. Redkey was without doubt the most prominent and outspoken American advocate of black migration in the years between the Civil War and the First World War".[2]

African Professor Edward Blyden, originally from the West Indies, having been enied entry into Rutger's Theological College, urged black people not to be a-hamed of their black skins and woolly hair; sought to foster the verification of all ue African people, rejected interlopers; stressed the fact that Liberia was a civi-zed state, a home for all black men; and unapologetically preached black repatria-on.

An Episcopalian priest, Alexander Crummell, born in New York in 1819, was one f the first black theologians to be critical of the agape doctrine of Orthodox Chris-anity: black people should espouse self-love in order to cast off the chains of oppression and gain the same equality as the white nations of the world. He was influential in articulating the responsibility of black intellectuals to the cause, and became the first president of the American Negro Academy.[3]

Another black theologian, Martin Delany, although a theoretician of black nationalism and emigrationism, "more than anyone else helped to clarify in the 1850s the cultural vocation of the black church, particularly its responsibility to assist in the redemption of Africa".[4]

In the late nineteenth century, black nationalism formed the praxis by which many black preachers in the US denied the inferiority of the black man, because many white churches used the Genesis story of Ham to formulate a racist ideology. Black clergymen who studied in the US returned to Africa to establish churches, such as the Rev. John Chilembwe of Nyasaland, who led his people in the Nyasaland rebellion in 1915. In South Africa, Ethiopian preachers were involved in the Zulu uprisings in 1906, and a Baptist preacher, the Rev. Lotin Same, organized anti-European agitation in the Cameroons. Garvey's philosophy and theology and ideas cannot be divorced from the influence of Booker T. Washington and many other persons who preceded Garvey.

Justice would not be done if this paper did not mention the black slaves on the plantations who presented the African religious culture, the Baptist Deacons – Sam Sharpe's uprising in 1831; the Morant Bay black struggle, led by another Baptist Deacon, Paul Bogle, in 1865; the successful guerrilla war of the Maroons against the British Army; the excellent work done by Baptist, Methodist and Moravian missionaries; and the three Anglican priests who were imprisoned for their anti-slavery views. It is crucial that we do not forget the black theology of Alexander Bedward, who was a threat to the status quo. Therefore, when Marcus Garvey's concepts began to be articulated, there was already a historical matrix, a socio-economic and political climate that concretized his views which have been documented. At this stage, it is vital that we define black theology, and examine Marcus Garvey's theological presentations in the light of some methodologies used by various liberation theologians in the Third World.

Black Liberation Theology

BLACK LIBERATION THEOLOGY is not a new theology, but a new way of doing theology, as all liberation theologies in the South are connected to the praxis of the oppressed and marginalized people. In other words, in examining the theology of Marcus Garvey you cannot separate black power from black religion or black nationalism from black liberation theology. Social beings inform social consciousness, matter should not be separated from the Spirit and the material problems of the black race are inextricably bound up with the religious dimension. James H. Cone argued that

> The task of black theology is to make Christianity really Christian by moving black people with a spirit of black dignity and self determination so they can become what the creator intended.... Black theology

> is a theology of the black community and is thus opposed to any idea which alienates it from that community. Since it seeks to interpret black power religiously, black theology endeavours to record the Christian tradition in view of the black predicament and to destroy the influence of heretical white American Christianity. In this sense, it is nationalistic. It attempts to provide black people with a sense of nationhood, knowing that until black unity is attained, black people will have no weapon against white racism.[5]

Marcus Garvey's concept of God is very vital in how we understand black religion. Religion for Garvey was neither mere philosophy nor ideology, but a relationship and an identity with the divine where the black man was not only an individual but a *person* made in the image of God, with dignity and self-esteem. In other words, the black man who is made in the image and likeness of God is truly human.

Let me quote from the Philosophy and Opinions of Marcus Garvey to show how he viewed the Divine:

> If the white man has the idea of a white God let him worship his God as he desires. If the yellow man's God is of his race let him worship his God as he sees it. We as Negroes have found a new deal. Whilst God has no colour yet it is human to see everything through one's own spectacles and since the white people have seen their God through white spectacles we have only now started out (late though it be) to see our God through our own spectacles, the God of Isaac and the God of Jacob. We Negroes believe in the God of Ethiopia, the everlasting God, God the Father, God the Son and God the Holy Ghost. The one God of all ages. That is the God in whom we believe, but we shall worship him through the spectacles of Ethiopia.[6]

In an article which appeared in the *Sunday Gleaner,* 1 February 1987 ("Garvey and Black Liberation Theory"), I mentioned that it has always been my firm belief that we have inherited a defective concept of God in the English-speaking Caribbean, which has derailed our ethics and emasculated black consciousness from our theological relationships:

> For me, God was realized neither in idealism nor in metaphysical cocoons, but through the process of liberation, when He revealed Himself to Moses as one who sided with the oppressed, the exploited, the marginalized, and one who was committed to their liberation from the oppressors. Black people have always been dehumanized, so if we as black people are serious about identifying with the Divine, then God for us is a black man.[7]

I strongly object to the view that God is "colourless", because for me this God does not exist – if He does, then I am an *atheist,* because a colourless God cannot be identified with anyone.

James Cone agreed with Garvey's theological reflections, when he reiterated that:

To suggest that Christ has taken on a black skin is not *theological emotionalism,* and if the church is a continuation of the Incarnation, and if the church and Christ are where the oppressed are, then Christ and his church must identify totally with the oppressed to the extent that they too suffer for the same reasons persons are enslaved. In America, blacks are oppressed because of their blackness. It would seem, then, that Emancipation could only be realized by Christ and church becoming black. *Thinking of Christ as non-black in the 20th Century is as theologically impossible as thinking of him as non-Jewish in the first Century. It is the job of the church to become black with him and accept the shame which white society places on blacks.* Black is holy, that is, it is a symbol of God's presence in history on behalf of the oppressed man".[8]

Marcus Garvey had to create a religious structure (a Christian church) which incorporated black nationalism, black consciousness, and a Christian church which had a black theology. Religion can either domesticate or liberate, and so is able to subvert or enhance the economic development of the black race. Garvey recognized this fact very early, and being a Catholic and also having an excellent knowledge of African religious psychology, he appointed a prominent Anglican (Episcopalian) priest, the Rev. Alexander McGuire, to be the Chaplain General of the Universal Negro Improvement Association in 1920. The Rev. McGuire (an Antiguan) was consecrated Bishop of the new African Orthodox Church on 28 September 1921. This church developed relations with the Ethiopian and Russian Orthodox Churches.

The *Negro Churchman,* the monthly magazine of the African Orthodox Church, reported that churches were established in Canada, Cuba and Haiti. Wilmore, in his book *Black Religion and Black Radicalism,* reported that by 1942 the had 30,000 members in the USA and overseas, 239 priests, 5 bishops, the Endrich Theological Seminary in New York and the George A. McGuire Seminary in Miami, USA.[9]

One of the features of all liberation theological processes, as outlined by José Miguez Bonino, is that having reflected on the praxis of the oppressed black man, "we must critically re-read and repossess biblical and theological tradition and also the Christian community in which we belong".[10] Bishop McGuire started to revolutionize Christian tradition, exhorting all negroes to remove pictures of the white Christ and the Virgin Mary from their homes and instead put up the Black Madonna and the Black Christ. The bishop declared that Christ was reddish brown in colour, and that we have characterized the devil as being black, and so from henceforth the Negro's devil should be white. The concept of the Black Madonna is traced to hieroglyphics on stone found in Egypt (Upper Nile) in 6000–5900 B.C.[11] This research was done by George C.M. James and Yosef Ben-Jochannan and documented in 1982. An interesting situation developed at the 4th International Conference of the Negro Peoples in 1924, when UNIA members marched with a large portrait of the Black Madonna and child.

This was very significant, because it was making a theological point: not only that man should demonstrate the feminine nature of God, but also that the black woman can rise to great heights and is also equally human. In other words, this movement began to assert the primacy of women in black religion. In the late 1960s two South African theologians were very critical of Western art as portrayed in Western theology, which viewed God as masculine and white. Women were despised, and black people had no God that reflected their black identity. These South African writers assert that Western theology inculcates a "person symbol"; it also attracts a sexist concept that is masculine and also a racist image.

Marcus Garvey's use of the Black Madonna was to demasculinize Western theology and liberate theology from a false view of women. In terms of other doctrinal changes, the UNIA printed a Catechism that not only underlined Catholic theology but exposed all the prominent black people in the Bible, black saints and early church fathers who were black and came from Africa (Tertullian and Augustine). An Ethiopian Orthodox clergyman supported Garvey and Bishop McGuire in their efforts to concretize black religion when he declared that the Negro would one day produce a Bible, illustrating black saints and black angels. At this stage of development, we must understand that black theology was responding to a particular socio-economic situation, and so it was inevitable that the early theological position had to be radical and sometimes extreme. *All liberation theologies must be situational.*

When Marcus Garvey referred to Ethiopia as the spectacles through which we worship God, it must be realized that in Biblical language he was correct, in that Ethiopia was used to represent Africa. The early black theologians quoted Psalm 57, which showed how Zion, the mother of nations, incorporated Ethiopia and Egypt as nations which accepted her as such. Ethiopia and Egypt are crucial to the study of the historical authenticity of black consciousness. L.S.B. Leakey and Richard E. Leakey have documented research material showing that it was in Ethiopia that the first human remains were found – five million years old.[12]

Recent research has also proven that the Egyptians were the first to accept the concept that there was one creator and the Trinitarian doctrine was reflected in Africa first, not by the Jews.[13] Marcus Garvey, although he never visited Africa, read widely and so was cognizant of the importance of Ethiopia and Egypt to black theology.

Black Consciousness and Black Theology

GARVEY WAS INFLUENCED by Catholic theology, and so in order to appreciate the real depth of black consciousness we should understand classic Western theological dimensions with regard to how Marcus Garvey interpreted the doctrine of creation when he affirmed that God created all men equal. He did not create one race to be superior and another to be inferior, and so He inspired the black man to chart his own destiny.

The Rev. Allan Boesak, a South African theologian from the Dutch reformed tradition, linked black consciousness with liberation theology, which was similar to the views expressed by Marcus Garvey. Allan Boesak declared that

> Liberation theology in South Africa is a human consciousness that we call black consciousness. Through black consciousness black people

> discover that they are children of God and they are part of history and that they have rights to exist in God's world. When I discover that God had made me a human being though I am not white it means that I have a right to be here; I am not less in God's eyes.[14]

Allan Boesak uttered these words in 1979, while Garvey said in the 1920s that he could not conceive of a God who would differentiate between any of the children he made to live on His earth. An impartial God meant an impartial heaven, so one of Garvey's devotional poems had a cover design of a Negro angel.

The Bible as a Theological Base

GARVEY'S USE OF THE BIBLE was not only revolutionary, but demonstrated that he understood theological terminology and re-interpreted theology in order to raise the consciousness of the black man. Garvey's speech delivered at Liberty Hall, New York, on 24 December 1922 – "Christ the Greatest Reformer" – revealed that he was cognizant of the Incarnational implications and what certain Christological forms imply. Garvey declared: "Christ was the first great reformer. Christ did not go exclusively to the classes. He devoted his life to all: the classes rejected Him, because He was not born in their immediate circle. He was not born of the physical blood royal, therefore they could not follow such a man".[15]

Therefore, it is not surprising how the Rastafarians have tried to interpret Garvey, in terms of situational theology, by enunciating their own incarnational views with regard to Haile Selassie. I must state categorically that Garvey did not try to divinize Haile Selassie but said that "man and God are to settle the world.... God works through the agency of human action".[16]

Garvey's Christmas message to the Negro peoples of the world, December 1921, juxtaposed the crucifixion of Jesus Christ and the sons and daughters of Africa, whose forbears "bore the cross for [them] up the heights of Calvary to [their] crucifixion"![17] The black man has to understand that liberation involves sacrificing one's life for justice, and the conflicts can be positive for development, not necessarily negative.

Another intriguing use of the Bible was Garvey's Easter Sunday sermon, delivered at Liberty Hall, New York, on 16 April 1922, when he used the Resurrection of Christ to demonstrate the importance of the resurrection of the Negro. Garvey stated emphatically, "We ourselves reflect God's greatness, we ourselves reflect the Trinity, and when we allow ourselves to be subjected and create others as superior, we hurl an insult at our Creator who made us in fullness of ourselves".[18]

His prophetic materialism was very visible in how he described "God as a War Lord".[19] All liberation theologies seek not only to liberate man but also to liberate the Gospel. Garvey sought in his own way to liberate the black man and also to liberate the theology which he inherited from his colonizers. In terms of Christian materialism Garvey emphasized that *matter cannot be separated from spirit,* which was evident in his Easter Sunday sermon when he declared that, "*Because* the teaching of Jesus sought to equalize the spiritual and even the temporal rights of man, those who hold authority, sway and dominion sought His liberty by prosecution, sought His life by death".[20] This same dialectical tension is now being waged between the liberation theologies of oppressed peoples and the Armageddon theologies of the TV evangelists.

Garvey's Christian materialism was very clear and precise, as he affirmed that, "Some of us seem to believe that Christ and God the Father are responsible for all our ills – physical ills. They have nothing to do with our physical ills.... Make your interpretation of Christianity scientific – what it ought to be – and blame not God, blame not the white man for physical conditions for which we are responsible".[21] He was very Biblical when he reminded us that, "God created you masters of your own destiny, masters of your own fate, and you can pay no higher tribute to your Divine Master than function as man, as He created you".[22]

His approach to Christians was not only pragmatic but reflected the Gospel message, when he said, "No hungry man can be a good Christian, no dirty naked man can be a good Christian, for he is bound to have bad wicked thoughts, therefore, it should be the duty of religion to find *physical as well as spiritual food* for the body of man".[23]

The South American liberation theologian, Gustavo Gutierrez, echoed similar ideas in the 1970s when he stated that "Poverty is not caused by divine intervention but by the economic structures". The economic structures make you rich or poor, not God.

Conclusion

IN ADDRESSING GARVEY and black theology, I did not elucidate extensively the *emigration* aspect, because although this was integral to the situation in Garvey's period, I think we should focus not so much on "going back to Africa" as on appreciating our African heritage, re-affirming the dignity and self-esteem of the black man, and showing that he is capable of controlling his own destiny. Most important, we must participate in the struggle to liberate South Africa from apartheid.

The black and brown middle-class intelligentsia who have ridiculed Garvey's ideas should remember that it is impossible to liberate the Caribbean man if we fail to understand the racial and political aspect, the folk-religious black culture, and especially that slavery was synonymous with being black and the African religious culture was suppressed during slavery. In other words, you cannot neglect the question of *race*.

Garvey's theological vibrations are a challenge to the churches in Jamaica, and to the rest of the Caribbean, to develop a theology of liberation. They are a challenge to liberate not only Jamaican men/women, but the theology which has been imported from the North which seeks to destroy *Koinonia* (community) and to reflect values that are demonic. Garvey's theology has demonstrated, though not necessarily in systematic form, that:

(a) There is no direct route from divine revelation to theology; the mediation of some praxis is inevitable;

(b) The area that defines this praxis and hence the critical plane on which reflection should take place is projected, not only in the socio-political one, but in black nationalism, the Rasta class division of race, emigration theories and what is basic for black liberation in our situation;

(c) Starting from this basic outlook, Jamaican churches must critically *re-read* and *repossess* biblical and theological traditions that are not only African, but are indigenous to the Christian community to which we belong.

Marcus Garvey's contribution to black theology is imperative for all seminaries, as they seek a new method to do theology. The deductive method is extremely idealistic and metaphysical, where the Scriptures are deemed to provide all the universal answers independent of history and hierarchically determined. Using the inductive approach to Garvey's theological ideas we notice that it is impossible to neglect historical events and that it is the human experience that determines how we look at the Bible and also provides the data for theological reflection. The inductive method impels us to question the structures of society which dehumanize the human person and force us to participate in transforming these structures for the purpose of creating a person who is truly human.

In this context Marcus Garvey's contribution to black theology is not only inextricably bound up with the liberation of the churches in Jamaica, but is as authentic as any other liberation theology in the Third World today.

Marcus Garvey did not set out originally to formulate a liberation theology, but what this paper is trying to show is that his ideas reflect the views of liberation theologians in all the Third World countries.

NOTES

[1] Gayraud S. Wilmore, *Black Religion and Black Radicalism* (New York: Anchor Books, 1973), pp. 184-185

[2] Edwin S. Redkey, *Black Exodus* (New Haven: Yale University Press, 1969), p. 24.

[3] Gayraud S. Wilmore, *Black Religion,* pp. 186-187.

[4] Ibid., p. 153.

[5] James H. Cone, *Black Theology and Black Power* (New York: The Seabury Press, 1969), pp. 130-131.

[6] Amy Jacques Garvey, *Philosophy and Opinions of Marcus Garvey,* Volumes I and II (New York: Atheneum, 1977), p. 44.

[7] Rev. Ernle Gordon, "Garvey and the Black Liberation Theory", *Sunday Gleaner,* Feb. 1987.

[8] James H. Cone, *Black Theology and Black Power,* p. 69.

[9] Gayraud S. Wilmore, *Religion and Black Radicalism,* p. 208.

[10] José Miguez Bonino, "Historical Praxis and Christian Identity", in *Frontiers of Theology in Latin America* (New York: Orbis Books, 1979), p. 262.

[11] George C.M. James, "Stolen Legacy", Julian Richardson, San Francisco, prepared by JAMIA Consultants, 1982.

2 Yosef Ben-Jochannan, *The Black Man's North and East Africa* (Alkebu-Lan Books, JAMIA Consultants, 1982).

12 L.S.B. Leakey, *The Progress and Evolution of Man in Africa* (Oxford University Press, JAMIA Consultants, 1982).

13 Ivan van Sertima (ed.), *Journal of African Civilization*, Rutgers University, New Brunswick, New Jersey, JAMIA Consultants, 1982.

14 Allan Boesak, "Liberation Theology in South Africa", in *Third World Liberation Theologies* (Mary Knoll, New York: Orbis Books, 1986), pages 266-267.

15 Garvey, *Philosophy and Opinions*, p. 29.

16 Ibid., p. 16

17 Ibid., p. 86

18 Ibid., p. 81

19 Ibid., p. 43

20 Ibid., p. 88

21 Ibid., p. 33

22 Ibid., p. 91

23 *Garvey and Garveyism*, p. 61.

The Religious Thought of Marcus Garvey

Philip Potter
United Theological College of the West Indies
Mona, Jamaica

Introduction

IT IS A DAUNTING TASK to speak on the religious thought of Marcus Garvey. While it is generally recognized that Garvey was a religious thinker, little emphasis has been given to this in Garvey studies. One exception is the pioneering book of Randall K. Burkett, *Garveyism as a Religious Movement,* in which he has a chapter on "Garvey as Black Theologian".[1] There are two reasons why I dare to venture in this field.

On 31 October 1937, just fifty years ago, I saw and heard Garvey speak in my home island, Dominica, in the course of a visit to the eastern Caribbean. There was quite a flourishing branch of the Universal Negro Improvement Association, some 800 strong, in Dominica, under the leadership of J.R. Ralph Casimir – a man who was close to Garvey and whom I knew and admired and with whom I had long conversations, the last being in September 1987. Garvey held us spellbound as he challenged us to think for ourselves and to have pride in ourselves as made in the image of God. We must throw off the shackles of dependency and of being objects of occasional charity. We must affirm ourselves as black people, assert our right to self-determination, and develop self-reliance if we are to play our part in the world and particularly with our fellow black sisters and brothers in Africa and the Americas. We must overcome our captivity to the divide-and-rule policy of the colonial powers and learn to act together in solidarity politically, economically and in mutual upliftment. The fact that Garvey spoke as a Christian and as one whose inspiration came from the prophetic message of the Bible had a powerful effect on me which has remained to this day. Alas, I never availed myself of the opportunity of making a study of Garvey until coming here two years ago. During the past year, especially, I have been immersed in the Garvey literature. I have also been supervising an M.A. student's research paper: "Towards a Theology of Marcus Garvey". Thus, early inspiration and later study have led me to consider Garvey's religious thought.

Marcus Garvey was baptized and grew up in the Methodist Church in St Ann's Bay, Jamaica. There is evidence that among the many books which his father had and which were at his disposal was the Bible, with old Garvey's many marginal annotations and comments. But in his early teens he had a rude shock.

As a child he played with the daughter of the minister, a Methodist missionary from Great Britain, and with other white children in the neighbourhood. When the time came for the family to return to Europe, this girl accosted Marcus and said, no doubt under parental instructions, that she would not write to him or try to get in touch with him, nor should he with her, because he was a "nigger". This incident led the teenage Marcus to sever regular links with the Methodist Church. It certainly made him determined to devote his life to the struggle for the dignity and independence of black people as made in the image and likeness of God and beloved of God.

The extraordinary thing about this traumatic experience is that it did not turn Garvey away from God or from the Church as the community of the Christ who came to serve and not to be served, and through whom there is neither Jew nor Gentile, slave nor free, male nor female, but we are all one in him. When Garvey came to Kingston as a printer and a dedicated advocate for his people, he frequently visited the churches in the corporate area, particularly the Baptist Church in East Queen's Street, where he met his first wife, Amy Ashwood, and Coke Methodist Church, where he would listen to the Rev. Theophilos Glasspole, that eloquent and prophetic preacher and the father of Jamaica's present Governor General.

When Garvey formed the Universal Negro Improvement Association in 1914, he adopted as its motto: "One God! One Aim! One Destiny!". Later it was expressed in Latin: "*Pro Deo Africa et Justitia*". The guiding principle was the commitment to "the universal brotherhood of man" growing out of "the universal fatherhood of God", in the spirit of the Sermon on the Mount and of the Golden Rule ("Do unto others as you will that they do unto you"), which Garvey later described as "the bedrock of God's philosophy". The meetings of the UNIA were begun and ended with hymns and prayers, and Garvey's exhortations were often based on Scripture and had a strong theological element about them. In 1921 appeared a *Universal Negro Catechism.* Its contents were in four parts: Religious Knowledge, Historical Knowledge, Constitution and Laws of the UNIA, and Declaration of Independence. The section on religious knowledge had questions and answers with appropriate biblical texts on God, Christ and his teaching, and on Ethiopia representing Africa in God's plan of redemption.[2] There was also *The Universal Negro Ritual,* with hymns, prayers and orders of worship. These two were largely drafted by the Antiguan, George Alexander McGuire, an Episcopalian priest who became the first Chaplain-General of the UNIA in 1920.

The Bible and Garvey Theology

RECENTLY, TONY MARTIN, to whom we are all indebted for many illuminating monographs on Garvey, has made available Garvey's *Message to the People: The Course of African Philosophy* (1937). This course contains twenty lessons, including the following: God, Christ, Man, the Universe, Personality, Winning the World for Kindness, Living for Something.

It is abundantly evident that Garvey's life-long struggle for racial identity and justice, and for the redemption of Africa, was grounded in his belief in the revelation of

God in the biblical message. At the UNIA Convention in Toronto in 1939 he declared:

> As a religionist, I feel 100 per cent a Christian and shall always act 100 per cent a Christian. I shall always believe in my God and I shall always know my God and I know my God to this extent, that whatever commands he gives to the individual he gives it but once and does not repeat it. God told man, when he made him, what the functions of man should be and from the day that he told man his function he has not altered that by any change at all.[3]

Marcus Garvey's faith was based on the Bible, but he was painfully aware that the Bible had been misused, especially with regard to black people. He expressed his understanding of the Bible on two occasions, in March and August 1921, as follows:

> You think now that I have sense I believe everything in the Bible. You people don't know how to diagnose and analyse things. What is the Bible? It is the Holy Word of God but God never wrote every word in the Bible. Inspiration came to the prophets and good men of the world and they wrote certain things and gave it to the Christian world....
>
> I am not one of those Christians who believe that the Bible can solve all the problems of humanity. It cannot be done; the Bible is good in its place, but we are men; we are the creatures of God and we have sinned against God, and therefore it takes more than the Bible to keep up with the age in which we live. Man is becoming so vile; man is becoming so criminal that you have to write other codes besides the Bible.[4]

For Garvey, the Bible is a book which has to be read with discernment and discrimination from the core of its message about God, Christ, and humanity. The Bible is a guide which obliges us to face our concrete situations in an existential way. And the concrete situation of the Blacks was the use of the Bible to denigrate them as children of Ham and "hewers of wood and drawers of water", rather than as made in God's image and likeness and sharing the same blood relationship with all human beings. Garvey was in fact calling for a new hermeneutic, or interpretation, of the Bible which is based on the central tenets of our faith and which provides, where necessary, a critique of the Scriptures themselves and points to the unity in diversity of the human family in justice and mutual well-being and peace.

The significance of Garvey's understanding of biblical interpretation is all the greater, because it is only in the last forty years or so that biblical scholars have been articulating this hermeneutical key. Garvey found this key in the second decade of the twentieth century. Today, women are using it in feminist theology and biblical exegesis to assert their right as sharing in the divine life which is both male and female. Indeed, this has been the hermeneutical method adopted by black and liberation theologies. It is in this sense that I agree with Ernle Gordon in his quotation from José Miguez Bonino that "we must critically re-read and re-possess the biblical and theological tradition and also the Christian community in which we belong".

Garvey's Understanding of God

WHAT THEN WERE the central faith convictions that Garvey constantly evoked? The best and simplest way to describe Garvey's deepest thought about God is to reproduce what is in the *Universal Negro Catechism*:

> *Q. What is God?*
> A. God is a spirit, that is to say, He is without body, or visible form.
>
> *Q. Are there more Gods than one?*
> A. No; there is but one living and true God.
>
> *Q. Mention some of the attributes of God.*
> A. He is everlasting, omnipotent, omniscient, omnipresent, and of infinite wisdom, goodness, truth, love, holiness, justice and mercy.
>
> *Q. By what title do we address God?*
> A. "Our Father in Heaven".
>
> *Q. Why is God called "Father"?*
> A. Because He is the Creator of all beings, visible and invisible, and the Maker of all things in the natural world.
>
> *Q. Are all human beings then the children* of God?
> A. Certainly; He is the great All-Father, and all members of the human race are His children.
>
> *Q. How did God create man?*
> A. Male and Female created He them after His own image, in knowledge, righteousness, and holiness, with dominion over all the earth and lower animals.
>
> *Q. Did God make any group or race of men superior to another?*
> A. No; He created all races equal and of one blood, to dwell on all the face of the earth.
>
> *Q. Is it true that the Ethiopian or Black Group of the human family is the lowest group of all?*
> A. It is a base falsehood which is taught in books written by white men. All races were created equal.
>
> *Q. What, then, is the chief reason for the differences observed among the various groups of men?*
> A. Environment; that is, conditions connected with climate, opportunity, necessity, and association with others.
>
> *Q. What is the color of God?*
> A. A spirit has neither color, nor other natural parts, nor qualities.

Q. But do we not speak of His hands, His eyes, His arms, and other parts?
A. Yes; it is because we are able to think and speak of Him only in human figurative terms.

Q. If, then, you had to think or speak of the color of God, how would you describe it?
A. As black; since we are created in His image and likeness.

Q. On what would you base your assumption that God is black?
A. On the same basis as that taken by white people when they assume that God is of their color.[5]

In this masterly catechetical description of God we see how Garvey and the UNIA effectively used the basic texts of Scripture. The question is: Did Garvey articulate a black theology? I would say he was articulating a theology which affirmed that humanity in all its racial variety finds its source and life in God. We are the image or icon of God. It is not that God is like us. It is rather that God's creation – human beings in their various environments and with their varied gifts – reflect the many-sidedness and richness of the Godhead. What is idolatrous and damnable is that anyone should exclusively claim God in terms of his/her form and character. That is the unforgivable sin of whites. What is true and right is that each and all of us as sexes, races and persons participate in the being of God and therefore have the responsibility to be as all-including as God is and to affirm our identities as given by God.

The significance of Garvey's understanding of God is that he passionately thought, spoke and struggled for and with the black people as God's beloved children, because, when our people – the black – are excluded from God's purpose for the good, it is a denial of the very existence of God and therefore of humanity itself. Particularity and universality are not opposed realities. They are reality itself. That is the divine economy. That is why Garvey had no difficulty in appreciating different peoples, including the Whites. In *The Negro World, Blackman,* and *The Black Man,* he wrote about what was happening in the world as he saw it, in whatever corner of it and in whatever way. He championed the causes of the Jews seeking a homeland; the Irish fighting to throw off their 700 years' yoke; the Indians, like all people under imperial rule, massively struggling for independence; and the Vietnamese independence movement, through his personal influence on the young Ho Chi Minh in New York. And he saw these struggles in relation to the black struggle. All had their own racial and national particularity, but they were one in their yearning for human dignity and solidarity. Out of the depths of the agony of the oppressed Black, Garvey identified himself with the agonies of the other oppressed peoples of the world.

This can be seen in the role which Garvey played during the conference on disarmament that took place in Washington in November 1921. World War One had taken a heavy toll of life, in senseless carnage. It is estimated that some two million Blacks from Africa, the Caribbean and North America had been involved in various fronts and on behalf of imperial Western nations, with much loss of life, in the name of opposing claims of justice. And yet, after the war, the Blacks were brutally denied their just claims to independence and fair play. Garvey spoke in Philadelphia and then in Washington itself during the conference. The message he wanted to convey to the statesmen gathered together was: "There can be no abiding peace until we (Blacks) are fully emancipated". But he went on to say:

> For us to have peace we must have equality, justice to all mankind. And that includes whom? It includes white, yellow, and black. Equality and justice to Whites alone will mean war from yellow and black. Equality and justice to Whites and yellow will mean war from the black. I want the world to understand that. There is not only an Eastern problem, an Asiatic problem – there is also an African problem. After you are through settling the problem of Europe, after you are through settling the problem of Asia, please remember that you are not through. There is a problem of Africa to be settled. And not until then will we have peace.[6]

A few days before, Garvey had said at Philadelphia: "The world will never disarm until the spirit of the man, Jesus Christ, is promulgated throughout the world. And not only promulgated, but practised in every respect by mankind everywhere".[7]

The Significance of Jesus Christ

FOR GARVEY, THE CENTRE of faith and the motivation for the devotion of his stormy life to the liberation of the black people and of humanity were found in the revelation of God in Christ. It was in Kingston in March 1921 that Garvey affirmed:

> Jesus Christ is the Son of God who took our physical form; that physical form bore in it a link of every race. The line from which He came had connection with every race existing, hence Jesus Christ is the embodiment of all humanity, otherwise He could not have been the Christ.[8]

In his writings and speeches, Garvey has helped us Blacks to capture the significance of Jesus Christ for us and for the world in a very arresting way. In the story of the incarnation, one of the three wise men or kings, who came from far to pay homage to the infant Jesus, was named by tradition Balthazar. He was black. The infant Jesus was received in Egypt as a refugee from the destroying rage of Herod the puppet king. In his ministry Jesus identified with the poor, the oppressed, the outcast. He prophetically challenged the religious and political authorities in the name of human dignity, justice and love. He was despised, hated, hounded, and finally condemned to death. It was an African, Simon of Cyrene, who carried his cross for him to Golgotha, while the religious powers and the crowds cried, "Crucify him!" and his disciples hid themselves in disappointment and fear. "Christ", wrote Garvey, "had in his veins the blood of all mankind and belonged to no particular race". But Garvey also observed that it was the Africans who were sensitively close to Jesus and it is Blacks who, with ever-renewed dignity and determined hope of redemption, are enduring rejection and ignominy by the perverted powers of the world. The resurrection of Jesus was, therefore, the sign and promise of the resurrection of the black race:

> As Christ, by his teachings, his sufferings and his death, triumphed over his foes, through the resurrection, so do we hope that out of our sufferings and persecutions of today we will triumph in the resurrection of our newborn race.[9]

It is this conviction which sustained Garvey to the end of his life.

In his Christmas and Easter messages, and on countless occasions, Garvey spoke with adoring passion about the Jesus Christ who gave himself for us human beings and for our salvation and liberation. And Garvey spoke and wrote as one who shared in the experience of Jesus. He too was hated, betrayed, wrongly condemned, and he experienced crucifixion in the destruction of his plans and projects for the redemption of his people. And yet, he would bounce back in the power of the risen life in Christ. In a poem, "Our Day" (1934), Garvey gives very moving expression to his faith in God in Christ, when he reflects on the eucharist of Christ's body and blood given for us and our response to give our body and blood for others:

> The Bread of life is gift of God to man,
> The blood of Christ is solace grand:
> To eat the food of Love Divine,
> Brings hope that leads to glory's land.
> The glorious Sacrament of Christ,
> Is tonic to the soul each day;
> A ransom in the blood of love,
> Is gain for those who humbly pray.
> As sons of Ham we eat the Bread,
> And drink the Holy Christian Blood;
> Our hope is in the Grace of God,
> For sufferings thus understood.
> Our day will come with showers true,
> For God on evil things will frown:
> Almighty love is all we claim,
> Though man destroys and keeps us down.[10]

It is in this spirit that Garvey spoke of Christ, in his 1922 Christmas Eve address, as "the first great reformer". He went on to say:

> Christ did not go exclusively to classes. He devoted his life to all; the classes rejected him because he was not born of high birth, of high parentage, because he was not born in their immediate circle; he was not born of the physical blood royal, therefore they could not follow such a man.... But there is one lesson we can learn from the teachings of Christ. Even though man in the ages may be hard in heart and hard in soul, that which is righteous, that which is spiritually just, even though the physical man dies, the righteous cause is bound to live....

> God is just, god is love, God is no respecter of persons; God created mankind to the same rights and privileges and the same opportunities, and before man can see his God, man will have to measure up in that love, in that brotherhood that he desired us to realize and know as taught to us by his son Jesus.[11]

Christ as reformer is the one who made most clear in himself and in his words and deeds that God is just, God is love, and that God's purpose for all people, and especially the oppressed black people, is that they may live in and practise justice in peace and love.

Garvey's Perspective on Humanity

IN THE PERSPECTIVE of the being and revelation of God in Christ, Garvey wrestled with the contradictory character of human beings. In a speech on "God and Man" delivered at Edelweiss Park, Kingston, in July 1929, Garvey said:

> God's greatest work is the making of man. In the making of man by God he grants a sovereignty to the individual that has never been in dispute; but which is still existent. That sovereignty places man in a position to so create, to so work, to so achieve, that in this accomplishment follows God's blessing....[12]

Garvey went further eight years later, speaking in Halifax, Nova Scotia, by making use of Psalm 8: 4-5: "What is man that thou art mindful of him, and the son of man that thou dost care for him? Yet thou hast made him a little lower than God, and dost crown him with glory and honour". Garvey asserted:

> God made man to be master of the world and this is the world of which man is master. Those who have mastered the world receive the compliment of the Creator, and God blesses them to rise to the height of being Lord and Master, to use the world and occupy the world as he sees fit.[13]

Ten years before, in 1927, Garvey had written a poem. "God in Man", in which he spoke forcefully of human beings as manifestations of God:

> Thou art the living force in part,
> The Spirit of the Mighty I;
> The God of Heaven and your heart
> Is Spirit that can never die.
> In each and every one is God,
> In everything atomic life;
> There is no death beneath the sod,
> This fact, not knowing, brings the strife.[14]

These bold, and almost pantheistic, statements about human beings were intended to remind the black race of its God-given rights and responsibilities. In his early *Dis-*

sertation on Man, he made it clear that he was challenging his people to assume their high calling – a challenge which is as relevant today as it was over sixty years ago when he articulated it:

> Man is the individual who is able to shape his own character, master his own will, direct his own life and shape his own ends.... He [God] never intended that that individual should descend to the level of a peon, a serf, or a slave, but that he should be always man in the fullest possession of his senses and with the truest knowledge of himself....
>
> After the creation and after man was given possession of the world, the Creator relinquished all authority to his lord, except that which was spiritual. All that authority which meant the regulation of human affairs, human society, and human happiness was given to man by the Creator, and man, therefore, became master of his own destiny, and architect of his own fate.[15]

Garvey not only believed this calling of Blacks, but acted on it. That was the basis of the very existence and activities of the UNIA, like the Black Star Line and various commercial and social projects. Garvey was merciless in castigating black folk for passively lamenting their terrible history and their ghastly condition. He constantly called them to know themselves:

> For man to know himself is for him to feel that for him there is no human master. For him Nature is his servant, and whatsoever he wills in Nature, that shall be his reward....
>
> To me, a man has no master but God. Man in his authority is sovereign lord. As for the individual man, so of the individual race.... So few of us can understand what it takes to make a man – the man who will never say die; the man who will never give up; the man who will never depend upon others to do for him what he ought to do for himself; the man who will not blame God, who will not blame Nature, who will not blame Fate for his condition; but the man who will go out and make conditions to suit himself.... If 400,000,000 Negroes can only get to know themselves, to know that in them is a sovereign power, is an authority that is absolute, then in the next twenty-four hours we would have a new race, we would have a nation, an empire – resurrected, not from the will of others to see us rise, but from our own determination to rise, irrespective of what the world thinks.[16]

Experience, however, taught Garvey the harsh reality of the awful sinfulness of human beings, and of the socio-political and economic structures which they erected and to which they became enslaved. He had to suffer the humiliation of his own black people letting him down and playing their part in his arrest, trial and imprisonment in the USA. Wherever he turned, up to his comparatively early death in 1940, he had to face this failure and betrayal. He used to quote Booker T. Washington, who described us Blacks as crabs in a basket, pulling each other down all the time. "That", commented Garvey, "is our peculiar psychology".[17] But Garvey saw that this sinfulness was inherent to human beings as such, of whatever race or nation. After an extensive tour of Europe in 1937, where Mussolini, Hitler and Stalin reigned, and which was gravitating to the inevitable catastrophe of World War Two, Garvey decided to create "The School of African Philosophy" for which he wrote the *Message to the People*. Lesson 11, "Man", begins thus:

> Man, because of his sin which caused him to have fallen from his high estate of spiritual cleanliness to the level of a creature, who acts only for his own satisfaction by the gift of freewill, must be regarded as a dangerous creature of life....
>
> When he can profit from evil he will do it and forget goodness. This has been his behaviour ever since the first record of his existence and his first contact with his fellows....
>
> The history of the world shows that man has been the chief murderer or killer. He has killed more creatures than any other being. He plans his murders which he may execute on individuals or on large groups of men and he generally does this for profit; national profit, racial profit, political profit or economic profit.
>
> He is so vile that he no longer depends upon his physical strength to execute his vileness or to defend himself. He manufactures the most deadly weapons to do the deed quickly, while seeking self-protection from a similar attack....
>
> The mind that makes TNT (high explosives), the mind that makes mustard gas, the mind that invents the Krupp Gun, the Winchester Rifle, the fast proof calibre pistol and poisons; all calculated to kill his brother. Do you want anything more wicked? Now, can you realize how bad man is? If you do, then always be on guard, because you know not when the evil genius cometh.[18]

Garvey's clear-eyed realism is a sharp reminder of who we are and where we are tending with our "evil genius", personal and collective. Garvey did not live to hear of the atomic bombing of Hiroshima and Nagasaki. But what he wrote showed great insight into its possibility. Today, we live in the constant threat of a nuclear holocaust and of the end of planet earth.

How, then, is humanity to be saved? This was not an easy matter for Garvey. He had declared that God was only encountered in the spiritual sphere. He used to say: "The spiritual is always God's, but the physical is your own property". The material sphere is where humanity was in control, for good or ill. Garvey was himself very ambivalent about this human sovereignty, because of the abject condition of his people. Garvey's love of rhetoric led him to give some curious examples of human sovereignty. In his speech on "God and Man" (1929), he declared: "It was Benjamin Franklin who said, 'God gives all things to industry'. It was Napoleon who, in the midst of one of his campaigns was interrogated, and asked the question, 'On whose side is God in this war?' Napoleon turned and answered, 'God is on the side of the strongest battalion'. That was a confirmation of Franklin's thoughts".[19] Did Garvey not know that Franklin, as one of the founding fathers of America, excluded Blacks from the benefits of the Declaration of Independence? Did he not know that, apart from his aggressive wars in Europe and North Africa, Napoleon cleverly got Toussaint l'-

Ouverture kidnapped and imprisoned in the Jura mountains, where he froze to death? What kind of examples was Garvey lifting up to his people?

In 1937 Garvey said in Canada:

> There is no part that man has played from the Garden of Eden that you, when you become conscious of yourself, cannot play. The part that Wolfe played in Quebec, the part that Abraham Lincoln played in signing the Proclamation [of the abolition of slavery]; the part that David Lloyd George played in the last bloody war, that McKenzie King is playing in Canada, that Stalin is playing in Russia, that Hitler is playing in Germany, you can play if you select that which is your function in life.... Man thinks and there is a kingdom, there is an Empire.[20]

Garvey was a man of his time. It was thought that, if people were intelligent, knowledgeable, industrious and determined enough, they would be a success. Garvey was apt to say: "The man who knows walks the world a colossal success". And he went on to lament about his people: "Your misfortune is the result of your lazy mentality".[21]

But, in fact, Garvey realized that humanity's autonomy was a cul-de-sac. In his *Message to the People* he writes:

> The mission of Christ, therefore, was to redeem man from sin and place him back on the pinnacle of goodness as God intended when he made the first two creatures.
>
> The life of Christ is intended to show man that by obedience he can lift himself to the highest soul expression in keeping with the Holy Spirit of God, of which he is a part, but only with free-will.[22]

Garvey expressed himself explicitly in verse, "Hell's Back Door" (1936), having in mind the cruel tyrant Mussolini, who raped Ethiopia:

> To close completely Hell's back door,
> We have to turn our faces round.
> And this should be for rich and poor,
> If man's best virtues must be found,
> We'll have to change the Hero's mark,
> And set examples good, in deed:
> The deeds of Jesus should be wooed,
> To make of life a course more true.
> To glorify the beast in man,
> And set it up in marble, tall,
> Is way to crucify each one,
> Who under tyrants often fall.
> When we do cease to honour sin,
> And praise but that of Christian love,
> We'll find a world worth living in,
> As pattern of the realm above.[23]

The question may well be asked, how do people "turn"? Incidentally, this word "turn" is in Hebrew *shuv,* which in the Old Testament means turning away from self to God and taking the way of righteousness, that is, right relations with God and with one another. Certainly, Garvey had no use for a pious faith in Jesus which did not motivate people to "set examples good, in deed". When he spoke in Kingston in 1921, Garvey said a word which needs to be said today:

> You negroes in Jamaica pray too much! With all your prayers you have hurricanes, earthquakes, droughts and everything! You know why! Because God is not satisfied with prayers alone. God says you must work and pray! And you people seem to give up the world to the white man and take Jesus! The white man has the world and gives up Jesus! Don't you know the white man has a right to Jesus, too? Jesus belongs to everybody, so you are foolish to give up the world and take Jesus only. You must take part of the world and part of Jesus, too! You negroes have not got into your head the scientific idea of worshipping God!
>
> Emotion and sentiment does not count in a world like this. They cannot move the world. This world can only be moved by practical achievements. Unless you work with your prayers, you will be too late here or anywhere else.[24]

Garvey and the Church

GARVEY SAW ONE MEANS by which people could be helped to be on the right course. It was through life in the fellowship of the church as a healing, redeeming and caring community of faith and action. In 1929, he wrote in *Blackman*:

> The Church is the most beneficent institution, the greatest civilizing agency; the institution which is begetter and ward of the rights and privileges, the freedom and liberty, not only of the community, but of the individual. It is the power protective of life and property. It is positive in its effect and of a potency unequaled by any other service of which our civilization boasts....
>
> Many atrocities are committed in the name of the Church – shameful scenes of persecution have been enacted and executed thereby, but the man who is prepared to isolate himself and live in open disregard of the Church, is inviting the greatest disaster that can befall him.[25]

Garvey had an astonishingly high view of the church as the community where, in mutual solidarity in Christ, we receive the judgement and mercy of God, so that we can become truly ourselves and therefore truly for one another in each place and all places. The "base communities" in the church in Latin America are a living example of how the church can be a liberating force for the people. Garvey understood this very early. That is why the UNIA was, in a sense, a precursor of the "base com munities". Its catechism and rituals, its whole ethos were intended to strengthen the churches in their calling to enable black people to emancipate their spirits and find ways of demonstrating their integrity as the people of one God, with one aim and one destiny – justice for the oppressed people of Africa as a sign of justice in the whole world.

There has been a tendency to associate Garvey and the UNIA with one church – the African Orthodox Church, the founder of which was George Alexander McGuire, the first Chaplain-General of the UNIA. This is far from the truth. In fact, just when McGuire was, in his absence in the Caribbean, appointed Bishop of the new church, the editorial page of *The Negro World* had a letter from the Assistant President-General of the UNIA under the caption: "UNIA Favours All Churches, But Adopts None as UNIA Church":

> I want it to be distinctly understood that the UNIA is not a church, and it does not intend to be one. So far as the present signs are, there will be no church connected with the UNIA. I wish to say if anyone comes around and tells you of a church bearing the name of the UNIA, repudiate it from start to finish, for it is absolutely false. There is no such church as authorized. We favor all churches, but adopt none as a UNIA church. Let the presidents and officers of the various locals take notice and govern themselves accordingly.[26]

The following year, at the Third International Convention of the UNIA (1922), Garvey is reported as follows:

> It was not the desire, he explained, of the UNIA to dictate any one's religious faith or religious belief; that was to say, we were not assuming to tell any one to become a Catholic or Baptist or Episcopalian or Seventh Day Adventist or Holy Roller or anything else. The idea was to bring to the Negro a scientific understanding of religion. What was desired was one great Christian confraternity without regard to any particular denomination, believing ourselves to be religious Christians.[27]

In his *Message to the People*, Garvey lists what the UNIA had done from 1917 to 1937. Among the 34 points he makes is this: "13. The UNIA taught the Negro how to support his own church".[28]

The important point here is that Garvey was concerned that the UNIA be a forum for all Blacks of religious faith sharing the same aims as the UNIA. While Garvey shared McGuire's theological understanding of the black people as made and loved by God and having a destiny blessed by God, he was convinced that, in the circumstances, the UNIA would be divided if it opted for one denominational expression. Nevertheless, McGuire continued to play a significant role as Honorary Chaplain-General of the UNIA.

African Redemption and Human Hope

WHAT GARVEY and McGuire believed fervently in common was undoubtedly vibrant hope for the redemption of the black peoples and especially of Africa. The both inherited from black preachers since the eighteenth century the promise of Go that Ethiopia – i.e., Africa and all black people everywhere – would be fulfilled i justice and peace. The classical biblical passage was Psalm 68: 31: "Let bronze b brought from Egypt, let Ethiopia hasten to stretch out her hands to God". This wa enshrined in the *UNIA Catechism,* which was largely drafted by McGuire:

> *Q. What prediction made in the 68th Psalm and the 31st verse is now being fulfilled?*
> A. "Princes shall come out of Egypt, Ethiopia shall soon stretch out her hands unto God".
>
> *Q. What does this verse prove?*
> A. That Negroes will set up their own government in Africa, with rulers of their own race.[29]

Psalm 68 is textually the most difficult of all the psalms and no one quite know what is supposed to come out of Egypt. The earliest English version was "princes" Others say "messengers"; yet others, more recently, say "bronze". A modern inter pretative translation is: "The noblemen come to thee from out of Egypt; Cus [Ethiopia] hastens to come before God with hands full of gifts". Despite the fact tha this psalm is made up of bits and pieces from different periods of Israel's history an in different states of the Hebrew language, commentators do remark that it is th most glowing, the most spirited and the most powerful of the psalms that speak o the universal saving power of God who cares for and delivers all who are in need an in distress. This is what the black preachers, and particularly Garvey, understood Even more important is the fact that not only Egypt but the more Negro Ethiopi played a leading role in ancient Near Eastern history, pointing to a highly develope civilization. But what Garvey was insisting on is that God's plan (a favourite expres- sion of his) is that Ethiopia, representing Africans at home and abroad, will in a spe- cial way find a welcome place before God as it presents its rich gifts. It will be remembered that Garvey often recalled the tradition that the black king, Balthazar, brought gold as a gift to the new-born Jesus.

Another crucial biblical text (Acts 8: 26-40) recounts the story that the first iden- tified non-Jew to be evangelized was an Ethiopian high official, a delegate from Can- dace, queen of Ethiopia. He was reading Isaiah 53, which tells of the saving work of the suffering servant of God – a fate which later the black race has endured as suf- fering and despised people. Philip the Evangelist expounded the fulfillment of the prophecy in Christ. The Ethiopian believed and was baptized. Through him the Gospel came to black Africa before it reached Europe and other continents outside the Jewish diaspora of the Middle East. Africa is therefore conspicuously present in God's purpose for the redemption of the world. Garvey was rightly bold in claiming that unless Africa – that continent so despoiled and abused by the so-called Christian West – is redeemed, the world will not be redeemed. Indeed, Garvey frequently quoted the words of the Book of Revelation: "After this I looked, and behold, a great multitude which no one could number, from every nation, from all tribes and peoples and tongues, standing before the throne and before the Lamb, clothed in white robes, with palm branches in their hands, and crying out with a loud voice, 'Salvation belongs to our God, who sits upon the throne, and to the Lamb!' " (7: 9-10). Garvey saw in it evidence that there would be no racial separation in heaven. He also often referred to Revelation 21, in which the peoples, overcoming obedience, bring their riches into God's open city, New Jerusalem, where none is excluded except those who exclude themselves. Garvey comments: "This story of Revelation ought to be the chart to every man, to every race and nation to measure self". [30]

In his editorial in *Blackman* in 1929 on "The Redemption of Africa", Garvey writes:

> The Redemption of Africa is a great commission, not only to recover Africa for the Africans, but to rescue the souls of Africa's sons and daughters from social, political, economical and spiritual bondage, and place them on a ground of vantage to secure the true uplift of the race, and the general good of the human family. The cause is profound in its depths, immense in its extent, and dazzling in the heights of its ambition....
>
> Where they [Negroes] find themselves, they can be absolutely loyal citizens, and at the same time absolutely loyal to the Cause of Africa redeemed. They may build up the nation and government just where they are with great success. They may build up their social, intellectual, political and economic independence, a common consciousness and a great confraternity of all Negroes all over the world.[31]

For Garvey, the redemption of Africa will secure "the general good of the human family".

When Garvey wrote and spoke on the redemption of Africa, only two countries were independent nations states: Ethiopia and Liberia. From the 1880s, apart from the old Portuguese and Spanish colonies and the occupation of South Africa, there was a ruthless scramble for Africa by European powers. Garvey grew up with the plight of a raped Africa, on top of the denuding of its population earlier by the slave trade.

While in England (1912-14) Garvey would have heard and read about the Zionist movement. In 1896 Theodore Herzl had published *The Jewish State,* which was widely read and hotly debated in Europe and North America. It was based on earlier Jewish thinking on "self-emancipation" and a "national home" for the Jewish people. There was considerable division among Jews at the time about the wisdom of a Jewish state. However, at a congress in 1911 an official programme was adopted:

> Zionism seeks to secure for the Jewish people a publicly recognized, legally secured home in Palestine for the Jewish people. For the

achievement of its purpose the congress envisages the following methods:

1. The programmatic encouragement of the settlement of Palestine with Jewish agricultural workers, labourers and those pursuing other trades.

2. The unification and organization of all Jewry into local and wider groups in accordance with the laws of their respective countries.

3. The strengthening of Jewish self-awareness and national consciousness.

4. Preparatory steps to obtain the consent of the various governments necessary for the fulfillment of the aims of Zionism.[32]

There is a close affinity between the Zionist movement and its programme and Garvey's idea of a homeland in Africa and of the relation of Blacks everywhere to Africa. Of great interest is the fact that Zionism was the response to Caucasian white racism against a Semitic people whose language had some kinship to Ethiopia's.

In 1923 Garvey wrote:

> It can plainly be seen that in the question of self-preservation and self-interest the Whites nowhere, whether in America, England or France, are going to give way to the Negro to the detriment of their own. We need not look for constitutional protection, or even for philanthropic Christian sympathy, because if that is to be shown it will be to the race that is able to bestow it.
>
> Hence, the Universal Negro Improvement Association has but one solution for this great problem, and that is to work unceasingly for the bringing about of a National Homeland for Negroes in Africa, so that when this wholesale declaration against Negroes takes place we can have a National Home of our own to look to.[33]

In 1925, in a statement on "African Fundamentalism", Garvey exhorted his people:

> Our union must know no clime, boundary or nationality. Like the great Church of Rome, Negroes the world over must practise one faith, that of Confidence in themselves, with One God! One Aim! One Destiny! Let no religious scruples, no political machinations divide us, but let us hold together under all climes and in every country, making among ourselves a Racial Empire upon which "the sun shall never set"....
>
> Never forget your God. Remember, we live, work and pray for the establishing of a great and binding racial hierarchy, the founding of a racial empire whose only natural, spiritual and political limits shall be God and "Africa, at home and abroad".[34]

The Garvey scholar Rupert Lewis tells us that "*The Negro World* of April 9, 1932 continued to advocate that UNIA members should 'establish bases' in independent African countries like Liberia and Ethiopia from which to spread the gospel of 'a united and liberated Africa' ".[35]

The deep significance of Garvey's eschatological thought – the vision of God's fulfillment of history – is that he never succumbed to the kind of religiosity which in its crudest form peddled the consolation of "pie in the sky when you die". He was the first leader to inspire millions of Blacks in the Caribbean, North America and Africa to grasp their hope in God as revealed in the crucified and risen Lord and work together for concrete goals – establishing a world-wide organization and network, the UNIA; fostering the development and deployment of their intellects and skills to become self-reliant; acquiring the political will to found governments in Africa, to struggle for their rights outside of Africa where Whites were dominant and domineering; maintaining the keen assurance that their struggle was aimed at justice and peace not only for Blacks, but for all peoples.

Garvey's confidence in the destiny of the black race finds eloquent expression in the words of the renowned black American theologian, James H. Cone, who acknowledges the debt of American Blacks to Garvey. Writing in 1984 and assessing where we are and where we are going as Blacks, he concludes his book in a way which would have delighted Garvey's heart:

> I belong to a Christian community whose members believe that we Blacks have come "this far by faith", leaning on the God of our slave grandparents. We have survived slave ships, auction blocks, and chronic unemployment because the God of black faith has bestowed upon us an identity that cannot be destroyed by white oppressors. It is the knowledge that we belong only to God that enables black Christians to keep on fighting for justice even though the odds might be against us. We firmly believe that Jesus heals wounded spirits and broken hearts. No matter what trials and tribulations blacks encounter, we refuse to let despair define our humanity. We simply believe that "God can make a way out of no way"....
>
> The eschatological hope found in black faith is not pie-in-the-sky religion. It is not an opiate. Rather it is born of struggle here and now because black Christians refuse to allow oppressors to define who we are:
>
> O, nobody knows who I am,
> Till the judgement morning.[36]

Conclusion

THIS PAPER HAS BEEN a tentative attempt to outline Marcus Garvey's religious thought. For me, the greatness of Garvey as a thinker, and especially as a religious thinker, is that he always related thought to strategy and action. The leitmotiv of his dedicated and incredibly productive life was, in the words of the Epistle of James, "faith without works is dead", and thought and action without a transcendent grounding is a recipe for ideological and existential opportunism and mimicry. Garvey was a man of faith in God in Christ and he perceived this faith as a means of radically unmasking the enslaving religion of both Whites and Blacks, and of challenging black people to rise up with their risen Lord and take a firm hold of their heritage as made in God's image, expressed in the soil of Africa, and act courageously to become fully human, inferior to none, and at the service in love to all. This radicalness of faith had to be constantly applied to our own self-understanding as Blacks. On the anniversary of Emancipation in the English-speaking Caribbean in 1929, Garvey said a word which is pertinent for us as we observe in 1988 the 150th anniversary of the final abolition of slavery: "We must create a second emancipation – an emancipation of our minds".

Moreover, Garvey was the first leader and thinker in this century to discern, from the action of God in Israel and from the ministry of Jesus, that God has always given preference to the poor, oppressed and downtrodden. Writing in Blackman in September 1929, Garvey declared:

> God seems to save from the bottom upwards. That he is as it were given a chance first of all to make what he can of the abandoned and the helpless is proof of his ability to save the better off.[37]

The liberation of the oppressed will be the liberation of the oppressors. It was Booker T. Washington who had said: "You can't keep a person in the gutter without remaining there".

The abiding relevance of Garvey's religious thought can be summed up in the preamble to the constitution of the UNIA:

> The motto of the organization is One God! One Aim! One Destiny! Therefore, let justice be done to all mankind, realizing that if the strong oppress the weak confusion and discontent will ever mark the path of men, but with love, faith and charity toward all the reign of peace and plenty will be heralded into the world and the generation of men shall be called blessed.[38]

And Marcus Garvey challenges us today as he did in 1939: "The end is not in our day, but in our time we can make a certain contribution to it".

NOTES

[1] Randall K. Burkett, *Garveyism as a Religious Movement* (New Jersey and London: Scarecrow Press, 1978), pp. 45-70.

[2] Robert A. Hill (ed.), *The Marcus Garvey and Universal Negro Improvement Association Papers* (Berkeley: University of California Press, 1983-1985), Vol. III, pp. 302-319.

[3] Marcus Garvey (ed.), *The Black Man,* Vol. III, No. 11, November 1938.

[4] Hill (ed.), *Garvey and UNIA Papers,* Vol. III, pp. 284, 601.

[5] Ibid., pp. 302-303.

[6] Ibid., Vol. IV, pp. 206-207.

[7] Ibid., p. 173.

[8] Ibid., Vol. III, p. 283.

[9] Amy Jacques-Garvey (ed.), *Philosophy and Opinions of Marcus Garvey* (New York: Atheneum, 1986), Vol. I, p. 62.

[10] Tony Martin (ed.), *The Poetical Works of Marcus Garvey* (Dover, Mass.: The Majority Press, 1983), Vol. I, p. 62.

[11] Amy Jacques-Garvey (ed.), *Philosophy and Opinions,* Vol. II, pp. 29-31.

[12] Amy Jacques-Garvey & E.U. Essien-Udom (eds.), *More Philosophy and Opinions of Marcus Garvey* (London: Frank Cass, 1987), Vol. III, p. 3.

[13] Ibid., p. 13.

[14] Martin (ed.), *Poetical Works,* pp. 43-44.

[15] Jacques-Garvey (ed.), *Philosophy and Opinions,* Vol. I, p. 24.

[16] Ibid., pp. 38-39.

[17] Jacques-Garvey & Essien-Udom (eds.), *More Philosophy and Opinions,* Vol. III, p. 19.

[18] Tony Martin (ed.), *Marcus Garvey: Message to the People: The Course of African Philosophy* (Dover, Mass.: The Majority Press, 1986), pp. 92, 94.

[19] Jacques-Garvey & Essien-Udom (eds.), *More Philosophy and Opinions,* Vol. III, p. 3.

[20] Ibid., p. 14.

[21] Ibid., pp. 15-16.

[22] Martin (ed.), *Message to the People,* p. 52.

[23] Martin (ed.), *Poetical Works,* p. 94.

[24] Hill (ed.), *Garvey and UNIA Papers,* Vol. III, p. 282.

[25] Jacques-Garvey & Essien-Udom (eds.), *More Philosophy and Opinions,* Vol. III, pp. 5-6.

[26] Burkett, *Garveyism as a Religious Movement,* p. 94.

[27] Ibid., p. 97.

[28] Martin (ed.), *Message to the People,* p. 174.

[29] Hill (ed.), *Garvey and UNIA Papers,* Vol. III, p. 307.

[30] Garvey (ed.), *The Black Man,* No. 2, January 1934.

[31] Jacques-Garvey & Essien-Udom (eds.), *More Philosophy and Opinions,* Vol. III, p. 140.

[32] Walter Laqueur, *A History of Zionism* (London: Weidenfeld and Nicholson, 1972), p. 106.

[33] Jacques-Garvey (ed.), *Philosophy and Opinions,* Vol. II, p. 49.

[34] John Henrik Clarke (ed.), *Marcus Garvey and the Vision of Africa* (New York: Vintage Books, 1974), pp. 158-159.

[35] Rupert Lewis, *Marcus Garvey: Anti-Colonial Champion* (London: Karia Press, 1987), p. 169.

[36] James H. Cone, *For My People: Black Theology and the Black Church* (Maryknoll, New York: Orbis Books, 1984), pp. 206-207.

[37] Garvey (ed.), *Blackman*, September 17, 1929, p. 1.

[38] Hill (ed.), *Garvey and UNIA Papers,* Vol. I, p. 256.

Pan-Africanism and other Ideological Issues in Garveyism

Garveyism, Pan-Africanism and African Liberation in the Twentieth Century

Horace Campbell
Faculty of Arts and Social Sciences
University of Dar es Salaam, Tanzania

Introduction

THE MARKING OF the centenary of the birth of Marcus Garvey in 1987 provides another opportunity to underscore the importance of the place of Garveyism in the long struggle for African liberation in this century. There are many elements in what is considered to be African liberation, and the specific content is defined by the differing social forces in search for liberation. But by any criteria, Garveyism laid the foundations for many of the important turning points in the long battles of this century. Garveyism was itself one component of the intense political and ideological struggles around the future of Africa and the relationship of this future to the dispersed African peoples.

Many demands have been presented in the struggle for black liberation this century. Questions of dignity, self-respect, independent statehood, social and economic freedom, religious freedom, freedom of movement, freedom of expression, economic co-operation, and social transformation have all been placed on the agenda as elements of African liberation in this century of liberation and revolution. Even though the century is not yet complete, the intense conflict in political, military and ideological terms over the future of Africa ensures that the problem of African redemption will be an important theme to reflect on in this year.

Political conferences or centenaries may reflect one level of the ideological struggle over Africa and her dispersed peoples, but the ultimate importance will be tested in the way in which the commemoration of Garvey accurately reflects the strengths and weaknesses of the profound struggles for the rights and dignity of the African peoples. Whichever direction the centenary takes, it is occurring at a time when popular struggles continue from day to day at many different and more profound levels. Probably the most intense point of this struggle is the confrontation with the ideation of white superiority which is today engulfing the whole of southern Africa in war and mass resistance. In this region, the confrontation with white racism reinforces the fact that the future of African liberation is linked up to the ending of white rule in Africa as a precondition for the return of African people to history.

Even though the present question of African liberation is still posed in terms of the requirements of independent statehood and the end of racism towards the African person, the rise of Garveyism was concerned with the fundamental principle of correcting the falsifications of the place of Africa, which is at the base of the intellectual culture of Europe. If Africa had been the cradle of human social transformations, then the changes in Africa were inextricably bound up with the processes of transformation on earth. But the requirements of slavery and colonialism meant that the written history of the transformations which took place hid the real place of Africa in the civilizations of the past. Garveyism was one attempt by a section of literate Africans at the turn of this century to reverse the falsifications which have been presented in the history books.

This elementary fact is now slowly being documented by a new generation of scholars who are beginning to place their own stamp on a new Pan-African intellectual culture. Garveyism, studied in empirical terms – e.g., conventions, membership of the UNIA, the economic ventures of the Black Star Line or the role of *The Negro World* – can and does shed light on the place of Garvey in the twentieth century. But the importance of Garvey and Garveyism can be analysed not only in the thrust of the UNIA in its form, but also in terms of the content of the real philosophical basis of the challenge which was essentially taken up by a movement of poor oppressed blacks: house servants, migrant labourers and a sprinkling of African nationalists.

These social forces were in the forefront of the Garvey movement and they took up the challenge of the question of African liberation without the hindrance of the internalization of the narrow history of Europe. The black intellectuals who were at the forefront of the Pan-African conferences were Africans who had come to the question of Africa out of their own contradictions with the process of knowledge production. The real cultural aggression that they faced was merged with the social and political oppression of the African peoples. The merger was reflected in the agenda of the five major African conferences, which was a response of the African people to their oppression. Garveyism was Pan-Africanism at the level of popular mass organization to confront the ideology of racism, and its programme was distinctly different from the Pan-African conferences. In content, the place of Garveyism was also different in that the conception of African liberation was linked to the organization and self-mobilization of the African masses.

In the closing decade of this century it is now possible to analyse the achievements of the African liberation struggle. Political independence has rolled back the frontiers of colonialism and new Pan-African organizations such as the Organization of African Unity have become a living part of this century. The OAU Liberation Committee by its existence also ensures that the programme for armed liberation of the African continent is the target of the peoples of Africa. However, the thrust of independent state power and the form of liberation thus far have proven inadequate to reverse the cumulative regression which had been deepening in Africa since the period of the slave trade, cemented during colonialism, and is now being entrenched in the period of neo-colonialism. Drought, famine, desertification, hunger, militarism, the trampling of democratic rights, destabilization and social distress dominate the contemporary news of the African continent, while the struggles in southern

Africa attempt to reverse the imagery of the helpless starving African. But even in this dramatic struggle the very recent antecedents of popular mass struggles now demonstrate that liberation must be conceptualized beyond the seizure of state power by Africans.

After the first period of constitutional decolonization, the leadership of the armed liberation movements declared for socialism and made Marxism-Leninism a state ideology. The demobilization of the popular mass organizations after the ascendance of state power meant that the dynamic of capital accumulation took precedence over alternative forms of economic and political organization. Once the conception of economic development and modernization was predicated on catching up with the factory relations of Western Europe or the model of catching up and surpassing capitalism, which has so far been defined as socialist development, the conditions of the African deteriorated, given the place of Africa in the international division of labour. The process of modernization was based on intensifying the old economic directions of colonial society. For the African masses to be able to redefine the purpose and meaning of liberation now requires new independent organizations from among the popular classes.

In this sense Garveyism, despite its weaknesses, represented a phase in the African liberation struggle where the masses were organized independently of the state. It is primarily in South Africa, where the nature of state power effectively blocks popular participation and expression, where the workers, the students, the progressive clergy, the women and farm workers are organized outside of the state. It is for this reason that the South African process offers one direction for the path of social emancipation. Social emancipation in Africa now requires the total dismantling of the old state apparatus and the building of a new basis of production and association based on those social forces that are capable of defending the rights of the poor.

This new requirement of social emancipation has also been sharpened by the contemporary crisis of capitalism, with its devastating effects on the peoples of the earth. Militarism, war, mass unemployment, declining standards of health care, mass underemployment, homelessness, and poverty form the opposite of the wealth and glitter of the third technological revolution. Old conceptions of white supremacy are developed in new and more subtle forms after the period of the post-World War Two boom and the civil rights revolution in the USA. For a while the strong assertion of racial pride and African origin took the same form as the thrust of the UNIA in the 1920s. Out of this manifestation of black self-dignity a small core linked the search for civil rights in the USA to actual support for armed liberation in Africa. The pivotal organization which carried this new Pan-African heritage was the African Liberation Support Committee. But the Pan-African and internationalist spirit of the ALSC did not survive the ideological poverty of the USA, and the ALSC shattered over the question of the relationships between race and class in the USA.

American capital, which took care to harness and nurture the negative aspects of racial consciousness, sought to mobilize part of the African identity of the Afro-American community in the anti-communist crusade of American imperialism, especially in the war in Angola. Just as the conservative and anti-black forces in Jamaica were willing to invoke the name of Garvey in the anti-communist hysteria of the 1980s, the thrust of present US foreign policy in Africa is to mobilize part of the African identity of US blacks to serve new imperial interests, and in the age of thought control to be able to trivialize the Pan-African spirit. Certain European powers seek to recolonize Africa with a Pan-African military force.

Elsewhere in the Americas, the experiences of the Rastafari culture among the Caribbean masses was another thrust towards perpetuating the traditions of Garveyism. As long as the social and cultural organization of Caribbean societies continued to ape Euro-American cultural values, there was a gap between the culture and language of the masses and that of the ruling classes. In opposing this relic of slavery and external overrule the Rastafari, through their song of racial memory called reggae, provided a major challenge to the impossible task of modernizing the society on the basis of "cultural pluralism". At the same moment the spokespeople of the Rastafari, through their music, awakened mass consciousness on the imperatives of African liberation. In this respect it was not insignificant that the most recent popular reawakening of the place of Marcus Garvey in African liberation came from the reggae artists in the 1970s. This effort at the popular level to reintroduce the ideas of Garveyism among the young was a bold effort to distinguish the view of Garvey as a defender of the poor from the wish of the state to gain legitimacy by placing the image of Garvey on the devalued coinage.

All over the African continent the search for cultural transformation and a decent life now takes place in differing manners among the popular masses. A great deal of information flows on the objective conditions in Africa but far less on the subjective elements of the new struggles. New and diverse forms of organizations are emerging in the process of elaborating a new framework for emancipation, which involves the rediscovery of the cultural unity of Africa. This search for a new basis of Pan-African solidarity takes many forms, and in a slow imperceptible manner new social forces are registering a different conception of liberation from the unity of states, which hinders real Pan-African unity. More and more, this search forces the pro-people intelligentsia to break with the established intellectual framework, which began and ended with Europe, and with the philosophical traditions of Europe to begin with. Frantz Fanon was most emphatic in his appeal for this break in the conclusion of his statement in *The Wretched of the Earth.*

This paper locates the struggle for African liberation this century against the objective conditions of European expansionism, which led to the political partitioning of Africa at the turn of the century. In so far as Garveyism was one response of the dispersed African poor, the paper seeks to conceptualize the differing periods and the ways in which the ideas of what constitutes African liberation have changed. The major shifts in the process of capital accumulation, the depressions and war provide the background for the profound political changes that galvanized nationalist politics and led to political independence. World War Two and the Italian invasion of Abyssinia called forth new responses from every section of the African population.

The liberation posture of the nationalists changed once they took over the organs of the old colonial states. At the continental level the compromise of the OAU survived, while the inherited borders of the Berlin Conference and the inherited economic structures reinforced regional differences. To entrench these differences, religious and ethnic politics were exploited to divide the poor while international capital found new ways to deepen the domination and exploitation of the African continent. Overt colonialism was replaced by new methods of domination as the global economic crisis engendered a new scramble for Africa.

In this scramble the USA, which was left out of the Berlin Conference, now moved with vigour to use her influence in multilateral bodies, such as the International Monetary Fund and the World Bank, to speed the process of the recomposition and reconstitution of capital. Economic management through the IMF and political destabilization became the overt forms of recolonization in the last quarter of the century.

It is in this period that the reflection on Garvey and Garveyism takes on a new meaning. For at the end of the First World War Garveyism represented the self organization of the oppressed masses. The UNIA, though constrained by the ideology of progress under capitalism, was the most dynamic mass movement across territorial borders among the African peoples this century. Now, one hundred years after the birth of Garvey and seven decades after the founding of the UNIA, it is still possible to say that Garveyism occupies a central place in the struggle for democracy, dignity and social transformation.

Given the limits placed on human development by capitalist expansion, it was difficult at that time to conceptualize development outside of the framework of kingdoms and business enterprises of the kind which the UNIA attempted. The present technological revolution, plus the embryonic breakthroughs already beyond capitalism, now enable us to conceptualize the possible transformations towards a new social order where the full capacity of humanity will be shorn of the deformities of race.

Garveyism in the Period of the Military Partition of Africa

MARCUS GARVEY was born in Jamaica in August 1887, two years after the Berlin Conference had formally divided Africa among the major European powers. This political partitioning had been dictated by not only the economic imperatives of the world capitalist system but also by the element of racism within the capitalist superstructure.[1] The Jamaican society into which Garvey was born had been nurtured on the deformed system of racial degradation where the ideas of racial inferiority/superiority were interwoven with the pseudo-science of social Darwinism to justify the crude subjection of the black majority. As children of the former slaves, the memory of Africa formed an indelible part of the consciousness of the poor. There was a distinct difference between the production of formal knowledge of the schools, where the ravages of the imperial order were praised in poetry and prose, and the informal process of knowledge production of the rural village communities, where the importance of African roots was disseminated through oral literature, songs, stories, dances and other cultural mediums.

Growing up in this society, where the legacies and monuments of slavery and resistance were stamped in all forms of social relationships and interactions, Garvey soon learnt the realities of the nature of class selection and racial hierarchy of the country. In his own struggle to escape the mediocrity and social oppression of the plantation society, Garvey, like thousands of others, came into contact with the intensity of the expansion of capitalism which was completely reorganizing societies in the whole world. His life and experiences in Central America, Britain and the USA brought home to him the connections between the processes of expansion, domination and partition which had their roots in monopoly capital. At the ideological level the process of expansion deepened the element of racism in European and American cultures.

The process of the complete division of the world had been engendered by the tremendous changes in the organization of production in Europe. The application of science and technology to production had taken a firm base in the system of social reproduction. Changes in the economic field had their impact on the area of communications, and the development of the wireless and television gave Europe a wider audience for its ideology of progress and free enterprise. Having completed the seizure of the "unoccupied" territories of our planet, the ideologues of European expansion claimed universal validity for the ideas of progress under capitalism. This universalism was to demonstrate the superiority of the capitalist mode of production and its corresponding philosophical, cultural and religious ideas. Ideas of human nature and the philosophical views of the European Renaissance (called Enlightenment) were linked to ideas of white superiority, and these views set the intellectual climate which brutally deleted the role played by Africans in the contributions to science, culture and religion. Empirical scientific practice in agriculture, animal husbandry, navigation, medicine, construction and handicrafts is as old as humanity; and since Egypt had been the cradle of human civilizations this society had been preeminent in the development of a scientific culture.[2]

When Europe built upon the foundations of these scientific advances of humanity, the development of a scientific approach in the realm of abstract ideas was fused to develop a scientific theory, and later this accelerated the processes of social reproduction. The intellectual and ideological culture of Europe then affirmed that the progress towards capitalism was the logical path of human development. Such a reading of history could not explain the contributions made by non-European societies such as China and Egypt to scientific practices, nor why these societies did not engender the social relations which would usher in capitalism. How to confront this powerful ideology with its military and economic consequences was the challenge the Garveyites took up.

The rise of the Garvey movement was a response to the ideological system of imperialism and the clear manifestations of the rape of Africa under the name of Christianity and civilization, the lynching of blacks in North America and the dehumanization of the southern African peoples in the Caribbean, Central America and South America. The nature of the response of Garveyism and the claim of universalism was one indication of how the opposition to racism and racial domination had internalized the intellectual culture of the West. Thus, though Garveyism was one brand of Pan-African thought which sought to build a tradition of liberation in the African cultural roots of the masses, the Universal Negro Improvement Association by its very nomenclature accepted the philosophical tenets of Western Europe and North America. It was not insignificant that in this context the most vibrant period of Afro-American culture was called the Harlem renaissance.

The cultural outpouring of the oppressed blacks in the USA in the period after World War One was one of the high points of American culture this century, for it was a period when the spirit of liberation opened up the appetite of the oppressed masses for self-discovery. Garveyism was one component of this self discovery and the vibrancy of the UNIA was dictated by the way in which the Garveyites were able to mobilize the most oppressed sections of the black community. Garveyism brought together diverse working people, independent trade unionists, pacifists, cultural nationalists, women liberation fighters, militant self-help groups, socialists, members of church organizations, and a whole host of unorganized black folk. Black workers in the USA had acquired the social weight and the little organizational experience to support the claims of the UNIA in its *Declaration of the Rights of the Negro People.*

Garveyism used the propaganda and organizational techniques available at that time to give meaning to the claim that the UNIA spoke for the liberation of all blacks and for the liberation of the African continent. Through *The Negro World,* with a brand of radical journalism unsurpassed at that time, Marcus Garvey carried the theme of redeeming the African motherland.[3]

Numerous accounts of the role of the UNIA in the cementing of race consciousness have been documented, and in this centenary year there will even be more scope for reflections on the work of Garveyism and the foundations for the politics of liberation among oppressed Africans this century. On the specific question of the liberation of Africa, this was a central platform in the programme of the UNIA. This question was addressed programmatically and politically in the work of the UNIA and it was instilled in the minds of the Africans in the West that their freedom was inextricably bound up with the freedom of the African continent.

It can now be understood, with the help of historical hindsight, why the Garvey programme did not have the mass following in Africa it had in the USA or the Caribbean. The limited amounts of capital expended in the process of incorporating African labour into the world system meant that naked force was the principal instrument used in capturing and pacifying the continent. Thus, in the spontaneous rebellions in every area of the continent (whether Ashanti, Bambata, Maji Maji, Nyabingi or other revolts) there was no real attempt to link up the local resistance wars to the wider continental problem of European overrule. The African National Congress, which was formed in the Union of South Africa in 1912, was one of the first organizations to emphasize the fact of Africa in its task of political mobilization. South Africa at this time was an area of intense capitalist penetration. It was therefore not accidental that the UNIA took deeper roots in that society than elsewhere on the continent.[4] The UNIA was in effect one of the first organizations to have branches and adherents all across the continent of Africa all focusing on the question of liberation from white rule.

The empirical studies on the branches of the UNIA in Africa have thus far failed to analyse the subjective element of African politics between 1916-1930 which would ensure that it would be primarily the literate Africans who would have the most access to the ideas of the Garvey programme.[5] As revolutionary as Garvey's programme was at this time in calling for the freedom of Africa by force, the oppressed masses did not have the organizational capacity, the required experience or the resources to carry forward this programme. Colonial African society did not allow the rudimentary freedoms, such as the right of assembly or freedom of expression, that workers were fighting for in Europe. In this context the programme of Garvey and Garveyism was taken seriously by imperialism, hence efforts to undermine the possible links between Garveyism and incipient African nationalism.

Even though the poor African masses were locked out of the wider world of ideas of the printed word, the urban workers, seamen, small traders and the few educated were attracted by the symbols of racial pride of the UNIA. The commercial enterprises of the movement and the launching of the Black Star Line were followed with eagerness by many Africans and this information reached a wider community than the literate few. Garvey's concept of sovereignty and statehood found a fertile place among all classes of Africans. As an all-class concept, the idea of independence meant different things to different social classes, but even at that period the initial links with Liberia demonstrated to the Garveyites that blacks from the West could convey the negative ideas of individualism and private property in their relationship to the local African population. The form of association of the UNIA with the ideas of economic co-operation and collective action by the downtrodden represented a higher form of organization than the Liberian state. Thus after the initial overtures by the UNIA to establish free communities in Liberia, the Liberian ruling class, plus the external colonial rulers in Europe, did everything to undermine the attempt to set up a base in a nominally independent African state.[6]

Because of the major effort to launch a programme for African liberation for a long time the scholarship on Garvey sought to denigrate the movement as Zionist, escapist and millenarian. For those who accepted the view that Africa was backward and not linked to the future of human development, the programme of Garvey was idealistic. This view of the UNIA was shared by both Marxists and non-Marxists, so that Garveyism was opposed from both the right and the left: by the FBI, the American state apparatus, and the left intelligentsia. At this period the experiences of the Bolshevik revolution had already suggested another path to liberation beyond capitalism. However, the supporters of the cause of socialism had internalized the ideas of white chauvinism to the point where some white communists believed that blacks could only reach socialist ideas through white tutelage.[7]

The polarization between race and class effected at the time of Garvey was to have a lasting negative effect on the intellectual culture of black liberation in this century. Garvey and the UNIA had used the conception of redemption to convey a powerful meaning to ex-sharecroppers in the USA and to cane cutters and banana loaders in the Caribbean. For those who envisaged a leap in the consciousness of the poor, which was not yet possible by the first quarter of the century, Garvey was a charlatan who was leading the masses astray. They looked grudgingly at the organizational capacity of the UNIA and never really appreciated the full impact of racial repression.

For the poor workers who understood the world in the biblical and spiritual terms of their exposure to the Bible and the church, Garvey was a prophet. These social forces thus accepted the leaderism in politics which was a component of Western individualism. This fact was to have a devastating effect on the movement when Garvey was removed from his mass base in New York in 1925. In breaking the material base of the movement and dispersing the leadership, the mass organization was severely weakened. Garveyism as a political appeal continued to be a major force, but in organizational terms the movement suffered a decline when Garvey moved to Jamaica and later to the United Kingdom. Even though in decline during the Depression, the Garvey appeal for African redemption served as a beacon for a generation that used the ideas of the UNIA as the reference point for the struggle for political independence.

Garveyism and Pan-Africanism

IN THE LONG STRUGGLE for liberation on the African continent, the forms of consciousness of the oppressed masses changed, given their awareness of the objective conditions and the efforts towards self organization. Garveyism in its thrust pointed to a form of independent mass organization that was emulated all over the continent by aspiring nationalists. However, the clarity of purpose that was embodied in the programme of the UNIA was severely affected by the Depression of the 1930s, with its destructive effects on Africa, the Caribbean and the producing classes worldwide, and coercion became the norm all over the colonial world as the initial spread of capitalism expanded. In this period of crisis all the European powers sought super profits from African labour to counter the falling rate of profit in the capitalist centres. It was therefore in this period of economic crisis that Italy undertook the invasion of Abyssinia in 1935.

This act was important politically, and at the same time symbolic, in that Abyssinia stood as the oldest independent African society. Positive references to Ethiopia in the Bible have struck a responsive chord among Christianized Africans everywhere, so much so that Ethiopianism could be called the precursor to the idea of Pan-Africanism.[8] Poor and rural Africans responded to this war as a further act of aggression, and the spiritual, political and cultural bonds between Africans everywhere were increased subsequent to the invasion and war. Garveyites who were still active took a leading role in denouncing the Italian aggression, but for many in the Caribbean the emphasis of the UNIA on titles, kingdoms and rituals had led many Jamaicans to oppose the Italian invasion by deepening their identification with the leader of Ethiopia, His then Imperial Majesty, Haile Selassie.

The response of educated blacks all over the continent to the invasion precipitated the formation of social movements calling for independence. The pre-eminent organization at this time was the International African Service Bureau in London. This group mobilized support for the cause of Ethiopia and brought together the leading Pan-African intellectuals who articulated the demands for self-determination in Africa. To be able to use the historical analysis of the process of change in Africa as a weapon in the struggle for self-determination, scholars such as W.E.B. Du Bois, George Padmore, C.L.R. James, and many others wrote critical tracts on the foundations of African history. Du Bois was one of the most prolific writers and intellectuals of this genre, and he was at the same time one of the leading spirits behind the five major Pan-African conferences held between 1900 and 1945.[9]

As a corollary to this intellectual thrust of the English-speaking Pan-Africanists, the Negritude movement among the French-educated Africans exalted the African past and the African personality. Negritude, like Pan-Africanism, struggled with the ideas of race by replacing one set of myths on the inferiority of the Africans with another set of myths and accepted the fundamental distinction between the races which became part of European culture. The unscientific assumptions about race and the romantic basis of Negritude became clearer when some of the exponents took power in Haiti and in Senegal. In Haiti, Negritude was the intellectual cover for brutal exploitation. This exploitation continued for more than two decades, and it is now becoming increasingly clearer that the artificial classification of the division between whites, blacks and mulattoes imposes a distortion of human history.

Pan-Africanism and Racism

AT THE TURN OF the twentieth century, W.E.B. Du Bois had declared that "the problem of the twentieth century was the color line". As one component of the battle against oppression, the struggle around the race question occupied a significant place in the political struggles this century. Yet the category of race was itself created historically in the process of exploitation. It required a materialist intellectual framework to be able to perceive the fact that the division of the world into races has been one way of justifying unequal human relations. Individual Pan-Africanists attempted this break, but this was not possible at the level of individual enlightenment; it was only possible given the maturation of the social forces most able to generate the intellectual framework of the materialist history of humanity.

Such a history is now possible, for not only have the African masses retaken their places in history and are they in the process of closing the last chapter of settler colonialism in southern Africa, but there is also enough evidence, documents and scientific breakthroughs in the field of archaeology to be able to write a clear history of humanity. Moreover, the West is today fully aware of this, but, in the words of the historian Diop, it lacks the intellectual and moral courage required, and this is why the textbooks are deliberately muddled. "It then devolves on us Africans to rewrite the entire history of mankind for our own edification and that of others".[10]

In the absence of this historical knowledge, Africans in their struggles against Europe developed a consciousness connected to their understanding of that particular moment. Religious and cultural resistance, in the form of the Rastafari, Kimbangoism, the John Chilembwe movement and others, represented a clash with the secularization of Western religious ideas, which conformed to the requirements of commodity production. Garveyism, with its emphasis on the creation of autonomous religious institutions – e.g., the African Orthodox Church – also connected the cause of liberation to the need for spiritual and religious freedom.

The philosophical and spiritual basis of the social consciousness of the African masses was transformed by the impact of World War Two. War transformed the military demand for personnel and labour, and the compulsion of the colonial state intensified as defence regulations were invoked to demand greater sacrifices from the African people. With the absence of democratic rights and the use of brutal coercion, colonialism dropped its thin veneer of the civilizing role even though its propaganda against fascism sought to present a liberal image of the principal colonial states.

World War Two was itself one of the major disasters for humanity. The ideas of racism that had festered over 400 years had taken root in Europe to the point that the hallmark of civilization was to put other human beings into gas ovens. Nazism as a contradiction of capitalism exploded, as the whole of the continent of Africa was mobilized to meet the requirements of war production. Out of this process of intensified exploitation, new social forces emerged in Africa to oppose colonialism. It was the spontaneous and organized activities of the workers, the poor peasants, the school teachers and traders that sped the process of political independence.

During this period the view was that African liberation was co-terminous with political independence. But it was only for a brief moment, for the mass of producers learned that independence could not be built on the basis of the old colonial economy. This lesson had to be learned, and it was only from this lesson that new goals were placed in the conception of what constituted liberation.

Garveyism, Pan-Africanism, Independence and Development

MARCUS GARVEY as an individual focused his attention during his lifetime on the redemption of Africa, but he was keenly aware of the importance of drawing the masses into democratic and active participation in the rebuilding of their societies. This was clear during the Italian invasion of Abyssinia, when Garvey separated support for the people of Abyssinia from support for Haile Selassie. Writing in *The Black Man* in 1936, Garvey castigated the emperor for the callous neglect of the poor peasantry in Ethiopia and for his dependence on European advisors.[11] This distinction made by Garvey between the Africa of the rulers and the Africa of the ruled is even more urgent 30 years after the independence process began. Outstanding leaders of the Pan-African congresses who formulated militant declarations had gone home to join the independence movement and carried with them the conception of modernization and Westernization as part of their ideological baggage.

Independence, to these leaders, meant the strengthening of the old organs of the colonial state, expanding and Africanizing the bureaucracy and building big projects. Because history for these leaders was the history of the ruling classes of former African kingdoms, they conceptualized development on the basis of the strengthening of the African ruling class, changing the personnel in the police and in the army and religious institutions without fundamentally breaking with the old forms of governance or with the extraction of surplus from the village communities to the towns and then to the capitalist metropolis.

Modernization theory was the dominant perspective and this formulation was tailored as socialism or as capitalism, depending on the rhetoric of the leadership. This approach looked on the masses as backward and "traditional", standing in the path of nation building and industrialization. It was not part of the calculation of this leadership that the collective knowledge accumulated over 10,000 years should be the basis for the launching of a new society in Africa.

Recent Egyptian history provides an excellent example of how the leadership of the post-World War Two era failed to mobilize the people on the basis of the history and collective experience of the society. For a short while, the leadership under Nasser provided a radical alternative, partly because of the confrontation with the West over the Suez Canal, over the question of Israel and the rights of the Palestinian people. But Nasserism, in the confrontation with the West, did not fully mobilize the people to the point where the social aspirations of the people could carry them to new heights. Nasser spoke of socialist construction, but he did not entrust this task to the people; instead he deepened his dependence on external forces while building monuments of modernization: dams, airports, armies, and industrial projects depending on foreign expertise. Without a coherent social and political plan Nasserism did not survive Nasser, in spite of the positive legacies of the anti-imperialist thrust of his leadership. During the period of Nasser, Egypt was the cultural centre for the Middle East and North Africa, but the advances that were made during this period were eroded so long as the development programme was predicated on external expertise. The political heirs of Nasser showed concretely that dependence on capitalist states or socialist states was equal to the underdevelopment and depoliticization of the masses. The lessons of regression in Egypt, where religious fundamentalism now holds sway, are replicated all over the continent.

It can now be understood why the small educated elite that took over the organs of the colonial state was swallowed up by the very state machinery it inherited. In the words of Walter Rodney:

> Owing to the low level of the development of the productive forces in colonized Africa, it fell to a small privileged educated group to give expression to the mass of grievances against racial discrimination, low wages, low prices for cash crops, colonial bureaucratic commandism and the indignity of alien rule as such. But the petty bourgeoisie were reformers and not revolutionaries. Their limitations were stamped upon the character of the independence which they negotiated with the colonial masters. In the very process of demanding constitutional independence, they reneged on one of the cardinal principles of Pan Africanism, namely the unity and indivisibility of the African continent.[12]

The limitations of the class and the compromises that led to the formation of the OAU showed that the conception of liberation and African unity were based on the unity of states and not on the real cultural unity of the peoples from Cape to Cairo and in the islands of Africa. Kwame Nkrumah's career as a disciple of Garvey and one of the leading exponents of Pan-African liberation this century was one of the clearest demonstrations of this fact.

All over the continent in the early 1960s Ghana, like Egypt, provided a beacon for those still under colonial rule, by her militant claims for liberation and the militancy of the popular classes on the eve of independence. Ghana's initiative in convening a conference of independent African states in 1958 brought the formal concept of Pan-African conferences home on African soil for the first time. The All African Peoples Conference was a genuine platform for revolutionaries, and not simply for the new leaders of the emerging states. Freedom fighters from Algeria, trade unionists from East Africa, anti-apartheid fighters from southern Africa, and nationalists of all shades met in Accra, and above all it was the platform from which Patrice Lumumba brought forth the centrality of the Congo to Pan-African liberation.

The issue of the Congo was to be a real test for whether those who conceptualized real liberation would give material support to Lumumba and the Congolese people. Instead the task of defending the heart of Africa was handed to the United Nations, which was at that time dominated by the Western powers. United Nations troops stood by while Patrice Lumumba was kidnapped and murdered. The compromise of the OAU became a reality after the continent suffered the setback in the Congo.[13]

Out of the efforts of Pan-Africanism at the level of governments came the Organization of African Unity. In practice not only has the OAU been committed to the maintenance of the inherited colonial boundaries but it also supports and buttresses the exploitative social systems that prevail. Because of the clause of non-interference in the internal affairs of member states, leaders such as Idi Amin, Jean Bokassa, and Sékou Touré carried out brutalities and no other African state could intervene. When Tanzania did intervene to repulse an invasion by Amin in 1978, the OAU equivocated and many leaders actively supported Idi Amin. In practical terms this means that the most conservative elements of the African leadership are protected by the OAU charter:

> One of the cardinal principles of Pan-Africanism is that the people of one part of Africa are responsible for the freedom and liberation of their brothers and sisters in other parts of Africa; and, indeed, black people everywhere were to accept the same responsibility.[14]

The OAU denies this, apart from the areas of South Africa and Namibia. By doing so the OAU accepts that the objective conditions that impelled the African masses to fight the colonialists have since been transformed. The realities of the present crisis show that not only does the African leadership stand in the path of liberation but in some cases Africans try to colonize others, as in the case of Morocco and the Western Sahara. This brazen form of colonialism was too much for the more conscious leaders, and when the Moroccan leadership could not advance its claims for OAU recognition of the Saharwi Arab Democratic Republic, Morocco left the OAU. It is not insignificant that the leadership of Morocco also wants to become a member of the European Economic Community.

As in the area of political cooperation, the field of Pan-African economic cooperation at the level of the present African states is equally bare. Many forms of informal trade continue across borders, but this kind of Pan-African trade is frowned upon as the revenues from this trade circulate among the people instead of among the ruling classes or through the transnational banking system. Experiments such as the East African Community collapsed and the Economic Cooperation of West African States remains basically an entity to create a bigger market for the transnational corporations.

The East African Community could not have survived the fact that Kenya was the regional epicentre for imperialism in East Africa, now unrepentantly so with military and naval facilities for the Rapid Deployment Force of the USA. Moreover, even before the breakup of this community, while capital was sheltered workers were expelled from one territory to the next. Restrictive employment and immigration practices abound to block the freedom of movement of the rural people, and in the past decade the most brutal expulsion of Africans (outside of the brutal removal of Crossroads in South Africa) took place in Nigeria. It was ironic that it was from this very state that the future plans for economic development and cooperation were tabled as the Lagos Plan of Action for the OAU.

The generals and bureaucrats who dominate the OAU offer subsidies to foreign capital while the working people are prevented from collectively organizing for better conditions. Divisions among the poor culminate in civil wars as the process of militarization engulfs the continent. The politicization of region, religion, and tribe accelerate, as economic regression is compounded by political authoritarianism.

In the absence of real forums for democratic expression and participation, the people lost the political experience they gained in the period after the Second World War. With this demobilization and depoliticization, thinking became subversive, to the point that the foremost African intellectuals became exiles from their societies.[15] Intellectual impoverishment and cultural repression meant the youths that were born after 1960 were unaware of the contributions of Marcus Garvey or W.E.B. Du Bois in the struggles for African liberation this century. It is in the area of combat in South Africa that a new political and intellectual culture is emerging consistent with the emergence of the popular masses on the centre of the politics of the globe.

Liberation and the Self-Mobilization of the Masses

IN THE MIDST OF the contemporary crisis of capitalism, the political and economic changes in Africa have given rise to the recognition that political independence could not be meaningful without economic and cultural freedoms. Popular demands for a decent life, even the right to life, were met with force as external forces sought to regenerate the old forms of agricultural production which the poor have been resisting since the period of political self-rule. The view that the peasant was traditional was shared by all shades of the ideological spectrum. At the same time the strengthening of the old state machinery so that it could speed the proletarianization of the peasantry meant the destruction of popular organizations such as producer cooperatives. Farmers' organizations, trade unions, independent churches, and student organizations were banned or kept under strict state control. Schemes for progressive farmers, responsible entrepreneurs, livestock producers who used modern drugs, and non-political trade unionists were organized to ensure that the social questions of housing, education, health, and the provision of clean water took second place to the production of tea, coffee, groundnuts, cotton, and minerals for export.

With the deteriorating terms of trade for primary products and in the context of the untransformed colonial economies, the wealth of the continent remained submerged beneath the ground while the ruling classes wallowed in conspicuous consumption in the midst of poverty. African peasants were losing their accumulated skills and experience in the midst of successive food crises. The poverty and hunger of the African poor formed the dialectical opposite of the food surpluses in capitalist Europe and America.

By the end of the 1960s, when this tragedy was already unfolding, Pan-Africanists and Garveyites called for the convening of a Sixth Pan-African Congress to chart a new course for liberation. The euphoria surrounding the possibility of such a meeting soon abated when it was clear that the meeting was to be another OAU-type conference with class allies from the Caribbean. This much was clear when the serious Pan-Africanists from the Caribbean, engaged in the struggle for liberation in the Caribbean, were excluded from the conference.

More and more it was becoming clear that nationalism had become a negation of itself. The nationalist leaders had negated the ideals for which the people were struggling: for a better life, indeed the right to life, and the right to live on this planet with dignity as human beings.

Frantz Fanon was perceptive as far back as 1961 to see that the nation-building and state consolidation of the nationalist leaders represented a stumbling block for the development of the liberation of Africa. Nationalist rhetoric had led to reversals and cynicism, and all over the continent, through songs and other forms of cultural expression, youths, small farmers, students, and workers declared that what was needed was a radical break with the past so that the foundations could be laid for social transformation and a transition beyond colonialism and neo-colonialism.

The nationalist leaders had reached the summit of their achievement with the Africanization of the state. The producers, however, wanted the creation of new democratic forms of association to dismantle the old state and so be able to develop a new person. In this quest the search for liberation and Pan-African solidarity embraces a wide variety of social groups with the cultural workers at the forefront. It was in this context that the Rastafari revival of Garveyism should be understood.

Most of the urban youths in the Pan-African world would not have heard of Garvey or the programme of the UNIA but for the spread of reggae music in Africa. Reggae found a fertile base among a section of the African population that was mobile, alert and groping for ways to understand the contemporary realities. This section of the population was aware of the cultural onslaught of the West and it was ironic, in reality part of the unity of opposites, that it was through the same Western media complex that the African people came to learn of reggae and the resistance of the Rastafari.

The power of North American films and communications media had hoped to use the cultural reservoir of Africans in the Americas to further the cause of cultural imperialism. This continues to be most evident in the way in which the USA uses the creativity of her black population to sell the American dream of the enterprising nature of capitalism and the possibility of progress. Hence memoirs of slavery, such as *Roots,* or the essential unity of the struggles of the African woman, as depicted in the novel *The Color Purple,* are packaged as products of capitalist culture.

But as in all areas of culture – art, music, dance, poetry, prose, etc. – the anti-capitalist and anti-racist component of black American music, theatre and film forced itself on the world stage and became one very important aspect of Pan-African expression in the last quarter of the century. It was within this complex of information and disinformation that cultural spokespeople such as Miriam Makeba, Fela Ransome Kuti, Stevie Wonder, Mbilia Bel, Franco, Alpha Blondy, Bob Marley, and scores of others maintained the traditions of militant resistance to racism. In particular, reggae music in its link to the traditions of Garveyism was able to occupy a special place in the African liberation struggle.

So popular had reggae music become in Africa that the Ivorian reggae artist Alpha Blondy used his talent as a linguist to ensure that the message of freedom and struggle reached as wide an audience as possible in states that have deep political and trade ties with Israel and South Africa. Bob Marley, one of the most dynamic of reggae artists, endeared a generation of youths in Africa including freedom fighters. Progressive Pan-Africanists who did not dismiss the cultural expressions of the Rasta as millennarian recognized the contribution of this music. In the words of one of the foremost Caribbean Pan-Africanists, Eusi Kwayana:

> The power of art that Bob Marley's music represented had done more to popularize the real issues of African liberation than several decades of backbreaking work by Pan-Africanists and international revolutionaries.

To be able to strengthen the cultural links that were developing among the scattered African peoples was one of the ambitions of Marcus Garvey and the UNIA. Rasta culture and reggae music strengthened and reasserted these links at a time when the struggles in southern Africa generated internationalist support and exposed those African leaders who co-operated with apartheid against the oppressed majority in South Africa and Namibia. The South African struggles underlined the essence of the mobilization and organization of the people so that they carry themselves to higher levels of struggle.

Youth and the South African Struggle

YOUNG AFRICANS in their daily struggles to affirm their dignity ensured that the questions that kept the OAU together were the questions of the transformations after apartheid and the full independence of Africa. The South African struggles and the ensuing military destabilization of the whole region reinforced the Pan-African dictum that "No African is free as long as one inch of the African continent is under foreign domination". The politicization and mobilization of South African youth in the anti-apartheid struggles represented the pivot of the repoliticization of the oppressed masses in Africa.

That the question of apartheid became the number one question before humanity was in no small measure because of the spread of self-organization and self-mobilization among the youths, the workers, students, and other grass-roots organizers. The rise of grass-roots forces of governance as people struggled against the military occupation of their neighbours dictated that the conception of liberation now went beyond the question of Africans replacing the whites in the old state apparatus.[16]

Political struggles, ideological debates, armed confrontation, and the international campaign against sanctions sharpened the internationalist tenets of Pan-Africanism and exposed the limits of the negative brands of nationalism based on a narrow all-class racial appeal. Many African leaders quivered at the potential of the South African struggle, for if the present resources used for war and resistance were mobilized for reconstruction and transformation many of the present regimes could not survive the changes that would emerge in a post-apartheid society. In this period it was clear that apartheid served not only to strengthen and lengthen the life of racists but served international reaction in general.

Consequently, many members of the OAU may vote for sanctions at the annual Pan-African summit, paying lip service to liberation, but provide landing and other communications facilities for the apartheid regime and seek solutions and compromises that would reform apartheid and take the initiative out of the hands of those in combat. Dialogue with apartheid, which was begun by conservative leaders in Malawi and the Ivory Coast in the 1970s, assumed new and sophisticated forms while the front-line states supported a limited guerrilla campaign against the Boer leadership. In this regard, the call for a Pan-African defence by some leaders could be seen as another technique to constrain the struggle in a manner that would not threaten the future of the present form of capital accumulation.

Pan-Africanism and Garveyism continue to be relevant in the search for African liberation, but the intellectual and ideological formulations on development, growth, structural adjustment and technological transfers are now inadequate to ensure that the processes of emancipation continue into the twenty-first century. At the same time it showed that the struggle against racism cannot be carried out from the same philosophical plane as those of Western cultural values. The South African process of establishing the dignity and self worth of the black person went through the motions of the kind of race consciousness of Garvey and developed to the point where it was seen that what was necessary was a non-racial society. The ideological and political tools for the harnessing of this kind of society are slowly being sharpened by the mine workers, the metal workers, the segregated farm labourers, the students, the cultural workers, and the militant freedom fighters of southern Africa.

So profound has been this struggle that all the old slogans and forms of struggle of the century are now being put under scrutiny. As early as the 1960s another African freedom fighter, Amilcar Cabral, had recognized the ideological weakness of those who sought to lead the national liberation struggle. Cabral asserted that

> The ideological deficiency, not to say the total lack of ideology, within the national liberation movements – which is basically due to ignorance of the historical reality which these movements claim to transform – constitutes one of the greatest weaknesses of our struggle against imperialism, if not the greatest weakness of all.[17]

This fact emerges even more clearly after those states who fought for independence retreated from the power of the popular masses once in power. Guerrilla movements, whether in Mozambique, Zimbabwe, Angola, or Uganda have been able to win military victories, but these victories did not empower the mass of the producers, for the thinking behind armed guerrilla struggles did not link these struggles to wider popular political struggles. It is also now clear that the espousal of Marxism-Leninism as a state ideology will remain empty as long as this attempt at a scientific doctrine is not based on the real history and culture of Africa. Too often, history for the state is the history of certain movements and the state attempts to select for the people what should be remembered and what should not.

Mozambique, in its present crisis of war, destabilization and economic crisis, offers a spectacle of untold suffering in a state which in the past twenty years has been a symbol of the revolutionary potential of Africa. At this writing the South African war of aggression plus the anti-communist crusade of the West threaten the sovereignty of that state. Pan-African military intervention by Tanzania and Zimbabwe after the assassination of Samora Machel in 1986 preserved the integrity of the Mozambiquan state.

However, the crisis in Mozambique and in southern Africa enables those concerned with African liberation to analyse the pitfalls of socialism by declaration; that is, socialism without the transformation of political power to dismantle the old colonial economic and authoritarian structures. The dynamic of destabilization, war IMF management, external subversion, and psychological warfare exist all over the continent and the people have shown that their collective political and organizational power can advance the African liberation struggle beyond the present quagmire of underdevelopment, political repression and desertification.

Conclusion

GARVEYISM AND PAN-AFRICANISM emerged out of the nineteenth century against the background of the transformation of capitalism into imperialism, with the resulting partition of Africa. At that time the symbols of racial pride were linked to nation building and statehood. The Garvey movement mobilized the poor to challenge the domination of Africa and the denigration of African peoples worldwide. At the ideological level, Garveyism confronted the falsification of African history, challenging black intellectuals to break with the Euro-centric conceptions of human development. For this period of the century Garveyism represented the most militant tendency of Pan-Africanism and at that stage was progressive. More so because this social movement was a concrete manifestation of the potentialities of the oppressed masses.

The Depression and the war underlined the barbarity of capitalism as a social system. New forms of consciousness appeared as the gut response of the masses in Africa to the spread of commodity production. Ideas of spirit worship, the recourse to African religious forms were the manifestations of the subjective condition of the African attempting to hold onto the pre-colonial cosmic world as one method of resistance. This kind of consciousness could not take the people forward and was soon overridden by the social questions generated by the war and its aftermath. Brutal exploitation, forced labour and racial exploitation galvanized the workers, peasants and the educated to join hands to call for the end of alien rule.

Many of those who offered themselves as leaders of this anti-colonial phase had been schooled in the organizational techniques of the Garvey movement. Kwame Nkrumah will go down in this century as the most influential of this generation. However, the lessons of the rise and fall of Nkrumahism need to be studied without rancour to underline the pitfalls of national consciousness. Western scholarship which is pre-occupied with the place of the individual in history, will castigate individual leaders but a new intellectual culture is now required, one that can situate these leaders within the social movements and ideas from which they emerged.[18]

Without this kind of approach it becomes difficult to separate the place of the Nyereres or Nkrumahs from the Bandas, Mobutus or Senghors. Yet it can be said that the process of class formation and class selection after independence forced the crushing of autonomous organizations of farmers, workers, students, and even independent churches. One-party states copied the socialist form of organization without the ideological content to unleash the creativity of the producing masses. Instead, these states, along with the militarists who dominate the OAU, continued the anti-democratic traditions of the colonial order.

Democracy was termed united nations-African even when the village communities struggled for forms of democratic control and accountability that went far beyond the formal democratic practices of the West. But in the main even these formal democratic practices were absent, for democracy could not exist when the whole basis of economic relations depended on force and the transfer of surpluses outside of Africa. Not even the proclaimed socialist leaders who called themselves African liberators attempted to support democratic forms of association. Imprisoning Marxism as a state ideology, these leaders proclaimed themselves the originators of emancipatory ideas, forgetting that it was the power of the organized masses that made history.

Garveyism was an important part of the intervention of the masses in the making of the history of black liberation in this century. Garveyism as a social movement was internationalist and shook the foundations of racism, but as part of the movements of this century it did not and could not transcend the ideological constraints of Europe or the arrogance of Western claims to universalism. The battle against racism accepted the unscientific category of race. In the struggles toward the twenty-first century, it is important to study Garveyism and Pan-Africanism so that the strengths of this form of social movement can be separated from the weaknesses. This would provide a firm base for those continuing the struggle for the full liberation of Africa.

Already the experiences of this century have sharpened the idea of liberation beyond the achievement of political independence. Popular participation, cultural freedom, democratic practices and the development of new forms of social existence remain a part of the project to move beyond the concept of nationhood. Capitalism sharpened national formation in Europe but forced the cultural, religious and ethnic diversity in Africa to fester in very unhealthy forms. The crisis in Africa is now forcing young people to recognize the potential offered to humanity by real social transformations.

At the base of this transformation is the need for the fundamental reorganization of society so that the concepts of agricultural production, work, culture, and leisure can relate to genuine collective endeavour, so that human beings can discover work that provides satisfaction and the full realization of human potential. The technological advances of the past twenty years belong equally to Africa and the rest of humanity. These developments, if properly built upon the real capacities of people instead of on the impossible conception of modernization, offer wider scope for the democratization of production. Inside Africa, where humans still face elementary problems of dealing with the natural environment, a scientific culture democratically based would be a major step towards freedom. But racism hinders real vision, as is evidenced by the reliance of the present ruling class on foreign experts. This racism also affects scientific research and medical science. This is best expressed by the way some scientists make unsubstantiated claims about the African origins of AIDS.

Garveyism developed before the maturation of the socialist alternative. African liberation since the period of independence holds both positive and negative lessons from the attempts to build a form of society beyond capitalism. The socialist rhetoric of some Pan-African leaders was already an acknowledgement that capitalism could not develop the productive forces of Africa. Now, African liberation is not only linked to the quest for a social order higher than capitalism, but also one in which the development of productive forces is not linked simply to the production of goods but also to the creation of new human beings. This perspective of free men and women, of cultural freedom, of the harnessing of the positive knowledge of the African past now forms part of the conception of the struggle for African liberation in the twenty-first century.

As long as capitalism exists, with its handmaiden, racism, the ideas that gave rise to Garveyism and Pan-Africanism will be part of the consciousness of Africans. The search for self-definition, which is at the core of Pan-Africanism, will survive. Moreover, Pan-Africanism will thrive as long as oppressed Africans can make the link between the exploitation of Africa and those Africans dispersed by slavery. In this regard, the African population of South America will be a major force for the restatement of Pan-Africanism. For in this region, the sophisticated racism of racial democracy hides real prejudice, as well as the historical foundations of the contacts between Africa and the American continent before the arrival of Columbus.

From the continent of Africa, new challenges are being presented before the world. At present, the challenge is formulated in the closing of the laboratory where the virus of racism was developed: South Africa. Youths in South Africa are developing an antidote to this virus, which will affect the whole of the continent of Africa. For even up to today, social relations in Africa are organized around racial classifications. To be able to place other questions on the agenda, apartheid and the notion of white superiority are being vigorously challenged.

The struggles in Africa are all part of the struggle for liberation. Mankind sets itself new goals when old goals are reached. For the Garveyites and other Pan-Africanists the goal was political independence and self-rule. It can be said that even political independence is not now guaranteed in the present scramble for Africa. This makes Garveyism very relevant as we approach the end of the century. And the experience of the period after the Second World War ensured that the new struggles for emancipation must be carried out by the self-organization and political leadership of workers, poor peasants and other oppressed classes.

This is the elementary requirement to move beyond the cumulative reversals of the past four centuries.

NOTES

[1] Walter Rodney, "The Imperialist Partition of Africa", *Monthly Review,* April 1970, 99, 103-114. This element of racism was also discussed by W.E.B. Du Bois in "The African Roots of the War", *On The Importance Of Africa To World History* (New York: Black Liberation Press, 1978).

[2] Chiek Anta Diop, *The African Origin Of Civilization: Myth or Reality,* ed. Mercer Cook (Lawrence Hill and Co., 1974).

[3] For a glimpse of the style and content of *The Negro World* see Amy Jacques Garvey (ed.), *The Philosophy and Opinions of Marcus Garvey,* Vols. 1 and 2 (London: Frank Cass., 1967).

[4] Robert Hill and Gregory A. Priro, "Africa for the Africans: The Garvey Movement in South Africa, 1920-1940", in *The Politics of Race, Class and Nationalism in Twentieth Century South Africa,* ed. Shula Marks and Stanley Trapido (London: Longman, 1987).

[5] Many studies focus on the "petty bourgeois" nature of the leadership of the UNIA in Africa. See Robert Edgar, "Garveyism in Africa", *Ufahamu*, Vol. VI, No. 3, 1976; Helen Bradford, "Class Contradictions and Class Alliances", in *Resistance and Ideology in Settler Societies* in *Southern African Studies*, Vol. 4, ed. Tom Lodge (Johannesburg: Ravan Press, 1986); J.A. Langley, "Garveyism and African Nationalism", *Race* XI (11), 1969; R.L. Okonkwo, "The Garvey Movement in British West Africa", *Journal of African History*, Vol. 21, 1980.

[6] The contradictions involved in the liberation settlement are discussed at length in Tony Martin, *Race First: The Ideological and Organizational Struggles of Marcus Garvey and the Universal Negro Improvement Association* (Greenwood Press, 1976).

[7] When one Jamaican Garveyite sought to learn from the experiences of the USSR and moved there to help to build socialism, white comrades from the USA attempted to drown him in the Volga River. For an account of this incident see James R. Hooker, *Black Revolutionary: George Padmore's Path From Communism to Pan-Africanism* (London, 1967). Padmore's own life mirrored the contradictions and polarization between race and class in the period of the birth of the communist movement in the inter-war years.

[8] For a discussion on the links between Ethiopianism and African liberation see Horace Campbell, *Rasta and Resistance: From Marcus Garvey to Walter Rodney* (New Jersey: Africa World Press, 1987). See especially Chapter 2.

[9] Vincent B. Thompson, *Africa and Unity: The Revolution of Pan-Africanism* (London: Longman, 1969). A useful book, inspired by the work of George Padmore, is *The Pan-African Movement,* by Immanuel Geiss (London: Methuen & Co., 1974).

[10] Chiek Anta Diop, *The African Origin of Civilization: Myth or Reality,* p. 115. The pioneering work of Diop in the attempt to reconstruct the African past to prepare for the future has been one of the most outstanding contributions to the freeing of the African mind from the limits placed on the perceptions of human transformations. Unfortunately, most of his work is not yet available in English.

[11] *The Black Man,* July/August 1936.

[12] Walter Rodney, "Towards the Sixth Pan-African Congress. Aspects of the Class Struggle in Africa, the Caribbean and America", in Horace Campbell (ed.), *Pan Africanism: Documents of the Sixth Pan-African Congress* (Toronto: Afro Caribbean Press, 1975).

[13] Kwame Nkrumah, who at the time militantly championed the cause of Lumumba, hesitated to place his forces at the disposal of Patrice Lumumba and instead placed them in the hands of the United Nations. The same troops which gained counter-revolutionary experience in the Congo were involved in the overthrow of Kwame Nkrumah and the CPP in 1966. For his account of the Congolese struggles, see Kwame Nkrumah, *The Challenge of The Congo* (London: Pan Af Books, 1967). The importance of the Congo and the part played by the USA in the political destabilization of the efforts for real independence is underscored in B. Kalb, *The Congo Cables* (London: MacMillan, 1982).

[14] Walter Rodney, "Towards the Sixth Pan-African Congress", *op. cit.*, p. 12

[15] Ngugi Wa Thiongo, *Decolonizing the Mind* (New Hampshire: Heinemann, 1986).

[16] The place of the programme of the liberation movements in the present struggles is the subject of a major debate in South Africa. This debate transcends the old discussion on which is the most correct liberation movement. For example in the last year the discussions on socialism at the Congress of the National Union of Metal Workers demonstrated the ideological sophistication of the workers. See a summary of the discussion in *Work in Progress,* No.48, 1987, "South Africa: Different Roads to Socialism".

[17] Amilcar Cabral, *Revolution in Guinea* (New York: Monthly Review Press, 1969), p.92.

[18] One of the leading Pan-Africanists of the century, C.L.R. James, fell into this pitfall of Western individualism in his commentary on the place of Walter Rodney in the Caribbean struggle. See his statement, "Walter Rodney and the Question of Power", *Race Today* pamphlet, 1984. For an alternative view of the struggles of the Guyanese people, of which Rodney formed a part, see Eusi Kwayana, "Walter Rodney", *Working Peoples Alliance* pamphlet, 1986.

Marcus Garvey and Nigeria

Adebowale Adefuye
High Commissioner for Nigeria
Kingston, Jamaica

THE SPIRIT OF MARCUS GARVEY lives on not only in the minds of Jamaicans but also in the minds of peoples of the world who have had a history of slavery, imperialism and colonialism. Garvey represented a reaction against the above injustices and stood for the implementation of the principles of the equality of all races.[1] Garveyism as an ideal is international in scope and character. As Tony Martin pointed out, the colonial system to which Garvey was opposed affected not only peoples of African descent but also Asians, Arabs and Europeans.[2] The ideal of Garveyism was intimately connected with humanism and nationalism. Garvey in his lifetime sent messages of solidarity to freedom fighters even in territories outside Africa.[3]

But there can be no gainsaying the fact that the African continent has a much longer history of slavery, colonialism and all other manifestations of man's inhumanity to man. Marcus Garvey in the early part of the present century added his voice to the rising tide of protests against injustices and sought to inculcate self pride and dignity in the minds of the Africans. By espousing the richness of African culture and rejecting notions of inferiority to others, Garvey attacked the philosophical basis of slavery and colonialism. His call for solidarity and unity of action among the black people of the world was an incalculable asset to the ideals of Pan-Africanism. This paper attempts an analysis of the connection between Marcus Garvey and the men and events that had to do with Pan-Africanism. It begins with a history and definition of the concept and goes on to see how Garvey's ideas, thoughts, and actions influenced Pan-Africanism. The concrete achievements of the movement are then analysed on a continental level before seeing how it contributed to Nigerian nationalism. The paper concludes with an examination of the effects of Garveyism on Nigeria's posture in Africa and world affairs.

Pan-Africanism

PAN-AFRICANISM is a powerful ideal and a sophisticated ideology. It has its roots in history. George Shepperson described it as a gift of the new world of America to the old world of Africa[4] because it began as a reaction to the maltreatment of the black man during the slave trade and the racial doctrines and attitudes that marke the era of abolition. European actions and attitudes forced Africans to unite an think of ways of solving the problems in which they found themselves. When it be came clear that the Europeans would not accept the freed slaves into their societie some individuals of African origin proposed emigration to the African continent As early as 1788 a Negro Union of Newport, Rhode Island, contributed money an sent one of their members to visit Sierra Leone to explore the possibility of takin free exiles back to the ancestral continent. The physician, Delany, MartinDr Marti Delany, sailed to Liberia in 1859, where he spent a year negotiating for the settle ment of black Americans. It was he who first publicly used the expression "Afric for Africans".

Thus in effect Marcus Garvey was neither the first apostle of Pan-Africanism no was he the first person to propagate the back-to-Africa idea. Other, earlier pioneer included the Barbadian Dr Albert Thorne, who between 1897 and 1920 sought t promote a movement for colonizing central Africa. William Ellis led an expeditio to Ethiopia in 1907, while Alfred C. Oklahoma in 1912 sought to link his back-to Africa venture with the Akim Trading Company on the Gold Coast. Dr Edwar Blyden, the foremost exponent of the doctrine of African personality, migrated fron the West Indies to Liberia. Long before Garvey established the Universal Negro Im provement Association, a Jamaican couple, the Rev. John and Letitia Ricketts lef Kingston in 1895, went to Colwyn Bay in Wales, and joined the Baptist mission in es tablishing churches in the Agbowa area of Lagos State, Nigeria. From missionary ac tivities, the Rickettses established farm settlements and were later joined by thei children. It was the Rickettses who built the first canoes that linked the Lagos Lagoo with the Nigerian interior.[6]

Garvey and Pan-Africanism

THE ABOVE INDIVIDUALS and Garvey were all Pan-Africanists in one way or th other. But Marcus Garvey is of special significance in that he was the one perso who in a more intense manner than anyone preached Pan-Africanism and sought t "practicalize" it as a movement. Arising from his personal qualities of eloquenc and perfect understanding of crowd psychology, which made an observer describ him as the greatest mass leader to appear on the American scene since Frederic Douglass,[7] Garvey's speeches and activities were the most intense. Their effect were felt more in Africa and the rest of the Third World than those of any other Pan Africanist. This is not to underestimate the contributions of men like Du Bois, Syl vester Williams, Edward Blyden and others. They were all Pan-Africanists an promoted the ideals of Pan-Africanism, which includes the emphasis on the rehab ilitation of the African past to counter the European charges of African rootlessness the vision of a united glorious Africa, solidarity among men of African blood, th belief in a distinct African personality, and a respect for African culture and tradi tions. These were ideals for which Garvey stood. Details of his life and activities i the implementation of the ideals are sufficiently familiar. What is important is tha even those who initially disagreed with Garvey's approach, such as Du Bois, later o came to appreciate his stand and described him as an extraordinary leader of men. The UNIA itself was described as one of the most interesting spiritual movements of the modern world.[8]

Of relevance to this paper is that Garvey during his lifetime consciously strove to get Africa involved in his movement. When, in August 1920 at his convention in New York City, plans were worked out for the establishment of a negro state in Africa, Garvey sent messages to the Emperor of Ethiopia and the President of Liberia among many other Africans.[9] Events connected with the UNIA were closely followed, and the ideas preached by Garvey were being circulated to the Africans. This explains the establishment of branches of the association in several parts of the continent. The Nigerian branch of the UNIA was formed in 1920 under the leadership of eminent Nigerians such as the Rev. W.B. Euba, first African principal of Wesleyan Boys' High School, Lagos, founder and first principal of Eko Boy's High School. Other co-founders were the Rev. S.M. Abiodun, the superintendent of the Egbado and Awori districts of the Church Missionary Society, and Earnest Sisei Ikoli, journalist, politician and company director. He was eventually one of the founders of the first national political organization, the Nigerian Youth Movement.[10] The *Lagos Weekly Record* of 27 November 1920 reported the unveiling of the association's charter on Friday, 26 November, and commended the orderliness of its proceedings and the evidence of a quiet internal strength among the leaders of the movement and its general membership: "The speakers struck a high note. They all stressed the need for the negro to co-operate in order for him to secure his upliftment in the order of things by his own independent effort". The association during its lifetime generated ideas which continued to act as a leaven to the political, national and race consciousness already developing in Nigeria. Nigeria's debt to Garvey was acknowledged by the *West African Pilot,* when at his death the paper declared:

> Marcus Garvey has lived and died leaving an indelible impression of his foot prints on the sands of time which neither the forces of space nor those of time could obliterate for ever. He refused to admit the alleged inferiority of the Africans. And throughout his life he inspired Africans to regard their black complexion with pride and to develop race consciousness so as to look forward to a place under the sun. Marcus Garvey was the fountain from which springs other scientific, constructive and effective ideas of Pan-Africanism.[11]

The last sentence of the foregoing quotation pinpoints the exact nature of the importance of Garvey to Pan-Africanism and Nigerian nationalism. It is interesting to note that the founder and editor in chief of the *West African Pilot* was Dr Nnamdi Azikiwe, who after his education at Methodist Boys' High School, Lagos, proceeded to the United States and attended Howard, Lincoln and Columbia Universities. While there, "Zik" confessed to having been exposed to racial discrimination, the influence of Pan-Africanism and the Garveyite movement. The publicity the negro press gave to Garvey attracted Azikiwe's attention. He became race conscious and completely internalized all that Garvey said and wrote. He was to become the most dreaded opponent of British colonialists on his return to Nigeria. At independence, he was one of the three recognized political leaders and the influence of his political party, which was a part of the first post-Independence government, partly account for the pre-occupation of Nigerian foreign policy with African unity and the con tinued struggle against colonialism and racism.

Garvey's call on the negroes of the world to unite into one great body was alread being hearkened to by 1925. People of African descent in the United Kingdon formed organizations with the aim of providing solace for themselves in the environ ment in which they found themselves. The most famous of the organizations was th West African Students Union (WASU), formed by Ladipo Solanke. He was a lav student from Abeokuta. On his arrival in Britain, he was exposed to forms of racia prejudice. But he had all along read about Garvey and exchanged correspondenc with him. Solanke was resolved to contribute his own quota to the emancipation o the negro. He was imbued with the idea that until Africans at home and abroa develop the principles of self help, unity and co-operation among themselves, the would continue to suffer the effects of colour prejudice and remain hewers of woo and drawers of water for other races of the world.

Solanke therefore established the WASU with the following aims:

(a) To act as a centre for information and research on African history, culture an institutions;

(b) To promote goodwill and understanding between Africans and other races;

(c) To foster a spirit of self help, unity and co-operation;

(d) To foster a spirit of national consciousness and racial pride among its mem bers;

(e) To publish a monthly magazine called *WASU.*[12]

The organization acquired a hostel, which became the centre for social activitie political education and propaganda for West African students. According to Profes sor Coleman, the first WASU hostel in London, acquired in 1928, was a present fron Marcus Garvey.[13] WASU also published a pamphlet titled *The Vanished Glor* which indicated the glory of the African past, its kingdoms and societies. That glor was destroyed by the slave trade. The pamphlet represented as it were a fore-run ner of Walter Rodney's *How Europe Underdeveloped Africa.* During the Secon World War, WASU pressed for the implementation of the Atlantic Charter in Wes Africa and sponsored a West African delegation, led by Azikiwe, to protest the ex clusion of Africa from the provisions of the charter. The shabby treatment th Colonial Office accorded the delegation left a permanent imprint on Azikiwe. H became implacably hostile to colonialism and acquired more militancy in his attitude

It is necessary to remember that the West African Students Union and Pan African organizations inspired by Garvey's ideas functioned alongside similar or ganizations which had existed before them. There were the series of Pan-Africa Congresses organized by Du Bois,[14] the first of which was in 1919. There was also i existence the National Congress of British West Africa, which came into existenc in 1920 and had been pressing for the opportunity for peoples of African descent t participate in the government of their country. The Pan-African Congress did con tinue after Garvey's death but by the time the Manchester Conference was held i

1945, it had among its participants notable Garveyites like Jomo Kenyatta and Kwame Nkrumah. It was Jomo Kenyatta who led the Mau Mau War against the British in Kenya when it became clear that the British had no intention of granting independence to the territory.

Kwame Nkrumah, like Azikiwe, was educated in America. While there, he attended meetings of the UNIA in New York. He was a president of the WASU in London. He came back to lead his country to independence and adopted the flag of the UNIA as his country's national flag and Garvey's black star as the national emblem. The Ghanaian national football team has been called the Black Star, as has the country's national shipping company, the Black Star Line, ever since Nkrumah's days. Perhaps Nkrumah's most important contribution to Pan-Africanism was his implementation of Garvey's emphasis on Pan-Continentalism in contrast to the tendency in some quarters to describe Garvey's emphasis on the Black as excluding Arabic- and Berber-speaking North Africans.

The fact was that Garvey himself dreamed and spoke of a Pan-African Union from Cape to Cairo. As he once said, "The whole world is my province until Africa is free". Kwame Nkrumah was particularly instrumental in bringing the north and south of the continent together as it never was before. The Nasser coup of 1952 acted as the inspiration for nationalist activities in North Africa. Although Nasser was by then apparently more concerned with Arab than African unity, Egyptian radio broadcasts, called the Voice of Free Africa, called for the overthrow of imperialist dogs in Kenya and Somaliland. The broadcasts were later on extended to West Africa and the Belgian Congo. The impact of these broadcasts was tremendous. Indeed, by 1955, an African Association had been formed in Egypt. It consisted of representatives of the various African nationalist groups who were being assisted by the Nasser regime.[15]

Kwame Nkrumah, after serving as WASU president, arrived in the Gold Coast in 1947. He first joined the United Gold Coast Convention. He later resigned to form the Convention People's Party, with which he led the Gold Coast to independence. On the occasion of independence, he declared that independence was meaningless while the rest of Africa was under colonial rule. He immediately put in motion a plan for a meeting of representatives of independent African countries to deliberate on continental unity and assistance to African peoples still under colonialism. He sent two missions to Cairo to consult the Egyptian government on the issue (he later on married an Egyptian woman). The independent African states of Egypt, Ghana, Liberia, and Ethiopia met in 1958 and 1959 at the instance of Kwame Nkrumah and deliberated on strategies for continental unity and liberation. When in 1958 Sékou Touré decided to reject de Gaulle's offer of freedom with France and voted for complete independence, Nkrumah led Ghana into a union with Guinea and offered a $10 million loan to tide over initial difficulties. Thus, the post-1958 era, largely due to Kwame Nkrumah, is according to Thompson characterized by efforts to express "the African personality", the need for economic and social development, and popularization of the United States of Africa which Marcus Garvey originally elaborated in the first phase of Pan-Africanism.[16]

The following decade saw the independence of many African states and the emergence of two schools of thought on the approach to African unity. Basically, Nkrumah, along with the presidents of Guinea, Algeria, Egypt and Mali, believed tha Africa should first seek political unity and form a central government under one president, as this would facilitate economic development and provide solutions to the problems of the continent. The other states, mainly the former French colonies together with Nigeria and Liberia, wanted a functional approach to unity: African states should first consolidate their independence and co-operate functionally before thinking of political unity. The latter group, known as the Monrovia powers, were not prepared to surrender a part of their newly won sovereignty for continental unity while the former group, known as the Casablanca powers, were prepared to do so The emergence of a continental organization, the Organization of African Unity (OAU), with the declared objective of promoting unity and development of African states represents a triumph for the ideals of people like Marcus Garvey. The charter of the organization is an attempt to reconcile the Casablanca and Monrovia approaches, although the tilt to the Monrovia doctrine is quite noticeable.

Nigerian Nationalism

THAT NIGERIA COULD PLAY a role in the emergence of the OAU is in part a tribute to the contributions of Nigerians influenced by Garvey in the development of Nigerian nationalism and the ultimate attainment of independence. Reference has already been made to the establishment of the UNIA in Lagos. Apart from the activities of the association, which generally stimulated nationalist thought, the contribution of individual members of the league was remarkable.

The first national political organization in Nigeria, the Nigerian Youth Movement (NYM), was begun in 1934 by three men, one of whom was Earnest Ikoli.[17] Ikoli had earlier on received his nationalist baptism when he joined two others to establish the Lagos branch of the UNIA. The aim of the NYM was the development of a united nation out of the diverse elements that made up Nigeria and the achievement of complete autonomy for the country. The movement advocated compulsory and free education, adult suffrage, and equal economic opportunities and treatment for Nigerians as compared to Europeans. The body engaged in a number of protests against aspects of colonial rule and one of its most notable successes was the agitation against the Cocoa Pool in 1938.

One of the effects of the Second World War in Africa was the intensification of nationalist struggles. After contributing immensely to the success of the allied forces, Africans suffered considerable hardship as a result of the wartime measures. Price controls and the high price of food, coupled with the agony of physical separation of the soldiers from their families, made Africans generally dissatisfied with colonialism. Perhaps the most important reason for the intensification of nationalist struggles was the reluctance of the allied powers to extend the ideals of democracy to their colonial subjects. But the anti-German war propaganda unleashed by the British let loose a ferment of ideas and there arose an increase in political awakening which made people conscious of their rights. There arose a new political awakening in Nigeria led by a group of young, educated nationalists, the most notable of whom was Nnamdi Azikiwe. His familiarity with American politics, negro journalism, and Garvey's ideas and a strong race consciousness put him in the forefront of nationalist agitation. His newspaper, *The West African Pilot,* gave vent to the grievances of the people. Having acquired, like Garvey, a gift of oratory and an uncanny mastery of crowd psychology, Azikiwe became the idol of the masses, who regarded whatever he wrote and spoke as the gospel truth.

By 1943, Azikiwe and a number of articulate new-generation Nigerians came together to form a national front in order to weld the aspirations of the youth to nationhood by exerting unified mass pressure. A series of meetings were held. Several organizations, such as the NYM, the Union of Teachers, and the Trade Union Congress participated. At the end, an all-embracing organization known as the National Council for Nigeria and the Cameroons (NCNC) was established on 24 May 1944, with the basic aim of exerting mass pressure in order to accelerate the political development of the country. Herbert MacAuley was elected President and Nnamdi Azikiwe was made Secretary. With the formation of the NCNC, says Olusanya, the real battle against British colonial rule could be said to have started.[18]

It was in his capacity as Secretary that Zik led the NCNC protest against the Richards constitution on the grounds that what the constitution provided was an opportunity for Nigerians to *discuss* their affairs. What the party wanted was an opportunity for Nigerians to *participate in* the affairs of their country. When the colonial governor refused to listen to their objection, the NCNC decided to send a delegation to the Secretary of State. Before the delegation left for England, Zik toured the United States. He was received by the deputy mayor of New York on the steps of City Hall, and a dinner was held for him at the Hotel Pennsylvania, where he made a speech in which he passionately pleaded for the emancipation of Nigeria from the political thraldom, economic insecurity and social disabilities imposed on it by Britain. He received a great deal of publicity from the press. The widely read weekly *Time* carried an article by him in which he was described as the "acacia thorn in the British Lion's paw".[19] The NCNC delegation was shabbily treated by the British Colonial Secretary, who advised them to return to Nigeria and co-operate in the working of the constitution. This only made Zik and the NCNC more resolute in their determination to rid Nigeria of colonialism.

In 1945, Nigerian workers embarked on a general strike. Zik used the *West African Pilot* to support the strikes. So popular did Zik become that parents named their babies after him and his name became a household word. When, towards the end of 1945, Zik alleged that the colonial government was planning to assassinate him, his anti-colonial credentials had become so strong that people believed the story. In an apparent appreciation of Zik's commitment to Nigeria's emancipation an organization known as the Zikist Movement was formed.[20] It was socialist in inclination and placed emphasis on positive action to rid the country of colonialists. It organized strikes and took advantage of a shooting incident at Enugu coal mine to embarrass the colonial government. Although the movement did not exist for long, it created an impact on the Nigerian populace.

It should be pointed out that Nnamdi Azikiwe, popular as he was, was not the first Nigerian nationalist. There were a number of earlier nationalists who, along with some of Zik's contemporaries, disagreed with his strategy. Like Garvey, Zik by his style aroused the suspicion and jealousy of some of his fellow nationalists. Some of them even accused Zik of being biased in favour of his Ibo tribe. Indeed, by 1951 a notable feature of Nigerian nationalism was the emergence of ethnic and regional division. The MacPherson constitution of 1951, which formally established federalism, acknowledged the need to recognize the diversity of Nigerian society. The three regions into which the country was divided – North, East and West – appointed delegates who participated in the various constitutional conferences that led to the attainment of independence in 1960.

It is important to note that many of the delegates from two of the regions, East and West, were influenced directly or indirectly by Garvey. They had either read and assimilated Garvey or participated in the activities of the WASU. Among these were Nnamdi Azikiwe, Mbonu Ojike, Eni Njoku from the East, and Bode Thomas and Samuel Akintola from the West. The first post-Independence government in Nigeria was made up of an alliance between the Northern People's Congress and the NCNC, led by Azikiwe. The Pan-African foreign policy posture of that government was influenced by Zik's belief that Nigeria had a historic and manifest destiny on the African continent.[21] This assertion is supported by the fact that with an area of 91,307,264 square kilometres and a population that is close to 100 million, the country has over 20 per cent of the entire African population. One out of every five Africans is a Nigerian. It is the most populous black nation on earth.

Successive Nigerian governments have identified the restoration of human dignity to black men and women all over the world as a major component of our national interest. Africa has therefore been the cornerstone of our foreign policy. In the conduct of our African diplomacy some broad stands have emerged. The first is the support for the OAU, which arises from our conception of the organization as the foremost continental machinery for the articulation of African interests. There is also the anticolonial pre-occupation and total identification with the anti-apartheid front.[22] This involves a moral and political commitment to the restoration of human dignity, particularly the black man's dignity in southern Africa. Another noticeable strand is our commitment to the notion of intra-African economic co-operation and the efforts at peaceful settlements of inter state dispute and conflicts. Nigeria played a crucial role in the emergence of the OAU and has been the biggest single financial contributor to the running of the organization. We led the battle for the expulsion of South Africa from the Commonwealth in 1963 and recognized the MPLA government in Angola in 1975, following South Africa's intervention on the side of the FNLA and UNITA. Our pressure on Margaret Thatcher's government contributed substantially to the independence of Zimbabwe. Since 1975, our contributions to the OAU liberation fund have been quite significant. Nigeria has always promoted inter-African economic co-operation. The Economic Community of West African States (ECOWAS) came into being mainly as a result of our joint effort with Togo, and the first ever African economic summit was convened by President Shehu Shagari in 1980 and resulted in the Lagos Plan of Action. The Lagos Plan of Action has remained the blueprint for African's economic integration.

The spirit and ideals of Garvey are strongly manifested in the activities of the present government. The background and character of the directors of foreign policy are such that its Africa-centred nature continues to be implemented in more vigorous manner without necessarily neglecting the need to encourage friendship and understanding with all the nations of the world. The Babangida regime, which officially declared a commitment to the maintenance of fundamental human rights of all citizens, cannot but be vigorously opposed to apartheid and all forms of racial discrimination. The government therefore sees apartheid as a vivid affront to its conscience and has made the restoration of fundamental human rights to all black peoples of the world an article of faith. The regime has been quite active in the struggle against apartheid and has consciously promoted African integration. So visible has our contribution to ECOWAS become that the president has been appointed the chairman of the subcontinental organization for a record three-year period. When Angola was attacked by the racist regime in 1986, the Nigerian government made a huge cash donation to Luanda to enable the African country to recoup part of its losses. We participated in the Eminent Persons Group and led the boycott of the 1986 Commonwealth Games in protest against British attitudes to sanctions. It was the Nigerian proposal at the Harare Summit of the non-aligned states in 1986 that led to the creation of the Africa Fund to assist frontline states. In late 1987, our president launched the Technical Aid Corps Programme, in which young Nigerian professionals would be sent to needy sister African and Caribbean countries.

Our concern with Africa has not diminished our interest in the promotion of peace and understanding in the wider world. Nigeria has initiated the coming together of a number of neutral states with regional influence to meet at regular intervals, discuss and offer suggestions on major world issues. The Lagos Forum, as the group is called, is designed to break the deadlock existing in the discussion of issues of relevance to world peace and progress by involving states from the developed and developing world and from both sides of the pole.

In conclusion, I would like to congratulate the Jamaican government and people and the University of the West Indies for honouring the spirit of Marcus Garvey. A society that does not cherish its past cannot make progress. By paying the Pan-Africanist hero his just tribute, Jamaica is appreciating its past and marching forward to the future.

NOTES

[1] See R. Nettleford, "The Spirit of Garvey, Lessons of the Legacy", *Jamaica Journal* (Vol. 20, No. 5, August-October 1987), p. 3.

[2] See Tony Martin, "International Aspects of the Garvey Movement", *Jamaica Journal, op. cit.,* p. 11.

[3] See V.P. Thompson, *Africa and Unity: The Evolution of Pan-Africanism* (Longman, 1969), p. 35.

[4] Ibid., p. 3.

[5] P.O. Esedebe, "The Emergence of Pan-African Ideas", in O. Otite (ed.), *Themes in African Social and Political* (Fourth Dimension Publishers, 1978), pp. 80-82.

[6] For details, see Ade Adefuye, John Gershion, and Joshua Ricketts, "Jamaican Contribution to the Socio-Economic Development of the Colony Provinces of Nigeria", in G.O. Olusanya *et al., Studies in Yoruba History and Culture* (University Press Ltd., 1983), pp. 135-152.

[7] W.E.B. Du Bois, *Dusk of Dawn: An Essay Towards an Autobiography of a Race Concept* (New York: Harcourt Brace, 1940), quoted in V.B. Thompson, *Africa and Unity*, p. 278.

[8] See G.O. Olusanya, *The Second World War and Politics in Nigeria, 1939-1953,* p. 32.

[9] Ibid.

[10] See *The Lagos Weekly Record,* Nov. 27, 1920.

[11] See *West African Pilot,* May 23, 1940; also quoted in G.O. Olusanya, *The Second World War.*

[12] See J.S. Coleman, *Nigeria: Background to Nationalism* (Berkeley, 1960), p. 204.

[13] Ibid., p. 458.

[14] See W.E.B. Du Bois, *The World and Africa* (New York, 1964).

[15] See V.B. Thompson, *Africa and Unity,* pp. 69-71.

[16] Ibid., p. 135.

[17] See G.O. Olusanya, *The Second World War,* p. 39.

[18] Ibid., p. 74.

[19] Ibid., p. 109.

[20] For details see G.O. Olusanya, "The Zikist Movement: A Study in Political Radicalism", *Journal of Modern African Studies,* No. 114, 1975.

[21] Nnamdi Azikiwe, *Zik* (Cambridge University Press, 1960), p. 7. For further details on factors which influenced the formulation and execution of Nigeria's foreign policy, see A.B. Akinyemi, *Foreign Policy and Federalism* (Nigeria: Ibadan University Press, 1974).

[22] A.J. Idong, *Internal Politics and Foreign Policy, 1960-1966* (Nigeria: Ibadan University Press, 1974).

The Ideology and Practice of Garveyism

Judith Stein
Department of History
The City College of New York, USA

THE EXPLOSION OF RESEARCH on Garvey and Garveyism during the last twenty years has restored the man and the movement to their place in history and, in the case of the United States, ended the view that the movement was a curiosity, marginal to the "mainstream" of Afro-American history. Today, no one serious about the subject can conclude with the American Theodore Draper that the programme of the Garveyites had "little or nothing to do with their immediate lives, with their own time and place".[1]

Nevertheless, I think that an alternative to the old school has not been reached because of a Whiggish racial tradition which makes Garvey a prophet of the future. This tendency is understandable because the renewed interest in Garvey took place during the resurgence of nationalism in the 1960s and 1970s, when there was an obvious political interest in earlier figures and movements. Although much new research was initiated by such an agenda, I think that it suffers from its virtues. Meanings from the contemporary period slip into the past, often unconsciously. Words like nation, race, people lose their historical meanings. The way Garvey and Garveyism function in contemporary politics is a distinct phenomenon, related but not identical to the historical movement.

I think that a way to resolve this problem is to pay more attention to the social practices of the Universal Negro Improvement Association, which I think have been slighted in the literature. Before I do this, I would like to discuss how dangerous it is to assume that these key words in all nationalist politics mean the same thing. I will use examples from the United States, but others from Jamaica or Africa could be used as easily. Then, I will talk about the circumstances which encouraged a movement based upon racial identifications – the UNIA – at a particular time and place. Finally, I will discuss how the practices of the movement clarify its ideology.

The Issue of Definition

POPULAR IDENTITIES, whether racial or non-racial, are constructed as people define their social and political objectives. For instance, in 1848, the abolitionist Frederick Douglass took for granted that Blacks were Americans: "I would ask you, my friends, if this is not mean and impudent in the extreme, for one class of Americans to ask for the removal of another class?"[2] This assumption was essential to Douglass's campaign against the American Colonization Society's attempt to remove Blacks to Africa. A few months later, he asserted that Blacks were a people and a nation: "We are one people – one in general complexion, one in a common degradation, one in popular estimation".[3] Addressing Northern Blacks, who evidently did not identify with the slaves, he attempted to mobilize them behind the cause of Southern bondsmen by asserting their oneness. Nevertheless, the identities were compatible. Douglass believed that Blacks, like the Germans and Irish, could be a people and Americans.

The same words can signify different meanings. In 1880, sugar workers in St John the Baptist Parish, Louisiana, also assumed Blacks constituted a nation: "The colored people are a nation and must stand together".[4] When the sugar workers declared themselves a nation, they were not defining a people but using a metaphor to unite a group of Blacks trying to win a bitter strike. One would assume that six years afterwards, when the Knights of Labor came into Louisiana's sugar fields and organized both Blacks and Whites, the manifestos were different. The sugar workers' definition of a nation was different from Douglass's and also from Cyril Briggs's.

Writing in 1919, Briggs thought of Blacks as a people and a race. They had "race traits" and a "race genius", which distinguished them from non-Blacks:

> The surest and quickest way, then, in our opinion, to achieve the salvation of the Negro is to combine the two most likely and feasible propositions, viz.: salvation for all Negroes through the establishment of a strong, stable, independent Negro state (along the lines of our own race genius) in Africa and elsewhere; and salvation for all Negroes (as well as other oppressed people) through the establishment of a Universal Socialist Co-operative Commonwealth.[5]

Unlike Douglass, Briggs believed that a people required a nation-state of its own. Although unique, Blacks were similar enough to other people to require a state and also socialism. Briggs's ideas were embodied in the African Blood Brotherhood, a short-lived organization he helped create during World War One. He joined the Communist Party in the early 1920s.

In 1919, a group of striking longshoremen in Key West, Florida, were less theoretical. They called themselves "honest workmen". Their self-conception was probably related to their newspaper appeal to the citizens of the city, "especially the working classes like the members of this union who have to earn their living by the sweat of their brow".[6] Another definition was implicit in the letter of the president of their local union to the National Association for the Advancement of Coloured People: "The principle involved means so much not only to these Negroes who are on strike but to our race in general".[7] The first stressed membership in a class; the second, in a race.

The different appellations and meanings undermine the common belief that racial identity or consciousness is fixed. The ways people define themselves are determined by their history, politics, and class. They change. The same words have conveyed vastly different meanings and encouraged diverse actions. They mean less and more than they seem. People employ strategic fictions which can only be understood in a context. They always must be understood as one element with other ideological beliefs which have nothing to do with race. And they interact with definitions made by other people, especially those who exercise power.

Therefore, in order to understand a complex phenomenon like Garveyism, paying attention to words and rhetoric, which are similar in all nationalist movements, cannot elucidate its rise and fall, its particular appeal to some Blacks and not others. Thus, I cannot share Robert Hill's definition of Garveyism as a "unique moral and political discourse".[8] First, I do not think the strength of Garveyism can be explained in terms of a unique language. Indeed, I would argue that its strength was its ability to incorporate ideas common among black elites and bring it to people who had been outside of political life. Moreover, the quest for the unique discourse tends to achieve it at a level of abstraction that makes it impossible to understand how the movement functioned in the actual world, where people joined for concrete reasons that had to do with their lives. Seeking consistency, statements which do not fit so comfortably are ignored, rather than seen as opportunities for fresh thinking.

The best example of this is Garvey's changing opinions of the Ku Klux Klan. But there are many more. In 1919, for instance, when American black leaders were supporting a loan to Liberia, Garvey refused to fall in line with them. He argued that the United States, because it too was a white nation, would support "England and France to crush any rising colored race".[9] In 1923, Garvey praised "philanthropic and liberal America, whose honesty in international politics should be better trusted than the ravenous white nations of Europe".[10] What is Garvey's position on the great powers? Analyzing Garvey's words cannot explain the differences. One would have to know that in 1919 Garvey was full of self-confidence, heading a growing organization. By 1923, the UNIA was faltering. Garvey supported a United States loan and altered his rhetoric accordingly. One could not figure that out by examining discourse and language, or an ideal blueprint of nationalism.

Just as we could not understand the politics of the striking sugar workers simply from their manifesto of racial unity, so we cannot understand the meaning of Garveyite discourse through its language. Instead, it is the everyday activities of Garvey and Garveyites that define the language and rhetoric of the movement. We are brought back to the need for social analysis. Examining rhetoric is essential but it becomes dangerous when interpreted without context.

The Idea of Black Nationalism of the Black Nationalist State

WE NEED TO analyse the UNIA as a nationalist movement, similar to other nationalist movements of the time but shaped by the specific experiences of a group of black men and women. Racial ideology is not an expression of racial identity, nor is it an arbitrary invention. It arises, like all ideologies, out of the need to make some sense of complicated social and political arrangements. Its first assumption is that race and nation are the major forces moving world history, and that ultimately a people need a state.

The notion that a people need a state was a new idea in human history, a child of the French Revolution. Most people of course were attached to a piece of land they called home, which was the locus of a real community with real social relations. But that is not the meaning of modern nationalism, which took over these associations of kin, associates, and home territory for land and people of a size and scale which made them "imagined communities".[11] Even so, the notion was slow to take hold about the masses of peoples who lived in empires ruled by others. It was also slow to take hold within the black community.

But basically the principle is too abstract to form the basis for a popular movement. Every movement, racial or non-racial, which hopes to take root among the masses of people must intersect with their concrete needs and hopes. All popular movements possess social, economic, and political ideas, often not elaborately articulated but present in the kinds of activities undertaken. Because specific programmes among all peoples tend to be based on concrete social experience, the social class that initiates the politics is important and its ability to marshal other groups behind its programme is crucial to its success as a popular movement.

The first nationalists were not founders of mass movements. Imperialism in Africa and the Jim Crow and disfranchisement movement brought a group of Blacks together at the first Pan-African Conference in London in 1900. One American participant, the churchman Alexander Walters, declared that "in matters of race there were no geographic or national limitations" to racial consciousness. The men who gathered in London were modern men, cut loose from traditional communities in Africa, the West Indies, and the United States. Like all nationalists, they claimed that Blacks composed a unique community, which should have a state at some point in the future. Nineteenth-century nationalists, unlike those of the twentieth century, assumed that a state must be modern, not simply independent.

The Pan-Africanists were not representative of most Blacks. They were an elite and their racial consciousness was shaped by their class experiences. These educated, and mostly professional, men saw the new racism closing off the opportunity that the Western civilization of an earlier day had promised. Thus, W.E.B. Du Bois, another American participant, feared that the problem of the twentieth century would be a colour line, meaning "a white effort to limit black progress and development". Although they excoriated the conditions of the new imperialism in Africa and growing disfranchisement and Jim Crow in the United States, their solutions accommodated to the changes but mandated heavy doses of racial self-help – schools, churches, and economic development.[12]

Du Bois's fears revealed the intellectual tradition and social position these men represented. The words progress and development were code words for Western civilization, propelled by the engines of capitalism. The men who met together in London were lawyers, teachers, journalists, civil servants, and churchmen – men who made up only a small minority of the black world. Men like them have traditionally been nationalists, particularly in its early, elite phases.[13] They occupied an ambivalent position between state and society. They held the values professed by the modern state, but most of the black society that the state controlled did not share them. Their very social security and position turned upon places within state institutions – in schools, courts, administrative bodies – which were being closed to them.

They viewed their exclusion both as a betrayal of principles concerning merit and as a denial of a firm position in the state and in society.

Nationalism provided a new identity, which contained and fused images of an ideal state and society in which they would have secure, respected and leading positions. Whereas they earlier thought that Western civilization was both desirable and open to all, they now learned that progress was not universal but wielded by nation-states, and that Western dominance mandated racial inferiority. Educated, urban, and sophisticated, their own lives revealed the limits being placed before them. Their solutions were, in the words of Wilson Moses, "civilizationist",[14] creating racial institutions embodying the new values, for themselves and for the uplift of the masses.

But most Blacks were farmers, peasants, and sharecroppers. Most sought autonomy or independence, not progress. For them, Western civilization was not benign. Initially, during the era of Emancipation, some had been optimistic. Even before the new imperialism and era of Jim Crow they had become suspicious as their independence was eroded or, in the United States, their citizenship limited.

The nationalists would not get a hearing from this vast majority who knew who they were and what they wanted, even when they could not effectively get it. They would have better luck with men who were uprooted from traditional communities, homes, values, and goals. Marcus Garvey would eventually be a recruit, but his early experience in Jamaica did not make him a nationalist or a pan-Africanist.

Born in the northern part of the island in 1887, Garvey was the son of a proud artisan unable to maintain his own status or promote his son's in the years of the depression of the 1890s and the general stagnation of the Jamaican economy. Like other sons of declining rural areas, Garvey went to the big city, Kingston, where he practised his printer's trade. Prospects were no better in Jamaica's capital city. Garvey, like other Jamaicans, sought careers off the island. Jobs and travels through Central America, however, yielded little. During this period, Garvey dabbled in local politics and expressed dissatisfaction and restlessness, but there is no evidence that he developed a coherent political ideology.

For instance, on a trip to England, he published an article on Jamaica which reflected his early thinking. He protested the preferment that Whites received on the island and praised the sons of slaves for their heroic efforts to prosper. The masses were hard-working, thrifty, and improving.[15] A later article, published in a British magazine and later reprinted in *The Daily Gleaner,* took a different tack. Arguing that Blacks and Whites lived harmoniously on the island, he said that the mass of Blacks "are in darkness and are really unfit for good society ... dwelling in villainy and vice of the worse kind".[16]

While in London, Garvey had learned the latest ideas and practices of pan-Africanism from the international black community which gravitated around Dusé Mohammed Ali's journal, *The African Times.* Concluding that the black majority would determine the prospects for its elite minority, Garvey blueprinted an immense project to uplift the masses through a vast complex of racial institutions – the Universal Negro Improvement Association and the African Communities League. He attempted to solicit aid from Blacks and Whites.

Like Dusé Mohammed Ali, Edward Blyden, and Booker T. Washington, Garvey now assumed that racial institutions modeled on the dominant ones of Western society were solutions, for himself and the race, to the new problems posed by the new imperialism in Africa and Jim Crow and disfranchisement in the United States, and the older ones of Jamaica. Garvey had become a nationalist, in particular a pan-Africanist. But the resources and will in Jamaica were inadequate to produce the schools which Garvey first thought were the key institutions. His Jamaican projects were neither distinctive nor credible enough to mobilize a significant number of people on the island. He went to the United States and stayed because the ingredients for civilization and the space for political advocacy there were a lot more plentiful.

When he first arrived, he was impressed with the racial institutions Afro-Americans had created. And business became a surer route to progress than the Jamaican school he had initially planned to build. All the while, Garvey became part of the new agitation in Harlem. Critics of the limited changes of World War One, these young men – Garvey, Cyril Briggs, Hubert Harrison, and A. Phillip Randolph – were bright, restless, and astute. They observed and attempted to assimilate the mass militancy of the war period – socialism, Bolshevism, trade unionism, and nationalism. They used the soapbox to debate elites – white and black. All lacked political organizations of weight. Although there were ideological differences among them, all placed a new emphasis on the political potency of the popular classes as the agents of transformation.

Garvey's basic ideas and methods, however, had not changed. The politics during the war confirmed his nationalism and led him to stress the need for a nation-state. Both political leaders in the halls of Versailles and Irish revolutionaries on the streets of Dublin put forward statehood as a solution to people's problems. Although Garvey frequently asserted the right of black self rule in Africa, and employed militant, and occasionally martial, rhetoric, his political practices were identical with those he had used in Jamaica.

Nationalism as a Popular Movement

GARVEY HAD formed a branch of the UNIA, a fraternal, and also the ACL, a business, corporation in New York. At UNIA meetings there was much talk about the new economic opportunities which the war had opened up in places like Harlem, the home of a growing number of Blacks. In February 1919, the UNIA opened its first business, a restaurant. But it was clear from the beginning that Garvey had something more in mind. A restaurant could not carry the weight of Garvey's programme of racial progress. A shipping line, announced in May 1919, could and did.[17]

Because the line failed, there is a tendency among scholars to note its ambitions and goals but to underestimate its role in the rise of mass Garveyism. But the doctrines of nationalism are very abstract. Garvey's notion that the UNIA represented the nation required concrete evidence that its practice bore some relation to its assertions. It was the Black Star Line that elevated Garvey from his position as a local leader into a world leader. Its role in the creation of UNIA locals in 1919 and 1920 is indisputable. New locals often appeared in the wake of stock-selling campaigns. In the American South, Garveyites were known as Black Star Liners.[18] Commerce and business are often vehicles for the transmission of modern political and economic ideas. In the case of Garveyism, the Black Star Line was a literal carrier.

Shipping lines in Western culture in the early twentieth century were symbols of national power, more-benign equivalents of nuclear weapons in the late twentieth century. This was especially so in the United States. The creation of an American merchant marine and navy, previously a satellite to the British fleet, had received the highest priority in the nation's mobilization during World War One. Most American men and *matériel* went to war on foreign ships, but the establishment of the US Shipping Board and a shipbuilding auxiliary in 1916 revealed the government's commitment to commercial expansion and naval power. The new fleet was to be the core of a string of American shipping lines capable of retaining and expanding the foreign markets American businessmen had captured from European nations during the war.[19]

While the huge profits reaped by shipping corporations during the war made a shipping enterprise promising, the political link between ships and national power, the heart of the American government's propaganda, was equally attractive to Garvey and his supporters. Hubert Harrison, echoing Admiral Alfred Mahan's 1890 treatise on sea power, proclaimed: "Nations and people never rose to power without ships".[20] Thus, by building a shipping line, the UNIA became the embodiment of the nation, a theme which became prominent in the Garveyite argument. When Garvey said the UNIA represented 400 million negroes of the world, he was correct from his point of view. Garvey's precise projects, beginning first with the Black Star Line, however, reflected the immediate interests of a particular stratum of the black community, its underemployed skilled and educated men and women, who had conceived the project.

Initially, the Black Star Line was to be the property of the small group of UNIA members in New York. Requiring capital, however, Garvey brought this project to the masses. Garvey took the elite and popular demands of the time and attached them to the Black Star Line. The line could meet the needs of merchants in the Caribbean and Africa, who charged that the British Elder Dempster discriminated in favour of European traders. Earlier, during the war, Dusé Mohammed Ali's *African Times* had resurrected economic pan-Africanism when it appealed to Afro-Americans to turn their attention to the "Racial Motherland" to aid native shippers and merchants with "capital, industry, and commerce".[21]

Thus, the Black Star Line won the interest and approval of West African elites, individually and together, at the National Congress of British West Africa meeting in 1920. Indeed, the initial success of a pan-African project was possible because the elites of three areas were using an economic strategy. Although Africans often overestimated the wealth of Afro-Americans, there were more Blacks in the modern economy of the United States, currently earning more wages than in the past. The Black Star Line also promised work for many underemployed, skilled Blacks, just beginning to experience the unemployment of the post-war economy. And, it promised profit. Despite these many virtues, Garvey added more. He wove the social battles of 1919 into his appeals for funds and managers.

Historians of all camps associate the rise of the UNIA with the race riots of World War One. I would modify this consensus somewhat. The black response to the race riots varied: some urged self-defense, palliatives like amusement places, socialism or caution. There is no correlation between UNIA strength and the occurrence of race riots. Moreover, the particular expressions of Garveyism – the Black Star Line and the UNIA – cannot be deduced from race riots. The race riots produced an opportunity but did not dictate the character of the UNIA. Rather, Garvey wove that issue, with others of 1919, into his appeals. Earlier he had asked Blacks to prepare for action; he called them now to act by buying stock. If the problem was lynching, he argued that Blacks would continue to be lynched until the Black Star Line was built.[22]

Thus, nationalist ideology under certain conditions can bring into being an imitation of its own ideas. Insofar as nationalism is successful it appears to be true. Because there was a certain plausibility about his efforts in relationship to existing social and political grievances, Garveyism had a currency. As other groups within the boundary of the nation saw some relevance to Garvey's objectives, they joined the nation.

In 1920, George Goodwyn, a black organizer for the American Federation of Labor, appealed to R.R. Moton to help oppose the open shop movement in American industry. Among the dividends the race would receive from prosperous black workers would be the ability to support "ships for Mr Marcus Garvey ..., if found worthy".[23] Goodwyn's appeal revealed several characteristics of the popular politics of the era. First, the organizer did not make a distinction between Moton and Garvey. Moton at this time was the head of the National Negro Business League, an organization founded in 1900 by Booker T. Washington to encourage black business. Political divisions at the top were often unappreciated at the bottom. Second, the popular notion of racial progress often lacked standard ideological differences. At least initially.

To Goodwyn, the prosperity of labour was the prerequisite to racial enterprise and progress. In practice, Garvey's ability to accumulate capital depended upon the earnings of black workers.[24] To Garvey, progress emerged not from them but from racial leaders who would accumulate and use the surplus to create the institutions capable of uplifting the masses. To Garvey, black entrepreneurs would enlighten the race; to Goodwyn, the organization of black workers would be the means for their self-improvement.

The new mass upsurge that Garvey had observed in the United States did not essentially change his theology of progress. In Jamaica, he had appealed to leading Whites for money to create institutions of uplift. When he first arrived in the United States, he solicited leading Blacks. The growth of a militant black working class in the United States temporarily freed Garvey from depending upon Whites and elite Blacks but did not alter his fundamental conception of racial progress.

And R.R. Moton, Booker T. Washington's successor at Tuskegee, accepted the validity of comparisons between his National Negro Business League and Garvey's UNIA. To Moton, the differences were social, not ideological. Moton saw his own followers as "the most thoughtful and intelligent groups of colored people", code words for Blacks with property, businesses, and social connections.[25] Over time, and after the failure of the Black Star Line, Moton's distinctions would become valid. Social boundaries were more fluid in 1919 and 1920. Even when the black elite doubted

Garvey's achievements and questioned his methods, they did not criticize his view of racial progress, which was their own. W.E.B. DuBois wrote in 1920:

> What he is trying to say and do is this: American Negroes can be accumulating and ministering their own capital, organize industry, join centres of the South Atlantic by commercial enterprise and in this way ultimately redeem Africa as a fit and free home for black men. This is true.... It is feasible.... The plan is not original with Garvey but he has popularized it.[26]

And Garvey frequently criticized the behaviour of the elite and the lack of financial support of the Black Star Line, but not the significance of their achievements. In 1920, Garvey proclaimed that "the greatest enemy to the Negro race is the successful business and professional man who is satisfied", a mild definition of racial treason.[27]

Unlike other leaders who also believed that racial enterprises were critical for racial development, Garvey tried to organize Blacks through the line. At a minimum, the financial requirements of the Black Star Line forced UNIA leaders to mine a broader base of black support than elite Blacks. But the masses were potentially disruptive and difficult to contain. Attracted to the Black Star Line on the basis of Garvey's appeal, they often brought their own agendas to the organization. Thus, the initial enthusiasm of Cuban longshoremen, many of whom were black, vanished when they went on strike the next year.[28] And the militancy of plantation workers in Central America, occasionally supported by local UNIAs, conflicted in 1921 with Garvey's attempt to raise capital for the Black Star Line, which required accommodation with colonial powers.[29]

We have two phenomena going on here. First, the post-war period often blurred organizational lines and political agendas, as we saw in the case of George Goodwyn. More generally, in the immediate post-war period, socialists, race-first men, militants often co-operated. Organizational and ideological divisions were weaker than they would become.

The government transformed this co-operation into a grand conspiracy. Thus, the US Department of Justice proclaimed in 1919 that all groups, "be they Socialist, revolutionary, nationalist, communist and anarchist have dropped their differences of opinion on detail for the common purpose of securing a change of Government in the United States".[30] The theory explained why one informer for the Military Intelligence Division of the US Army imaginatively linked Morris Lewis of the NAACP, Republican Congressman Oscar De Priest, Ida Wells-Barnett, and Marcus Garvey together in one socialist bomb-making factory in Chicago.[31] (This example should also caution historians to distinguish the panic elements of the government from reality.)

Second, the meaning of political ideology and words like independence, nation, and race in the New York headquarters of the UNIA was not always the same as its meaning in Florida or South Africa. Thus, the Miami division reported that "its members ... are yet making untold sacrifices for this cause". The Floridians interpreted the cause as ownership of "houses from which they derive rentals and on which not one penny is owed".[32] To the men and women of the branches, independence was often property ownership free of debt, a traditional goal for working people.

On the other hand, the millennial goals of Wellington Butelezi in the Transkei reflected the social experiences of South Africa, not New York or Florida. Intensified rural impoverishment, proletarianization, and the migrant labour system had created a crisis in traditional culture which made the Transkei peasantry open to outside political influence. But the millennial thrust of the people, even though the agents of redemption were Afro-Americans on ships, reveals the politics of a peasantry in distress, not the modernizing values of the UNIA in New York.[33] The UNIA here as in so many places did not reshape as much as assimilate regional politics. That is one of many reasons why historians should not uncritically accept the government theory of outside agitator. Not every popular protest in the era was a manifestation of Garveyism, even those which included a Garveyite or a copy of *The Negro World.*

From the beginning the differences between the goals of the parent body in New York and the locals were sources of conflict, even when the differences were not expressed in ideological terms. The leaders of the Los Angeles division seceded not out of ideological disagreement but simply because they wanted to use UNIA financial resources for local developments on the West Coast.[34] With the demise of the Black Star Line in 1922, the problem became acute. And the UNIA was never able to produce another vehicle which could justify its pan-African structure. Where divisions remained, and many did through much of the 1920s, they were small, locally oriented, except for rituals, and diverse, lacking the vanguard role in local communities that Garvey had hoped they would play.

Like other racial movements, Garveyism asserted that race was the most important characteristic of black people, and the UNIA was the instrument of the race. Empirically, it was not. The Liberians chose nation over race. In the United States, the Los Angeles division chose region over race. Eventually, the UNIA in Jamaica chose nation over race. And in hundreds of ways individuals chose community and class over race. What I am saying here is not that these conflicts must inevitably fracture racial movements. Simply, one cannot assume the unity of movements based upon race. Black people have other characteristics than their descent, which are the critical ingredients for sustained organization.

The Decline of the UNIA as a Mass Movement

THE UNIA WAS a mass movement insofar as many people joined the hundreds of divisions. Unlike his early years in Jamaica, Garvey found that the new migrant communities in the Northern cities of the United States offered favourable organizing terrain. The process of migration had ended old relationships and thus provided a point of entry for new political groups. The war itself provided long-time residents with many new experiences and contacts which led them to seek alternative organization and authority. Moreover, despite its limits, the war had produced new work in factories, new black businesses, and new power in numbers. It is under these kinds of circumstances, when identity and place are no longer a given, that new political ideologies can become relevant. Having established itself in the United States, the logic of success facilitated the UNIA's entry into other areas of the Caribbean and Africa.

At the same time, other ideologies and movements took hold as well – communism, trade unionism, etc. Although there was an upsurge of black trade unionism and socialism during the war, the post-war recession and repression against the labour movement, the Socialist party and the new Communist party had destroyed many popular movements. Although the UNIA survived this period, the favourable environment for popular politics had disappeared, which Garvey acknowledged in 1924: "1914 and 1919 up to 1922 presented the one glorious time and opportunity for the Negro.... The world has practically returned to its normal attitude".[35]

The political climate of the 1920s, which was worldwide, not simply American, and Garvey's principal goals and methods explain why the UNIA did not mobilize the masses for political objectives. Garveyites paraded and petitioned; they did not demonstrate. The organization was hierarchical, not democratic. Its bonding was loose because Garvey did not require programmatic action, only loyalty and support of UNIA projects. The great 1920 convention was an eloquent bill of racial complaint that ranged from protesting discrimination in public hotels to decrying the treatment of Africans under imperialist rule. The declaration was vague about methods and priorities. Some delegates celebrated their local progress while others, like the Rev. Thomas Harten, stated that Blacks should use force to improve their condition in the United States.[36]

The convention offered very little that was new in substance. It restated historical black demands and routes to racial progress. Its novelty was the assertion of UNIA hegemony in the black world: "We hereby demand that the governments of the world recognize our leader and his representative chosen by the race to look after the welfare of our people under such governments".[37] Because the UNIA lacked a unified political strategy, increasing its membership depended upon Garvey's ability to conquer the marketplace with the Black Star Line, which over time he could not do. And exhortation was not powerful enough to impose the discipline or elicit the financial support that was necessary to maintain an organization of Blacks with different social experiences and objectives.

In the beginning, Garvey promised concrete benefits. After 1922, he asked for loyalty. Charisma had its limits. The effectiveness of Garvey was waning even before his imprisonment in 1925. His attempt to keep the organization together through his own person was heroic but ultimately unsuccessful. Nationalist movements often use leaders as symbols when the bonds of community are weak and objectives capable of uniting the group are absent.

After the failure of the Black Star Line in 1922, many, especially the prominent, left. Without a pan-African project, surviving divisions turned their attention to local matters. Many attempted to encourage local businesses in the northern cities of the United States and in urban areas everywhere; some turned to local politics. Even though the organization became socially more homogenous, the divisions steadily declined in numbers, despite the devotion of small groups. They simply took their place as one of many community organizations, generally reflecting the agendas of middling strata in black communities. Garvey's return to Jamaica was a tonic to the

UNIA there. But Garveyism was a minor player in the labour rebellions of 1938 and the subsequent creation of a politics of Jamaican nationalism. In some instances, former Garveyites joined the new organizations, which battled more effectively. In other instances, Garveyism laid the seeds for more radical and less political cults.

The motivations of Garveyites offer a clue to the weakness of the organization. The most active Garveyites were those with the steadiest work, which was usually modest. They were ambitious but pursued their goals singly. The UNIA opened up a more sophisticated world for many. The divisions were forums for intellectuals and activists who spoke on black, but also world, culture and politics. If the Black Star Line mined the black community deeper than many other enterprises, one result was to bring modern ideas to people for the first time. (Most churches, except for those of the elite, were provincial, parochial, and often anti-intellectual.)

But the diverse and loose motivations explained the high turnover. The UNIA was a voluntary organization, not a cult. Its values were not sharply delineated from other racial organizations of the 1920s. Indeed, they were shaped by the same trends. One evidence of this is that Garveyites of all classes usually belonged to other organizations as well as the UNIA. Changes in the locals and divisions were often mandated by people's traditional expectations of what fraternals offered. Thus, the UNIA was forced to offer death benefits. The ceremonies and parades of UNIA gatherings affirmed achievement, ambition, and solidarity, like other fraternals of the 1920s. However satisfying to participants, they were not collective mobilizations for particular goals or actions.

For other Garveyites, the UNIA expressed and confirmed their experience of injustice. Through most of the 1920s, these experiences lacked outlets for redress. Those locals which survived into the 1930s became somewhat more active when they, like most racial organizations, absorbed the new politics of that decade. Thus, Captain A.L. King, head of one New York division, admitted to Garvey in 1935 that the branch was "deviating from our past politics. Our policy of self-help will continue to be the same, but existing circumstances make it necessary to accept other methods".[38]

Garvey had learned during World War One that the masses could be a potent force, but because he held an elite model of progress, the masses were a necessary but passive part of his politics. The model had been created by black elites in the late nineteenth century, but was embraced by other, more impatient, less established men like Marcus Garvey. During the war he and others attempted to incorporate the militant masses, with imperfect success. On the other hand, by championing their legitimate role, history and culture, he sharply broke from the past. But the difficulty he had in organizing the masses to alter the societies that oppressed them reveals that his own transition to modern politics was partial. Subsequent black leaders would mobilize the masses more effectively because they did not ask them to defer their immediate needs to build elite institutions. This change was not fostered simply by the devastating impact of the Great Depression on racial enterprises, but also by new relationships in the broader society.

Just as Garvey's early politics were grounded in the models of British social imperialism and then those of American nationalism, so black strategies of the 1930s and 1940s were influenced by a new labour movement, radical politics, and a transformed state compelled to intervene in the affairs of civil society on the side of its working classes because of the militancy of organized workers – the labour rebellions in the Caribbean and the new Congress of Industrial Organizations in the United States. The new sphere of legitimate state action was a necessary bulwark to constitutional and moral arguments, while the social power and demonstration of effective working class organization provided a base from which to demand civil rights legislation in the American South, more equitable practices in the American North, or independence for colonial nations. Racial leaders no longer appealed to the masses, as Garvey once did, to support elite institutions by buying stock and deferring immediate popular needs. Quite the contrary: a Jamaican nationalist in 1940 argued that

> So long as our propaganda for the realization of our immediate task – political independence – remains on the plane of our "inalienable rights" and fails to show the connection between the struggle for political independence and the bread and butter interests of the classes we hope to draw into the struggle, we cannot expect to arouse their serious enthusiasm. We must get our roots deep down in the grievances of these classes and demonstrate clearly that before any real progress can be made in their alleviation, we must first win political freedom.[39]

Even then, it was not easy to convince people. But the ingredients necessary to produce a mass movement were clear in a way they were not during World War One and the 1920s.

NOTES

[1] Theodore Draper, *The Rediscovery of Black Nationalism* (New York, 1970), pp. 48-56.

[2] "Prejudice not Natural", 8 June 1848, in Howard Brotz (ed.), *Negro Social and Political Thought, 1850-1920* (New York, 1966), p. 213.

[3] "An Address to the Colored People of the United States", 29 September 1848. Ibid., p. 210.

[4] Cited in William Ivy Hair, *Bourbonism and Agrarian Protest: Louisiana Politics, 1877-1900* (Baton Rouge, 1969), p. 173.

[5] Cited in Theodore Draper, *American Communism and Soviet Russia* (New York, 1960), p. 324.

[6] "Open Letter", Key West, Florida, 18 January 1919, copy in C-319, National Association for the Advancement of Colored People papers, Library of Congress.

[7] L.A. Gabriel to James W. Johnson, 26 January 1919, ibid.

[8] Robert A. Hill, "General Introduction", *The Marcus Garvey and Universal Negro Improvement Association Papers* (10 Vol. projected: Berkeley, 1983–), I, xxxv.

[9] Cited in "Negro Agitation", 10 December 1919, file 10218-364/16, Military Intelligence Division, in RG 165, Records of the Department of War, National Archives, Washington, D.C.

[10] *Negro World*, 20 May 1923.

[11] Benedict Anderson, *Imagined Communities: Reflections on the Origins and Spread of Nationalism* (London, 1983).

[12] Owen Charles Mathurin, *Henry Sylvester Williams and the Origins of the Pan-African Movement, 1869-1911* (Westport, Connecticut, 1976), pp. 76, 165-69.

[13] Men similar to the group in London were members of the Frankfurt Parliament of 1848 and the Indian National Congress prior to 1918.

[14] Wilson J. Moses, *The Golden Age of Black Nationalism, 1850-1925* (Hamden, Connecticut, 1978).

[15] "Marcus Garvey, The British West Indies in the Mirror of Civilization", in John Henrik Clarke (ed.), *Marcus Garvey and the Vision of Africa* (New York, 1974), pp. 77-82.

[16] Marcus Garvey, "Universal Negro Improvement Association: Address Delivered by the President at the Annual Meeting", Kingston *Daily Gleaner*, 26 August 1915.

[17] Ida Wells-Barnett, *Crusade for Justice: The Autobiography of Ida B. Wells*, ed. Alfreda M. Duster (Chicago, 1970), p. 391; Amy Ashwood Garvey, "Marcus Garvey: Portrait of a Liberator" (typescript in possession of Lionel Yard, Brooklyn, New York), 11-12; *Negro World*, 1 March 1919.

[18] *Baltimore Afro-American*, 20 July 1923.

[19] Judith Stein, *The World of Marcus Garvey: Race and Class in Modern Society* (Baton Rouge, Louisiana, 1986), pp. 64-68.

[20] Cited in "Negro Activities", 20 October 1919, file 10218-364/12, MID, RG 165.

[21] J. Ayodele Langley, *Pan-Africanism and Nationalism in West Africa, 1900-1945* (Oxford, 1973), pp. 91, 127,129; G.O. Olusanya, "Notes on the Lagos Branch of the Universal Negro Improvement Association", *Journal of Business and Social Studies* (Lagos), I (1970), pp. 133-43.

[22] "Negro Agitation", 17 October 1919, file 10218-364/11, and 7 November 1919, file 10218-261/50, MID, in RG 165.

[23] George Goodwyn to R. Moton, 19 August 1920, R.R. Moton papers. Tuskegee Institute.

[24] Thus, neither Garvey's Midwest tour nor aide William Ferris's New England campaign had yielded much in early 1921, a time when the nation was still suffering from the sharp post-war depression. Ferris reported that people could not "invest money in extraneous business propositions". *Negro World*, 19 February 1921.

[25] R.R. Moton to Ida A. Tourtellot, 4 October 1920, Phelps-Stokes Fund papers, Schomburg Center for Research in Black Culture.

[26] W.E.B. Du Bois, "Marcus Garvey", *Crisis*, XXI (December 1920), pp. 58-60.

[27] Marcus Garvey, *Negro World*, 11 September 1920.

[28] Harold Williamson to Secretary of State, 25 June 1920, file 850.4, in RG 84, Records of the Foreign Service Posts of the Department of State; report, 2 February 1922, file 2655-q-53. MID, RG 165.

[29] Wallace C. Thurston to Secretary of State, 22 January 1921; Stewart McMillin to Thurston, 29 April 1921, file 840.1, RG 84; A.P. Bennett to Secretary for Foreign Affairs, 9 May 1921, F.O. 371/5684, Public Record Office (London).

[30] "Radicalism and Sedition Among the Negroes as Reflected in Their Publications", in *Investigation Activities of the Department of Justice*, Senate Documents, 66th Cong., 1st Sess., XII, 163-87.

[31] Chicago operative to Mr Kenny, 15 October 1919, file 10218-377/1, MID, RG 165.

[32] *Negro World*, 28 February 1925.

[33] Robert A. Hill and Gregory A. Priro, "Africa for the Africans: The Garvey Movement in South Africa, 1920-1940", in Shula Marks and Stanley Trapido (eds.), *The Politics of Race, Class & Nationalism in Twentieth Century South Africa* (London, 1987), pp. 238-42.

[34] *California Eagle,* 10, 24 September, 29 October, 3, 17 December 1921; see also Emory J. Tolbert, *The UNIA and Black Los Angeles* (Los Angeles, 1980).

[35] *Negro World,* 23 August 1924.

[36] Amy Jacques Garvey (ed.), *Philosophy and Opinions of Marcus Garvey* (2 vols., 1926; rpr. New York, 1969), II, pp. 135-43.

[37] Ibid., 140.

[38] A.L. King to Marcus Garvey, 19 December 1935, UNIA Papers, Schomburg Center.

[39] Ken Post, *Strike the Iron: A Colony at War: Jamaica, 1939-1945* (2 Vols., The Hague, 1981), I, 122.

Garveyism: Organizing the Masses or Mass Organization?

William A. Edwards
Formerly in the Department of Black Studies and Sociology
University of California – Santa Barbara, USA

ANY DISCUSSION of the Garvey movement is likely to refer to it as a mass movement. While there is general agreement that it *was* a mass movement, the term is more likely to be descriptive than analytic. That is, it is used both as a quantitative and qualitative description of those who can be considered Garvey followers. It is frequently used as a pejorative term by the critics of the Garvey movement. Sociologically, the term refers to spontaneous behaviour by a large number of people towards some goal. In its narrowest sense, it refers to those who were actual members of the Universal Negro Improvement Association.

Why should a designation concern us if it is presumed to be commonly understood? Is it merely quibbling over distinctions that have no significance outside of academic discourse? In the case of the Garvey movement, the term mass movement takes on an inclusive meaning that lies at the core of a nationalist ideology. Its designation refers to more than a distinction of kind and numbers, but compels our attention to that aspect of the movement that defined its historical significance.

A mass is defined as a collectivity of individuals characterized by their heterogeneity, anonymity and lack of organization.[1] In a political context, the term "masses" refers to those excluded from power and privilege in a political order. Garvey made extensive use of both the sociological and political meanings of the term when he variously referred to Blacks as "scattered Ethiopia" and "400,000,000". While these constituents may have lacked organization and were collectively excluded from power and privilege, Garvey did not conceive of them as heterogeneous or anonymous regarding their birthright or their destiny. Thus, the prevailing designations of "mass movement" do not facilitate a clear understanding of the Garvey movement.

Garvey's perception of the black "masses" and the universal application he made of the term were efforts to give his movement a rationality which is often slighted in an analytic context. While the movement was an example of a mass organization, Garvey's universalism gave it the texture of an organization of masses. This distinction seems especially relevant for a conceptual view of the Garvey movement and its appeal. Before taking up this issue at greater length, a brief comment on nationali and consciousness is considered as a backdrop for further development.

As a social movement, the Garvey movement demonstrates the essential chara teristics of any movement. It was a form of collective action designed to resolve conflicting status situation, define or redefine a sense of identity, and create a mo satisfying and acceptable social order. Largely considered a movement of redem tion or revitalization, the Garvey movement was also a movement of resistance. I this sense, resistance meant a willingness to defy status relations with a domina power. For Garvey, resistance carried with it the implication that the collective de tiny of a race depended upon its capacity to coalesce racial consciousness into liberation strategy in defiançe of a dominating power.

Race consciousness, in the Garvey context, was synonymous with the "we-co sciousness" associated with the transition from an unorganized to an organized stat It was the necessary precondition for collective action. It was also the preconditio that defined the rational basis for collective action. Whether or not Garvey was awa of it (there is no evidence to conclude that he was), he was making an application a sociological idea formulated by Franklin Giddings.[2]

Garvey's model of a universal mass assumed that a common racial heritage woul provide the groundwork for collective organization. His nationalism was not th result of an identification with an existing nation-state, but the result of race co sciousness creating the nation-state. The nation-state would be the creation of people endowed with a sense of universal connection and common destiny. Garve saw the rationale of his movement in the emergence of a "new Negro", who woul sense the call of destiny and seize the mandate for organization.

An Indigenous Basis for Organization

GARVEY'S PERCEPTION of a universal mass of Blacks with a common raci heritage suggested more than a common basis for organization. His rhetorical us of divine destiny embraced the idea that each racial group was endowed with natur gifts. Although he did not necessarily spell out these gifts, Garvey clearly believe that the foundation of liberation resided within each racial group. Thus his call, "U You Mighty Race, You Can Accomplish What You Will", was a challenge to recog nize that there was an indigenous basis for organization. Nationalism was therefor not merely a response to an oppressive condition, but a compelling characteristic o racial and national groups. Garvey's view of the nationalist movement refutes in pa the argument that black nationalism is nothing more than a response mechanism t oppression. His contention suggested that nationalism is a latent aspect of racia groups.

Garvey's application of consciousness attempted to merge a collective sense o commonalty with a recognition of an inherent capacity for mobilization. Althoug he admired the accomplishments of the British, he challenged Blacks to rise to th same level of development. Just as a sense of collective consciousness and interes were the driving forces behind the success of the British, the same would be true fo Blacks. With a strong sense of consciousness and collective interest, Garvey believe it was no more irrational for Blacks to be nationalist than it was for the British, the Irish, the Jews, or the Germans. The logical extension of Garvey's thinking meant that nationalism in its purest form was racial in nature. The redemption of the race and Africa could, therefore, only be accomplished through a racial movement based upon the unique endowment of Blacks themselves.[3]

Garvey's use of the analogy with the British, the Irish, the Jews, and the Germans may have served his purpose politically, but it calls into question the comparison of a racial group with a national or cultural group. Notwithstanding their racial identification, Garvey mistakenly equated nationality with his belief in universal racial nationalism. Did the British act out of a sense of white racial nationalism or as Britain? Was Irish nationalism an expression of racial nationalism or nationality? These questions could not easily be answered by Garvey within the framework of racial nationalism. Neither could his belief in racial destiny explain these expressions. These disparities remained unresolved with Garvey; however, he resolutely maintained his commitment to the idea of a universal racial nationalism among Blacks.

Conceptualizing the Masses

THE FIRST INDICATIONS of Garvey's perception of a universal mass occurred during his first years in England.[4] His association with Dusé Mohammed Ali, African students and workers on the European continent, and fellow West Indians considerably broadened his view of Blacks in the world. He acknowledged his enlightenment in his essay, "The Negro's Greatest Enemy". More than anything else, Garvey envisioned a racial nation comparable to the nations of Europe and Asia. To effect this nation-state, a universal bond of brotherhood had to be established. In proposing this measure Garvey attempted to exceed, at least ideologically, any previous pan-African schemes. The first organizational name he proposed suggested the scope of his thinking – the Universal Negro Improvement Association.

Upon his return to his native Jamaica in July 1914, Garvey's enthusiasm for a universal brotherhood confronted the realities of racial heterogeneity. The two years he spent in England in 1912–1914 and the enlightenment he had gained apparently overshadowed the political education he acquired from his early mentor, Robert Love.[6] Even his inclusion of the word "negro" in the title of his new-founded organization ushered in an avalanche of criticism and rejection from segments of the Jamaican population.[7] While his vision may have been broad and pan-African in scope, an examination of his early speeches in Jamaica and the United States indicates that Garvey used the term "masses" to refer to both an underclass and a racial collectivity. However, Garvey quickly discovered from his first organizational attempt that racial nationalism was not self-evident among Blacks. As Amy Jacques Garvey recalled, "Garvey spent many months of hardships and disappointments by not getting the masses to unite and co-operate for their own good, but still he plodded on".[8]

Garvey indeed plodded along, frustrated but undaunted. In one of his earliest publications after the formation of the Jamaica chapter of the UNIA, Garvey concluded an open appeal to West Indians by saying, "Let us from henceforth recognize one and all of the race as brothers and sisters of one fold. Let us move together for the one common good, so that those who have been our friends and protectors in the past might see the good that there is in us".[9]

With very modest success in his first organizational appeal, Garvey turned to Booker T. Washington for assistance in soliciting funding for the support of the Jamaica chapter of the UNIA. In a letter to Washington on 8 September 1914, Garvey submitted an enclosure that was intended to familiarize Washington with his work and the objectives of the UNIA. The initial statement in the enclosure announced "Having organized ourselves into a Society for the purpose of helping the struggling masses of this community to a higher state of industry and self-appreciation, we take the opportunity of acquainting you of our aims, and we hereby beg to solicit your assistance in helping us to carry out our most laudable work".[10]

It is apparent from the above statement that Garvey was mindful of intra-racial class divisions. His description of the masses in this and other statements reveals not only class divisions but the extent to which he believed there existed a lack of race pride. As Garvey viewed it, there were two dimensions to the problem. In the first place, he argued that the disadvantaged and "lowly" among the race were victims of self-deprecation resulting from their particular place in the history of Jamaican society. Second, and perhaps most important, those who enjoyed a relatively high economic status felt little or no sense of moral responsibility to uplift the "fallen of the race". Before he could contemplate universal race nationalism, Garvey was confronted with the harsh reality of the legacy of colonialism. While the race may have existed ideologically as a foreordained group in Garvey's thinking, his organizational success depended upon his ability to bridge enormous gaps in history.

Garvey's appeal to Washington was not without cause. He was undoubtedly familiar with Washington and his influence in the United States. Dr Robert Love, the publisher of *The Jamaica Advocate* and Garvey's early mentor, had published a series of articles on Washington, his philosophy of industrial education and his views on the race question.[12] While employed with Dusé Mohammed Ali, publisher of *The African Times and Orient Review,* during his early years in England, Garvey again was exposed to Washington.[13]

When Garvey spoke of the disadvantaged black masses in Jamaica, he shared not only Washington's belief in self-reliance, he also shared a qualified perception of the need for uplift among their ranks.[14] The black masses, in this context, were perceived as a critical element in universal racial nationalism, but they were also recognized as a stratum with particular characteristics. They, nonetheless, were a part of the destiny ordained for the race.

North to Harlem: Continuity and Conflict

IF THE MASSES WERE to be uplifted and the race and Africa redeemed, the UNIA needed financial solvency. To that end, Garvey looked to Booker Washington and the United States. Although Washington died in 1915, Garvey followed through with his plans for a fund-raising trip to the United States. In the meantime, Washington's death had created a leadership debate and a national scrabble for organizational and ideological direction. Garvey arrived in the United States at one of the most critical junctures facing black Americans and this society during the twentieth century. If Harlem were awaiting a leader, "one done in black preferably", as Roi Ottley proclaimed,[15] Marcus Garvey was not the obvious choice.

Garvey did not enter the United States as the heir apparent to Booker Washington. Nor did he have any intention of thrusting himself into the national debate taking place among black Americans and white liberals. Ideological debates among black Americans were being waged on many fronts. Although Washington's philosophy of gradualism and accommodationism had its converts in the North, it was not a major preoccupation of the mass of black Americans. Economic opportunities, state and national enforcement of civil rights, disfranchisement, and an end to racial segregation and violence were national priorities for black Americans. Ironically, some of the strongest voices for self-help and self-reliance came from the black professional ranks who were trying to secure themselves against a society that segregated them despite their status attainment.[16]

Garvey was very impressed with the entrepreneurial success of black Americans, as well as their business acumen and production of such prominent figures as Booker Washington and Frederick Douglass. In a reflective essay written eight months after his arrival in the United States, Garvey heralded American Blacks as, "the peer of all Negroes, the most progressive and the foremost unit in the expansive chain of scattered Ethiopia".[17] However, as he traveled throughout the country and became more familiar with black America, Garvey began to qualify his applause of the professional class. He later criticized them for what he considered self-aggrandizement and doubted their capacity as race leaders. Despite this criticism, Garvey's statement above attested to his hope for a universal confraternity and for the potential leadership role of black Americans.

As noted earlier, Garvey's purpose in coming to the United States was to raise funds for the Jamaica chapter of the UNIA. He had no well-defined strategy and apparently had not given much thought to race relations in the American context. His first appearance before a Harlem audience was an inauspicious one. He was jeered by the crowd and during the delivery of his speech accidentally fell from the stage.[18] From his earliest initiation to black life in Harlem it was neither apparent that Garvey was a Moses nor that there was some natural affinity between himself and black Harlemites. His oratory contained none of the fiery call for universal racial nationalism that would subsequently characterize him.

A. Phillip Randolph, a well-known Harlem figure and an active member of the Socialist Party in 1916, recalled being interrupted during one of his street corner speeches with a request to allow Garvey to address the crowd. Randolph remembers that he was told that a Jamaican was there who wanted to address the crowd about establishing a back-to-Africa movement in America.[19] Garvey met with little success after his speech, but continued to learn more about the existence of Blacks in this country.

The East Saint Louis riots of 1917 afforded Garvey an opportunity to issue one of his most scathing attacks against racial injustice and the failed promises of democracy.[20] This speech earned Garvey considerable credibility, especially among those Blacks who were willing to affirm his assessment of racial injustice. By

February of 1918 Garvey had reorganized the UNIA and launched a Harlem branch that remained under his leadership until his imprisonment. A new militant voice was now exalting Harlem and black America to unite in a movement of revitalization. Garvey's message of race pride, uplift, and progress carried familiar echoes of nineteenth-century black nationalism. Garvey was not offering anything that was fundamentally new, but he did package his message in such a way that it had tremendous appeal among what was considered the "black masses". He was not afraid to challenge the class divisions that separated this group from the leadership of existing mass organizations. At the core of Garvey's challenge was the inclusive definition he gave to the term "masses", one that embraced Blacks of all strata, colours, and geographical locations.

Mass Organization and the Problem of Reaching the Masses

MASS ORGANIZATION had been a part of black life in America since the eighteenth century. These organizations particularly flourished during the nineteenth century following the Negro Convention movement. The use of the word "African" or the association with Africa frequently characterized these organizations and gave rise to a collective sentiment of racial nationalism.[21] The nationalism of David Walker, Henry Highland Garnet, and Martin Delany included strong elements of Africanism in their ideologies. During the last decade of the nineteenth century, Bishop Henry McNeil Turner sought to merge a strong African sentiment with a call for emigration. The rise of Booker Washington, however, submerged the nationalist agenda and it was not until Garvey's emergence in the United States that nationalism would again occupy centre stage.

Washington's rise to power not only influenced the national agenda regarding black Americans and colonial Africa; his ideology of accommodationism triggered numerous counter-organizational attempts. Among the most prominent of these organizations were William Monroe Trotter's National Equal Rights League, formed in Boston in 1908, and the National Association for the Advancement of Colored People, formed in 1909. In addition to these organizations, numerous small voluntary associations were formed, especially in the Northern states.

Prior to the formation of these twentieth-century organizations and in the wake of the death of Frederick Douglass, T. Thomas Fortune proposed the formation of a mass civil rights organization, the National Afro-American League, in 1887. The first meeting of the League took place in Chicago in December 1889, with delegates from 23 states. Citing the lack of mass support and funding, the League folded in 1893. Disappointed with the demise of the League, Fortune doubted the preparedness of the race for such an organization,[22] but, undaunted, he tried to revive the idea in 1898 with the formation of the National Afro-American Council. But once again the inability to attract the masses caused Fortune to become disenchanted, and he resigned as president of the organization in 1904. Fortune recalled that the organization "... never commanded the sympathy and support of the masses of the people, nor is there, or has there been, substantial agreement and concert of effort among the thoughtful of the race along these lines".[23] In 1923, Fortune would take up the cause of the mases when he served as editor of *The Negro World,* a position he held until his death n 1928. On his association with Garvey, Emma Lou Thornbrough observes, "There s no evidence that Fortune ever became a Garvey convert, but he admired Garvey or his ability to arouse and mobilize the black masses as no other leader had done".[24]

Fortune's comment above was a crucial observation in view of the context and ime of the statement.[25] The period between 1902 and 1915 is often described as the period of the great ideological debate between Washington and Du Bois. Yet overooked in this period was the contribution that Fortune was trying to make to organizational strategy. "There can be no healthy growth in the life of the race", said Fortune, "or a nation without a self-reliant spirit animating the whole body.... This pirit necessarily carries with it intense pride of race, or of nation, as the case may be, and ramifies the whole mass, inspiring and shaping its thought and effort...".[26]

Fortune was calling attention to the key elements that would eventually ignite the Garvey movement in 1918. In 1903, however, his call was unheeded. The leadership struggle that ensued was preoccupied with trying to deflate the enormous influence of the "Tuskegee machine". The leadership struggle was also being waged among a black intelligentsia which found it difficult to overcome class disparities for the sake of mobilizing the spirit that would inspire the "whole body", as Fortune described it. Further, it should be kept in mind that while the black intelligentsia was essentially ocated in the urban North, the vast majority of the black population lived in the South, where they constituted 30 per cent of the population. Of the nearly ten milion Blacks who lived in the United States in 1910, 73 per cent resided in rural areas.[27]

The challenge to black leadership was more than overcoming the gradualism of Washington. Constituting a very small percentage of the black population, the black ntelligentsia was removed from the day-to-day existence of the vast majority of Blacks. Could they depend upon race alone as a claim to leadership? How representative would the "exceptional men" be whom Du Bois envisioned as the leaders of the race? How would the emerging leadership be defined? What role, if any, would race pride and mass appeal have in formulating organizational strategies? These were questions suggested by Fortune's argument. Moreover they were questions which had to be asked in relationship to the realities of black life in the South.

W.E.B. Du Bois, one of Washington's greatest antagonists, hoped that the talented tenth would ideally bridge the gap between the black intelligentsia and the masses. It was this thinking that occasioned the call for the Niagara Conference in 1905. Du Bois's hope was that this gathering would germinate into a movement led by the best and brightest of the race. The movement was to be centred around, "a group of educated Negroes, who from their knowledge and experience would lead the mass. I never for a moment dreamed that such leadership could ever be for the sake of the educated group itself, but always for the mass".[28]

The Niagara Conference never became the vehicle of Du Bois's dream. While the conferees were fully committed to the struggle for equal rights, they never developed a strategy that incorporated the masses. Internal friction and personality clashes militated against the success of the Niagara Movement. Later in his life, Du Bois remained convinced that the idea of a talented tenth among black leadership was a good one, but expressed reservations that it could have easily become a class for itself.

With the demise of the Niagara Movement, most of its members became a part of the National Association for the Advancement of Coloured People in 1909. The dissolution of the movement also postponed, at least temporarily, the organization of a black vanguard which in principle recognized a critical relationship to the masses. The irony is that an experiment in black organizational leadership gave way to a national organization whose initial leadership was exclusively white, except for Du Bois. As the historian John Hope Franklin points out, the presence of Du Bois labeled the organization "radical". Franklin notes: "Many feared that it would be a capricious, irresponsible organization that would draw its main inspiration from the dreamings of the Niagara Movement".[29]

Fortune's prescription for organizational leadership did not receive a hearing within the NAACP. The nationalist sentiment that he expressed was overshadowed by an integrationist thrust. The question of race pride was taken up in part by Trotter, who was a member of the Niagara Movement but refused to join the NAACP because of its white leadership. But Trotter remained in Boston and his influence was most prominent in that city. The nationalist-emigrationism of Bishop Turner had faded and exerted no major influence on the ensuing debate at the start of the twentieth century. By the time of the United States' entry into World War One, the NAACP had established itself as the most influential organization of its kind. Its leadership was white and the direction of the organization reflected the composition of its leadership. A significant portion of the black population was uninspired by the NAACP, especially that segment of the population that could be called the "masses".

Reclaiming Scattered Ethiopia

THE RACIAL AGENDA in the United States during the second decade of the twentieth century was heavily influenced by a number of significant factors. A substantial migration of Blacks from the South to the Northern states intensified competition with immigrants for jobs and living space. Lynchings were accompanied by national indifference. Racial tensions heightened with the appearance of D.W. Griffiths' film *The Birth of a Nation* in 1915. Internationally, the spread of imperialism and the European scrabble for the resources of Africa forged a critical assessment of democracy in the world arena. The return of black soldiers from the war to a climate of racial discrimination dashed the hopes that racial equality would be an imminent reality.

Garvey was mindful of the implications of international events on the plight of Blacks everywhere. His vision of universal racial nationalism suggested to him and the collectivity of Blacks that they were faced with a "national question". The colonization of Africa and the treatment of Blacks in England, the West Indies, and in the United States were merely indications that Blacks were not destined to share the white world's view of democracy. Pride of race and consciousness of kind were the imperatives for racial salvation.

Garvey affirmed for the masses of Blacks a reality that they were experiencing. Contrary to those analysts who argue that his movement appealed to the crowd instinct,[30] there was a rational basis for his appeal. Where the masses of Blacks had been excluded from or peripheral to the organizations formed during the twentieth century, Garvey embraced them as no other organization had done. Fortune had seen the necessity for such an endeavour as well as the nationalists of the nineteenth century. Du Bois had recognized the importance of the masses but could not programmatically implement a scheme to attract them. The socialist urgings of A. Phillip Randolph and Chandler Owen received marginal attention. The Communist Party had not yet taken root in the United States. In either case, black workers held a skepticism about the racial tolerance of white fellow workers.

What is important to bear in mind in discussing Garvey's meteoric rise in the United States is that he did not create the conditions for his movement. In the decade in which he entered the United States, the national agenda, as reflected in the presidential election of Woodrow Wilson, gave a clear indication that Blacks could not expect a national commitment to racial equality. Neither would Wilson consent to place before the Paris Peace Conference a platform for human rights and racial justice. The civil rights-integrationist thrust of Du Bois and the NAACP depended upon the benevolence of the national government and a climate of conciliation. The radicalism of Randolph and Owen depended upon the derivation of a working-class consciousness that transcended racial barriers. Despairing of any hope that Whites would change their racial disposition, Garvey proposed that Blacks should "close ranks" among themselves and effect their own agenda for racial salvation.[31]

A persistent theme in Garvey's speeches prior to the first UNIA Convention in 1920 was that a "new Negro" must emerge in the collective sense. "The new Negro is no coward. He is a man, and if he can die in France or Flanders for white men, he can die anywhere else, even behind prison bars, fighting for the cause of the race that needs assistance".[32] Garvey proclaimed the rise of a transformed racial consciousness which would engulf the entire black world. Never in the twentieth century in the United States had the masses of Blacks been addressed as Garvey addressed them in the climate of the post-war years. Throughout the North, West, and rural South, the Garvey message of racial redemption reached an unprecedented number of Blacks, particularly with the newspaper, *The Negro World.* When Garvey launched the Black Star Steamship Line in 1919, it captured the imagination of thousands of blacks, as witnessed by the sale of five-dollar shares.

The phenomenal sale of shares in the Black Star Line and the international reception of *The Negro World* made Marcus Garvey and the UNIA a formidable influence in the United States and the world. As his influence mounted, so did his detractors. While they questioned Garvey's integrity and honesty, they never solidified a movement of race pride and self-determination as he was doing. The criticism that Garvey was offering nothing more than escapism and impractical schemes does not answer the question of why his detractors failed to mobilize the black masses. The criticism that Garvey was a charlatan does not explain the heightened sense of racial pride he engendered. Even Randolph admitted in his reflection on Garvey that "against the emotional power of Garveyism, what I was preaching didn't stand a chance".[33]

The first UNIA Convention, in August 1920, was in part a commencement of an unprecedented movement of pan-Africanism and racial unity. Randolph was correct to point out that Garvey's appeal was not divorced from its emotional power. But such is the nature of social movements. They are not devoid of emotional appeal They speak to the individual's sense of identity and seek to establish a "we-conscious ness". Identity is partly a sense of how we feel internally. Individuals who join o identify with a movement frequently are emotionally attached to the leader. Gar veyism attempted to extend the boundaries of "we-consciousness" and embrac thousands of persons who had previously felt unaffected by existing mass organiza tions. This is not to suggest, however, that emotionalism was the only way to attrac this segment of the black population.

Neither Harlem, the United States nor black America had ever witnessed any thing like the 25,000 who attended the first UNIA Convention. For one month delegates met to establish a racial agenda for the world community of Blacks. It ma have been an audacious endeavour, but many of the points adopted in the Declara tion of Rights of the Negro Peoples of the World[34] have figured prominently in dis cussions of race relations in the 1970s and 1980s. The fact that these points are stil relevant is testimony to the substantive basis of the issues discussed during that firs UNIA Convention.

Marcus Garvey offered no radically new ideas to the world. Practically every thing he said had already been said by someone before him. He was a student of his tory and borrowed liberally from seemingly contradictory sources. He moulded . brand of nationalism and a vision of racial redemption that captured worldwide at tention. Whether he could have been successful in leading millions of Blacks t Africa is a moot question. His claim to have been a spokesman for "400,000,00 Negroes" is debatable. To reduce the participation of millions of Blacks in a world wide movement to emotionalism or deception trivializes the significance of socia movements. It also begs the question of the rational means through which individual and groups try to manage the circumstances of their lives and project a new vision o the future. In the final years of his life, Garvey continued the message of universa racial nationalism. "We call upon the Negro peoples [*sic*] of the world to close ranks to stand together, to be in every way united to meet the future with a policy base upon self protection, the maintenance of that power that is necessary to safeguar our racial rights".[35]

Although a critic of Garvey, Claude McKay was moved to conclude: "Marcu Garvey's influence over Afro-America, native Africans and people of African de scent everywhere was vast. Whether that influence was positive or pervasive and in direct, Negroes of all classes were stirred to a finer feeling of racial consciousness".[3

NOTES

[1] See Herbert Blumer's discussion of the mass in his essay "Elementary Collective Groupings", in *Prin ciples of Sociology,* 3rd edition, ed. Alfred McClung Lee (New York: Barnes.& Noble, 1969), pp 85-89; J.B.S. Hardman, "Masses", in *Encyclopedia of the Social Sciences,* Vol. 10, eds. Edwin Selig man and Albert Johnson (New York: Macmillan Co., 1933), pp. 195-201.

[2] See Giddings's formulation of the term "consciousness of kind" in his book *The Principles of Sociol ogy* (New York: MacMillan Co., 1916).

[3] The idea of an indigenous foundation for a racial movement has been given theoretical development in recent discussions of the Civil Rights movement. None of the writers, however, argue that biological endowment is a basis for movement organization. See, for example, Doug McAdam, *Political Process and the Development of Black Insurgency, 1930-1970* (Chicago: University of Chicago Press, 1982); Aldon Morris, *The Origins of the Civil Rights Movement* (New York: The Free Press, 1984); Michael Omi and Howard Winant, *Racial Formation in the United States: From the 1960s to the 1980s* (New York: Routledge & Kegan Paul, 1986).

[4] The best discussion of Garvey's first years in England can be found in Robert Hill, "The First England Years and After, 1912-1916", in *Marcus Garvey and the Vision of Africa,* ed. John Henrik Clarke (New York: Vintage Books, 1974), pp. 38-70.

[5] *Current History,* 18 (September 1923), pp. 951-957.

[6] Garvey's early affiliation with Dr Robert Love is discussed in two important essays by Rupert Lewis. See Rupert Lewis, "Robert Love: A Democrat in Colonial Jamaica", *Jamaica Journal,* 11 (August 1977), pp. 58-63; Rupert Lewis, "Garvey's Forerunners: Love and Bedward", *Race & Class*, 28 (Winter 1987), pp. 29-40.

[7] In a lengthy letter to Robert Moton, president of Tuskegee Institute, following Booker Washington's death on 29 February 1916, Garvey bemoaned the inter-racial and intra-racial state of affairs in Jamaica. He especially denounced intra-racial divisions that militated against effective racial organization to improve the lot of the disadvantaged and dispossessed.

[8] Amy Jacques Garvey, *Garvey and Garveyism* (Kingston: A. Jacques Garvey, 1963), p. 13.

[9] "Talk with Afro-West Indians", in *Marcus Garvey and the Vision of Africa,* ed. John Henrick Clarke, pp. 86-87; Robert A. Hill (ed.), *The Marcus Garvey and Universal Negro Improvement Association Papers,* Vol. 1 (Berkeley: University of California Press, 1983), p. 61.

[10] Robert A. Hill (ed.), *The Marcus Garvey and Universal Negro Improvement Association Papers,* Vol. I, p. 68.

[11] Marcus Garvey, "The Negro's Greatest Enemy", p. 952.

[12] Rupert Lewis, "Garvey's Forerunners: Love and Bedward", pp. 35-36; Rupert Lewis, *Marcus Garvey: Anti-Colonial Champion* (London: Karia Press, 1987), p. 34.

[13] The August 1912 issue of *The African Times and Orient Review* published an article entitled, "Tuskegee Institute", with a Booker Washington byline, outlining the development and programme of industrial education at the school. A month prior to the appearance of this article, *The African Times and Orient Review* published a report, "The Negro in Conference was not primarily a race meeting. It was a meeting of all those who were interested directly or indirectly in the practical work that is being done to educate and uplift the Negro, either in Africa or America", p. 11.

[14] Washington clearly demonstrated a distance between himself and the black masses whom he proposed to uplift. See Louis Harlan, *Booker T. Washington: The Making of a Black Leader, 1856-1901* (New York: Oxford University Press, 1972), pp. 302-303.

[15] Roi Ottley, *New World A-Coming* (Cambridge, Mass.: The Riverside Press, 1943; reprinted New York: Arno Press and The New York Times, 1968), p. 70.

[16] See August Meier, *Negro Thought in America, 1880-1915: Racial Ideologies in the Age of Booker T. Washington* (Ann Arbor: University of Michigan Press, 1969), especially Chapters 8-9, pp. 121-157.

[17] Marcus Garvey, "West Indies in the Mirror of Truth", in *Marcus Garvey and the Vision of Africa,* ed. John Henrik Clarke, p. 89; Robert A. Hill (ed.), *The Marcus Garvey and Universal Negro Improvement Association Papers,* Vol. 1, p. 198. The original version of this essay appeared in *The Champion Magazine,* January 1917, pp. 167-168.

[18] An account of Garvey's first public address is given by W.A. Domingo in Robert A. Hill (ed.), *The Marcus Garvey and Universal Negro Improvement Association Papers,* Vol. 1, pp. 190-192.

[19] Randolph's account appears in Jervis Anderson, *A. Phillip Randolph* (New York: Harcourt Brace Jovanovich, Inc., 1972), p. 122.

[20] Garvey's speech took place at Lafayette Hall in New York City on 8 July 1917. The speech is printed in Robert A. Hill (ed.), *The Marcus Garvey and Universal Negro Improvement Association Papers,* Vol. 1. pp. 212-220.

[21] Sterling Stuckey has written a recent and compelling account of the relationship between the rise of nationalism among black Americans and the links with Africa. See *Slave Culture* (New York: Oxford University Press, 1987), especially Chapter 4.

[23] T. Thomas Fortune, "The Negro's Place in American Life at the Present Time", in Booker T. Washington *et al., The Negro Problem* (New York: Arno Press and The New York Times, 1969; reprinted, pp. 216-217.

[24] Emma Lou Thornbrough, "T. Thomas Fortune: Militant Editor in the Age of Accommodation", p. 35.

[25] Fortune's statement is extracted from the same book in which Washington reiterates his stand on the primacy of industrial education and Du Bois makes his famous declaration on the "Talented Tenth". The year in which these essays were published was 1903, shortly after Du Bois issued his seminal work, *The Souls of Black Folk.*

[26] T.Thomas Fortune, "The Negro's Place in American Life at the Present Time", p. 213.

[27] US Department of Commerce, Bureau of the Census, *The Social and Economic Status of the Black Population in the United States: An Historical View, 1790-1978,* Special Studies Series, p. 23, No. 80, 1979.

[28] W.E.B. Du Bois, "My Evolving Program for Negro Freedom", in *What the Negro Wants,* ed. Rayford Logan (Chapel Hill: University of North Carolina Press), p. 38.

[29] John Hope Franklin, *From Slavery to Freedom,* 4th ed. (New York: Alfred Knopf, 1974), pp. 328-329.

[30] See, for example, E. Franklin Frazier, "Garvey: A Mass Leader", *The Nation,* 18 August 1926, pp. 147-148; E. Franklin Frazier, "The Garvey movement", *Opportunity,* November 1926, pp. 346-348.

[31] Garvey used the term "close ranks" in a speech delivered in Newport News, Virginia. See *The Negro World,* 1 November 1919. The term was an obvious reference to Du Bois, who urged Blacks to "close ranks" in support of the war effort. His editorial of the same title is printed in *The Crisis,* July 1918.

[32] *The Negro World,* 14 June 1919.

[33] Randolph, quoted in Jervis Anderson, *A. Phillip Randolph,* p. 137.

[34] "The Declaration of Rights of the Negro Peoples of the World" can be found in Amy Jacques Garvey (compiler), *Philosophy and Opinions of Marcus Garvey,* Vol. 2 (London: Frank Cass, 1967), pp. 135-143. An extensive account of the first UNIA Convention is presented in Robert A. Hill (ed.), *The Marcus Garvey and Universal Negro Improvement Association Papers,* Vol. 2, pp. 476-656.

[35] "A Call to Action", in *The Black Man,* August 1937.

[36] Claude McKay, *Harlem: Negro Metropolis* (New York: Harcourt Brace Jovanovich, Inc., 1968), p. 177.

Garveyism and Race in Jamaica and Cuba

Garvey's Perspective on Jamaica

Rupert Lewis
Department of Government
University of the West Indies, Mona, Jamaica

MARCUS GARVEY made his name in the United States in the 1920s. His travels, the Universal Negro Improvement Association's organizational work, the Black Star Line, his newspapers, especially *The Negro World,* considerably enhanced his reputation in the Caribbean as an outstanding political leader of black people. However, American scholarship on the Garvey movement from the time of E.D. Cronon's book has a strong tendency to dismiss the post-1927 years.[1]

Race and Class Consciousness

FAILURE TO TAKE into consideration Garvey's response to the Caribbean, Jamaica in particular, robs any scholar or writer of a rich terrain of thought and action where we see Garvey coming to grips in his analysis with race and class factors. In 1916 he made a valuable sociological analysis in a letter to Major R.R. Moton of Tuskegee. Garvey wrote:

> Jamaica is unlike the United States where the race question is concerned. We have no open race prejudice here, and we do not openly antagonize one another. The extremes here are not between white and black, hence we have never had a case of lynching or anything so desperate. The black people here form the economic asset of the country, they number 6 to 1 of colored and white combined and without them in labor or general industry the country would go bankrupt.
>
> The black people have had seventy-eight years of Emancipation, but all during that time they have never produced a leader of their own, hence they have never been led to think racially but in common with the destinies of the other people with whom they mix as fellow citizens. After Emancipation the Negro was unable to cope intellectually with his master and per-force he had to learn at the knees of his emancipator.

> He has, therefore, grown with his master's ideals and up to today you will find the Jamaican Negro unable to think apart from the customs and ideals of his old time slave masters. Unlike the American Negro, the Jamaican never thought of race ideals, much to his detriment, as instead of progressing generally, he has become a serf in the bulk, and a gentleman in the few.[2]

The relatively low level of racial consciousness in Jamaica is one of the areas that preoccupies Garvey in his Jamaican writings. For Garvey, "the Jamaican Negro has been sleeping much to his loss, for others have gained on top of him and are still gaining".[3]

Colonial ideological policy consistently debased Africa as well as people and things African. The future, the colonizer claimed, belonged to Europe. Hence colonial subjects were made to identify progress with the ideals of their master. In the process of the formation of Jamaica as a nation the negation of Africa and blackness has been constant. And so has the resistance to it by black people.

Garvey's writings on race consciousness can best be understood as a response to the racial traditions embodied in the work of the Jamaica-based planter-historian Bryan Edwards, in the eighteenth century, and of Jamaica's first novelist, Herbert George de Lisser. Edwards, in his work on Haiti, which was published in 1797 during the revolutionary upheavals, frequently described the African population as savage. This image marked the colonial mind, so slavery was portrayed as civilizing. Rights naturally did not apply to Blacks. Moreover not only was economic exploitation the lot of Blacks, but contempt and degradation were attached to the race. A little more than a century later, de Lisser, who wrote an entire novel ridiculing the Garvey movement,[4] repeated the same clichés. In his book entitled *Twentieth Century Jamaica* (the introductory chapter was titled "Jamaica's Future: with England, Canada or the United States"), published in 1913, de Lisser wrote:

> Not more than a century has passed since the work of Christianizing the people of Jamaica was begun; at the beginning of 1800 the island was practically heathen. A great number of the people then living had been brought from Africa, most of the slaves born in the country had African parents; and it is a favorite saying among the white men who have lived in the Dark Continent that only a sheet of fine paper divides West Africa from Hell.[5]

De Lisser was Jamaica's Kipling and he set to work to shape national consciousness in a colonial way in a society where 630,181 Blacks, 15,605 Whites, and 163,301 Coloureds constituted the main ethnic groups. The two others were East Indians (17,380) and Chinese (2,111). For him, insofar as Jamaica was civilized, it was English. De Lisser said that Jamaica bore the indelible impress of English influence and that Jamaicans were proud of their connections with the British Empire. The truth is that most people were. So when de Lisser came to write Jamaican history through his novels, he portrayed that to be black was "to be savage at heart".[6] Paul Bogle, leader of the 1865 rebellion and later a national hero, was described as being "a brave man. But underneath the veneer of his religion lay deep the superstitions of the African savage".[7] Later on, the Jamaican writer Vic Reid, in his novels written between the 1940s and 1980s, provided an eloquent answer to de Lisser's racist prejudices. In a 1981 interview, Reid said: "The whole reason for my writing, the whole reason, is to have the black people proud of themselves and their history".[8] Reid's outlook and writings, however, are not characteristic of mainstream thinking among the Jamaican cultural intelligentsia of his generation. Mainstream thinking of the black middle class in Garvey's time was reflected in the reply of the prominent black educator D.T. Wint to Garvey's 1929-30 campaign speeches:

> Garvey said the labouring man should get 4/- per day with an eight hour day. Could the smaller people who had to employ labour send such an impossible man to the Council? If Garvey wants to go to Africa, let him go, but it is an insult to every Jamaican to tell him he should go back to African savagery – to darkest Africa – Garvey's Mecca.[9]

So we have come full circle from the African savagery of Bryan Edwards to that of D.T. Wint.

Garvey's newspaper criticized the Euro-centric bias of de Lisser's magazine. In *Blackman,* on 10 December 1929, Garvey pointed out:

> We are concerned at this moment with a number of photographs of ladies and gentlemen appearing in the magazine.... No doubt the Editor considers only men and women of their complexion are entitled to be regarded as representatives of Jamaica. What a misrepresentation! What an injustice to the Negro of Jamaica – full-blooded and otherwise.... We write on this occasion, to give a gentle reminder to those who have always attributed the fomentation of racial prejudice to the black man alone. In this instance it is quite perspicuous that there can be no reconciliation for the attitude of any Jamaican who would publish a book depicting the life [*sic*] Jamaican without the photographs of a single Negro, lady or gentleman – not the technical Negro; but those whose features are clearly and distinctly Negro, and have shone so brilliantly that the island can be justly proud of.... We are quite right in emphatically stating that the colour question is raised first and last by men of the type of the author of *Planter's Punch,* and not from the Negro, whom the blame is invariably placed on; in fact, if he [the Negro] raises the question, even though he is treated with contempt, sneer and derision, he is branded as the instigator of an [*sic*] universal calamity".

The self-assertion of black people, the rejection of the "contempt, sneer and derision", was in Garvey's time as in ours met with the criticism of "black racism". The name Garvey chose for his Jamaican newspaper seems to have created a stir of opposition, if not resentment. And this would have come not only from Whites but also from prominent Blacks. But Garvey defended his decision. The same editorial lambasting de Lisser contended:

> The very name "blackman" offended some people, but for all who will take the trouble to think, the name more accurately bespeaks its origin and its aim than any other that could be suggested.[10]

Thereby Garvey's newspaper stuck to its Afro-centric posture in a Euro-centric Jamaica.

Notwithstanding slavery and colonialism, many Blacks had illusions about England, the so-called "Mother-country". It was as if the racism in the colonies had no connection with the metropole and was generated by purely "tropical circumstances". A column he wrote on Una Marson, the Jamaican writer, is well worth quoting at length, for he uses the experience of racism in London and the bursting of the illusion of "equality" to illustrate a point made in *Philosophy and Opinions*. In that volume he had argued that "a race without authority and power is a race without respect".[11] Being powerless, the basis for reciprocal sanctions against racism was weak. This is not to say that organization and mass actions were not important, but there is a difference between fighting for state power and accepting a position of underdog. The latter was never on Garvey's agenda. Garvey wrote:

> Our countrywoman Miss Una Marson went to England some time ago to be disillusioned. She thought she was going to a country where she would be accepted on equal terms with those who built it, and made its civilization possible. Like most of our race, she thought we have nothing else to do than to project ourselves into the civilization of other people and to claim all its rights. When she found a contrary attitude, she rebelled and wrote some very nasty things about the English. She called them conceited.

Garvey associated her attitude with feelings which had characterized his first London visit in 1912, but he points out that a nation or people have a right to be proud of worthwhile achievements.

> If Miss Marson had gone to England representing a race that had equal accomplishments like the English, then her arguments would be sound but nobody who builds a house, beautifies it and adorns it could have somebody else just walk in and take possession without bearing any of the responsibility for its construction or any of the costs for its adornment.
>
> Miss Marson and ourselves are living in a borrowed civilization. We haven't contributed much to it , if anything worthwhile.[12]

Garvey also criticized Dr Harold Moody, in an editorial in *The New Jamaican,* and here he more succinctly developed his philosophy concerning Western racism. He contended that "the question of race hinges upon the progress of peoples. So long as certain races remain backward their colour will be very marked and very much so with the stamp of inferiority".[13]

Race and power were concepts which Garvey used to argue that advancement for black people was bound up with their struggles for self-determination. In his critical comments on Marson and Moody, Garvey was also criticizing the "white psychology" of the West Indian middle class. Garvey anticipated Fanon's important book *Black Skin, White Masks,* when in 1937 he argued:

> The West Indians generally, have developed more of the white psychology than of black outlook; but gradually, in some of the islands, the consciousness of race is dawning upon the people which may develop to place the competent Negroes there in the right frame of mind to be of service when needed. There is much hope for the West Indies as for anywhere else in the outlook of the Negro toward nationalization [*sic*] and independence".[14]

Garveyism went beyond anti-colonialism to advocate a programme of decolonization. His Jamaican experiences give us a good picture of his political thought and practice. It shows that Garvey was an exceptionally modern and secular thinker, which distinguishes him from some of the more religiously oriented movements – whether these be Rastafarian- or Muslim-influenced. For Garvey, Jamaica must take its place among the "progressive and successful nations of the world". Garvey's June 1921 letter to *The Gleaner* showed that he had given a lot of thought to the problems facing the island. He not only criticized the colonial rulers but tried to identify those factors among the black population which made them compliant. Garvey's method was to hammer away at them. In this respect he was frequently critical of his own people. The political thinking of this letter set the criteria for Garvey's political activities in Jamaica during the years 1929-35. Garvey argued that Jamaica needed to develop a national spirit and was critical of those Blacks who regarded England as the "Mother Country". He said that Jamaica needed a political awakening and it should come from within and not from without.[15] He recommended that "the poorer classes of Jamaica, the working classes get together and form themselves into unions and organisations and elect their members for the Legislative Council. With few exceptions the men in the Council are representing themselves and their class. The workers of Jamaica should elect their own representatives".[16]

Garvey's Economic and Social Reforms

GARVEY CONSISTENTLY represented the interests of the working class, the peasantry, the poor, the middle classes in colonial Jamaica. I have dealt with the role of the People's Political Party in other publications.[17] I would like to comment on the programme of the 1934 Permanent Jamaica Development Convention. The Jamaica Convention was held from 3 to 12 September 1934 in Kingston. The Convention focused on the economic crisis facing Jamaica. The world capitalist crisis of 1929-33 had very devastating effects on the West Indian economies and on the working class in particular. Many of Garvey's articles had exposed the conditions of the masses and had gone on to put forward proposals to ameliorate the conditions. Many were the petitions made to the Governors and to respective Royal Commissions. The Jamaica Convention called for a £10 million loan to be raised for economic and social development of the island. It also made proposals as to how the loan would be paid back.

Always emphasizing education, Garvey said that a university should be established in Jamaica, with a capital of £1 million, "for the higher training and education of those who desire to enter the professions and to prosecute complete academic courses in the Sciences and the Arts".[18]

He called for a land settlement scheme to assist farmers and peasants to secure cultivable lands and that attention be paid to the building of roads and ports to facilitate them. He called for a national steamship line which would facilitate farmers and producers "in transporting their products to the different available markets of the world". He also called for the setting up of trade commissioners and "marketing and advertising agencies in the principal countries where markets are available for the marketing of Jamaican products".

In order to promote and develop native industries Garvey called for the establishment of a Central Industrial Bank. The development of tourism also received his attention when he advocated that £1 million should be used to develop and improve the Milk River Bath and the St Thomas Bath to make them sufficiently attractive to health-seekers, at home and abroad. He also called for the development of seashore resorts. On the issue of social development he proposed the building of housing schemes and the improvement of hospital facilities and the adding of maternity sections to those hospitals that were already established.

The Resolution made specific proposals for repaying the loan. The loan was to be for a period of 40 or 50 years and would be repaid by establishing a sinking fund with interest. Garvey recommended that:

> A special commission of two and a half or five per cent ... be levied as an additional tax or commission on all properties sold in this island or transferred from one owner to the next within the period of the loan and this commission or tax shall not interfere with the death duties or any commission due Government under existing laws on the sale or transfer of properties and where properties have not been sold or transferred for a period of thirty years that the said tax or commission on such unsold or untransferred properties be levied, so that all properties within the period of the loan, will contribute to the repayment of the loan, in that all properties, voluntarily or involuntarily, will have benefited during the period of time by the expenditure of the ten million pounds in the scheme of General Island Development".[19]

These proposals were not Garvey's ideas alone. They were the product of a Convention and reflected the thinking of many who had worked with him during the 1930 election and who had supported him throughout the 1920s. The Rev. E.E. McLaughlin, who was also a Councillor of the Kingston and St Andrew Council along with Garvey, was Garvey's deputy at the Jamaica Convention. Nothing came of the Convention, but the ideas were absorbed by the Moyne Commission and by the political parties formed after the 1938 revolt. The economic, social and political ideas advanced by the Garveyites were the most progressive in the 1930s.

Garvey's Pan-Caribbeanism

NOT MUCH HAS YET been done to highlight the role that Garveyites played in the nationalist movements in the Caribbean in the last five turbulent years of that decade. The sad irony is that when the masses began to move to change their position in society, Garvey was past his political prime and in exile in London. He was a pan-Caribbeanist who had a view of the region as a whole. He did not have the narrow parochialism of so many other Jamaican political leaders who came afterwards. Garvey's regional ideas were sustained because the UNIA had divisions throughout the Caribbean and Central America, he had travelled through the region on several occasions, his newspapers were widely circulated, read and discussed and he had personal ties with people like T.A. Marryshow of Grenada and Captain Cipriani of Trinidad. Cipriani played host to Garvey during the latter's visit there in 1937.[20] In a newspaper article written in Kingston in 1932, Garvey said he was a great admirer of Captain Cipriani and expressed the wish that Jamaica should have men like him.[21]

In editorials and articles Garvey frequently commented on developments in the other English-speaking Caribbean territories. He was an advocate of Caribbean unity. In an article appearing in *The New Jamaican* on 23 August 1932 he commended Grenada, Trinidad, Dominica, and Barbados for standing up as colonial peoples through some of the members of the Legislative Council to protest against the maladministration of their respective colonial regimes. Garvey said that Jamaica could well take a leaf out of the book of these West Indian islands. He described Marryshow and Cipriani as "the bull-dogs of West Indian politics.... They have never been afraid to speak their minds, on behalf of their people, and their people have willingly supported them on every occasion".

In an article on West Indian federation Garvey argued that: "the West Indies were one from the geographical and economic standpoint. We showed that they had a single history of peoples of a common race, not indigenous, but of a solidarity of which there is a deep consciousness that grows and expresses itself in every step of their advance".[22] When he started publication of the *Blackman* newspaper in 1929, Garvey said that he wanted to have a daily newspaper in every important island of the West Indies.[23]

Garvey's conception of the Caribbean was not British. In an editorial on Haiti he stated: "We hope that the day will come when Haiti will be the centre of a group of West Indian nations capable in every respect of taking care of themselves".[24]

Garvey had long been a strong critic of the American occupation of Haiti.[25] In 1930 he advocated that "the best of Negro intelligence of America should migrate to Haiti when things become favourable, to assist in making a model country".[26] These articles by Garvey accompanied others on the struggles being waged, particularly in India. Garvey can count himself as being one of the most consistently aggressive defenders of Mahatma Gandhi in the 1930s.[27]

Garvey, in his role as Jamaican political leader in the 1930s, was a pan-Caribbeanist at the same time that he maintained his firm commitment to the liberation of Africa and the upliftment of black people wherever they were.

Working-Class Agitation

ALTHOUGH GARVEY HAD a high regard for the capabilities of the West Indian intelligentsia, their colonial mentality remained a major political obstacle not only to their individual advancement but to that of the people from whom they had come. In his journalistic agitation of the 1930s Garvey sought to encourage and build working-class organizations and to represent the interests of the workers on a variety of issues. Special attention was also given to West Indian migrant labour in the United States, Cuba and Central America who were being deported and repatriated in their thousands.[28] Garvey seemed to be looking more to the working class to give support to his programmes but also to develop more independently as a class. Garvey was actively involved with the formation of the Jamaica Workers and Labourers Association, which was organized in 1930. Garvey had been elected chairman; T.A. Aikman was vice chairman, S.M. DeLeon secretary, and J.I. Denniston treasurer. One of the first demands made by the JWLA was for the British government to appoint a Royal Commission "to make a thorough investigation of the working classes in the island" (*Blackman,* 26 April 1930). The issues raised by Garvey were a minimum wage, an eight-hour working day, housing and medical attention on the estates, prohibition of child labour, assurance against accident or failing health.[29] The 19 April 1930 issue of *Blackman* was devoted to labour, and in some instances the paper sounded Marxist. An editorial in the 10 June 1929 edition stated:

> The *Blackman* stands for the Emancipation of the working man from the shackles of the capitalists, for the economic progress and liberty of those who supply the muscle and brawn....

Garvey's vigorous pro-labour journalism and activism in the early 1930s helped lay the foundation for the modern trade union movement in the Caribbean.

From the standpoint of social and political theory in the Americas, Garvey in his writings understood very well the inter-relationship between race and class. In an editorial entitled "Labour in Struggle" *Blackman* contended:

> In many, such as the European countries, the question is discussed and fought out on lines of a clear and definite class issue, while the opponents in the struggle, set up the distinctions in varying terms of might against right, rich against poor, strong against weak, etc. In other countries the subject is complicated by the colour and race questions. It is in these places that the Negro enters the conflict, under the conditions intensified by the sentiment and feeling born of these elements – race and colour.[30]

In light of Garvey's strong pro-labour stance it is not surprising that he came out so militantly in defence of the Jamaican working classes when they revolted. Writing from London, he argued:

> The labouring classes of Jamaica have never had anything to be loyal about; they have been among the most brutally oppressed peoples of the British Empire. The employer has no sympathy for the poorer classes.... The classes in the island are visibly drawn. The man with money is on the top, and the man without can easily be seen as the unfortunate human being that he is. Money and colour count for more than anything else.[31]

In 1934, Garvey reflected on the state of Blacks in an article marking the centenary of Emancipation in the West Indies. His comments are caustic. He wrote:

> They, like the American Negroes who were freed in 1865, through the good efforts of Abraham Lincoln and the force of national urgencies, were set loose upon the world without a cent in their pockets or a bit of land to settle on that they could call their own. From the beginning they have had to fight their own way up to where they are today. Some have done well but the great majority are almost where they were when they came off the plantations. They are propertyless and almost helpless.[32]

As is so characteristic of his West Indian writings, Garvey emphasizes the socio-economic situation, but he is not just articulating economic advancement for a minority of Blacks within the framework of a British colony, nor is his preoccupation with the economic issue. Garvey goes on to say:

> The millions of Negroes of the West Indies, like the millions of Negroes of the United States, have not yet formulated a programme of racial preservation, nor have they any settled racial outlook. They are still drifting in the white man's civilization.[33]

The Anglo-philistine black and coloured middle-class that led the Caribbean to independence was, in terms of these criteria, profoundly anti-Garveyite. A racial agenda was not a central part of their thinking. They espoused an Anglophile orientation which included a false multi-racialism.[34] Britain was the acknowledged mother country, and black civil servants took their home leave in London. In the 1940s to 1960s the strength of the Garvey legacy rested on Rastafarians and ordinary working people in addition to Garveyite militants in the trade union movement and the political parties.[35] These social forces were, however, marginal to the decision-making process in the economy and in government. Garvey goes on to make an interesting comparison between American and West Indian Blacks:

> ... the organized prejudices against the American Negro have somewhat inspired in him some kind of racial consciousness. This is due to the fact that he is a minority in his country of adoption, while in the West Indies the Negroes are in the majority; and so it would not be good to encourage racial antagonism; therefore the West Indian Negroes have grown up without racial consciousness. This has contributed much to his weakness and his inability to accomplish much by himself. Some think that he is much better off than the American

> Negro in his midst – while the thoughtful think that the American Negro is far better off, because by the prejudice practised against him he has developed an independence in the different walks of life that may lead ultimately to his economic salvation. The two branches of liberated Negroes have grown up separate and apart without any recognition of their kinship.[36]

There is a lot to think about in these observations. Racial issues tend to be avoided in political discourse in Jamaica. No one who is progressive talks about racial consciousness. Class consciousness is acceptable, either from the standpoint of radical politics or as a reflection of social mobility. In Jamaican history since Garvey the only sector to consistently challenge the false multi-racialism has been the Rastafarians. The Garvey movement for a time brought together "the two branches of liberated Negroes" in collective action. That has not been achieved since the 1920s.

In looking at Garvey's use of the term "racial consciousness", one is aware of it less as a reactive, defensive consciousness and more as an assertion of the need for an active and independent programme of racial uplift. Garvey concludes his centenary article by stating:

> When the American and West Indian Negroes get to know their history, there will naturally spring up among them a better feeling of sympathy and comradeship, and when both of them become more conscious of their own origin they will have a greater love for the African from whom they have sprung. It seems very sad that these three units of the Negro race should have lived so long without the conscious knowledge of their relationship. It is hoped, however, that the Universal Negro Improvement Association will do much to cement them together in one bond of racial love and pride that will enable them to extricate themselves from the difficulties that now surround them in the countries of their dispersion.[37]

Garvey's Pan-African vision has been put aside and has been virtually forgotten by the political elites; instead, island nationalisms that eschew racial identity have been encouraged. Yet no doubt due to the high profile of Garvey in the centenary year he has been recognized as Jamaica's most outstanding hero in public opinion polls. In 1983 the polls ranked Jamaica's National Heroes as follows: Sir Alexander Bustamante, 37 per cent; Paul Bogle, 19 per cent; Marcus Garvey, 15 per cent; Norman Manley, 14 per cent. By 1987 Garvey had soared to 56 per cent, Bustamante was at 20 per cent, Manley 16 per cent, and Bogle 5 per cent.[38] A January 1988 survey indicated that 88 per cent of those polled agreed with the teaching of Garvey's life and work in all schools.[39]

The high profiling of Garvey at the official level has been marked by a concern to preserve racial harmony in keeping with the national motto: "Out of many, one people". The idealized view of race relations in Jamaica was a product of the colonial era. Garvey was fully aware of this. An editorial in *Blackman* on 23 December 1929 entitled "The Negro Question in Jamaica" noted:

> The generally accepted theory of the peaceful inter-course of the races and the proud boast, by those who know better, of the entire absence of the race question have only been in the interest of a propaganda which has deceived the world and seven-eights [*sic*] of the people of this country – probably nine-tenths of them.

The editorial went on to speak in a manner that many black Jamaicans would identify with in 1988, the 150th anniversary of emancipation:

> Recent developments have proven the fallacy of the argument and exposed the utter corruption of process and practice which working through deceit and subterfuge merely lulled into sleep and maintained inert the faculties that perceives [*sic*] such evils, and finally building up the consciousness of a people on a false conception and making them to believe their progress depended upon and rightly so, the goodwill and charity of those whom they were taught to revere as their masters in the flesh, and in many instances even in the spirit.

This editorial, though probably not written by Garvey, sums up the colonial mentality which still exists in the 1980s. Implicit in the thinking behind the editorial is the link between dependent psychology, race, class and property relations. In a recent essay, the Barbadian novelist George Lamming shows what this link means in the 1980s. He explains:

> The world of men and women from down below is not simply poor. The world is Black, and it has a long history at once vital and complex. It is vital because it constitutes the base of labour on which the entire Caribbean society has rested; and it is complex because Plantation Slave Society (the point at which the modern Caribbean began) conspired to smash its ancestral African culture, and to bring about the total alienation of man, the source of labour, from man, the human person.
>
> The result was a fractured consciousness, a deep split in its sensibility which now raised difficult problems of language and values; the whole issue of cultural allegiance between the imposed norms of White Power represented by a small numerical minority and the fragmented memory of the African masses: between White instruction and Black imagination. The totalitarian demands of White supremacy in a British colony, the psychological injury inflicted by the sacred rule that all forms of social status would be determined by the degrees of skin complexion; the ambiguities among Blacks themselves about the credibility of their own spiritual history.... Could the outlines of a national consciousness be charted and affirmed out of all this disparateness? And if that consciousness could be affirmed, what were its true ancestral roots, its most authentic cultural base?
>
> The numerical superiority of the black mass could forge a political authority on their own making and provide an alternative direction for

> the society. This was certainly possible. But this possibility was also the measure of its temporary failure.[40]

These concerns, which were so central to the Garvey movement, did not figure prominently on the agenda of the political parties formed in the post-1938 years. The alienation of Garvey in Jamaican society in the 1930s and the marginalization of Garveyite militants throughout the Caribbean in the post-World War Two years was bound up with the process of alienation which Lamming describes, but to add insult to injury, the fractured consciousness and psychological injuries have been elevated to national symbolic status in that the black in the Jamaican flag signifies hardship. The symbolism at the national level has served to reinforce a structure of property relations that was very familiar to Garvey. The dilemmas of being numerically superior and oppressed are at the heart of Garvey's writings on race consciousness in Jamaica. The return to Garvey in the 1980s therefore amounts to much more than a charting of a particular historical period. It is an effort at developing the lines of a national consciousness in keeping with the real interest of the black majority.

Garvey's vigorous political and cultural activities in Jamaica between 1929 and 1934 indicate the relevance of his thinking to modern Jamaica.[41] His work in founding a party in the pre-party phase of Jamaican politics, his development of a wide-ranging programme, which is in essence still relevant in the post-Independence era, his journalism and popular education, and his Afro-centric positions all make him relevant to the agenda of decolonization in the Caribbean. In the wake of the labour riots 50 years ago, Garvey expressed the hope that since 1938 was the centenary of Emancipation, radical changes would be effected in the condition of West Indian workers. The Caribbean working classes of the 1930s, through their mass actions, contributed to a change in the political status of the British West Indian colonies. Were Garvey alive today and assessing the 150 years since Emancipation and the 50 years since the regional labor actions, he would not have to change the basic questions he posed in 1934 and 1938. A retrospective glance at Garvey's Pan-African agenda suggests that his conception of racial consciousness is as important as class consciousness in assisting the process of changing the neo-colonial orientations of most Caribbean states.

NOTES

[1] E.D. Cronon, *Black Moses – The Story of Marcus Garvey and the Universal Negro Improvement Association* (Madison: University of Wisconsin Press, 1955).

[2] Robert Hill, *The Marcus Garvey and Universal Negro Improvement Association Papers,* Vol. 1 (Berkely and Los Angeles: University of California Press, 1983), p. 179.

[3] Ibid.

[4] For an interesting analysis of the Jamaican elite, see Louis Lindsay, *The Myth of Independence: Middle Class Politics and Non-mobilization in Jamaica* (Kingston, Institute of Social and Economic Research, 1981) and Herbert George de Lisser, "The Jamaican Nobility, or the Story of Sir Mortimer and Lady Mat", *Planter's Punch* (1925-26), pp. 9, 22, 23.

[5] Herbert George de Lisser, *Twentieth Century Jamaica,* (Kingston: The Jamaica Times, 1913), p. 107.

[6] Herbert George de Lisser, *Psyche* (London, 1952), p. 39.

[7] Herbert George de Lisser, *Revenge: A Tale of Old Jamaica* (1919), p. 18.

[8] Edward Baugh, "Vic Reid in His Own Words: An Interview", *Jamaica Journal,* Vol. 20, No. 4, November 1987–January 1988, p. 7.

[9] Rupert Lewis, *Marcus Garvey: Anti-colonial Champion,* (New Jersey: Africa World Press, 1988), p. 34.

[10] *Blackman,* 10 December 1929.

[11] Amy Jacques Garvey (ed.), *Philosophy and Opinions of Marcus Garvey,* Vol. 3 (New York: Atheneum, 1927).

[12] *New Jamaican,* 20 February 1933.

[13] Ibid., 9 June 1933.

[14] *The Black Man,* September–October 1936.

[15] Robert Hill, *The Marcus Garvey and UNIA Papers,* Vol. III, pp. 426-427.

[16] Ibid.

[17] See Rupert Lewis, *Marcus Garvey: Anti-colonial Champion,* Rupert Lewis and Maureen Warner-Lewis (eds.); *Garvey: Africa, Europe, the Americas* (Kingston, Institute of Social and Economic Research, 1986); and Rupert Lewis, "Garvey's Significance in Jamaica's Historical Evolution", *Jamaica Journal,* August–October 1987.

[18] *The Daily Gleaner,* 12 September 1934.

[19] Ibid.

[20] Rupert Lewis, *Marcus Garvey: Anti-colonial Champion,* pp. 268-269.

[21] *New Jamaican,* 1 September 1932.

[22] *Blackman,* 17 May 1929.

[23] Ibid., 30 March 1929.

[24] *New Jamaican,* 13 September 1932.

[25] *Blackman,* 16, 17 May 1924; *The Black Man,* 14, 28 February, 3, 17 March, 24 May, 27 September 1937.

[26] *Blackman,* 27 September 1930.

[27] Ibid., 12 April 1930.

[28] Ibid., 1 July 1929, 10 May, 23 August, 1 November, 13 December 1930.

[29] Ibid., 9 January 1930.

[30] Ibid., 21 January 1930.

[31] *The Black Man,* July–August 1938.

[32] Amy Jacques Garvey and E. Essien-Udom, *More Philosophy and Opinions,* Vol. 3 (London: Frank Cass, 1977), p. 92.

[33] Ibid.

[34] See Erna Brodber, "Marcus Garvey and the Politicization of Some Afro-Jamaicans in the 1920s and the 1930s", *Jamaica Journal,* Vol. 20, No. 3, August–October 1987, pp. 66-72.

[35] Research into the Black Power and Civil Rights movement in the United States and the Caribbean may modify this view.

[36] Amy Jacques Garvey, *More Philosophy and Opinions,* Vol. 3, p. 92.

[37] Ibid., p. 93.

[38] *The Daily Gleaner,* 8 July 1987.

[39] Ibid., 16 February 1988.

[40] George Lamming, "*In the Castle of My Skin,* Thirty Years After", *Anales del Caribe* (Havana), 3, 1983, p. 280.

[41] See Rupert Lewis, *Marcus Garvey: Anti-colonial Champion,* for further discussion of the Jamaican years. Also Beverly Hamilton's essay in this volume.

Race and Economic Power in Jamaica

Carl Stone
Department of Government
University of the West Indies, Mona, Jamaica

Introduction

GARVEYISM REPRESENTS an ethnic political movement in search of the liberation of Blacks worldwide. Like other such ethnic movements seeking to remove the bonds of political, economic and cultural oppression from a dominated race, Garveyism has emphasized the importance of Blacks' owning and controlling the economic forces that shape their lives.

Unlike the political movements that led most of the anti-colonial struggles in many Third World countries, Garveyism understood the harsh reality that political sovereignty and independence without real economic power in the hands of Blacks would perpetuate black subordination to minority ethnic control.

This paper attempts to examine the pattern of ethnic economic power in Jamaica to assess how far it has changed since the plantation period. The analysis examines the forces that underpin minority economic power in Jamaica and (by extension) tries to identify the conditions under which the present structure of minority ethnic economic power might change in the future.

Marxists have long understood (quite correctly) that capitalism tends to create a concentration of corporate ownership which produces enormous private power in the hands of those families who own and control the large corporations that dominate production, finance, markets, communications, and technology. The Marxists, however, mistakenly believed that big corporate power would eliminate petty capitalists and small entrepreneurs. Instead of the elimination of petty capitalists or smaller entrepreneurial enterprises, a division of labour has emerged in capitalism worldwide in which large numbers of petty capitalists coexist in an alliance with big corporations, employing considerably more labour than the big corporations and providing an important political and economic support that helps to maintain the capitalist system.

Where the Third World differs from many advanced capitalist countries is that the distribution of power, rewards and opportunities between big corporations, petty capitalists and workers is based largely on ethnicity, which was built into the very fabric of the colonial ethno-class structures.

Ethnicity or ethnic groupings are defined here as aggregates of persons who share an identity based on race, language, religion, tribal ties and core cultural institutions and differentiate themselves from other aggregates who do not share these attributes. The level of ethnic bonding or solidarity varies considerably between ethnic groups. It is influenced by such factors as small size or minority status, the importance of shared cultural institutions, the presence or absence of a strong ethnic ideology, shared experiences of discrimination or persecution, and the existence of intra-ethnic or intra-group networks of mutual support and common socialization or learning institutions that entrench ethnic loyalty.

Ethnic loyalties, where fully developed, often compete with and undermine the territorial nationalism or territorial bonding that seeks to channel citizens' loyalty around membership in a territorial state. Strong ethnic loyalties cut across national territorial boundaries and create transnational alliances, linkages and ties between members of the same ethnic group who belong to different nations.

Garveyism aspired towards creating a transnational or international definition of black ethnic bonding which challenged the established territorial nationalism of the Jamaican state. The idea of multi-racialism and of creating a society that denied the validity of ethnic bonding was a deliberate attempt to weaken the potential for black ethnicity to emerge as a central reference for political identity and political action among the majority of the black population in Jamaica.

The calls to ethnic bonding and solidarity among subordinate and oppressed ethnic groupings in colonial societies were inherently subversive of the power structure and the status quo because many of these societies were controlled by tight ethno-class structures of power built on top of a racial economic division of labour.

Europeans owned most of the wealth-producing assets in the colonial economy. The indigenous populations were allowed to engage in small-scale peasant farming on the fringes of large white-owned plantations but were mainly relegated to providing cheap labour for the white settlers in the expanding corporate economy. Where this posed problems, intermediary racial groups (Chinese, Indians, etc.) were brought in to fill the gaps in labour supply. As export staples increased the wealth base of the colonial economy and as some diversification into minerals, tourism and manufacturing increased that wealth base further, commerce and services expanded. This opened up opportunities for small-scale capital and smaller entrepreneurial firms to operate alongside the large white-controlled corporations.

The white settlers and the colonial administrations facilitated the intermediary ethnic groups' grasping of these business opportunities. In some cases migration inflows from an even more diverse set of intermediary ethnic groups flooded the opportunities for small-scale capitalism. These migrating ethnic groups either had prior traditions or experience in commerce (the Chinese, the Lebanese, the Jews, etc.) or had the advantage of strong extended family systems (the Chinese, the Indians, etc.) that facilitated rapid capital accumulation.

As some of these multi-ethnic Third World countries achieved political independence, their societies were stratified sharply between powerful Whites who controlled plantations and big corporations, an intermediary grouping of minority ethnic groups who dominated petty capitalist and small entrepreneurial sectors, and the majority ethnic group that comprised most of the wage labour force and most of the small peasant farmers.

Several countries in East Africa and Asia evolved according to this pattern. The granting of independence gave political power to the majority ethnic groups. The economically dominant Whites had hoped for the cementing of a partnership in which the majority ethnic group managed the state and occupied the government bureaucracies while the Whites maintained their control over the big corporations and the intermediary ethnic groups dominated smaller scale entrepreneurial activity. But political power in the hands of the ethnic majorities created pressures on both the Whites and the intermediary racial minorities to share economic power with the majority.

Where the Whites retreated in the face of insecurities created by strong indigenous nationalism, demands for greater state control of economic life and the widespread nationalization of foreign corporations, the intermediary ethnic groups expanded from petty capitalism to big corporate power, filling part of the vacuum left by retreating white-controlled corporate capital. In some countries where the Whites built a strong alliance with the political leadership of the majority ethnic groups, they entrenched their economic power after independence (Kenya, Ivory Coast). These economies are run and controlled by white-owned corporations with a supporting cast of middle- and small-scale black entrepreneurs.

In other multi-ethnic Third World countries, the pressures came down on the intermediary ethnic groups, which have often come under severe harassment, violence and racial hostility as ethnic majorities resent their economic dominance (Uganda, Fiji, Indonesia, Malaysia). The tendency has been for the intermediary ethnic groups to be seen as blocking opportunities for progress by the majority ethnic groups.

It is the intermediary ethnic groups rather than the Whites who often become the casualties of enraged and frustrated aspirations by the subordinate ethnic majorities for a better life because they are more visible, are easier targets and have no powerful international backing such as the Whites enjoy (e.g., in Kenya).

Wherever in Third World countries there is a large white settler community, as in Latin America or South Africa, white-controlled corporate capital still dominates as it did in the colonial period. Where that large or strong white settler presence is not in place, white corporate capital has tended to retreat and reduce its presence in the face of post-independence Third World economic nationalism and socialist state economic management trends. This was the case in many African, Middle Eastern and Asian states. In some of these countries, the intermediary ethnic groups assumed economic ascendancy.

In Indonesia, Malaysia and Thailand, ethnic Chinese dominate these economies, much to the resentment of the ethnic majorities. In Mauritius and Fiji it is the Indians who dominate economically. Fiji is a special case in that the Indians now outnumber the native Fijian population, combining economic dominance with a threat of political dominance. As a consequence, the native Fijians have dismantled parliamentary democracy, established a black-controlled military regime and declared the country a republic to keep the Indians permanently at a distance from political power. In Liberia and Sierra Leone, economic ascendancy is in the hands of Lebanese minorities.

The common condition of the inherited Third World ethno-class societies is that the majority ethnic groups tend to be economically powerless or dominated by minority ethnic control of land, capital and wealth-producing assets. This applies as much to the indigenous Indians in Peru, Bolivia and Guatemala as to Malays in Malaysia and Blacks in the Caribbean.

Political independence has not changed that pattern in that most of the new economic power has been appropriated by intermediary or minority ethnic groupings (Chinese, Indians, Lebanese, Jews etc.). The only countries where ethnic majority control of economic power is to be found in the Third World are those which are (relatively) ethnically homogeneous (South Korea, Singapore, Taiwan), those where private control of the means of production has been eliminated (Cuba, North Korea, North Vietnam), and those where ethnic nationalism has created a force hostile to foreign corporations, imperialism and minority ethnic economic power (Iran, Libya, Iraq).

In the case of the Caribbean, the indigenous Indian population was wiped out shortly after European contact. Black African slavery provided the labour force for the colonial plantation economies of the region and thus the Blacks became the majority ethnic group. Chinese and Indians were brought in as intermediary ethnic groups to fill gaps in the labour supply. Later streams of minority ethnic immigration (Jews, Lebanese, Portuguese, Indians, etc.) strengthened the intermediary ethnic minorities.

The racial mixtures between white and black, which created a brown middle class who inherited property and had privileged access to education, formed the beginnings of a minority intermediary ethnic group. Their ranks were expanded by the addition of the other primarily immigrant ethnic minorities (Chinese, Lebanese, Jews, Portuguese, Indians, etc.) who began by establishing a foothold in petty commerce and later used this as a basis to extend their economic power as big capitalists.

As the plantation economies gave way to tourism, mineral exports, and more diverse service and manufacturing activities, it was the intermediary ethnic groups that grasped many of these new opportunities and created a new owning class controlling significant corporate economic power alongside the traditional white planters, whom they largely displaced. It was the merchant class of ethnic minorities that emerged, along with new white-controlled foreign corporate capital in tourism, sugar, petroleum and bauxite, as the new capitalist class in the Caribbean, although they were joined by some survivors among the largely decimated and disappearing older white planter class.

In the Jamaican case, minority economic power and control over corporate wealth reflects a dual dominance of foreign capital and a strong presence of the successful intermediary ethnic-minority families (Jews, Lebanese, Chinese), with only a minority presence of ownership linked to the old white planter class.

The pattern of ethnic economic power in Jamaica has, however, fluctuated and changed over several periods since the nineteenth century. The place of Blacks and that of the intermediary ethnic groups has changed over these periods and is likely to change even further in the future. The main body of this analysis will now give a brief overview of these periods over which there has been a changing racial economic division of labour in Jamaica as a background against which to examine the present ethnic economic division of labour in the country and the conditions under which it is likely to either change or become further entrenched.

Background to the Current Situation

ALL SOCIETIES THAT came under Western European colonization developed ethnic economic divisions of labour, which were used to control and limit the role and power of the subordinate and the intermediary ethnic groups, to perpetuate the power and privilege of the dominant Whites, and to entrench a rigid ethnic hierarchy that limited and regulated competition between the ethnic groups. Order in colonial society was maintained by each ethnic group's knowing its place and its limits and by social and ideological doctrines which were used to legitimize ethnic inequality. Racism was therefore an integral part of all such colonial societies. The colonial state was used to maintain this racial hierarchy.

Change in this ethnic economic division of labour occurs where the following factors emerge either separately or in combination:

(1) Economic crises undermine the hegemony of the dominant ethnic group and create economic space for the increased economic power of the subordinate or intermediary ethnic groups.

(2) The subordinate ethnic groups threaten the status quo by demanding more power and the dominant ethnic groups are pressured into making concessions.

(3) Illegal, informal or underground economic activities (drugs, crime, black marketeering) emerge as a parallel or sub-economy which open up opportunities for the subordinate or intermediary groups to accumulate income and property, thereby removing or reducing blocked opportunities for accumulation that retard the life chances of the subordinate or intermediary ethnic groups in the mainstream or corporate economy.

(4) Rapid economic growth, modernization or diversification expand economic opportunities at a pace that cannot be accommodated by the rigid colonial ethnic hierarchy, and the intermediary or subordinate ethnic groups are allowed to move into positions beyond their traditionally prescribed economic roles.

Significant social and political change (as against cosmetic changes) only occur in these societies when there is some alteration or re-definition of the ethnic economic division of labour due to one or more of these factors.

All of these factors have operated in Jamaica to change the ethnic economic division of labour in the period between the emancipation of the black slaves and the post-Independence period. We can identify four major periods over which some significant changes occurred. These include the following:

(1) The period between Emancipation in 1838 and the Great Depression of the 1930s, when the economy stagnated and the ethnic division of labour re-

mained entrenched, only to be challenged by the political upheavals of th 1930s.

(2) The period between World War Two and Independence in 1962, when ther was very rapid economic growth.

(3) The decade of the 1970s, characterized by economic crisis and class and eth nic conflicts.

(4) The decade of the 1980s, characterized by efforts to reverse and inhibit th changes occurring in the 1970s.

In the hundred years between Emancipation and 1938, the black ex-slaves wer limited largely to small peasant farming, unskilled wage work at less than subsistenc wages, and limited artisan occupations. A few entered professional occupations suc as teaching, nursing, and dispensing drugs, and non-manual occupations such a clerks and policemen.

Blacks were discouraged from entering the field of commerce, which was domi nated by the intermediary ethnic groups (Chinese, Browns, Lebanese, Jews), whil the Whites controlled large-scale plantation agriculture, the dominant area of eco nomic activity. The Indians occupied a position indistinguishable from the black sub ordinate ethnic group.

Table 1. Overall Ethnic Balance in Jamaica in 1938

Group	%
Dominant ethnic group	
Whites (%)	1
Intermediary ethnic groups	
Browns	17
Chinese, Lebanese, Jews	2
Subordinate ethnic groups	
Blacks	78
Indians	2
TOTAL:	100

At the end of this period the overall ethnic balance in the country was as show in Table 1.

Over the period, the plantation economy declined as estates became less profit able, earnings from export agriculture dropped and many Whites sold out famil lands and migrated. As a result, between Emancipation and the 1930s the white population declined from some 3 per cent of the population to one per cent.

The decline of the white-owned family estates and the overall state of depression in export agriculture opened up opportunities for both the Blacks and the intermediary ethnic groups to acquire land. The economic crisis within the plantation sector facilitated the emergence of a vibrant black rural middle class built around medium-sized holdings concentrating on export crops such as banana, pimento, coffee, citrus and, later, sugar (when it was revived). Some of the Jewish and Lebanese urban merchant interests among the intermediary ethnic groups acquired large holdings to recover delinquent loans extended to planter families. This helped to consolidate their growing economic power in the Jamaican class structure. The economic decline of the traditional family estates weakened the power base of the dominant white ethnic group and started the process of class reformation that was to be completed in the post-war period, when the centre of economic power finally shifted from the plantation sector to the urban areas.

Education at the time was an accurate index of class. The level of opportunity for education beyond primary school was a reliable indicator of the extent of ethnic inequality in the society at the end of this period. In the late 1930s, 62 per cent of the Whites had experienced education beyond primary school. Among the more well-off Jewish and Lebanese intermediary ethnic groups, the level of post-primary educational exposure was 60 per cent and 45 per cent, respectively. The level for the Browns and Chinese was considerably lower — 10 per cent and 12 per cent, respectively. The subordinate ethnic groups had the lowest levels of post-primary education, which amounted to 1.5 per cent for the Blacks and 2 per cent for the Indians. The intermediary ethnic groups (and especially the Jews and Lebanese) were therefore much better equipped educationally than the Blacks or Indians to grasp any new opportunities that emerged from the later post-war diversification and expansion of the Jamaican economy.

Only a small proportion of the Chinese and the Browns could be considered part of the middle class, in contrast to the Jews and Lebanese, who were relatively more privileged and were mainly middle class by the end of the 1930s. Only a tiny fraction of the Blacks and the Indians could be classified as middle class. The small black rural middle class that developed invested heavily in educating their children so that they would move up into respectable professions. Their attempt to accumulate through agriculture was frustrated because a large proportion of what should properly have been profit for the farmers was appropriated by urban produce dealers, middle men, traders, distributors, and government agencies and commodity-board bureaucracies. In time, the search for a stronger lever of economic power led the younger generation of this black rural middle class to migrate to the urban areas, where incomes from professions and public service jobs combined with investments in urban real estate became the basis on which they entered the new urban middle class. Black social protests triggered by a new political awakening and economic discontent brought this period to a close by ushering in political changes. These political changes led to representative government, mass parties, strong trade unions bargaining on behalf of the working class, and a gradual drift towards political decolonization and democratization. Political leaders emerged mainly from the brown and black middle class (urban and rural) as power brokers negotiating with the white power structure over demands for change on behalf of the impoverished black masses. Black voters rejected parties and leaders that were visibly linked to the white planter class or the aspiring and upwardly mobile Jewish, brown and Lebanese urban merchant and commercial interests that saw themselves as the new ruling class. The Chinese lacked the ethnic confidence needed to enter the political arena. But the dominant among the intermediary ethnic groups sensed the power vacuum developing in the economy with the retreat of the traditionally dominant Whites and moved in the political arena to use state power to enhance their ambitions to become part of the new ruling class.

With the deep distrust of the more privileged ethnic minorities by the majority Blacks, the black and brown middle-class political leaders assumed the dual role of bargaining for the Blacks while protecting the interests of aspiring and economically powerful intermediary ethnic groups (Jews, Browns, Chinese, and Lebanese) whom they saw as providing the enterprise and entrepreneurial dynamism to move the economy forward. The idea of Blacks aspiring towards economic dominance or playing a key role in the entrepreneurial leadership to usher in the new economic order was not being articulated and had no place in the new scheme of things. Blacks were seen as a sort of supporting cast to provide support for ethnic minority economic leadership. The Blacks would provide the labour power and some of the professional skills, but the means of production was to be controlled by the dominant intermediary ethnic minority groups. That was the unstated and imbalanced economic ethnic power-sharing that formed the foundation of the new Jamaica that was to be shaped along democratic lines. The Blacks subscribed to this unstated understanding by aspiring mainly to move out of low-status agriculture into high-status urban professional jobs.

This dual role undertaken by the new political leaders became the basis for the multi-ethnic, multi-class coalitions around which the Jamaica Labour Party and the People's National Party were established in the period after the political upheavals of the 1930s.

Garveyism or black ethnic consciousness and nationalism, which had emerged in the latter part of the period between Emancipation and the 1930s, was pushed aside in favour of multi-racialism, non-ethnic territorial nationalism, and systematic attempts to politically disinfect the politics of the race issue. Garveyism was suppressed, although it played a key role in the political awakening in Jamaica that occurred as the prelude to the political protests of the 1930s. Concern with race (and especially as it affected the black majority) was seen as subversive of the new order of economic modernization that was promised by the emergent political leaders and that would be led by the intermediary ethnic groups, who were poised to join the white ruling class.

A new economic order was created in the second period in Jamaica, between the end of World War Two (1945) and Independence (1962). The major changes were as follows:

(1) Trade links were shifted from Britain to the USA.

(2) Bauxite, tourism and urban based manufacturing and services replaced export agriculture as dominant sectors of the economy.

(3) There was a large scale entry of US foreign capital and foreign corporations, which strengthened the new capitalist formations.

(4) Dominant economic power shifted from the rural-based planter class to the urban-based intermediary ethnic groups (Jews, Lebanese, Chinese and Browns), who reconstituted a new and powerful capitalism which included the Whites but eliminated the latter's ascendancy and dominance.

(5) Rapid economic growth replaced economic stagnation, but except for tourism and bauxite areas in the rural parishes, the growth was confined to the capital city of Kingston and St Andrew and adjoining urban St Catherine.

(6) New economic opportunities emerged as the public sector and the private sector expanded rapidly, new jobs and occupations were created, and the working class, the middle class and the entrepreneurial class in the growth regions of the country all expanded very rapidly. On the other hand, agriculture stagnated and black rural poverty became entrenched.

(7) Massive rural to urban migration was stimulated by this uneven development. Heightened aspirations for a better life, stimulated by this economic growth, were frustrated for the black majority, leading to a huge exodus of rural migrants to Britain.

How did these changes affect the ethnic economic division of labour in Jamaica? Blacks used the expanded educational opportunities created by the new political leaders to enter the middle class through white collar and professional employment in the public sector and in the independent professions (law, medicine, engineering, etc.). But the new opportunities for Blacks were limited to professional and white collar employment in the public sector and a few positions in the independent professions. This was due to continued racism, which reserved middle- and upper-level positions in the private sector for the upper and intermediary ethnic minorities (Whites, Browns, Chinese, Lebanese, and Jews). Blacks did not see themselves as challenging the dominant and intermediary ethnic groups for economic ascendancy. They were thankful for limited opportunities to move into the professional middle class, working for salaries and thereby escaping from the frustrations and tribulations of rural poverty.

But the rapid growth of the public sector facilitated a significant growth of the black middle class over the period. The one-per-cent black middle class in the 1930s expanded to a 10-per-cent level by the 1960s. The sheer size of the black population meant that Blacks now became the largest ethnic group within the middle class, broadly defined to include middle income earners. The upper middle class or more affluent layers of the middle class, however, was dominated by the non-black ethnic minorities.

Significantly, black protest against blocked opportunities for social and economic advancement was limited to vocal minority political tendencies over the period. These included the Rastafarian movement and the People's Political Party (PPP), which was led by a black lawyer, Millard Johnson.

The early Rasta movement in this period was the most militant political voice advocating black ethnic nationalism and black liberation. The movement openly challenged white dominance in the society and economy and explicitly rejected the social ideology of black inferiority to the majority ethnic group by putting forward the idea of black supremacy.

Millard Johnson's PPP argued the case against anti-black discrimination in private sector employment and for greater respect for Blacks in a society still heavily influenced by anti-Black colour prejudices. Although the PPP attracted widespread interest and frightened the JLP and PNP leadership, the party only earned 5,000 votes out of some 575,000 votes cast by the predominantly black electorate in the 1962 independence elections won by the Jamaica Labour Party. A prominent and well-known Rastafarian candidate (brother Sam Brown) ran against a JLP Lebanese (Mr Seaga) and a PNP black lawyer (Mr Dudley Thompson) in West Kingston, which was then the centre of urban-based Rasta cultural and political influences. Many Rastas refused to vote, defining elections as corrupt Babylon politics. The Lebanese JLP candidate won the election by 52 per cent of the vote and the black PNP lawyer received 46 per cent. Sam Brown obtained 78 votes, or less than one per cent of the vote.

The black middle class distanced itself from the Rasta movement, which became a minority expression of black lower-class racial protest. Middle class Blacks generally denied their black ethnicity and lost any trace of a black identity in the desire to assimilate into the mainly light-skinned upper middle class. The mainstream Blacks gave their support to multi-ethnic political alliances and parties (the JLP and the PNP), which tried to suppress black ethnic nationalism over this period. Indeed, middle class and PNP/JLP hostility to the Rasta movement set the stage for harsh laws against ganja and police harassment of the Rastas. A systematic effort was made to ostracize the movement and to identify it with criminality and mental illness.

For the majority of Blacks rapid economic growth merely heightened their limited aspirations for a better life but led to no real fulfillment of those aspirations. These frustrated aspirations resulted in massive outward migration to Britain and a large-scale exodus from rural to urban areas, which translated rural poverty into urban ghettos and urban poverty.

Some marginal increases in black economic power were achieved through upward mobility into the middle and the upper layers of the public service bureaucracy and the independent professions. Even here, however, the light-skinned ethnic minorities enjoyed most of the positions of greatest power and status in the professions and in the public sector. The non-black minorities dominated private and corporate ownership and middle- and top-level managerial and technical jobs.

The most important change, however, was the growth of a new urban capitalist class dominated by the Jews, the Lebanese and the Whites and to a lesser extent by the Browns and the Chinese. Large new corporate enterprises were created by new and old wealth in banking, insurance, manufacturing, trading and commerce, export agriculture, construction, tourism, and a wide variety of service industries. A modified ethnic economic division of labour emerged but for most Blacks the situation remind unchanged.

The intermediary ethnic groups achieved a significant increase in their economic power that pushed them upwards and out of the intermediary grouping into becoming part of the dominant ethnic grouping in the Jamaican economy. They were the principal beneficiaries of the changes in the Jamaican economy over this second period. Most Blacks were left behind and the seeds of racial and class resentment were sown in this second period, between World War Two and Independence. This set the stage for the political and racial turbulence of the 1970s, which opened up wider opportunities for Blacks to enter the managerial and entrepreneurial classes on an unprecedented scale.

In the third period, which covered the decade of the 1970s, when the PNP was in power, the Jamaican economy experienced continuous negative growth. This decline in national income and production was accompanied by class and racial militancy as well as by the rise of leftist or Marxist articulation of demands for change within the PNP and from the minor Marxist party, the Workers' Party of Jamaica.

Violent crime escalated as the power contention between the JLP and the PNP assumed the character of a street war. Organized gangs engaged in orgies of excessively violent crime against the middle class and the rich, who became victims of rapes, robberies and beatings that seemed designed to settle scores with the privileged classes and ethnic groups.

A younger generation of urban-based youth became highly politicized in the late 1970s, due to the fledgling Abeng and Black Power movements, led by young university intellectuals who emerged as the first generation of the black and brown middle class to openly question the economic hegemony of the dominant ethnic minorities. This new wave of radicalism accused the Jamaican political leaders and the economically dominant ethnic groups of conspiring to perpetuate the poverty and powerlessness of the Jamaican masses.

These new militant political tendencies were incorporated into the PNP under the new leadership of Party President Michael Manley. Their influence and Manley's assumption of intellectual leadership of this new wave of class militancy shifted the PNP towards a leftist course and weakened severely the party's links with the economically dominant ethnic groups, who now saw the PNP as promoting an enemy cause. Party Secretary Dr D.K. Duncan was seen as symbolizing a great political threat to their economic dominance, while Manley was seen as being a captive of the new leftist inclinations and as being manipulated and stage-managed by Marxists in his party.

The PNP's multi-racial and multi-ethnic alliance was fractured by this development and its traditional minority ethnic support stampeded towards the JLP. The PNP therefore became (especially during the second half of the decade) the mouthpiece through which pockets of radical black tendencies were articulated.

The economically dominant ethnic minorities retreated in fear. They exported capital, closed down enterprises, and migrated in large numbers to the USA and Canada in much the same way as the plantation Whites had retreated earlier in the century. The motivating factors were a combination of political threats, increased black racial militancy, political challenges to their class dominance, violent crime, intensified class struggles waged through militant strikes and trade union action, and deep fears that the black majority and their political leaders no longer accepted their economic leadership. The dual class role of the party leaders to negotiate for the poor and protect the privileged, entrenched in the unstated political pact of the early 1940s, was now shattered.

This combination of economic and political crisis and threats dislocated many business enterprises and destroyed the earlier class confidence of the ethnic minorities. This dislocation of the established and economically dominant ethnic groups created unanticipated and unexpected new openings for black entry into the entrepreneurial class and facilitated large-scale entry of Blacks into the middle and upper levels of private sector management.

By the end of the decade the Blacks, who had been largely excluded from top jobs in the private sector, emerged to occupy an estimated 40 to 50 per cent of top- and middle-level technical and managerial jobs in the private sector, alongside the Whites, the Jews, the Browns, the Chinese and the Lebanese. The bigger corporate enterprises (both local and foreign) shifted their policy towards hiring and promoting Blacks into top positions. The rapidity of the change is well illustrated by the commercial banks, which had only a handful of Blacks in clerical and non-manual jobs in the early 1960s. By the end of the 1970s some 60 per cent of the top jobs in banks were occupied by Blacks.

This rapid mobility by Blacks into private sector management was facilitated by several factors. First of all, the supply of qualified Blacks expanded through the growth of higher educational opportunities at the University of the West Indies and the College of Arts, Science and Technology, especially in both management training and the applied sciences. This was augmented by streams of returning Jamaican black students who were educated overseas but were motivated to return home by white racism in Canada, the USA and the UK.

Outward migration by frightened ethnic minorities forced some enterprises to promote Blacks into top positions and many discovered (contrary to their earlier assumptions) that the experienced and educated Blacks could handle private sector management responsibilities. The widening of these top employment opportunities in the private sector motivated many gifted, highly trained and experienced Blacks in the public sector to abandon public sector careers in favour of more lucrative private sector employment. In some cases the hiring of Blacks to fill top positions was a deliberate strategy to defuse the issue of race and questions about racism in the private world of corporate power. Some multinational corporations used this strategy to disguise and reduce the visibility of their foreign presence and to attempt by this symbolism and tokenism to appease and soften local economic nationalism and strident calls for nationalization from radicals by increasing the social and political integration into the Jamaican polity.

Black entry into the urban entrepreneurial class was also significant but less successful. Big corporate capital continued to be monopolized by the ethnic minorities but a small number of large corporate enterprises employing hundreds of workers and owned by Blacks emerged during the period in manufacturing, construction, business services, tourism, commerce and agriculture. The typical new black entrepreneur was a small businessman hiring 20 to 50 workers.

Large-scale emigration of Chinese, brown, Lebanese, Jewish and white businessmen during the 1970s opened up unprecedented opportunities for Blacks to enter the entrepreneurial class in smaller and medium-scale enterprises. The economic and political crisis, by dislocating the dominant ethnic groups, created more economic space, which came to be occupied by the Blacks in the business sector and gave the Jamaican private sector less of a non-black appearance.

The routes to black acquisition of enterprises were many. Some bought out firms that were being sold by migrating owners. Others saw market opportunities left open by collapsing enterprises and went in search of investment funding. Some top-level managers and technical staff bought out enterprises where they worked but which the previous owners had decided to close. Some started entirely new enterprises to meet needs that could not be filled by importation due to the shortage of foreign exchange. The foreign exchange crisis by itself was inducing and motivating increased import substitution and manufacturing activity pioneered by several young and enterprising black entrepreneurs.

Financing was made easier because of the PNP government's take-over of the local Barclay's Bank, which was turned into the state-owned National Commercial Bank. NCB became an aggressive and expansionist lender to small- and medium-scale businesses starting up new ventures and continuing the life of old ventures that would otherwise have folded up. The entry of many middle class Blacks into managerial jobs in the commercial banks opened up access to bank loans to black entrepreneurs in the 1970s.

The 1970s witnessed the most far-reaching changes in ethnic economic division of labour in Jamaica. Blacks became well established within the corporate managerial elite. Black entrepreneurship was finding a foothold in many sectors of the economy alongside the still dominant minority ethnic groups. But perhaps the most far reaching changes occurred at the level of higgler trading and black marketeering on the one hand and illegal production of and trading in drugs on the other.

Foreign exchange shortages created an opening for several thousand women, mainly from the lower socio-economic groups, to establish themselves as higglers in import trading. They travelled overseas, earned or acquired foreign exchange and produced scarce goods, luxury goods, banned goods or whatever the local market needed but the established merchants could not supply. They aggressively took over a considerable market share of the import trade from the established merchants in clothing, footwear, household articles and some small strategic areas of imported food. A minority became very wealthy and bought their way into middle class living, but the majority made enough money to live comfortably and reduce the impact of the economic downturn on their families.

Foreign exchange shortages in the 1970s, combined with the liberalization of ganja use in the USA, motivated a new breed of entrepreneurs to open up the illegal drug trade into the USA on a big scale. Large fortunes were accumulated by many Chinese, brown and black entrepreneurs. They abandoned the restraints and constraints of professions and legitimate businesses to make their fortunes in drugs. A few used drug money to finance or expand legitimate enterprises, thereby providing themselves with access to investment funds they would otherwise be unable to realize by more conventional and legal channels. The lucrative ganja trade helped to finance a significant entry of some Blacks into businesses, as some laundered drug money by buying farms and agricultural land, hotels, supermarkets, service stations, and high priced real estate.

By the end of the decade, therefore, Blacks had established unprecedented access to money, a visible presence within the private sector, a wide range of new, small- and medium-scale black-owned enterprises and a few large black companies owned and controlled by the more successful. The Browns, the Chinese and the Lebanese no longer dominated ownership of medium-scale and smaller manufacturing and commercial enterprises in the Jamaican economy.

The big corporate sector enterprises in insurance, banking, distribution, manufacturing, hotels and services remained, however, under the predominant ownership of the economically dominant ethnic minority of Jews, Whites, Lebanese and Browns. These larger enterprises made handsome profits in the 1970s and their owners were not sufficiently intimidated by political and class threats to go into retreat. Instead, there appears to have been a consolidation and expansion of corporate ownership, as the owners of the more successful enterprises expanded and bought out smaller firms and enterprises abandoned by migrating families. This was especially the case in the areas of big finance, distribution and services, where high profit margins were used to diversify and expand into other enterprises.

It was mainly the weaker and smaller enterprises owned by the ethnic minorities that were dislocated in the 1970s. Large numbers of Chinese, Browns and Lebanese migrated and closed or sold businesses over the period. The more established Jews and Whites were only marginally affected by these developments.

Instead of leaving the country, big business families spearheaded the political attacks on the PNP government and did everything in their power to get Mr Seaga's JLP elected in 1980 to turn back the threat they thought the PNP government posed to their interests. Much of what they identified as class threats was little more than an excess of rhetoric, but their fear was that it inflamed the black masses and put them under class and racial pressures. Fundamentally, however, the PNP in the 1970s under Michael Manley broke the unstated pact of the 1940s whereby party leaders defined a dual role for themselves: protecting the privileged and negotiating and engineering benefits for the poor.

The PNP's rhetoric was too populist for the economically powerful ethnic minorities, and although Manley protected and assisted some of his friends (Grace Kennedy, Alkali, ICD, the Matalons, etc.) in the big corporate sector in the 1970s, the overall climate in the political system gave the appearance of threatening to undermine their economic leadership position and their power position in the political system. Reality and appearance are often quite different, however, as in this case.

In contrast to the 1970s, when there was an unbroken pattern of negative economic growth in Jamaica, the decade of the 1980s has witnessed two periods of steady growth (1980–83, and 1985–87) interrupted by a period of negative growth (1983-85) that was induced by IMF stabilization designed to reduce imbalances in the economy caused by the drastic decline in bauxite earnings. In both the growth periods and the recessionary, negative-growth years, black business and black accumulation of capital have come under severe pressure. Overall, some ground has been lost, but most of the black ownership expansion of the 1970s has not been reversed.

The return to a pro-business political atmosphere that accompanied the change of government to the JLP in 1980 stimulated a return flow of some migrants who had left during the 1970s. Where premises were leased or rented to new black owners this return flow of ethnic minorities from the USA displaced some black owners. The market share of commerce that was aggressively taken over by the black higgler women was reduced as big borrowing by the government and massive inflows of aid money removed the severe foreign exchange shortages that facilitated the initial growth of the higgler trade. The big established merchants were restored to power. Instead of competing with the big merchants, some higglers now joined forces with them, operating as their wholesale suppliers in areas such as garments. Many higglers have, however, been able to stay in business by underselling the merchants and targeting their sales to low income buyers.

Dependence on US loans forced the government to mount the most large-scale and systematic anti-ganja campaign ever attempted in Jamaica, as dissatisfied US interests threatened to cut off aid if no effective anti-ganja measures were developed. The new government initiated a programme of legal and tax harassment of suspected or known ganja dealers. Some were charged with multi-million-dollar tax claims. Others were imprisoned on real or manufactured drug or criminal charges. The intensive anti-drug surveillance increased the losses incurred by the drug operators and cut the export outflow of ganja to the USA. As a result, this source of illicit capital accumulation that was accessible to some Blacks was reduced.

The new economic policies of the JLP government tried to promote an open-economy strategy that emphasized exports over domestic production and opened up the economy to a larger inflow of imports. Both the import deregulation policies and the more easily accessible supply of foreign exchange threatened many local manufacturers and farmers with competition from imports. Manufacturing and farming ventures that were viable and lucrative in the conditions prevailing in the 1970s ceased to be viable. Some of these enterprises had to go out of business due to competition from imports. Several businesses established by smaller black entrepreneurs in the 1970s folded as a consequence.

This reversal was further aggravated over the post-1983 period, when high interest rates (exceeding 30 per cent) were used to cool down and stabilize the economy. The high cost of money and the massive increases in business debt, added to increased competition from imports, drove a number of black-owned business enterprises into ruin and bankruptcy. Black businesses were obviously not the only interests that were adversely affected, but because many had recently come into business, had borrowed heavily to make this move, and were operating in very vulnerable sectors, the effect was greater on black businessmen as a whole than on the other ethnic groups owning enterprises. A significant number of Blacks who borrowed heavily at low interest rates to run businesses that were viable under the conditions of the 1970s experienced bank foreclosures and bankruptcy in the 1980s. On the other hand, many of the big corporations owned by ethnic minorities profited from the devaluations of the dollar carried out during the 1983-85 period. The big corporations thrived and made unprecedented high profits while the smaller, vulnerable enterprises, where there was significant growth of black ownership, came under severe pressure.

Some critics have accused the JLP government of deliberately attempting to undermine the growth of black private enterprise in Jamaica. There is no evidence for this contention, except in one case where race and party politics have combined to encourage the JLP government to undermine one of the largest black corporate enterprises established in the country. The overall trend is one in which policies adverse to recently established smaller manufacturing enterprises have served (by largely unanticipated consequences) to weaken many small businesses. In the 1970s, black business expanded by similar unintended consequences of policies, politics and the overall economic climate. In the 1980s, the effect has been reversed, with similar unintended consequences hurting many recently established small businesses owned by Blacks. The fact is that no Jamaican government to date has ever developed economic policies with any intention to promote black business.

On the other hand, the JLP government's emphasis on private sector growth and privatization has encouraged a further expansion of black business in areas such as export manufacturing, horticulture and non-traditional export agriculture. The larger flow of credit, foreign exchange and investment money has encouraged many small enterprises owned by Blacks to emerge. More than 60 per cent of the new export enterprises sponsored by the Jamaica National Investment Programme are small businesses, and at least half of them are owned by Blacks, some of whom are venturing into business for the first time. This continued growth of black-owned smaller businesses has served to neutralize some of the effects on black businesses due to the unintended consequences of policies and economic trends adverse to many small businesses.

Two other developments in the 1980s convinced many critics of the Seaga-led JLP government that it was undermining black interests in Jamaica by its policies. These included the heavy emphasis and expenditure on foreign consultants, which was seen as discrimination against local black professionals, and secondly the over 30,000 lay-offs and employment cut-backs in the public sector, which shrunk and dried up a large part of the job market that traditionally provided jobs and income for the black lower middle class. That policy, combined with the tight restrictions on public sector wages and salaries and the high cost of living increases caused by big devaluations during the 1983-85 period convinced some middle class Blacks that the government was systematically and deliberately weakening their economic opportunities. Again, it seems that policies adverse to lower middle class public sector workers (teachers, nurses, civil servants, etc.) created great hardships in areas dominated by Blacks, but there was no racial intent. The fact that the Prime Minister is a member of the ethnic minorities and seems in the eyes of some to be more ideologically attuned to the needs and interests of the minorities rather than the needs of the black majority has given birth to this perception. But objectively, it seems to me that it has no real basis and is more perception than reality.

The Contemporary Situation

THE FOREGOING OVERVIEW of the ethnic economic division of labour in Jamaica since Emancipation suggests that there have been some important changes due to economic growth, economic crises, blackmarketeering, and sporadic political pressures which have opened up opportunities for black ex-slaves to move into professional, managerial and entrepreneurial roles in the Jamaican economy. These changes have enhanced black economic power but it is the original intermediary ethnic minorities (Browns, Chinese, Jews, and Lebanese) that have benefitted most. A new, urban-based capitalist class has emerged over the period, with Whites, Jews, Browns, and Chinese located in dominant positions of ascendancy. Blacks for the most part occupy positions of great influence in the top public sector jobs and institutions, in the independent professions and more recently in key private sector managerial positions. Black ownership of capital, while experiencing significant growth in the 1970s and to a lesser extent in the 1980s, lags behind and is in contrast with the high concentration of corporate ownership and power in the hands of Jews, Whites, Lebanese, and to a lesser extent Browns and Chinese. Blacks have made it into majority ownership of small enterprises, but a significant entry into the big corporate sector continues to elude black entrepreneurs in Jamaica.

Over the 1970s and 1980s there has been a consolidation and increased concentration of ownership by the economically dominant ethnic minorities. Among the larger enterprises in the economy, these ethnic minorities own and control companies whose total sales exceed those of the big foreign corporations in Jamaica.

Table 2. 1986 Sales of Largest Private Sector Companies

Company	1986 sales (US$ million)
Grace Kennedy	200
Desnoes & Geddes	103
Jamaica Banana Producers	82
Industrial Commercial Development	68
Jamaica Flour Mills	45
T. Geddes Grant	39
J. Wray & Nephew	35
Pan Jamaican Investments	31
Lascelles Demercado	27
National Continental Corporation	18
CMP & Wisynco	13
Gleaner	12
West Indies Glass	10
Alkali	9

SOURCE: *South* magazine, April 1987, pp. 91-92

Among the 30 largest privately owned, non-financial corporate firms in Jamaica, 19 are owned mainly or exclusively by these ethnic minorities and 11 mainly or exclusively by foreign interests. In terms of sales in US dollars for 1986, the locally owned corporate entities represent some 64 per cent of the total sales and the foreign enterprises 36 per cent of total sales generated by these 30 largest companies. The largest among these locally owned private-sector companies, selling a minimum of US$9 million or J$50 million in 1986, are shown in Table 2.

These big companies and the other major locally owned financial, manufacturing, distribution and service companies are controlled mainly by the following 23 prominent and strategic ethnic minority family interests: Ashenheim, Matalon, Henriques, Hart, Issa, Clarke, Kennedy, Facey, Mahfood, Williams, Lalor, Ewart, Stewart, Hendrickson, Panton, Thwaites, Chen Young, Hadeed, Dacosta, Desnoes, Geddes, Delisser, Rousseau.

Only three black businessmen or business families in legitimate enterprises have established large corporate enterprises. These include Ellworth Williams and brothers (merchant banking, food processing, construction); Richard Morgan (manufacturing); and Denis Morgan (hotels, car rentals, real estate). The Williams manufacturing enterprise was put into receivership and the merchant bank closed

Table 3. Percent Share of Gross Profits in the Jamaican Economy in 1982, by Sector

Sector	Share of Gross Profits (%)
Agriculture (%)	13
Bauxite	8
Manufacturing	13
Construction	4
Distribution	37
Finance	6
Real estate	22

SOURCE: National Income and Product 1982 *(Statin)*

Note: Due to rounding, the percentages add up to more than 100%.

after the Free Zone-located food processing business was refused entry into the Jamaican market and cash flow problems developed. The evidence suggests that two of the big corporations owned by ethnic minorities played a key role in orchestrating pressures on the company to facilitate a takeover. The owners, who support the PNP, have accused the JLP government of acting to facilitate those interests in putting the food processing company into receivership and in closing the bank.

The Broadway Company, owned by Richard Morgan, is in deep financial trouble and might end up in receivership for large overdue loans owed to NCB. Of the three big black-owned enterprises, only the Denis Morgan interest seems likely to survive and grow into a major black corporate enterprise.

An examination of gross profits flowing through the Jamaican economy in 1982 gives a clear picture of the concentration of economic power in the hands of the ethnic minorities. Black ownership concentrates in agriculture and manufacturing, where some 26 per cent of the overall flow of gross profits were earned. The major share of the 26 per cent in fact accrues to the big companies owned by the ethnic minorities.

The bulk of the gross profits flowing through the Jamaican economy in 1982 was generated in distribution, finance and real estate. These together represent 65 per cent of total gross profits in legitimate private business in the Jamaican economy. The greater proportion of that 65 per cent was generated in big enterprises controlled by the ethnic minorities (see Table 3).

The corporate power of the ethnic minorities extends to their strategic location in sectors that determine whether smaller enterprises survive. They control the ownership of the financial institutions and dominate the boards of directors. They therefore determine which interests get big loans and how enterprises are treated when they run into financial problems. They also control the big distribution firms, which determine which goods produced reach the mass market through their distribution networks. They therefore operate as the gate-keepers of the private sector, who control exit and entry and exercise enormous private power over the fate of smaller business enterprises owned by Blacks. Black business interests are therefore intimidated by their awesome power and seek to court their favour.

Access to drug money through the ganja trade has been the illegitimate alternative channel which has facilitated Blacks getting access to big financing. While much of the drug money is banked overseas and dissipated in excessive consumption, in a few important cases (I am unable to cite them for legal reasons) successful black businessmen have used drug money to finance legitimate enterprises and thereby bypassed the power and stranglehold exercised over big corporate financing by the ethnic minorities.

The issue that some commentators have raised is whether these powerful ethnic minority interests act in accordance with anti-Black racist positions (like Whites in South Africa) or whether they discriminate against black entry into the business sector on purely class grounds. Their exclusiveness and defensive use of their corporate power to protect their class interests could be so interpreted. But such a view strikes me as being misinformed.

My evidence of their social behaviour suggests that while they have daily and intimate business contacts with Blacks, there is a tendency to operate socially within their narrow ethnic groups. Close social contact with Blacks is therefore taboo among the older generation of these ethnic minorities. The younger generation, however, is breaking out of this narrow social world and is developing social ties with Blacks.

There is no evidence that the racial groupings operate as tightly knit ethnic formations that avoid close linkages (business or social) with other non-black, ethnic groups. On the contrary, marriage patterns, intimate social relationships and friendship ties tend increasingly to cut across these ethnic lines to a point where it makes sense to regard them as now constituting a single social agglomeration with networks of alliances and family and social ties that knit and integrate the powerful and ethnically varied family interests together.

They have a strong sense of common interests and always rally to each other's defence when under political attack. Intra-group disagreements are usually arbitrated by informal leaders, as occurred in a public dispute between Senator Hugh

Hart and hotelier Butch Stewart. And they try to avoid a public display of intra-group contentions. In that sense the Browns, Whites, Jews, Lebanese and Chinese are evolving into a single unified ethnic minority of powerful families controlling the country's corporate sector. A few Blacks will be admitted to the inner circle over time as the economy expands, because their small size does not allow them to monopolize potential opportunities for corporate growth and expansion. Such likely cooptation of Blacks into the ruling class is likely to be on terms that will preserve intact the dominant power position of the ethnic minorities.

The ethnic minorities have not had to practise racism because they have not really been challenged by a sustained effort by Blacks to break into corporate power. What the ethnic minorities do is simply to use their corporate power to protect their interests by keeping out challengers, supporting each other in cartel-like fashion, tying up and monopolizing intra-enterprise business transactions to the exclusion of outsiders and using their financial power to perpetuate their class hegemony.

In exercising that power they are building up networks of black support by promoting and utilizing black managerial talent and developing client relationships with small black businessmen, who are grateful for the help they receive. The need for them to mobilize a defence of their interest by racial actions and offensives (overt and covert) does not arise because there is no real black challenge to their hegemony. Claims about racial attacks amount to little more than isolated incidents of racial abuse of individuals or sporadic political appeals to black political identity that pose no real threat to most of the more confident ethnic-minority families, who know that they enjoy real power in the society and can mobilize pressure against interests that choose to challenge them.

Their strategy is to accuse all persons who raise the race issue as being racist and as undermining Jamaican multi-racial nationalism. There can be no challenge to their class hegemony unless the issue of minority ethnic control is put on the political agenda as it has been in Uganda, Kenya, Malaysia and Indonesia. To date race has not been an item that has attracted political interest or support from the mainstream political parties or political tendencies in the country since the earlier Garvey period. Until that issue is put on the political agenda, the ethnic minorities will remain unchallenged in exercising their hegemony over the corporate economy.

The more important question is whether this seemingly entrenched ruling class can be displaced and dislodged to make way for black control or a greater black presence in the corporate sector of the economy. Given the entrenched character of the increasingly unified ethnic minorities who control the corporate private sector of the Jamaican economy, it is most unlikely that their economic ascendancy and power will decline in the near future. That fact, however, will not prevent black entry into the big corporate sector. Such black entry to the big corporate sector would have the effect of diversifying the ethnic elements controlling the corporate economy and changing the present ethnic division of labour that limits black economic power in the corporate sector to the occupation of managerial authority under the ownership control of brown, white, Chinese, Jewish and Lebanese family interests.

Significant black entry (beyond tokenism) into ownership in the corporate sector could be facilitated by four major factors. These include the following:

(1) Black ethnic nationalism challenging the economic dominance of the ethnic minorities.

(2) The mobilization of external black financing in Canada, the UK and the USA to establish a black venture-capital market for the long-term financing of new black enterprises.

(3) Policies which encourage drug dealers to accept legal amnesty in exchange for channeling their overseas hard currency into legitimate local business enterprises and providing a new stream of black business financing.

(4) Sustained rapid growth of the economy, which would open up wider opportunities for entrepreneurship than have so far emerged and on a scale that would force the small ethnic minority to open up its inner circle to trained, experienced and enterprising black entrepreneurs.

If all four factors were set in motion, reinforcing each other, the impact would be to significantly blacken the complexion of the dominant corporate owning families in Jamaica in one generation.

The black population as an ethnic majority has the power to act on and change the first or the most political of these four factors. It is a necessary and crucial ingredient if the country is to achieve a significant ethnic-majority presence in the Jamaican privately owned corporate sector. Several factors, however, militate against this issue becoming a political demand articulated by large numbers of Blacks in the society across the various class divisions.

Unlike the ethnic minorities, the Blacks reveal very weak ethnic bonding or solidarity. Part of the problem is that the social, cultural and historical forces making for strong ethnic bonding are largely absent among Jamaican Blacks. Apart from a common racial coloration and physical features, the Blacks in Jamaica have very few attributes and characteristics which they share uniquely and which set them apart from other ethnic groups as is the case with majority ethnic groups in many Asian and African countries where ethnic bonding is very strong. They have no common and distinctive language, religion, or core cultural institutions and ethnic leadership that sets them apart from other ethnic groups. They are sharply divided by income, class and education.

Many have overcome the negative stereotypes about black inferiority generated in the country's colonial period and which still operate at some levels in contemporary Jamaica. But the typical response of the Jamaican Blacks to their inherited position of social inferiority is to fight against the system militantly as a tough, rugged individual articulating total confidence – as is exhibited by higglers, gunmen, ghetto militants, black intellectuals, professionals, entrepreneurs and others. These struggles for personal mobility, accumulation and power become individualistic and personal triumphs, where they succeed, but provide no basis for enhancing and moving forward the collective situation of other Blacks in the system. This very rugged and aggressive individualism of confident Blacks is often used against the ethnic group by those in ascendant positions of power as the aggressive and individualistic Black can be induced to block and destroy efforts by other Blacks to survive and progress.

The single and fundamental problem facing black Jamaicans at the political, economic and social levels is the fact of weak ethnic bonding. It is reinforced by the suppression of black ethnic identities and nationalism in favour of multi-racial territorial nationalism among the country's mainstream political movements, sharp intra-black class divisions, the absence of shared ethnic institutions, and tendencies to seek individual progress without any collective concern for the ethnic group. These realities make it most unlikely that the issue of race will be put on the political agenda in the near future unless these factors change. Such a change is crucial to pressuring the economically dominant ethnic minorities to accept the validity of the case for seeking after a blackening of the coloration of private corporate ownership in the country as a legitimate and worthwhile objective.

The other major issue is that the powerful corporate controlling ethnic minorities are too numerically small as a class to provide the range and depth of economic leadership and private sector dynamism needed to move our economy forward to fuller employment, greater production and better living standards for the black masses. To expand the country's still narrow productive and economic base, the inner circle of the corporate ruling class must be widened. Given the ethnic balance in the country, this can only happen by promoting large-scale black entry into the corporate sector.

REFERENCES

[1] Pierre L. Van Den Berghe, *Race and Racism: A Comparative Perspective* (New York: John Wiley, 1967).

[2] Colin Clarke, *Kingston, Jamaica: Urban Development and Social Change 1692-1962* (Berkeley: University of California Press, 1975).

[3] Gisela Eisner, *Jamaica 1830-1930: A Study in Economic Growth* (Connecticut: Greenwood Press, 1974).

[4] Cynthia H. Enloe, *Ethnic Conflict and Political Development* (Boston: Little, Brown, 1973).

[5] Adam Kuper, *Changing Jamaica* (Kingston: Kingston Publishers, 1976).

[6] Rupert Lewis, *Marcus Garvey: Anti-Colonial Champion* (London: Karia Press, 1987).

[7] Rex Nettleford, *Mirror, Mirror: Identity, Race and Protest in Jamaica* (Collins and Sangster, 1970).

[8] Carl Stone, *Class, State and Democracy in Jamaica,* 1986 World Bank Monograph.

[9] Carl Stone & Aggrey Brown (eds.), *Essays in Power and Change in Jamaica* (Kingston: Teachers Book Centre, 1977).

Race, Class and Social Mobility in Jamaica

Derek Gordon
Department of Sociology and Social Work
University of the West Indies, Mona, Jamaica

Introduction

"If you were to go into all the offices throughout Jamaica you would not find one percent of black clerks employed. You will find nearly all white and coloured persons, including men and women; for proof please go through our Post Office, Government Offices and stores in Kingston, and you see only white and coloured men and women in positions of importance and trust and you will find the black men and women as store-men, messengers, attendants and common servants. In the country parts you will find the same order of things. On the Estates and Plantations you will find the black man and woman as the labourer, the coloured man as clerk and sometimes owner and the white man generally as master. White and coloured women are absent from the fields of labour. The professions are generally taken up by the white and coloured men because they have the means to equip themselves".[1]

GARVEY MADE these observations on Jamaican society during World War One. Although it is generally conceded that the correlation between race and class position, in which light-skinned people are concentrated at the top of the class structure and black Jamaicans are concentrated at the bottom, remains a feature of contemporary Jamaican society, there is considerable debate about the contemporary extent of this correlation and its significance.

While conceding that racial differentials in economic position and opportunity continue to exist, Adam Kuper has argued that these differentials can be reduced to prior class differences between racial groups. As he puts it:

> If your ancestors were poor you will be much less likely to be well-off than another man whose ancestors were rich. The average black is worse-off than the average coloured Jamaican; but then, in England, the average descendant of a mill-hand is no doubt worse-off than the average descendant of a mill-owner.[2]

This paper considers the extent of changes in the position of the major racial groups in the post-World War Two period, one of important qualitative and quantitative changes in the economy and class structure of the country. It also examines Kuper's thesis by presenting new data on racial differentials in social mobility from the *1984 National Mobility Survey*.[3] Finally, the paper offers some reflections on the nature of the relationship between race and class in Jamaica.

The Classification of Race

THE ANALYST using existing racial classifications or attempting to develop a racial classification is already faced with fundamental theoretical problems about the nature and significance of race in Jamaica. The racial classification developed for the *1943 Census* and used with modifications thereafter is a good example. As Lloyd Braithwaite pointed out in his classic article, "Sociology and Demographic Research", the census classification mixes biological, social, cultural and geographical principles in an unsatisfactory way.[4] The boundaries between the various "mixed" and "pure" groups are unclear, and the classification of race depends in part on the social context.[5]

While we start from the view that purely biological classification of races is an enterprise of doubtful scientific validity, the social and cultural existence of discrete social groups based on phenotypical and real or imagined social and cultural differences is not generally denied, whatever the difficulties in classifying them, and whatever the differences among theorists in accounting for their existence and significance.

In Jamaica, the phenotypical features of significance are well described by Henriques:

> "Colour" is evaluated in terms of actual colour, hair formation and skin texture. All these are assessed in relation to their nearness to European characteristics and distance from the African.[6]

At one level, obviously, these features span a "colour" continuum. At another level they lead to the identification of discrete racial or ethnic groups, which have a definite social and cultural existence with real consequences for the individuals within these groups.

At the most general level, the colour continuum takes a discrete form in the threefold distinction Black, Brown and White. Or it may be reduced to the dichotomy Black and Non-Black or Light-Skinned. Both of these constitute popular conceptions of the social structure, which are not based purely on perceived physical features but also on perceived social and cultural differences.[7] This may be complicated by the recognition of distinct ethnic and racial minorities like the Chinese, "Syrians" and Indians.

In the analyses that follow, we shall be using two related classifications. The first is an abbreviated version of the *1943 Census* classification, used for purposes of historical comparison between the *1943 Census* data and our sample survey. In this classification we collapse all the ethnic minorities, except Indians, into one minority group. This does some injustice to the distinctions between them, but is unavoidable given the small numbers in our sample survey. While we attempted to maintain comparability with the 1943 inquiry in our instructions and training of the interviewers for the 1984 study, caution needs to be exercised in drawing conclusions from the comparisons, as the basis for racial evaluations has changed.

For consistency with the analysis of historical trends, we also use this classification, dichotomized into Black and Other racial groups, to assess mobility differential by race in the 1984 sample. A second classification, developed for the more detailed analysis of race in the *1984 Mobility Survey,* is used in this study as a check on the validity of our mobility findings. Interviewers were asked to rate respondents on three 5-point scales. The three characteristics – hair, skin colour and facial features – were chosen to represent the main features used to evaluate colour and race in Jamaica. A score of 1 represented "African" features and a score of 5 represented "European" features. For the purposes of the analysis, persons with a score of either 1 or 2 on all of the three characteristics constituted the Black group, while all others

	Black	Indian	Mixed	White, etc.	
Black	5,946	59	710	3	6,718
Brown	616	114	899	38	1,667
	6,562	173	1,609	41	8,385

Table 1. Two Alternative Racial Classifications

constituted the residual Light-Skinned group. An analysis that treated the scores on the three characteristics as a continuum was possible but was not attempted here. While there is some evidence that the latter classification is slightly less subject to a social-class contextual effect (in which the racial classification of upper- and middle-class respondents is "upgraded"), we should not lose sight of the fact that the conception of an African or European racial type – i.e., black skin colour/white skin colour, curly/straight hair, and broad/narrow nose, thick/thin lips, etc. – also has an ideological dimension.

The relationship between the two classifications in our *1984 Mobility Survey* is given in Table 1. The discrepancies in this table should correct any impressions of spurious "natural" objectivity in the classifications. Although the vast majority of those classified as Black in one classification are also classified similarly in the other, it is clear that the social context has an influence on the attribution of race. A large proportion of those classed as Mixed or Brown in one classification are classed as Black in the other.

Finally, it should be pointed out that the gross classifications we use, while having social validity, overlook finer distinctions which play a role in social life, and understate the racial differentials at the extremes. If we do find racial differentials that cannot be attributed to class background, for example, we would almost certainly find sharper differentials with a finer classification or the use of continuous variables.

Race and Occupational Status in the Post-War Period

AN INDISPENSABLE SOURCE for analyzing changes in the position of the racial groups in the post-war period is the *1943 Census of Jamaica and Dependencies.* This census is generally acknowledged to be the first modern Jamaican census, and the quality of its data is generally recognized. It was therefore with some surprise that we discovered an important omission in the presentation of the tables on race and occupation. Generally, the census presented occupational data by age and education, broken down by sex and by employment status (employer, own-account worker, and wage workers), but when presenting similar data by race, only data for wage workers were presented. Own-account workers and employers are unaccountably missing.

This does not seem to be an oversight, as race figures as an important variable in this census. The introduction, for example, discusses the distribution of race by employment status in percentage terms, although there is no companion raw table of figures in the main body of tables. This is a severe disappointment, because it means that we cannot get an overall breakdown of the racial composition of employers or the many own-account occupations in which the ethnic minorities play a part.

Was this a deliberate omission? Elsewhere in the farm census, there is data on the racial composition of farmers by acreage, which has proved invaluable to other researchers. But nowhere in the census can we get a comprehensive breakdown of the racial status of the workforce. Perhaps some official memo has the answer.

What we have done is therefore limited in some respects. We have compared the racial makeup of the wage-earning occupations in 1943 with the wage-earning occupations in our *1984 Mobility Survey.* Two large groups make up the wage-earning population: the middle class and the working class. We know from other data that the relative percentage of the wage-earning class has not changed dramatically in the 40-plus years since 1943. An analysis of the changing composition of these large groups and the role of the different racial groups within them can tell us a great deal about changes in racial opportunities in the post-war period.

All groups except the ethnic minorities have undergone a relative shift in the composition of their wage-earning population, expanding their middle classes dramatically (Table 2). But some have started from a much lower base than others. In 1943, the black middle class made up only 3 per cent of all black wage earners. Only the Indians, with 4 per cent, were close to them. Twenty-one per cent of coloured wage earners were then in the middle class, and a two-thirds majority (65 per cent) of the ethnic minorities.

Since then, the Indians appear to have enjoyed the most dramatic advances. About 47 per cent of their present-day wage earners are in the middle class. In 1943, nearly two thirds of Indians were agricultural labourers. The coloured middle class has also expanded dramatically, maintaining the advantage which they have historically had over the black population. Forty-four per cent of all coloured wage earners are at present in the middle class, compared to 25 per cent of black wage earners. The ethnic minorities have maintained their middle-class character, as two out of

Table 2. The Changing Occupational Composition of Racial Groups: 1943–1984

	Black		Indian		Coloured		White, etc.		TOTAL	
OCCUPATIONS	1943	1984	1943	1984	1943	1984	1943	1984	1943	1984
Higher Mgmt., Prof.	0.12	1.27	0.24	6.25	1.26	5.23	8.72	19.44	0.48	2.33
Lower Mgmt., Sup.	0.26	2.09	0.22	4.17	1.60	3.56	5.53	8.33	0.58	2.48
Lower Prof.	1.01	9.00	0.37	12.50	4.31	14.23	8.36	19.44	1,68	10.23
Acctg., Sec. Clerks	0.16	4.37	0.47	9.38	3.35	9.73	6.76	11.11	0.82	5.63
Other Clerks	0.72	4.26	1.05	6.25	6.64	6.90	13.91	5.56	1.95	4.86
Sales Clerks	0.80	3.89	1.79	8.33	4.15	4.39	21.67	2.78	1.78	4.08
TOTAL MIDDLE CLASS	**3.07**	**24.89**	**4.15**	**46.88**	**21.30**	**44.04**	**64.96**	**66.67**	**7.28**	**29.62**
Foremen, Hi Serv.	1.51	2.96	2.09	1.04	4.00	3.45	6.41	2.78	2.02	3.02
Operatives	10.82	23.50	7.23	19.79	17.01	19.14	7.86	19.44	11.68	22.50
Service Workers	2.71	15.77	1.87	9.38	5.20	13.70	6.30	5.56	3.16	15.13
Unskilled Manual	19.46	10.67	12.02	4.17	10.43	6.59	1.62	5.56	17.47	9.65
Domestic	22.10	12.78	8.40	7.29	21.01	8.47	10.12	0.00	21.36	11.68
Agric. Labourers	40.34	9.42	64.26	11.46	21.05	4.60	2.74	0.00	37.03	8.40
TOTAL WAGE EARNERS	**100.00**	**100.00**	**100.00**	**100.00**	**100.00**	**100.00**	**100.00**	**100.00**	**100.00**	**100.00**
N	*262,408*	*3,544*	*7,814*	*96*	*53,624*	*956*	*6,492*	*36*	*330,338*	*4,632*
I.D.	*49.00*		*62.81*		*33.36*		*44.47*		*46.11*	

Table 3. The Changing Composition of Wage-Earning Occupational Groups, 1943–1984

OCCUPATION	YEAR	Black	Indian	Coloured	White	%	N	I.D.
Higher Mgmt., Prof.	1943	19.90	1.21	42.91	35.98	100.00	1,573	
	1984	41.67	5.56	46.30	6.48	100.00	108	29.51
Lower Mgmt., Sup.	1943	36.00	0.88	44.50	18.62	100.00	1,928	
	1984	64.35	3.48	29.57	2.61	100.00		30.95
Lower Professional	1943	47.96	0.52	41.71	9.80	100.00	5,538	
	1984	67.30	2.53	28.69	1.48	100.00	115	21.35
Acctg., Sales Clerks	1943	15.66	1.37	66.67	16.30	100.00	2,694	
	1984	59.39	3.45	35.63	1.53	100.00	474	45.81
Other Clerks	1943	29.26	1.28	55.41	14.05	100.00	6,428	
	1984	67.11	2.67	29.33	0.89	100.00	261	39.24
Sales Clerks	1943	35.81	2.38	37.85	23.96	100.00	5,873	
	1984	73.02	4.23	22.22	0.53	100.00	225	39.06
Foremen, Hi Serv.	1943	59.22	2.44	32.12	6.22	100.00	6,684	
	1984	75.00	0.71	23.57	0.71	100.00	189	15.78
Operatives	1943	73.57	1.46	23.64	1.32	100.00	38,576	
	1984	79.94	1.82	17.56	0.67	100.00	140	6.73
Service Workers	1943	67.99	1.40	26.70	3.92	100.00	10,442	
	1984	79.74	1.28	18.69	0.29	100.00	1,042	11.75
Unskilled Manual	1943	88.50	1.63	9.69	0.18	100.00	57,698	
	1984	84.56	0.89	14.09	0.45	100.00	701	4.67
Domestic	1943	82.17	0.93	15.97	0.93	100.00	70,568	
	1984	83.73	1.29	14.97	0.00	100.00	447	1.92
Agric. Labourer	1943	86.52	4.10	9.23	0.15	100.00	122,336	
	1984	85.86	2.83	11.31	0.00	100.00	541	2.08
TOTAL	**1943**	**79.44**	**2.37**	**16.23**	**1.97**	**100.00**	**330,338**	
WAGE EARNERS	**1984**	**76.51**	**2.07**	**20.64**	**0.78**	**100.00**	**4,632**	**4.41**

every three wage earners remain in the middle class. If we use a more restrictive definition of the middle class, including only professional and managerial personnel, we find that coloured and Indian wage earners are twice as likely to be middle class as Blacks (23 *vs.* 12 per cent) and that Whites and other minorities are twice as likely as the coloured wage earners to be middle class (47 *vs.* 23 per cent). Indeed, if we consider only the higher managerial and professional positions, the advantages of the ethnic minorities in contemporary Jamaica stand out in even sharper relief. Nearly one in five (19.44 per cent) of the Whites and other minorities were from this higher stratum, compared to 5 per cent of the coloured group and 6 per cent of the Indian group, respectively. Only 1.27 per cent of the black group reached the higher reaches of the middle class. Of course, an important factor facilitating the expansion of the minority ethnic groups is their small size relative to the majority group. Even if Blacks occupied all positions in the higher managerial and professional ranks, this would still represent a very small percentage of the black population.

The expansion of middle-class occupations, then, has affected all racial groups, but it has not led to the elimination of differentials between them. The black middle class remains in relative terms much smaller than the middle class of other racial groups, although, as we shall see, the majority of the middle class is *now black.*

Table 3 gives us more information on the racial composition of the major wage-earning groups. We can see, reading across and comparing 1943 percentages with 1984 percentages in each occupational or class group, that the black middle class has moved from being an absolute minority of the middle class to an absolute majority. They are still under-represented, however, in relation to the size of their population.

The situation in particular middle-class occupational groups is revealing. Blacks are still not a majority in the upper reaches of the middle class, in the higher professions and in senior managerial positions, but they have increased their representation from one in five in 1943 to two in five in 1984. As these occupations have expanded, Whites have maintained their relative positions in them, compared to 1984, but are unable to make the significant numerical impact they made in 1943, when, for example, Whites and other ethnic minorities were 36 per cent of the higher professions and managers.

The areas of strongest representation for Blacks in 1943 (48 per cent) and 1984 (67 per cent) were the mass professions, particularly teaching and nursing. The area of greatest change has definitely been in the clerical professions, once a stronghold of the coloured population. In 1943, for example, only 16 per cent of secretarial and accounting clerks were black, while coloured clerks accounted for two thirds. By 1984, just under 60 per cent of these clerks were black, while a little over a third were coloured. In these occupations in 1943, Whites and other ethnic minorities accounted for proportions far in excess of their numbers in the population. For example, they made up 16 per cent of secretarial and accounting clerks, the same as Blacks, who outnumbered them in the population forty to one in 1943!

The Index of Dissimilarity in the last column of the table gives us a simple summary measure of the change in racial composition of the occupational groups. It represents the positive percentage-point difference between the 1943 and 1984 racial contributions in each occupation. The greatest change in composition in favour of the black majority came in the clerical occupations.

Generally, the racial composition of the working-class occupations did not change greatly. Blacks were generally somewhat over-represented in manual occupations. Exceptions to this were foremen and higher-grade service workers, like policemen, and service workers, which were both areas of the working class where Blacks were historically under-represented and where they made gains between 1943 and 1984.

Race and Social Mobility

We have already shown, with regard to the wage-earning population, that the light-skinned population is more likely to be middle class than the black population. This remains strikingly true when we consider the whole work force, including those who are small proprietors or employers. In this section we collapse the more detailed wage-earning categories into three middle-class and three working-class groups, giving us a ten-group classification. As Table 4 shows, 30 per cent of the present-day experienced labour force of light-skinned complexion are middle class, compared to 15 per cent of the black work force. Of interest is the greater concentration of the black work force in small farming and other own-account occupations compared to those of lighter complexion. Twenty-five per cent of the former were farmers, compared to only 19 per cent of the latter.

Table 4. Class Origins and Destinations, by Race

Class Category	BLACK Origins	BLACK Destinations	BROWN Origins	BROWN Destinations
Higher Mgmt., Prof.	0.46	0.75	1.87	3.88
Lower Mgmt., Prof.	2.32	6.78	5.88	12.02
Clerical	1.23	7.67	4.26	14.15
TOTAL MIDDLE CLASS	**4.01**	**15.20**	**12.02**	**30.04**
Employers	1.19	1.00	2.45	1.87
Artisans	6.38	7.33	5.10	6.40
Traders	7.10	5.71	9.50	5.30
Small Farmers	52.70	24.86	41.99	19.44
TOTAL PETITE BOURGEOISIE	**67.38**	**38.90**	**59.04**	**33.01**
Foremen, Hi Serv.	1.77	1.87	3.04	2.07
Operatives, Service	9.93	23.81	13.18	21.71
Unskilled	16.91	20.22	12.73	13.18
TOTAL WORKING CLASS	**28.61**	**45.91**	**28.94**	**36.95**
TOTAL	5,761	5,761	1,408	1,408

Of more interest to us is whether these differences existed in the past, in terms of the class origins of these two broad groups. Looking at social origins and comparing the two groups, we find that these differences existed in the past and were even slightly sharper, although the comparison of past and present class origins within each group reveals that there has also been substantial mobility out of small farming and into the middle class and the working class in both cases. The view that the current

Table 5. Inflow Mobility of Major Racial Groups

		Present Occupation											
HEAD'S OCCUPATION	RACE	1	2	3	4	5	6	7	8	9	10	%	N
1. High Mgmt., Prof.	Black	7.1	4.8	4.8	7.1	9.5	9.5	26.2	2.4	23.8	4.8	100.0	42
	Other	13.3	28.3	6.7	5.0	0.0	13.3	15.0	3.3	13.3	1.7	99.9	60
2. Lower Mgmt., Prof.	Black	1.3	9.5	2.9	4.6	5.8	12.1	41.1	2.4	10.5	12.9	100.1	380
	Other	4.8	12.4	7.5	6.5	2.7	11.3	29.0	3.8	15.1	7.0	100.1	186
3. Clerical	Black	1.9	5.6	4.4	1.2	6.3	9.5	30.7	2.6	16.0	18.8	100.0	430
	Other	3.7	11.9	11.0	1.7	4.1	11.9	21.0	4.1	19.2	9.6	100.2	219
4. Employer	Black	0.0	5.4	1.8	8.9	5.4	21.4	37.5	1.8	7.1	10.7	100.0	56
	Other	0.0	10.3	0.0	6.9	3.5	13.8	41.4	3.5	10.3	10.3	100.0	29
5. Artisan	Black	0.7	1.5	0.2	0.7	12.2	7.8	50.1	1.2	7.8	17.8	100.0	411
	Other	1.0	2.0	3.0	0.0	9.1	6.1	41.4	1.0	13.1	23.2	99.9	99
6. Trader	Black	0.9	1.6	0.3	0.3	5.6	11.3	50.6	1.6	11.6	16.3	100.1	320
	Other	0.0	3.7	3.7	1.2	3.7	14.6	39.0	6.1	9.8	18.3	100.1	82
7. Farmer	Black	0.0	0.6	0.3	0.7	3.9	4.4	77.6	0.4	3.2	9.0	100.1	1,394
	Other	0.3	3.8	1.9	3.8	5.7	11.4	41.9	5.7	12.4	13.3	99.9	10
8. Foreman, Rel.	Black	0.0	3.8	1.9	3.8	5.7	11.4	41.9	5.7	12.4	13.3	99.9	105
	Other	0.0	3.1	12.5	3.1	9.4	9.4	43.8	0.0	15.6	3.1	100.0	32
9. Operative, Service	Black	0.3	2.2	1.7	1.7	7.3	7.4	40.0	1.9	15.7	21.8	100.0	1,335
	Other	0.6	3.0	2.7	0.3	6.3	8.3	40.8	4.4	17.6	16.1	100.0	33
10. Unskilled	Black	0.0	1.1	0.4	0.6	6.8	4.9	53.5	1.4	8.7	22.5	99.9	1,134
	Other	0.0	1.0	1.5	2.9	5.9	11.3	47.5	1.5	11.3	17.2	100.1	204
TOTAL	**BLACK**	**0.7**	**6.8**	**7.7**	**1.0**	**7.3**	**5.7**	**24.9**	**1.9**	**23.8**	**20.2**	**100.0**	**5,607**
	OTHER	**3.9**	**12.0**	**14.1**	**1.9**	**6.4**	**5.3**	**19.4**	**2.1**	**21.7**	**13.8**	**100.0**	**1,548**

Table 6. Outflow Mobility of Major Racial Groups

HEAD'S OCCUPATION	RACE	Present Occupation 1	2	3	4	5	6	7	8	9	10	%	N
1. High Mgmt., Prof.	Black	11.5	19.2	30.8	0.0	11.5	11.5	0.0	0.0	15.4	0.0	99.9	26
	Other	27.6	31.0	27.6	0.0	3.4	0.0	3.4	0.0	6.9	0.0	99.9	29
2. Lower Mgmt., Prof.	Black	1.5	27.7	18.5	2.3	4.6	3.8	6.2	3.1	22.3	10.0	100.0	130
	Other	18.7	25.3	28.6	3.3	2.2	3.3	4.4	1.1	11.0	2.2	100.1	91
3. Clerical	Black	2.9	15.9	27.5	1.5	1.5	1.5	5.8	2.9	33.3	7.2	100.0	69
	Other	6.1	21.2	36.4	0.0	4.5	4.5	3.0	6.1	13.6	4.5	99.9	66
4. Employer	Black	4.5	9.0	7.5	7.5	4.5	1.5	14.9	6.0	34.3	10.4	100.1	67
	Other	7.9	31.6	21.1	5.3	0.0	2.6	10.5	2.6	2.6	15.8	100.0	38
Artisan	Black	1.1	6.1	7.5	0.8	14.0	5.0	15.1	1.7	27.1	21.5	99.9	358
	Other	0.0	6.3	11.4	1.3	11.4	3.8	20.3	3.8	26.6	15.2	100.1	79
6. Trader	Black	1.0	11.6	10.3	3.0	8.0	9.0	15.3	3.0	24.9	13.8	99.9	398
	Other	5.4	14.3	17.7	2.7	4.1	8.2	10.9	2.0	19.0	15.6	99.9	147
7. Farmer	Black	0.4	5.3	4.5	0.7	7.0	5.5	36.6	1.5	18.1	20.5	100.1	2,955
	Other	1.4	8.3	7.1	1.8	6.3	4.9	32.0	2.2	21.1	14.9	100.0	650
8. Foreman, Rel.	Black	1.0	9.1	24.2	1.0	5.1	5.1	6.1	6.1	26.3	16.2	100.2	99
	Other	4.3	14.9	19.1	2.1	2.1	10.6	8.5	0.0	31.9	6.4	99.9	47
9. Operative, Service	Black	1.8	7.2	12.4	0.7	5.7	6.6	7.9	2.3	37.5	17.8	99.9	557
	Other	3.9	13.7	20.6	1.5	6.4	3.9	7.4	2.5	28.9	11.3	100.1	204
10. Unskilled	Black	0.2	5.2	8.5	0.6	7.7	5.5	13.2	1.5	30.7	26.9	100.0	948
	Other	0.5	6.6	10.7	1.5	11.7	7.6	15.7	0.5	27.4	17.8	100.0	197
TOTAL	**BLACK**	**0.7**	**6.8**	**7.7**	**1.0**	**7.3**	**5.7**	**24.9**	**1.9**	**23.8**	**20.2**	**100.0**	**5,607**
	OTHER	**3.9**	**12.0**	**14.1**	**1.9**	**6.4**	**5.3**	**19.4**	**2.1**	**21.7**	**13.2**	**100.0**	**1,548**

Table 7. Inflow Mobility Percentages to Present Occupation from Head's Occupation at Age 14, by Race (Second Classification)

HEAD'S OCCUPATION	RACE	Present Occupation 1	2	3	4	5	6	7	8	9	10	%
1. High Mgmt., Prof.	Black	6.25	10.42	4.17	8.33	8.33	10.42	20.83	2.08	25.00	4.17	100.00
	Brown	14.55	25.45	7.27	3.64	0.00	14.55	18.18	3.64	10.91	1.82	100.00
2. Lower Mgmt., Prof.	Black	1.04	10.44	3.13	1.83	5.74	12.27	40.99	2.35	11.75	10.44	100.00
	Brown	5.46	10.38	7.10	6.01	2.73	10.93	28.42	3.83	12.57	12.57	100.00
3. Clerical	Black	1.37	5.72	5.49	1.14	6.18	11.21	30.43	5.26	15.79	17.39	100.00
	Brown	4.63	12.04	8.80	4.17	4.17	8.80	21.30	4.63	18.98	12.50	100.00
4. Employer	Black	0.00	8.47	1.69	8.47	5.08	18.64	37.29	1.69	6.78	11.86	100.00
	Brown	0.00	3.85	0.00	7.69	3.85	19.23	42.31	3.85	11.54	7.69	100.00
5. Artisan	Black	0.73	1.46	0.49	0.49	11.89	7.28	50.24	0.97	8.01	18.45	100.00
	Brown	1.02	2.04	2.04	1.02	10.20	8.16	40.82	2.04	12.24	7.69	100.00
6. Trader	Black	0.30	1.82	0.91	0.30	5.76	11.21	50.91	1.52	10.61	16.67	100.00
	Brown	2.78	2.78	1.39	1.39	2.78	15.28	36.11	6.94	13.89	16.67	100.00
7. Farmer	Black	0.07	0.61	0.34	0.75	4.20	4.07	77.83	0.61	3.19	8.34	100.00
	Brown	0.00	1.32	0.44	1.32	3.52	7.05	66.08	0.44	5.29	14.54	100.00
8. Foreman, Rel.	Black	0.00	3.74	1.87	3.74	3.74	10.28	45.79	3.74	14.95	12.15	100.00
	Brown	0.00	3.33	13.33	3.33	16.67	13.33	33.33	6.37	6.67	3.33	100.00
9. Operative, Service	Black	0.22	1.94	1.79	1.57	7.62	7.47	40.51	2.17	15.84	20.85	100.00
	Brown	0.90	3.89	2.40	0.90	5.09	8.38	38.62	3.59	17.07	19.16	100.00
10. Unskilled	Black	0.00	1.02	0.51	1.11	7.08	5.46	53.50	1.28	8.53	21.50	100.00
	Brown	0.00	1.80	1.20	0.00	2.99	8.38	46.11	2.40	13.77	23.30	100.00
TOTAL	**BLACK**	**0.36**	**2.40**	**1.41**	**1.27**	**6.51**	**7.19**	**53.17**	**1.74**	**9.95**	**16.02**	**100.00**
	BROWN	**2.41**	**5.97**	**3.84**	**2.34**	**4.10**	**9.45**	**39.13**	**3.27**	**13.42**	**18.77**	**100.00**

Table 8. Outflow Mobility Percentages from Head's Occupation, by Race (Second Classification)

HEAD'S OCCUPATION	RACE	Present Occupation 1	2	3	4	5	6	7	8	9	10	%
1. High Mgmt., Prof.	Black	14.29	19.05	28.57	0.00	14.29	4.76	4.76	0.00	14.29	0.00	100.00
	Brown	23.53	29.41	29.41	0.00	2.94	5.88	0.00	0.00	8.82	0.00	100.00
2. Lower Mgmt., Prof.	Black	3.62	28.99	18.12	3.62	4.35	4.35	6.52	2.90	18.84	8.70	100.00
	Brown	16.67	22.62	30.95	1.19	2.38	2.38	3.57	1.19	15.48	3.57	100.00
3. Clerical	Black	2.47	14.81	29.63	1.23	2.47	3.70	6.17	2.47	29.63	7.41	100.00
	Brown	7.41	24.07	35.19	0.00	3.70	1.85	1.85	7.41	14.81	3.70	100.00
4. Employer	Black	5.48	9.59	6.82	6.85	2.74	1.37	15.07	5.48	28.77	17.81	100.00
	Brown	6.06	33.33	27.27	6.06	3.03	3.03	9.09	3.03	9.09	0.00	100.00
5. Artisan	Black	1.07	5.87	7.20	0.80	13.07	5.07	16.53	1.07	27.20	22.13	100.00
	Brown	0.00	8.06	14.52	1.61	16.13	3.23	12.90	8.06	27.42	8.06	100.00
6. Trader	Black	1.21	11.35	11.84	2.66	7.25	8.94	14.49	2.66	24.15	15.46	100.00
	Brown	6.02	15.04	14.29	3.76	6.02	8.27	12.03	3.01	21.05	10.53	100.00
7. Farmer	Black	0.33	5.13	4.34	0.72	6.76	5.48	37.48	1.60	17.70	20.47	100.00
	Brown	1.81	9.44	8.35	2.00	7.26	4.72	27.22	1.81	23.41	13.97	100.00
8. Foreman, Rel.	Black	1.00	9.00	23.00	1.00	4.00	5.00	9.00	4.00	29.00	15.00	100.00
	Brown	4.35	15.22	21.74	2.17	4.35	10.87	2.17	4.35	26.09	8.70	100.00
9. Operative, Service	Black	2.09	7.85	12.04	0.70	5.76	6.11	8.20	2.79	37.00	17.45	100.00
	Brown	3.17	12.17	21.36	1.59	6.35	5.29	6.35	1.06	30.16	12.17	100.00
10. Unskilled	Black	0.22	4.33	8.23	0.76	8.23	5.96	13.33	1.41	30.23	27.30	100.00
	Brown	0.45	10.36	12.16	0.90	9.01	5.41	14.86	0.45	28.83	17.57	100.00
TOTAL	**BLACK**	**0.83**	**6.65**	**7.59**	**1.02**	**7.15**	**5.73**	**25.60**	**1.863**	**23.23**	**20.34**	**100.00**
	BROWN	**3.91**	**13.00**	**15.34**	**1.85**	**6.96**	**5.11**	**16.12**	**2.13**	**23.72**	**11.86**	**100.00**

differences between black and light-skinned Jamaicans are due to their different class origins would appear plausible.

We can explore this hypothesis by examining whether any differentials exist in the degree to which the different racial groups in the same occupational or class group are able to hold on to or inherit their positions, on the one hand, or to have better opportunities for mobility given the same class backgrounds, on the other. If we still find significant differentials in these two respects between the racial groups we would have to reject Kuper's hypothesis that present-day race differentials are a product of prior class differences between the racial groups.

Table 5 gives us the inflow percentages which map the patterns of recruitment of the different social classes. Reading across the table, we are comparing the two racial groups in each occupational group in terms of their social origins. At the highest levels of the middle class, there exist significant differences between the black and light-skinned sections. Nearly half (48 per cent) of the light-skinned professionals and managers have middle-class backgrounds compared to under one in five (17 per cent) of the black professionals and managers. Of course, this is also an indication of black mobility made possible by the expansion of opportunities in this stratum.

A similar pattern, but more attenuated, is revealed for the other middle-class occupations. For clerical labour, for example, the differentials are more modest. Twenty-seven per cent of the lighter-skinned clerical workers are from the middle class, compared to about 12 per cent of black clerical workers. This advantage that light-skinned persons enjoy in maintaining their middle-class positions is an important difference between the racial groups, but it does not challenge directly Kuper's thesis. This can more effectively be done by examining the outflow percentages, which indicate the relative chances of upward or downward mobility.

Regardless of class background, Table 6 shows that light-skinned persons are more likely to get into the middle class or to remain there once they started out there than their black counterparts. While anyone with a higher professional or managerial background was likely to remain in the middle class, light-skinned persons were more likely to do so than Blacks. Nearly nine out of ten with professional and managerial backgrounds (87 per cent), were able to do so, compared to just over three out of five Blacks with similar backgrounds. A similar pattern, although slightly attenuated, can be seen in the case of the other middle-class occupations. Seventy-three per cent of light-skinned respondents with lower managerial or professional backgrounds ended up in the middle class, compared to 48 per cent of Blacks with the same background.

If we compare those with working-class backgrounds, the differences are still quite striking. Thirty-seven per cent of light-skinned persons with a working-class background (operatives, skilled tradesmen and service workers) were able to end up in middle-class occupations, compared to 21 per cent of black people with similar backgrounds.

The pattern of outflows suggests that the racial differentials cannot simply be reduced to prior class differentials. These findings are not an artefact of the particular racial classification we adopt. Tables 7 and 8 make it clear that similar results are obtained when we use the racial classification peculiar to the 1984 survey. Although the analysis in this paper is mainly exploratory, and confined to the inflow and outflow percentage tables, it leaves us in no doubt about the existence of these differentials. Further analysis of the source of these differentials would reveal how much of the differential is due to the differing class composition of the major racial groups, how much to the ability to inherit social positions, and how much to the ease of mobility between positions.

None of this, of course, removes the fact that the black majority is composed of different classes. If the black majority is moving in the direction of expanding its middle class and capitalist class, it seems inescapable that this class development has not by any means exhausted its full potential, and is being held back by racial forces which operate directly in terms of economic power, as well as more indirectly through the medium of culture and ideology.

Reflections on Race and Class

THE ANALYSES we have carried out demonstrate that despite the tremendous changes in the location of black Jamaicans in the class structure, particularly in the wage-earning classes, stubborn racial differentials in position and opportunity remain. We have documented in some detail aspects of these changes, and remaining inequalities in the class structure and patterns of social mobility.

This is as far as this kind of empirical analysis can take us. Empirical associations between location in the class structure and race provide useful indications of underlying dynamic relations, but they cannot substitute for an analysis of these dynamic relations themselves. As Carl Stone put it in another context in his *Democracy and Clientelism,* "While demographic and occupational factors in the society reflect some of the major changes over the period, such quantitative data miss the more fundamental underlying factors at the center of the changes in the Jamaican class structure over the approximately half a century prior to 1978".[8]

It is not always appreciated that class and race are concepts at very different logical and theoretical levels. An analysis which proceeds as if they are at the same level – which uses race and class in the same breath, attempting to establish theoretical relations between them directly, as in the manner of empirical correlations – makes if difficult to understand the underlying relations between them. This is certainly so in many Weber-inspired analyses, which see class and race as basically two dimensions of the problem of distribution of resources: class in this case as the principle of allocation according to market forces, and race as the distribution of resources and values on the basis of particularistic criteria or on the criteria of racial dominance.

This approach basically leaves race as an unexamined, unexplained, *a priori* reality – either biologically or culturally based, but in either case unexplained. It leaves class as mere differential material position or opportunity, ignoring the basis of class relations in the mode of production. Racial and class antagonisms are then "explained" either by primordial sentiments or racial dominance, on the one hand, or, on the other, by the view that mere material difference produces conflict based on this difference.

Marxists in the Caribbean and elsewhere are not immune to this approach either: in our case, it takes the form of "reducing" racial oppression and racial antagonisms directly to class antagonisms, thus dissolving race into class. A much more subtle approach, but one which is still inadequate, situates "class" at the level of material relations and "race" at the level of ideological relations. This leads in some cases to a view that "race" is simply a distorted or insubstantial reality, produced and reproduced in the service of class relations and which can be overcome in the class struggle against racist ideology. Thus, this position may still deny the relative autonomy and historical validity of racial and national struggles.[9]

There are basically two sets of relations between race and class which must be explained. When they are adequately explained, the relationships between the two sets will be clarified. The first concerns the qualitative changes in the nature of social classes arising from changes in the mode of production in Jamaica. Race here is an organizing principle in the class relations of a slave plantation society which undergoes change in the course of the society's development. The second set of relations in which race appears is in relations of national oppression, in which this national oppression takes a racial form: the oppression of black nationalities by white nations. Race and nation never become and cannot become fully co-terminous, but our analysis of race here has to draw on the peculiar and extreme forms which national oppression takes when it fixes on physical features as a mark of the oppressed nationalities. In this case race is not merely an expression of nationalism but an element of nationality and ethnic identity, however weakly the latter is developed. Nationalities are led by classes, national struggles are a relatively independent form the class struggle takes, and classes are the classes of nationalities. This is the second link between race and class.

Some progress has been made in the analysis of the first set of relations from both Weber-inspired and Marxist positions. Stone has argued, for example, that "the most fundamental feature of the changes [in the class structure] involves the transition from a paternalist class system to a more competitive one. This transition is, however, still incomplete".[10] Stone goes on to show how the basic class premises of the mainly agrarian, plantation-based order entrenched racial privilege, limited the mobility of the black majority, and instilled an ideology of racial/cultural superiority. He describes how changes in the mode of production resulted in a "drift to a more competitive class system" with the ascendancy of a new merchant manufacturing sector over the old planter class, the expansion of the middle class and the formation of an organized urban working class. This necessarily changed the role and salience of race as an organizing principle of stratification and a medium through which class relations necessarily had to operate. Race and racially based struggles do not necessarily disappear, but, in Stone's view, they take on either diminished significance or appear racial in form, while remaining fundamentally economic or class-based in motivation and content. An issue Stone touches on but does not fully explore is the extent to which the remaining racial and national forms of the class struggle are stimulated by the continued economic and political dominance of imperialist nations.

Recent Marxist analyses that try to explain why class struggles take on a racial form are found in the work of, for example, Stuart Hall, Charles Mills and Diane Austin. Mills tries to show why the class structure of slavery must necessarily lead to a racial understanding of class:

> Just as capitalism tends to foster particular ways of seeing the world, quite independently of the conscious efforts of pro-capitalist ideologists, so the slave system produced its own characteristic ideational patterns, experientially based on the obvious correlation of race with social position and power. In capitalist societies that are (more or less) racially homogeneous, the subordinate position of the working class and the poor is explained through theories of attitudinal deficiency ... and lack of intellectual capacity.... In racially structured class societies like those of the Caribbean, however, the stigmata of putatively innate inferiority are phenotypically visible. Thus a racial interpretation of the class structure was the most natural ideological outcome.[11]

Austin tries to show, for contemporary urban class relations in Jamaica, that the class structure has not become as classically capitalist as might be conveyed by Stone's notion of a "competitive class system". Class is overlaid by cultural differences and antagonisms that still carry many of the ascriptive distinctions of early modes of production. Austin effectively explores some of the ways in which this weakens the ability of workers to develop their struggles against exploitation in a consistent manner. She argues that even the ideology of education has within it certain notions about the innate cultural inferiority of working people which profoundly affect their ability to develop modern class consciousness, even while they may be aware that their position is due to class exploitation.

> The identification of education with enculturation and of wage exploitation with slavery brings history into the present, and makes ascriptive distinctions a factor in contemporary class ideology. If the colour of Jamaica's middle class is mixed, the working class remains predominantly black, and when this class is associated with the original slaves and their condition it is easy to think of the working class as the inheritors of the slaves' position.... The blackness of the working class reveals them as the direct descendants of slaves, and therefore decultured and outside society.[12]

These views point the way towards an analysis of race as a factor in class relations. They suggest that while the changing class character of Jamaican society brings about a changed (and reduced) role for race, it does not eliminate race as an element in class relations.

What these views do not adequately deal with is the relationship of race to nationality, to national oppression and to national struggles against oppression, and of these to class. The struggles of Bogle and Gordon were surely both class struggles in the narrow sense and national struggles; not only in the sense that the classes they represented needed for their advancement to thrust aside the monopolies and privileges of the white landed class, but also because they were representing all the classes of a developing black Jamaican nationality which was being oppressed.

The same is true for Garvey. In his "Attachment", quoted at the beginning of this paper, Garvey makes clear that his remarks on Jamaican social structure were aimed at correcting the one-sided view (attributed to Du Bois on a trip to Jamaica) that the racial problem was basically solved in Jamaica because the black peasantry was developing. The task was therefore to ensure the continued economic development of this peasantry and this would deal effectively with the remaining racial problem. Garvey disagreed fundamentally with Du Bois and tried to show that the black Jamaican was oppressed not only economically but culturally and politically, and that a broader national struggle against white domination would be necessary. The national struggle that developed did not take quite the forms that Garvey was engaged in. In some respects it was far richer and more varied in form than the Jamaican struggle in Garvey's day; in others it is only now putting on the agenda and seeking to resolve many of the issues Garvey posed.

Here Caribbean Marxism still has some way to go. It remains true that it is the theorists of other schools who have held most steadfastly to this second aspect. It is M.G. Smith's theory of social and cultural pluralism, which despite its many obvious deficiencies puts the major focus on national and racial oppression.[13] For Smith, it is those "wider racial and cultural divisions which together constitute the corporate macro-structure" that are the fundamental units. Classes are subsumed within and subordinated to "these more inclusive, fundamental and intricately interwoven differences of race and culture, history and political power".[14] These societies are societies based upon the national and racial oppression of white, European nations, who conquered, subordinated and enslaved indigenous and African populations and continued to exercise their military and political dominance after slavery. To this day, even while relinquishing formal political power, these groups continue to oppress the black majority nationality.

This reality of racial domination and racial antagonisms, which Smith describes, still leaves fundamental questions unanswered. What explains the development (not simply the recurrence) of the struggle against national oppression, its changing character, goals and objectives? What explains the altered balance of power of the major racial and ethnic groups? What explains the changing role of social classes in this struggle?

Here Smith can help us very little, because he sees basically a one-sided relationship between national struggles and the mode of production and the classes based on this, in which it is the ethno-cultural groups or nationalities who shape the economy and the class structure. Smith simply replaces with his own one-sided approach the one-sideness of some Marxist analyses, which ignore the implications of the fact that classes – even the class which by its nature is potentially able to go beyond nationalism: the working class – are always the classes of particular nations or ethnic groups.

This is a gap that represents a real challenge for a revitalized Caribbean Marxism. This Marxism must learn to reject an abstract universalism which is really hiding behind its own great-power and racist nationalism, and to start from the struggles of our Caribbean people against oppression.

NOTES

[1] Marcus Garvey, in an attachment to a letter to Major R.R. Moton, February 1916, in Robert Hill (ed.), *The Marcus Garvey and Universal Negro Improvement Association Papers* (Berkeley: University of California Press, 1983), p. 180.

[2] Adam Kuper, *Changing Jamaica* (London: Routledge and Kegan Paul, 1976); M.G. Smith, *The Plural Society in the British West Indies* (Berkeley and Los Angeles: University of California Press, 1965); M.G. Smith, *Corporations and Society* (London: Duckworth, 1974); M.G. Smith, *Culture, Race and Class in the Commonwealth Caribbean* (Kingston: Department of Extra-Mural Studies, University of the West Indies, 1984); Carl Stone, *Democracy and Clientelism in Jamaica* (New Brunswick, New Jersey: Transaction Books, 1980).

[3] Adam Kuper, *Changing Jamaica,* p. 66

[4] Derek Gordon, *Class, Status and Social Mobility in Jamaica* (Kingston: ISER, 1987).

[5] Lloyd Braithwaite, "Sociology and Demographic Research in the British Caribbean", *Social and Economic Studies,* Vol. 6, No. 4, 1957, pp. 523-571.

[6] David Lowenthal, *West Indian Societies* (London: Oxford University Press, 1972), p. 94.

[7] Fernando Henriques, *Family and Colour in Jamaica* (London: Eyre and Spottiswoode, 1953), p. 54.

[8] Carl Stone, *Democracy and Clientelism,* p. 15.

[9] See, for example, Nancy Foner, *Status and Power in Rural Jamaica* (New York: Teachers College Press, 1974); and Jack Alexander, "The Culture of Race in Middle Class Kingston", *American Ethnologist,* 4, 1977, pp. 413-435.

[10] Stone, *Democracy and Clientelism,* p. 15.

[11] Charles Mills, "Race and Class: Conflicting or Reconcilable Paradigms?", *Social and Economic Studies,* Vol. 36, No. 3, 1987, pp. 70-108.

[12] Diane Austin, *Urban Life in Kingston, Jamaica* (New York: Gorcion and Breach, 1984), p. 156.

[13] Don Robotham, "The Way of the Cockatoo", *Social and Economic Studies,* Vol. 34, No. 2, 1985; and Charles Mills, "Race and Class".

[14] M.G. Smith, *Culture, Race and Class,* p. 141.

The Left and the Question of Race in Jamaica

Trevor Munroe
Department of Government
University of the West Indies, Mona, Jamaica
General Secretary, Workers' Party of Jamaica

THE ISSUE OF RACE is at the centre of Garveyism. In his philosophy, work and activity, Marcus Garvey rejected white racism and affirmed blackness – the need for black race consciousness, race pride, race solidarity. Garvey, nevertheless, recognized the element of class: particularly in his work in Jamaica and the Caribbean he had to take account of class division amongst Blacks and, in so doing, more often than not sided with the most oppressed amongst the Blacks.

From time to time, in relation to other events, Garvey forcefully expressed the importance of the class factor in politics. On the occasion of Lenin's death in 1924, Garvey said:

> It is impossible to expect that all the people will think kindly of any one individual in the world, because there is a division of interests in the world. All people are not interested in the same thing.... Each class has its own representatives. Each has its own leaders.[1]

Garvey went on to say that in expressing their class interests, "the governments of the capitalist class ... of the privileged class" refused to recognize the Bolshevik regime,

> ... but we of the UNIA ... without any hesitancy, without any reserve, could not but favour the existence of social democratic rule in Russia ... because we are of the class that rules in Russia.[2]

Class perspectives were clearly not absent within the framework of the primacy of race. Our concern in this paper, however, is not to trace that inter-relationship in Garvey's work, but to examine the race perspective within that section of the left which traditionally assigns primacy to class considerations.

Overview of the Jamaican Left

OUR EXAMINATION has to begin with the recognition that as yet no comprehensive or systematic study of the left in modern Jamaican politics has been done. Work

CRITERIA	REVOLUTIONARY NATIONALISM	REVOLUTIONARY SOCIALISM	REVOLUTIONARY CHRISTIANITY
Race	Primary	Secondary	Mixed
Ideological Foundation	Garvey	Marxism-Leninism	Christian Bible
Class	Secondary	Primary	Mixed
Philosophical Orientation	Materialism/Idealism	Materialism	Idealism
External Economic Relations	Reduce dependency	Reduce dependency	Reduce dependency
Internal Economic Relations	Subordinate big bourgeois/landowner property	Subordinate big bourgeois/landowner property	Subordinate big bourgeois/landowner property
Political System	Transcend two-party democracy	Transcend two-party democracy	Transcend two-party democracy
Culture	Anti-US imperialist culture/pro-Black	Anti-US imperialist culture/pro-Black	Anti-US imperialist culture/pro-Black

Figure 1. Criteria for delineating the left in Jamaica, 1965–1985.

has either been confined to one section of the left within a narrow time period[3] or, alternatively, the left is examined as part of the PNP Manley administration.[4] In another dimension, opinion polls allow us to estimate the support for left tendencies at different points in time.[5] Perhaps the only exception in the partial nature of these studies of the left is Horace Campbell's[6] – an excellent study as yet insufficiently noticed in the Caribbean.

This gap in studies of the left is no doubt partly a reflection of the marginality of explicit left challenge to state power in modern Jamaican politics. Whenever the left becomes a force in state power – as in Grenada (1979-1983) or under Michael Manley's PNP (1972-1980) – scholars run to catch up with numerous studies of varying value. As far as I know, there was no study of the New Jewel Movement prior to 1979. Now such are countless. In relation to Jamaica, an overall examination of the origin and development of the left is now very definitely on the agenda. This arises from a number of considerations: the obvious need for basic change in the interest of the majority; the reduction in the confidence amongst the majority that politics in general and the major established parties in particular can bring about fundamental change; the relative weakness of the left and its inability as yet to develop itself as a credible alternative.

Our discussion of the attitude of the left to the question of race, therefore, is set within the framework of an overview of what constitutes the left; aims to identify weaknesses in the attitude to race of one section of the left; suggests reasons for these weaknesses; and proposes some measures to avoid repetition of past mistakes.

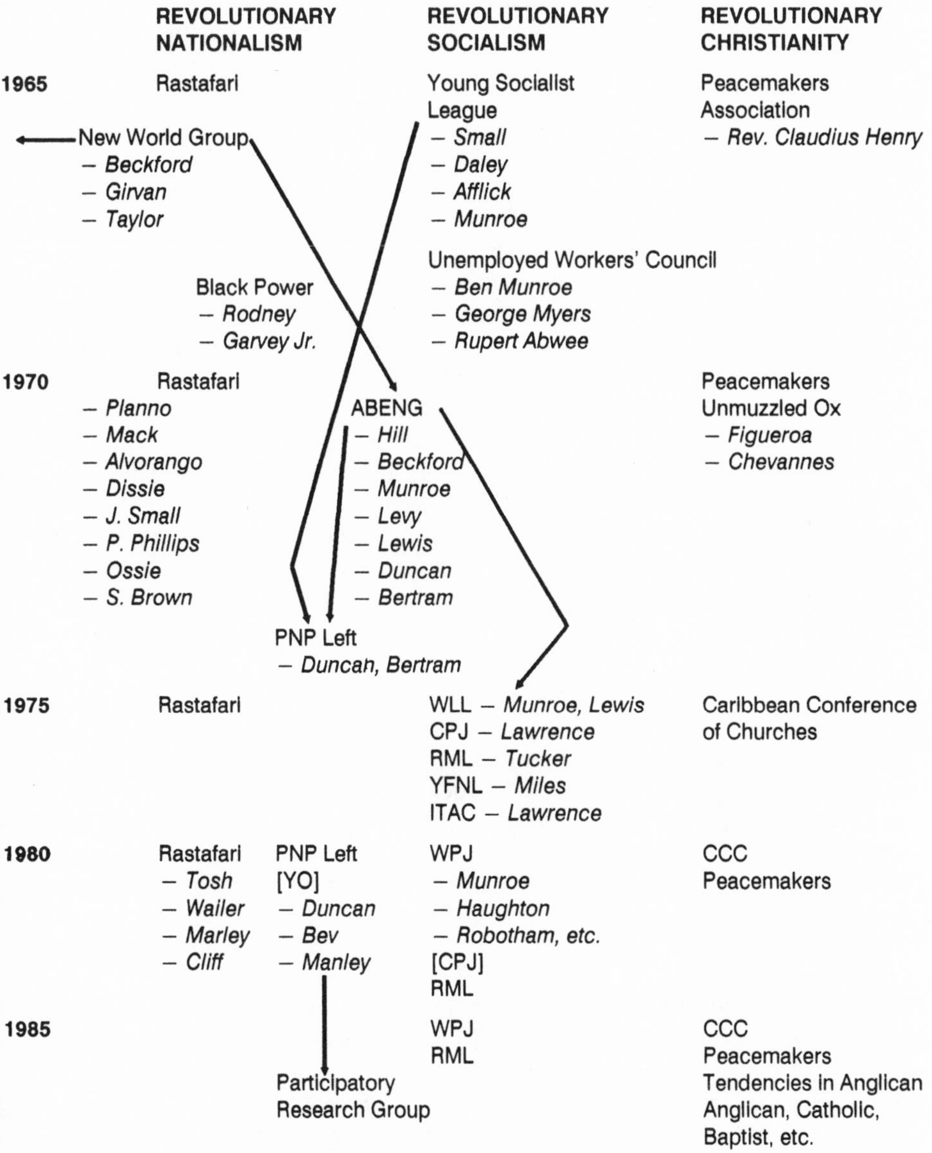

Figure 2. The left in Jamaica, 1965–1985.

Figure 1 proposes, tentatively, some criteria on the basis of which to identify and delineate the left as it has developed over the last twenty years or so. We identify three main revolutionary tendencies, using the term "revolutionary" in its most general sense: an interest, objective or subjective, in fundamental structural change for the benefit of the majority. Revolutionary nationalism, revolutionary socialism and revolutionary Christianity are thereby differentiated and related on the basis of varying or similar attitudes to race and class, varying or similar ideological foundations and philosophical orientations, as well as programmatic perspectives on external economic relations, internal economic relations, the political system and culture. Figure 2 identifies the tendencies, movements, organizations, groups and the more prominent personalities embodying these left tendencies and which assumed some significance in the last two decades.

A number of comments are in order. First, not all the tendencies are explicitly electoral or political, but all have political implications for radical change. Second, they each have much in common, both at the level of identifying criteria as well as in practical relations and development over the years. Third, because the categories are neither discrete nor mutually exclusive, often particular organizations/personalities partake of and contribute to different tendencies. Fourth, these tendencies came most to the fore in a period of intense neo-colonial subjection (the mid-1960s), grew to mass significance in a decade of high popular militancy (1968–1978), and have survived under the rightist Seaga administration and in the context of growth in reformist passivity amongst the masses. As is usually the case with revolutionary tendencies, the state power has, with varying degrees of success, used techniques of accommodation and repression to marginalize the independent left. Nevertheless, these tendencies have survived in one or another form, and there is reason to believe that the politics of the 1990s will provide a foundation for their strengthening.

The Marxist Left and Race

REX NETTLEFORD and M.G. Smith[7] have noted critically that the Marxist tendency in the Caribbean has hitherto failed to deal adequately with the factors of race and colour. To be fair, the Marxist activists, in particular Richard Hart, had a definite appreciation of the practical importance of racism as an ideological means of maintaining colonial rule, and of race pride as an ideological precondition for effective struggles by the black working class.

In this regard, from the early 1940s, Hart lectured on the revolutionary resistance of black people to slavery to help dispel "the formidable institutional legacy of a widespread lack of racial self-respect".[8] Despite Garvey's advances in this regard, Hart recognized that "the task of inspiring national self-confidence" remained a formidable one. For his efforts, we can recall that in October 1942 a detention order issued against Hart charged him, *inter alia,* with "the fostering of racial and class dissension in Jamaica".[9] Hart explicitly identified as one technique of British rule the establishment of "a system of education and indoctrination deliberately designed to promote a loyalty to the prevailing imperialism and an acceptance of the domination of whites over blacks".[10]

A review of the two basic documents influenced by the Marxist tendency in the left movement 40 years after – namely, the *Programme of the Workers' Party of Jamaica* (1978) and *PNP Principles and Objectives* (1979) – gives substance to the criticism of Nettleford, Smith and others. In the case of the WPJ *Programme,* race is certainly recognized as an important political issue. In the historical section, the document states: "under the whip and branding irons of the planter, a slave society built upon racial oppression and with the hateful ideology of racial superiority was forged on our land" (para. 90). It goes on to recognize that after the abolition of slavery, "racial oppression and prejudice continued unabated" (para. 27). Paul Bogle's struggle is identified not just as a "struggle for land, for high wages and an end to labouring service against oppressive, discriminating taxation for justice and political rights"; it is also recognized as a struggle for "an end to racial prejudice and oppression" (para. 32).

With the onset of imperialist capitalism, the *Programme* recognizes that with the consequent changes "the whole system of national and racial oppression was intensified" (para. 40). This "national subjugation and racial oppression led to a renewal of the national movement and the beginnings of a working class movement in Jamaica" (para. 48). Elsewhere, "the broad masses of the people were subjected daily to racial humiliation and hatred for black people by the imperialists and the local oligarchy" (para. 56). On the eve of Independence, the WPJ *Programme* says, "ethnic minorities continued to enjoy racial and socio-economic privileges. Racial prejudice, discrimination and oppression of people of African descent continued to pervade the society and hindered the consolidation of the nation" (para. 89). Following Independence, at the beginning of the 1970s, the *Programme* states:

> The black majority of the people continues, as in slavery, to be at the bottom in our society: under the guise of multiracialism, the minority ruling groups maintain their racial exclusiveness, imposing their hostility to people of African descent, to their culture and history in many areas of social life, and encouraging the persistence of racism as well as decadent imperialist culture. *(para. 115)*

The condition of the rural people is specifically singled out: "Race and class lines merge to separate the land gods from the rural masses. Racial oppression and accompanying racist ideologies and attitudes is an all-pervasive feature of rural life" (para. 127).

In the analysis of resistance to these conditions, it is stated that:

> The progressive elements in the Rastafarian Movement played a vital role in championing the struggle of the people against racism and imperialism. Revolutionary nationalism, under the slogan "Black Power" and led by the Abeng movement, became a force in Jamaican politics. *(para. 7)*

As far as Marxist parties and Marxist tendencies go, a relatively extended and positive assessment of Marcus Garvey is given:

> A second more radical trend led by our National Hero, Marcus Garvey, renewed the call of Bogle and Bedward for an end to racial oppression, founded the UNIA initially in 1914, and developed it after 1921 into the first real anti-colonial mass movement in our history.
>
> Persecuted, imprisoned and finally expelled from America, Garvey returned to Jamaica in 1927 and began to take an active role in politics. In 1929, Garvey founded Jamaica's first real political party –

> the People's Political Party; and in 1930, the Jamaica Labour and Tradesmen Association as a pressure group for sugar workers. In his programme, in addition to his call for an end to racial oppression, he proposed the establishment of an 8-hour day; a minimum wage; workmen's compensation laws; rent control; land reform; rural electrification and industrialization. Thus, Garveyism recognized, even though instinctively, the need for a national movement based on the alliance of the proletariat and the petty bourgeoisie, albeit under petty bourgeois leadership. Nevertheless, although Garvey awoke thousands of our people to political life for the first time, and laid the foundation for our present national movement, his struggle failed. (*paras. 60-61*)

Two reasons are given for the failure of Garvey's struggle, and it is in these two reasons that the programmatic weaknesses of the WPJ programme on the race question begin to be revealed. The first reason is what the *Programme* describes as the strength of "the reformist and colonial mentality, especially on the racial question ... amongst the national bourgeoisie and the middle strata" (para. 61). In respect of this national bourgeoisie and middle strata, it is they who later assumed leadership of the major political parties and guidance of the political system in post-Independence Jamaica. The considerable implications of "brown racism" at the helm of the state is insufficiently identified, and hence, in part, the failure of the *Programme* to specify adequate measures to eradicate racism against black people.

Thus, in a programme of 251 paragraphs and against the background of nominal recognition of racism being intertwined in the fabric of Jamaican society, two paragraphs deal with the "elimination of racism and racial discrimination". Those read:

> Deriving from slave society and reinforced by imperialism and neocolonialism, racial prejudice and discrimination, especially against the black majority as well as other minority ethnic groups, has constantly plagued our socio-economic and cultural life and retarded the formation of a Jamaican nation.
>
> The Programme of our Party abolishes the economic basis of racism, the Constitution would outlaw it and the cultural and educational programme would strive to eliminate it by developing and promoting the cultural heritage of the people on a broad and equal basis. (*paras. 236-237*).

Clearly, the proposals in the latter paragraph come close to repeating a crude economic determism by implying that the economic proposals of socialist orientation, together with unspecified cultural and educational measures, would lead to the withering away of racism. No specifically political action is indicated in relation to a specific struggle against racism. Needless to say, no such deficiencies are apparent in the *Programme* in respect of measures to democratize the state, reduce the role of foreign capital, strengthen the position of the working class, etc.

A second main weakness in the WPJ programmatic treatment of the race question is an exaggeration – in some measure a misrepresentation – of the significance of relations with the international working-class movement in respect of the struggle for national liberation and against racism. This is apparent in the second reason given for "Garvey's failing": "Garveyism failed to link up our national movement with the international workers and communist movement" (para. 62). "Thus, the Garveyite national movement ... unable to utilize the possibilities created by the Great October Socialist Revolution of strengthening the national movement by allying with the international working class movement declined" (para. 64).

To be fair, the *Programme* does recognize that Garvey's alienation from communism had to do with "racist and chauvinistic attitudes" in sections of the working-class movement. It should also have indicated, however, that while links between the communist movement – in particular the Communist International – and national liberation movements often had advantages for both and weakened world imperialism, nevertheless, particularly after Lenin's death, opportunism and political errors in the Comintern meant that national liberation struggles sometimes advanced despite, rather than because of, links with world communism.[11]

In relation to the PNP's *Principles and Objectives,* this document remains amongst the most comprehensive and far-reaching in its proposal for transformation of Jamaican society in the interest of the masses and was drafted under the influence of revolutionary socialist tendencies. It states bluntly:

> The objective of the PNP is the construction of a socialist society in Jamaica. Socialism is a method of social and economic organization in which the means of production are socially owned and/or controlled. This provides a basis for ending the exploitation of one class by another. *(p. 7)*.

It goes on to say that "as the entire socialist process deepens, the working class and small farmers will naturally play a more active role in national life and within the class alliance" (p. 11). Tasks of ideological struggle are set out, including "to combat the insidious campaign of imperialism, fascism, and local reaction, aimed at maintaining privilege, exploitation and inequality" (p. 17). The *Principles and Objectives* state the need to develop "a comprehensible and flexible economic and social plan" (p. 34). Twelve planning objectives are identified, including "combatting inequities in the distribution of wealth" (p. 36). Social goals for education are set out, including "developing in members of society a sense of community spirit, cooperation and concern for others" (pp. 42, 43). Principles and aims governing mass media policy are set out, including the need to "inculcate in our people a concrete patriotic orientation" (p. 43).

Nowhere, however, in the entire length and breadth of the 67 pages of the PNP's *Principles and Objectives* is the reality of racial oppression against the black majority identified and the eradication of racism or racial discrimination set as a goal. Specifically, the elimination of racism is not mentioned as a task of ideological struggle, a goal of economic policy, a guideline for reorganization of education, nor an objective of the mass media. In two places only is the term "race" even mentioned: first, "our Party is the heir to and the torchbearer of the fine revolutionary traditions of our people begun by Nanny, Tacky and Sam Sharpe ... continued by Garvey for national liberation, *racial dignity* and international solidarity of oppressed people" (p.

1; emphasis mine). The second and final place in which it is mentioned is in the international policy: "*Condemnation of all fascist and racist regimes:* The PNP condemns the practice of racism and fascism which continue to be the main instruments of the degradation of man by man" (p. 56; emphasis mine).

This document, *PNP Principles and Objectives,* is not only a key manifesto of the left movement; it also significantly reflected and guided PNP policy as government between 1974 and 1980.

We can therefore conclude that serious programmatic weaknesses reveal themselves on the race question, not so much in historical analysis, but in the complexity of the contemporary situation and in the appropriate goals of the left on this question. This clearly needs explanation as, in the 1960s and 1970s, the left – particularly at the revolutionary nationalist stage of its development – made relatively significant use of race in its publications, speeches and mass activity.

A Review of Left Publications and Agitation: The PNP, 'Abeng' and 'Struggle'[12]

WE START with the PNP. The 1972 electoral campaign saw Michael Manley making dramatic use of all the symbols, personalities and groups associated with the struggle against racism – both white and brown. The Black Power slogan "Power to the People" was a main rallying cry; the rod – allegedly received from Haile Selassie – a central symbol; Rastafari and the Rev. Claudius Henry main allies; and black music main campaign material. Activists from *Abeng* were co-opted into the PNP's campaign organization. It is not easy to explain, therefore, except on grounds of electoral opportunism, how the paraphernalia of the black struggle could so dominate an election campaign and yet the race question be so absent from a fundamental programmatic document which began to be elaborated little more than three years after by some of the very same personalities.

A second factor, however, undoubtedly had to do with ideological deficiencies taking shape in the revolutionary nationalists from *Abeng*, who evolved towards revolutionary socialism as leaders of the PNP left and of the Workers' Liberation League (WLL). The essence of this deficiency lay in a counterposing of race (of the *Abeng* period) to class (of the WLL/PNP left period). In retrospect, a major weakness in our understanding and application of dialectics is revealed. Race is negated abstractedly instead of dialectically. *Abeng*'s stress on factors associated with race is not integrated with the class factor, but displaced by it. This gross deficiency is revealed in a comparison of the 32 issues of *Abeng,* 1 February – 3 October 1969, and a corresponding number of issues of *Struggle,* 30 June 1977 – 14 September 1978.

To gain a quantitative measure of this deficiency, articles were classified according to whether their main content dealt with black culture, Marcus Garvey, the African liberation struggle, imperialism, party politics, scientific socialism, the working class (mainly unionism), the economy. The results are shown in Tables 1 and 2 and Figure 3. Briefly, *Abeng* devoted proportionately four times as much coverage to black culture and five times as much to Marcus Garvey as *Struggle*. Conversely, there is almost no mention whatsoever of scientific socialism in *Abeng,* whilst almost

	Abeng		*Struggle*	
	No.	%	No.	%
1. Culture	21	17.5	8	4.2
2. Garvey	19	15.8	6	3.1
3. African Liberation Struggle	13	10.8	10	10.5
4. Imperialism	8	6.6	19	10.0
5. Party Politics	39	32.5	36	18.9
6. Scientific Socialism	0	0.0	26	13.7
7. Working Class/ Unionism	8	6.6	56	29.5
8. Economy	8	6.6	9	4.7
9. Miscellaneous	4	3.3	10	5.2
TOTAL	120	100.0	190	100.0

Table 1. Distribution of selected articles by subject in ABENG (1969) and STRUGGLE (1977–1978).

14 per cent of Struggle articles are devoted to this subject. Similarly, there are over four times as many articles dealing with the working class in *Struggle* as in *Abeng*. A simple aggregation reveals that whereas *Struggle* devoted less than 18 per cent to articles that had themes of race, Abeng had 44 per cent. Eighty-two per cent of Struggle articles were devoted to themes associated with class.

No doubt this comparison may suffer from imprecision. For example, it could be argued that articles dealing with imperialism in *Abeng* should be associated with the race theme. But re-examination certainly of the headline treatment of imperialism indicates only in a minority of instances "Whites" being bracketed with imperialism. Furthermore, the differences in relative emphasis in the two papers may well reflect in part the high level of race-/nationalist-oriented activity in the 1969 period, compared with the high level of working class activity in the mid-1970s. In the latter

	Race (1, 2, 3)		Class (4–9)	
	No.	%	No.	%
Abeng	53	44.1	67	55.9
Struggle	34	17.8	156	82.2
TOTAL	87	28.0	223	72.0

Table 2. Distribution/Aggregation of subjects/articles in ABENG and STRUGGLE by main orientation.

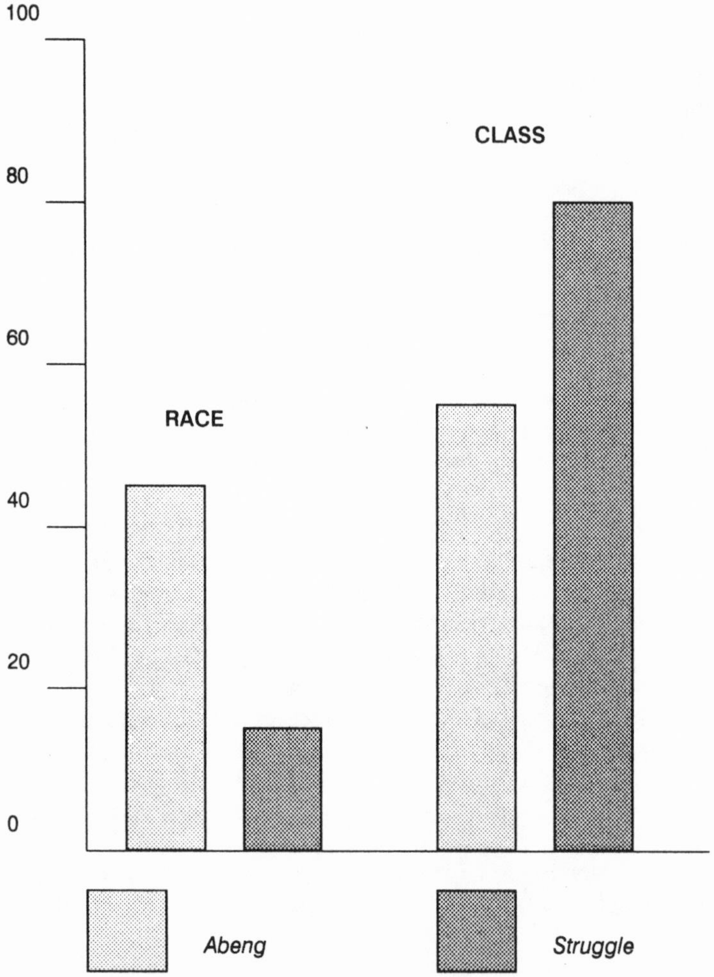

Figure 3. Bar graph of class/race orientation in ABENG and STRUGGLE newspapers.

period, the data do confirm that the working-class strike movement was at its highest since the 1938 uprising. Nevertheless, this cannot entirely explain the significant change in the content of the publishing and public education activity of the same people over a short period of time. There are other factors to be taken into account.

Factors Conditioning Inadequacies on the Race Question

A Dogmatic Approach to Marxism

In transcending revolutionary nationalism, the left approached Marxism more as a set of formulae we learned and applied to our conditions. Hence, research was carried out to aggregate our census data into Marxist class categories. This produced work on the Jamaican class structure that got behind the economic inequalities, which were obvious and which ranked amongst the highest in the world.[13] Little or no emphasis was put on Marx's dialectical materialist method and its essential openness to life and new realities. In coming to grips with class, we lost sight of race.

Relative Absence of Race Analysis in Classical Marxism-Leninism

Munck[14] estimates that only 2 to 3 percent of the writings of Marx and Engels deal with nationalism, as opposed to 25 per cent of Lenin's output. An even lesser proportion would deal with the specifically racial component of black nationalism. In any event, the classical assessments were carried out from two points of view: first, capitalism as the progenitor of racial and national oppression and, second, the necessity of the working class in advanced capitalist states opposing the colonialism and imperialism of its own bourgeoisie and defending the right of oppressed nations to self-determination. In either case, race is analysed not so much as an independent variable but in a relationship of dependence, in the first case on capitalism, and in the second case on its connection with the emancipation of the proletarians of Europe. Lenin it was who went furthest in identifying the relative autonomy of both the nationalism of the oppressed and the nationalism of the oppressor, as well as the need for the class-conscious elements within historically oppressive groups to bend over backwards in ridding themselves of national chauvinism.

The main point is, however, that the absence of anything substantial on race in the classics and a dogmatic approach encouraged the absence of anything substantial in our Marxism. What we should have sought, and did not, was a synthesis between our "old" revolutionary nationalism and "new" scientific socialism. We insufficiently heeded some voices that were grasping the embryo of this error as early as 1969: in a letter published in *Abeng* on 31 May 1969, Jerry Small wrote: "Learn and teach that ours is not merely a class struggle to be waged by a proletariat, but in addition and also, overwhelmingly a cultural, spiritual and mental struggle being waged by race, a nation Africa".

Moreover, few of the leading personalities of the left at the time were aware of, took seriously enough or viewed sympathetically a significant body of writing by progressive Blacks pointing to the deficiency of classical (as well as applied) Marxism on the race question. In some instances there was admiration of the work of C.L.R. James. This admiration, however, for reasons that need fuller explanation, was subordinated in the left as the 1970s progressed.

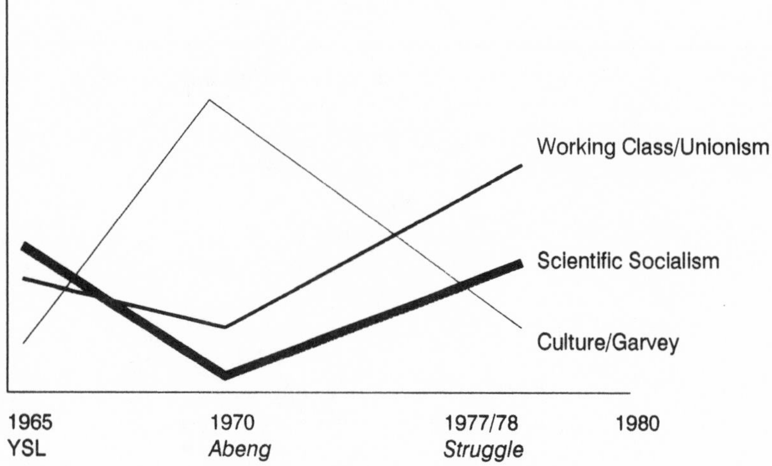

Figure 4. Graph of treatment of selected subjects at different points in the left movement.

The Degree of Manifestation of White Racism and Racial Subjection of Blacks

Clearly, throughout the period, racism and racial oppression have been evident. However, such was more manifest prior to 1972 under the Shearer Jamaica Labour Party (JLP) administration and, subsequently, since 1980, under the Seaga government. For many reasons, Blacks did make advances under the Manley government in overcoming self-denigration, in affirming race pride, in resisting imperialist cultural penetration, and in developing anti-imperialist culture. In addition, some advance was made in reducing the racial exclusivity of the managerial strata with the incorporation of a relatively significant number of Blacks into this area. This would have contributed to the delusion that the question was taking care of itself and needed no specific attention.

Linkages with National Reformism and the International Working-Class Movement

The left sectors who went into the PNP had to face objective limits on their blackness in the context of the "out of many one people" multi-racial ideology of the brown middle strata. The sectors that established the connection with the international working-class movement had to face continuation of the historical neglect of the race factor. In either case, neither sufficient self-confidence nor a sense of political independence existed to sustain adequate attention to race.

Taken together, these factors have given the Jamaican left a zig-zag, up-and-down character on race, class and associated factors over the last 20 years. Figure 4 tries to depict this graphically in relation to relative attention given these variables at different points in time – namely, the Young Socialist League in the mid-1960s; *Abeng* in 1970; and *Struggle* in the last part of the 1970s. At each turn, we suffered from not assimilating the best in our previous practice and carrying our work to a higher plane. So that, for example, almost every issue of *Abeng* contained relevant editorials, speeches, quotations from Marcus Garvey. Instead of taking this over and carrying it forward in a critical spirit, as well as combining it with concepts of scientific socialism, *Struggle* chose to abandon Garvey and to take up Marx, Engels, Lenin, scientific socialist concepts, writings, countries.

The left clearly has got to learn that throwing out the baby with the bath water at each juncture can only contribute to relative ineffectiveness.

Specific Deficiencies and Proposals on Race

TO ME, THERE ARE FIVE related failings in the Marxist left on race:

(i) White racism and its derivative, brown racism, has not been identified and elaborated as a relatively independent component of the consciousness of the ethnic minorities and the brown middle strata.

(ii) Discrimination based on race has not been identified and elaborated as a relatively autonomous factor maintaining Blacks in unequal positions vis-à-vis ethnic minorities with otherwise comparable or inferior qualifications, training, economic means, etc. Hence, in important spheres a big black land-owner is not equal to a white land-owner, even when the latter has less land than the former. Similarly, a black student and a white student in high school or, for that matter, a black cabinet minister and his counterpart from one of the ethnic minorities. By and large, all Blacks, regardless of class, experience this phenomenon.

(iii) A failure to recognize that racism and racial discrimination – particularly in the top reaches of the ownership of the corporate economy – will not simply disappear over time, as we supposedly draw closer to "out of many one people". Because of the relative autonomy of the race factor, even equality of opportunity between Blacks and the racial minorities is not likely to produce equality of result, particularly vis-à-vis ownership of big business.

(iv) Apart from Campbell and Rodney, the Marxist left has not explicitly recognized race pride and race consciousness as a necessary, though insufficient, element of class consciousness. In our concrete conditions, therefore, class consciousness amongst workers does not only require grasping the labour theory of value, understanding the class limits on working people's rights in plural democracy, etc. Class consciousness also requires a race consciousness to counter white and brown racism. This means that, unlike the British worker, the Jamaican worker and peasant needs to know the essence of Sharpe, Bogle, Garvey, Rodney, and Rastafari, in addition to Marx, Engels and Lenin.

(v) Inadequate measures on race have naturally followed on inadequate analysis. The left can and should move towards correcting this weakness. In essence, "affirmative action" suitable to our conditions and around which to mobilize a united front of Blacks is necessary. Amongst the measures I would suggest are:

- Preferential treatment for Blacks vis-à-vis ethnic minorities in access to resources in the financial system. So long as capitalism exists, and even under socialism, non-propertied Blacks need to support propertied Blacks in this sphere in our collective self-interest vis-à-vis the ethnic minorities. Ethnic solidarity among all classes of Blacks is needed to combat the continued hegemony of ethnic minorities who, unlike the Blacks, make their differences secondary and maintain a united front in the face of challenge.

- Drastic reduction in visual portrayals of racial minorities on the electronic media; proportional upgrading of Blacks in a positive light.

- Overhaul of the content of educational instruction to identify the manifestations and role of racism in the ethnic minorities as well as to inculcate racial pride and self-confidence in the black majority. An integral part of this would be the teaching of Garveyism in schools.

- Qualitative change in the "no discrimination" clause in Jamaica's constitution to facilitate effective legal action against discrimination based on race.

- National debate towards changing the motto of the country to express the fact that we are a black nation. "Out of many one people" multi-racialism, even non-racialism, is a desirable ideal, but it cannot, as now, be at the expense of the black majority.

- Establishment of a state structure to develop and monitor programmes against racism in the widest areas of national life as well as to bring to public notice acts of racism and racial discrimination.

- A bureau on race relations or a race relations ombudsman may be considered. One area of urgent attention is to ensure that foreign consultants are not utilized where competent black professionals are available. Another would be to put the tourism sector under a microscope to unearth manifestations of racism.

- A continuing programme of published research into the progress or lack of progress of the black majority. This could be the responsibility of the specific state structure and/or university institute.

These and other similar measures should not be at the expense of recognizing the legitimate role and place of the privileged ethnic minorities in a black Jamaica, but as minorities with equal rights. The measures would also be an extension to and not a replacement of the main programmatic points of the left concerning greater democracy and accountability in the political system, reduction in economic dependence, agrarian reform, and programmes to reduce youth unemployment in particular.

Conclusion

THE MARXIST LEFT in Jamaica has clearly failed to deal adequately with, to take up and consistently carry forward the positives in Garveyism. At the same time, it has clearly developed a reputation for honesty in affirming its ideological outlook and consistency in championing the cause of the oppressed. It has also developed organizations of national significance amongst the working class and fraternal relations with national liberation movements, as well as communist parties. Coming to grips with the race question cannot be at the expense of gains made, thereby repeating the historic error, and should be part and parcel of the process of ridding itself of dogmatism and sectarianism.

As such, dialogue with other left tendencies and the achievement of common positions with revolutionary nationalists as well as revolutionary Christians is a priority not only for the left in general, but for a more effective revival of the national liberation struggle. Towards this end, a re-examination of Garvey's own treatment of the inter-relationship between race and class in Jamaican society would undoubtedly be helpful.

NOTES

[1] Robert Hill (ed.), *The Marcus Garvey and Universal Negro Improvement Association Papers* (Berkeley: University of California Press, 1986), Vol. 5, pp. 550-51.

[2] Ibid., pp. 550-51.

[3] Trevor Munroe, "The Marxist Left in Jamaica" (Jamaica: ISER Working Paper No. 15, 1977).

[4] Evelyne & John D. Stephens, *Democratic Socialism in Jamaica* (London, 1986); Michael Kaufmann, *Jamaica Under Manley* (London, 1985).

[5] Carl Stone, *The Political Opinions of the Jamaican People* (Kingston, Jamaica, 1982), and "Political Trends in Jamaica in the 1980s" (unpublished) (Department of Government, UWI, Mona).

[6] Horace Campbell, *Rasta and Resistance: From Marcus Garvey to Walter Rodney* (London, 1985).

[7] Rex Nettleford, *Caribbean Cultural Identity: The Case of Jamaica* (Kingston: Institute of Jamaica, 1978), and M.G. Smith, *Culture, Race and Class in the Commonwealth Caribbean* (Mona, Jamaica: Dept. of Extra-Mural Studies, UWI, 1984).

[8] Richard Hart, *Slaves Who Abolished Slavery: Blacks in Bondage* (Kingston: ISER, 1980).

[9] Munroe, "The Marxist Left", p. 67.

[10] Hart, *Slaves,* p. 1.

[11] Ronaldo Munck, *The Difficult Dialogue: Marxism and Nationalism* (London, 1986); Robert Hill, *Marcus Garvey,* Appendix 3.

[12] *Abeng* (1969) was and *Struggle* (1976-1987) is an important publication of the left in Jamaica. They rank as possibly the most important left newspapers of the last 20 years. Each at its peak attained

circulations of 20,000. The first was in the tradition of revolutionary nationalism; the second of scientific socialism. There was, however, significant overlap in the personnel directing and working with both publications.

[13] Charles L. Taylor and Michael Hudson, *World Handbook of Social and Political Indicators* (London, 1976).

[14] Munck, *The Difficult Dialogue,* p. 76.

Garvey and Cuba

Bernardo García Dominguez
Professional Development and Cultural Studies
Casa del Caribe, Santiago, Cuba

When Marcus Garvey was born, slavery had already been abolished for almost fifty years in Jamaica. In Cuba, whose Sierra Maestra mountains could almost be seen from St Ann, slavery had lasted until less than fifty weeks before.

The exodus from Jamaica in search of work began in the late nineteenth century. Growing waves of immigrants from Jamaica and other West Indian islands arrived in Cuba – 125,000 between 1907 and 1927. Many stayed. In 1931 there were 40,000 Jamaican residents, and even though many returned to their native lands between 1932 and 1938, in 1969, forty years after the last massive immigrations, 18,000 Jamaicans still lived in Cuba. An even greater number of Haitians came to work in the canefields. Both Jamaicans and Haitians would bring to the Cuban nationality a new dimension of culture, a new bridge to universality for the suffering country which, after defeating Spanish colonialism, was now contesting, alone and without weapons, dependency.

In Cuba, racial discrimination at the beginning of the century was less stringent than in other countries with a white majority; but after a rebellion by Blacks was savagely suppressed in 1912, and all the radical black leaders had been killed, racial discrimination became much more virulent. The black generals who had led the country in the war against Spain had hardly obtained any political power in the Cuban government. The Morúa Law of 1909 had forbidden the establishment of political parties on a racial or religious base, and the "Guerra de los Negros" of 1912 had started as a propaganda action of Cuban black leaders to press for the removal of the Morúa Law. However, the José Miguel Gómez government had reacted with such violence that hundreds and maybe thousands of Blacks had been killed. The government had wanted to show Blacks their "place". After thirty years of revolution against Spain and ten years' experience of republican institutions, Blacks still felt quite sure of themselves, though few had risen to positions of prominence, and this was considered an intolerable state of affairs for the neo-colonial republic that was being established under US control.

When Garvey arrived in Cuba, it was only a year since some Jamaican families had been paid $10,000 by the Menocal government in compensation for a massacre of several Jamaican workers in Jobabo in 1917.

It has been generally considered by Garvey scholars that Garveyism was an exclusively West Indian affair in the Latin American countries. There are reasons to believe that in Cuba the influence of Garveyism was greater. Because of this, and also owing to certain impressions regarding Garvey's trip to Cuba and the subsequent development of Garveyism in the country, it seems necessary to expand on certain matters of detail that can show the importance of his visit.

Marcus Garvey boarded the S.S. *Governor Cobb,* property of the Peninsular and Occidental Steamship Company, at Key West, Florida, on Monday, 28 February 1921. The *Governor Cobb* sailed at 10:30 p.m., and entered Havana harbour the next day, Tuesday, 1 March, at 6:30 a.m. The skies of the Cuban capital were partly covered. Garvey was received at San Francisco dock by the House Representative for Matanzas province, Primitivo Ramírez Ros, who was to accompany him throughout his visit to Havana. Ramírez assigned his own residence in Centro Habana (San Rafael 281) to Garvey, his secretaries and his assistants, who preferred it to a hotel.

There were, however, clouds in the political skies. The national elections conducted in Cuba on 1 November 1920 had been denounced by the Partido Liberal, the main party of the opposition. The government, under American pressure, had consented to repeat them. They had been scheduled for 1 March, the day Garvey arrived, but were postponed to 10 March a week before, and again postponed till the 15th, when they were conducted throughout the country (except for Oriente Province, where they took place on 26 March). So electoral fever was at its height when Garvey arrived, and this circumstance had a favourable impact during the three weeks of his visit to Cuba.

Garvey did not come to Cuba in the *Kanawha*, nor in any ship of the Black Star Line, as is sometimes believed. He had decided to rename the *Kanawha* the *Antonio Maceo* in honour of the exceptional Cuban black general and national hero of Cuba, whose glorious mother Mariana Grajales had died as an exile in Kingston, Jamaica, in 1893, but the ship would not arrive in Cuba until 9 April, when Garvey was already back in Jamaica. This was the moment when Garvey's personal prestige was highest, when the Black Star Line appeared to be on a permanent rise, and when the Universal Negro Improvement Association was about to make a breakthrough in its Liberian project.

During his first day in Havana, Garvey met the main leaders of the UNIA branch in the city, and in the night, he delivered a two-hour speech from the ring of the Park of Santos y Artigas in Old Havana, in front of Martí Theatre. Garvey expounded his doctrine. The audience was made up of more than 500 people: Jamaicans, other West Indians, North American Blacks, and some Cubans.

Garvey spoke at the same place the second night, and again had a large audience that responded with enthusiasm. The papers described Garvey's public presentations in detail, considering them a display of high eloquence, and noted his red, black and green robe. While Garvey spoke, his secretaries sold bonds of the Black Star Line and of other Garveyite enterprises. The meeting began with Cuba's national anthem, then Congressman Ramírez Ros presented Garvey with a speech in Spanish that was translated into English. He also gave Garvey a large Cuban flag for the *Antonio Maceo.* Pablo Herrera, ex-president of Club Atenas, also delivered some words of welcome. The Cuban press recognized the great expectation that Garvey's visit had aroused, but wondered "how he would be received by the Cuban black race, whose problem is so different from that of the black Americans". Of course the problem of racial discrimination against black Cubans was not essentially different from that experienced by black Americans, but there is no doubt that Cuban nationalism, already powerful and distinctive, was immediately grasped by Garvey.

On the third day of his visit to Cuba, Garvey gave an interview to the newspaper *Heraldo de Cuba*. At that time, there were already 25 branches of the UNIA in Cuba. Garvey was very cautious in the interview, but when the journalist asked him insistently about the means to be used to accomplish the UNIA's purposes, Garvey calmly answered: "It is sometimes difficult to obtain the recognition of a right without fighting.... The independence of Cuba is an example of this". After the interview, Garvey, accompanied by Ramirez Ros, left the residence at noon for Cuba's Presidential Palace, to be received by President Mario García Menocal.

Almost exactly one year before, the *Yarmouth*, unofficially renamed the *Frederick Douglass*, had received an enthusiastic welcome in Havana, having arrived safely with a cargo of $5 million worth of whisky. President Menocal had given a banquet to the captain and crew, and had offered the support of the Cuban government to the Black Star Line. The ship, for various reasons, stayed 32 days in Havana. Garvey, then in New York and warmed by the magnitude of the reception and the success of the UNIA in Cuba, is reported to have said in a speech on 22 February 1920 in a rhetorical manner: "The people of Havana are far ahead of the people of this city and that is the reason for the transfer of the headquarters from New York to Havana".

Now, President Menocal received Garvey, and after what seems to have been a formal but cordial conversation, he was introduced to Alfredo Zayas, the presidential candidate for Menocal's party, who would win the 15 and 26 March elections.

Garvey visited three black clubs in his last hours in Havana: the Abraham Lincoln in the afternoon; in the evening the long-standing club Unión Fraternal, where its president and the director of the black magazine *La Antorcha* welcomed him; and Club Atenas, where he made a speech.

Garvey arrived at Club Atenas at 9 p.m. He had to leave by the 10 p.m. train for Ciego de Anila. In spite of time limitations, it was one of the crucial moments of Garvey's visit to Cuba. The Club Atenas building, its front ornamented with nine Greek faces, still exists. It belonged to the black and mulatto aristocracy of Havana. Garvey's words were considered somewhat radical, in spite of his moderation out of respect for the evident circumstanccs of the club. Its president, Dr Miguel Angel Céspedes welcomed Garvey, considering the club honoured by his visit. Céspedes minimized black discrimination in Cuba, but conceded that there were differences in the state of progress of Whites and Blacks that should disappear in the near future. Garvey, according to the *Heraldo de Cuba*, answered the address in these terms:

> [I] have noted with surprise that the Negroes that so brilliantly had fought for the independence of several countries viewed with indifference [the] Pan-African ideal, and the same efforts that were made to free Cuba are the ones that are needed to constitute the great African nation.

Céspedes answered that the black Cuban who had fought for the establishment of the Cuban republic "does not conceive of having any other motherland but the Cuban motherland and does not share the Pan-African ideal because he holds a cosmopolitan concept of the human spirit". He also endorsed a "civilizing mission" on the African continent. Garvey departed with grace from Club Atenas with a short address of great courtesy, and so ended the visit to Havana.

The first town he visited inside the country was Morón, a sea port in the north of Camaguey Province. There, Garvey went to the canefields and spoke, this time with more freedom, to the West Indian and Cuban canecutters, who gave him an enthusiastic welcome. From Morón, on 5 March, Garvey wrote two important editorial letters. In the first one, published in *The Negro World* on 12 March, there was a frank declaration in favour of force to fight the powers opposed to black progress.

> In the final analysis it will be found that the powers opposed to Negro progress will not be influenced in the slightest by mere verbal protests on our part. They realize only too well that protests of this kind contain nothing but the breath expended in making them. They realize too, that their success in enslaving and dominating the darker portion of humanity was due solely to the element of force employed. In the large majority of cases this was accomplished by force of arms. Pressure, of course, may assert itself in other forms, but in the last analysis whatever influence is brought to bear against the powers opposed to us must contain the element of force in order to accomplish its purpose, since it is very apparent that this is the only element they recognize.

Garvey continued by carefully identifying the world organization of Blacks under the UNIA banner as a combat force. The combative spirit of this letter is perhaps rooted in the open spirit with which Garvey spoke inside the country. His strategy was constrained by the capacity of the audience to understand and accept the revolutionary truth of his teaching.

In the second editorial letter, published in *The Negro World* on 19 March 1921, Garvey presented with great precision and coherence the aims of the Black Star Line, and concluded: "We need more ships and bigger ships. Cuba is loyally responding, and we ask the Negro peoples of the world to follow suit".

From Morón, Garvey continued his journey to Nuevitas, Camaguey, and from there to Preston, in Oriente Province, headquarters of the United Fruit Company, but also, in Garvey's words, "the great stronghold of the Universal Improvement Association". From Preston he went to the other great United Fruit Company plantation, Banes, which Garvey also considered "another great stronghold". Garvey had developed a very bad cold, and the Black Cross Nurses refused to let him out of bed to speak for a second day in Banes. The next stop was Antilla, in Nipe Bay, and the last journey was to Santiago de Cuba, the country's second city, capital of Oriente Province, where he stayed for a week, was received by the governor, and where he probably met Alexander Bustamante, who was then still Aleck Clarke.

Garvey, after concluding his successful visit to Cuba, arrived in Kingston, Jamaica, on 22 March. From there he travelled to Costa Rica and Panama and returned to Kingston on 7 May. He now had to go to Santiago de Cuba to solve a conflict between the members of the UNIA in Santiago and the captain and crew of the

Kanawha, which he brought back to Kingston on 17 May. The *Kanawha*, whose unfortunate history is well known, returned without Garvey to Cuba, having been abandoned in Antilla on 24 August. There its ruins have remained to this day, sunk in Nipe Bay. The port of the ship could still be seen in 1952.

Garvey's sojourn in Cuba and the Caribbean was in itself a great political and economic success. His doctrine was delivered as "a new religion and a new politics". Unfortunately, his absence from the New York headquarters was disastrous. His lieutenants quarreled among themselves, and the internal unity of the movement was gravely damaged.

In Cuba the UNIA developed greatly after Garvey's visit. In 1926 there were 51 branches of the UNIA (there appear 52 different membership cards in the Central Division files at the Schomberg Center, but one of the names seems to be repeated). Cuba was the second biggest country for UNIA activity in the world, after the USA.

Analysis of the UNIA's work has tended, erroneously, to regard Cuba as homogenous, and has had to ignore the reality that eastern Cuba has distinct historical and sociological peculiarities that distinguish it from western Cuba, and that the development of the UNIA in Havana may not be representative of the rest of the country. Forty of the 51 branches of the UNIA in Cuba were established in the old Oriente and Camaguey Provinces, which encompassed half the nation's territory and represented the part nearest to Jamaica and Haiti. The majority of the black population of Cuba lived in eastern Cuba, and that included the black soldiers and officers of the Liberation Army of the war against Spain.

The most powerful branches of the UNIA in Cuba in 1926 were: 1. Banes, 2. Camaguey, 3. Sagua La Grande, 4. Santiago de Cuba, 5. Guantánamo, 6. Florida, 7. San Germán, 8. Mariano, 9. Guanabacoa, 10. Jatibonico, 11. Central Elía, 12. Central Macareno, 13. Central Francisco, 14. Nuevitas, 15. Antilla, 16. Bartle, 17. Nueva Gerina, 18. Hatuey, 19. San Gerónimo, 20. Havana.

Of the twenty mentioned, 15 belong to Oriente and Camaguey, in eastern Cuba and to Las Villas in central Cuba, while 4 belong to Havana, in western Cuba. Ten per cent of the UNIA branches of Oriente and Camaguey included Cubans in their hierarchy. This did not happen in western Cuba.

During the Machado government there was a general crackdown on UNIA branches. In 1928 *The Negro World* was banned for some time. Its Spanish column was widely read by black Cubans who did not read English, and the main news of the paper was translated by the West Indians who had been established in Cuba for some time and spoke Spanish. In 1929 the UNIA was made illegal and that lasted for half a year. In 1930 Machado did not allow Garvey to visit Cuba. This action against Garveyism in Cuba coincided with the tyrannical climate which President Machado imposed and which led to the 1933 Revolution. As Rupert Lewis has explained, the movement disappeared in Cuba as

> ... a result of local repression and increased surveillance, the UNIA's own international decline, the repatriation and harassment of migrant workers in the thirties, and the fact that the first generation of Cuban-born offspring of West Indian parents were recognized as Cuban nationals with legal and political rights, so much so that special UNIA

sessions had to be conducted in private, out of their hearing. (*Marcus Garvey: Anti-colonial Champion. p. 113*)

However, the essential doctrine of Garveyism was simply internalized by the main Cuban black clubs.

The crisis of the UNIA in Cuba was part of the general crisis of the UNIA in the world, and its dissolution gives light to certain serious weaknesses within the movement. Disloyal employees and incompetent lieutenants are not enough to explain it. A constellation of opposing forces increased internal friction in the movement. Garvey had been right when he had thought seriously about an African base. He needed to govern a country and Africa was at least a possibility. With an African homeland – no matter how limited – it would be possible to sustain the UNIA during hard times, and generate with security and power the programme of liberation so elaborately implemented. Without a motherland there could be no guarantee against political persecution, economic sabotage and the divisive tactics of alien doctrines.

The amount of excitement unchained by Garvey's personal work in Cuba, the basic race pride that black Cubans had developed because of their massive role in the revolutionary wars against Spain, the relationship between West Indian immigrants and the Cuban population, especially in eastern Cuba, gave Garveyism an effect it did not have in other Latin American countries. Only major research of Cuba's black clubs after 1933 will be able to determine clearly the nature and extent of the impact of Garveyism on Cuban society. This remains to be done. However, at present there is enough circumstantial evidence to suggest that the doctrine overflowed from the West Indian community and to a certain extent reached the black Cuban population. Garveyism was a live element in the political and social black consciousness in Cuba, and it helped in the process of setting new standards for Blacks in Cuban society, in developing racial self-respect alongside the class awareness that the Cuban unions and progressive parties had helped develop. According to informants such as M. Barreras, an active member of black societies in Santiago de Cuba, black societies thrived in Cuba in the early 1940s and in their concerns one can easily perceive far-reaching understanding of race issues.

Further, the influence of Garveyism also radicalized West Indians themselves, some of whom had already developed political consciousness in the workers' struggles in Cuba.

In Cuba, nationalism has always been so strong that it has tended to assimilate social, ethnic and cultural distinctions. The black movement in Cuba had been crippled by the massacre that resulted from the 1912 rebellion, and the integrationist tendency of the mulatto intellectual stance in large cities did not have racial pride as an important part of its content. Garveyism put a mirror in front of black people's faces and forced them to look at themselves, urged them to know themselves and exhorted them to fight for themselves. Race nationalism had of course an inner connection with other liberation struggles, but the polar star of the movement was race consciousness, and that should never be understated, because of the problematic issues which negritude contains.

Garvey was a revolutionary leader fighting against huge odds. In the USA, where it was impossible to achieve political power, he was more of a reformist, but if his

Caribbean activity is closely examined and compared with that of other revolutionary leaders in the region, the common link is visible. There is the same projection into the future and the same vision of a future unfolding from the strife of the present, a charisma and instinct for mass leadership, moral idealism, a talent for political action, class consciousness, and an anti-colonial attitude that was pan-Caribbean in scope.

Garvey was one of the few Caribbean leaders in his time whose pan-Caribbean ideal embraced the entire region. *El ideal antillano* of the Puerto Rican revolutionaries Ramón Betances and Eugenio María de Hostos was exclusively oriented to the Spanish-speaking Antilles, and even José Martí, who did have a universal political grasp, for immediate political reasons, preferred to concentrate on *América nuestra* or limited his regional scope to *El ideal antillano* of Puerto Ricans. Máximo Gómez, however, the Dominican-born General-in-Chief of the Cuban Liberation Army in the war against Spain, did include in his conceptions of Caribbean unity all the Caribbean, and Antonio Maceo also expressed his ideal of a federation that would encompass more than the Spanish-speaking Caribbean. Garvey's legacy is the antecedent of modern ideas on Caribbean federation.

Fortunately, Garveyism has been vindicated by history. Many have insisted on poring over Garvey's follies and mistakes. José Martí would have said of him what he said of Bolívar:

> There are men that live in contentment even if they live without respect. There are others that suffer as in agony when they see that men live without honor around them. In the world there must be a certain sum of light. When there are many men without honor there are always others that have in themselves the honor of many men.... Men cannot be more perfect than the sun. The sun burns with the same light with which it warms. The sun has spots. The ungrateful speak of nothing else but the spots. The grateful speak about the light.

INTERVIEWS

M. Barreras, Santiago de Cuba, 1980
F. Boti, Guantánamo, 1987
H. Brown, Banes, 1987
M. Caballero, Santiago de Cuba, 1985
C.C. Durrant, Guantánamo, 1987
G. Hillhouse, Guantánamo, 1987
R. Lilly, Palma Sariano, 1985
D. Rubiera, Santiago de Cuba, 1985
R.C. Russell, Morón, 1985
R. Varona, Banes, 1987

Garvey's Legacy

Garvey's Legacy: Some Perspectives

Rex Nettleford
Director of Extra-Mural Studies
University of the West Indies, Mona, Jamaica

Introduction

THE CENTENNIAL of Marcus Garvey's birth has prompted a more serious look at one of the century's foremost visionaries, thinkers and political activists. He advanced discipline, education, economic self-reliance, cultural action, and international trade as modalities of actualization in the human struggle for survival and eschewed the embrace of models utilized by other races for their own mobilization and assertion, since the humiliation of the black African by the so-called civilized world was *sui generis* and required solutions forged by black people themselves in their own interest. This did not prevent him from acknowledging parallels and correspondences in the experience of others; and he was clearly influenced by tactics employed by others, without ever losing the core commitment of black liberation through the black experience and by the effort of black people.[1]

The popular press appropriately and accurately portrays Garveyism in action as a brand of Pan-African ideology which "transcended linguistic, national and professional boundaries, mobilizing the world's scattered Blacks into a community of spiritual and political hope".[2]

It is the mobilization of the world's scattered Blacks on the Continent and in the diaspora – Garvey's greatest achievement and one of his great legacies – which now challenges the black world, which is still groping for recognition, status and opportunity, despite the admittedly far-reaching gains of the liberation struggles since Garvey's time.

It is only fair to concede that many initiatives have indeed been taken over a long period to achieve this. Yet there remains a feeling that there is a conspicuous absence of any true ethnic solidarity in Africa and the black diaspora, despite the universally robust rhetoric against racial discrimination.[3] In fact, such solidarity is regarded by many Blacks themselves as an expression of bad taste, of racism in reverse, as an unrealistic strategy for a capitalist/socialist world which is divided more into bourgeois exploiters and exploited proletarians than into Whites and Blacks, and as inappropriate in a North–South, First World–Third World dispensation in which the race variable is regarded as peripheral.

All of this begs questions rather than providing answers. And consequent on the continuing powerlessness of Blacks economically and politically in the world at large, many are tempted to ask in Garvey's centennial year: what institutional link-up can now exist among peoples of African ancestry that is of a universal or global dimension dedicated to the cause of black betterment? Is there a political philosophy, some economic order or plan, or some cultural philosophy that is integrated, that carries its own inner logic and consistency, and speaks to the reality of the African presence on the planet? What is twentieth-century technology doing for the black populations of the world and they with, or to, it? We know how effectively the eighteenth- and nineteenth-century technologies were used to enslave and mutilate, to colonize and condition hordes of black humanity into self-doubt and subjugation. We also know that in response those hordes developed techniques to fight back and to survive after a fashion.

International initiatives in organizing and assembling have been among the strategies. There has been no shortage of funding, relatively speaking, for some of these initiatives designed to address questions of existence, survival and development. Particularly frequent of late have been such endeavours as international conferences and arts festivals, perceived by many a donor as the harmless indulgences of a reputedly rhetoric-happy and fun-loving race and exploited by many an opportunistic politician (black ones included) as part of the bread-and-circus escape from providing more lasting developmental programmes for the people.

There persists, then, the frustration of the unfulfilled – brought on by the absence of that classic vision bequeathed by Marcus Garvey, but which has been either ignored or discounted for a period that has turned out to be too protracted for everybody's good.

Some International Initiatives

A CONFERENCE of "Garvey scholars" drawn from the Caribbean, the United States and Africa (as a newspaper report of this conference states) held at the University of the West Indies, which may be accused of not spending enough of its 40 years' existence on many of the things that really matter to the black world (including the life and thought of Marcus Garvey), must clearly be seen as an international initiative, only this time one that is meant to mean business. The recent conference held at Miami's Florida International University on "Negritude and Ethnicity in the Americas" was another which may well turn out to be an historic and watershed affair.[4] Two other significant twentieth-century black thinkers and political activists, Aime Cesaire and Leopold Sedar Senghor, were there to review their creed while acknowledging their debt to the likes of Marcus Garvey.

A series of arts "festivals" since the 1960s has been focusing attention on that classic vision to which I refer – the Dakar Festival, spearheaded by Alioune Diop; FESTAC (the Festival of African Arts and Culture), hosted by Nigeria in the 1970s; and soon FESPAC (Pan African Festival of Arts and Culture), to be hosted by Senegal at the end of the decade. A conference of black intellectuals is being contemplated for Paris in 1989, the bicentennial of the French Revolution, a coincidence which is not lost on the organizers, who see the Haitian Revolution as part of the worldwide movement for freedom and equality at the end of the eighteenth century.[5] No doubt they will all find funding and there is promise that, as with past "assemblies", a good time will have been had by all. But Garvey keeps reminding us that behind the mass rallies, the conventions, and the manipulation of symbols in the display of pomp and circumstance, some hard sustained work must go on.

The initiatives mentioned did not develop accidentally. They all had ancestral forebears in the Pan-African Conferences, which started in London at the turn of this century, the most recent being held in Dar-es-Salaam (the first on the African continent) in 1976. Both Sékou Touré and the conference's host, Julius Nyerere, brought diasporic Africans to the realization that new challenges (of economic development of an oppressed continent) had to take priority over purely mythic considerations. Mythic considerations had long before that spawned creole Africanism or Afrocriollo – a movement which burrowed its way into the reality of the Caribbean and Latin America (with Haiti, Cuba and Brazil in the forefront, followed by some of the English-speaking islands. led by Jamaica). By the late 1960s it was Black Power, a protest movement with its source of energy in the belly of the beast that roamed the cities and rural South of the United States. It extended itself to the rest of the diaspora where racial injustice reigned and from which such patron saints as Frantz Fanon and Marcus Garvey could be drawn.[6] Still before that was the Negritude Movement, born in Paris but conceived in the realities of colonial Martinique, French Guyana and Senegal. It came to attract international attention, if only because it challenged many throughout the diaspora to yet another mode of self-definition in this awesome quest for authenticity. Yet the greatest of all of these in terms of global impact and holistic proportions was the movement led by Marcus Mosiah Garvey,[7] which flourished through the 1920s and 1930s. The Garvey movement has left behind a body of thought in Garvey's philosophy and opinions which defines the "classic vision" and in Garvey's ideas a programme of action that addresses the lot of the black man in the wider world. That programme of action sought not simply to explain or interpret that world but to change it in terms of the perceived interests of the people of African ancestry. It was a bold, unprecedented and still unequaled and unsurpassed achievement in the history of black liberation struggle, if not of mass movements for liberation anywhere.

The Garvey Legacy

SUCH IS THE LEGACY of Marcus Garvey, whose successes and failures in a world predicated on notions of the inferiority of non-Caucasian peoples can still give clues to the nature of the world and to the demands on strategy and tactics for the many black rulers who have emerged in Africa and beyond the continent. For the Universal Negro Improvement Association, which Garvey founded in 1914 in Jamaica and consolidated in the United States by 1920, was the target of attack for every major imperial power that existed at the time, with the Euro-centric United States thrown in for good measure. His achievement is yet the more remarkable since, as Tony Martin, one of the new-generation "Garvey scholars", reminds us, Garvey's UNIA in the 1920s could boast over 1,200 branches in over 40 countries, with 700 branches flourishing in the United States alone. The rest were to be found in the Caribbean, Central America, Canada, and West, Central and South Africa.[8]

Without the benefit of radio, satellite, television, or a worldwide news agency, Marcus Garvey used his several newspapers, especially *The Negro World,* to internationalize his movement, to educate the black masses to their self-worth and creative potential, and to set the teeth of the colonizing European powers on edge. The banning of *The Negro World* almost everywhere no doubt sharpened the curiosity of its readers. Yet fewer Blacks could read then than can now. Why, then, is there nothing comparable in intensity and impact in the African world today? Could it be that the battles fought in *The Negro World* by Garvey have already all been won?

The persistence of racism in the form of discrimination against Blacks everywhere tells otherwise and should logically result in a corresponding persistence of an organization like the UNIA. But the rather successful discrediting of Garvey by US courts and his rivals aside, other developments have conspired to defuse the force and power of the Garvey message. Most of us have lived through the effective tactics of the so-called master race, which in this century has responded to pressure from African peoples in the most ingenious of ways, giving with one hand while taking back with the other. In this the black world has not always been as astute to the tactics as it should; and the struggle indeed continued with much energy having to be mustered to repossess self each inch of the way, to fight over battles which were thought to have been won, to protect what piece of ground one has managed to lay claim to in the face of new attempts at penetration.[9]

The tactics turn in large part on systemic co-optation of would-be liberated Blacks into so-called mainstream agendas, whether in the field of education (there are black university professors in the West who are so flattered or intimidated by their membership in the hallowed fellowship that they forget how they got there and what role they are actually expected to play in liberating knowledge from its ethnocentric bondage in half-truths, prejudice and pseudo-science), or in business (the few managers who get recruited into the corporate structure take themselves terribly seriously, forgetting that they are not the owners). Even the call for building up an exclusive black business sector in a place like the United States has to guard against Blacks' being trapped in the bazaar segment of the economy – buying and selling, rather than establishing control over production segments and above all over the ideas behind manufacturing, etc.[10]

The same is true in the arts (especially entertainment), where the critical mass of a non-black market dictates the direction of the artist to the point where the Blacks deny the true value of their own contributions and wish to become "artists, dancers, writers" rather than be "black artists, black dancers, etc". In any case, the minstrelsy syndrome continues to be strong among Blacks in the diaspora. The market wants the jungle with tinsel, or the primitive innocence and uncontrolled, childlike energy of the noble savage.[11] The idea that Mother Africa has a civilization that developed its own aesthetics, its own ways of harmonizing form with feeling, its own classicisms is not part of the consciousness of the "White world" in its myriad manifestations in Europe, the Americas, and among the ex-colonized Third World elites. The minstrelsy syndrome stretches to that other great performing art: sport. Blacks continue to be the players in and never the "owners" of the teams. The co-optation in the name of survival persists with a vengeance. So much for Garvey's dream of black control over the destiny of black people in the fields of education, business and culture.

In seemingly less vulnerable circumstances, promise has yet to blossom into fulfilment. The political liberation of most of black Africa has been achieved, judging from the number of such nations that now sit in the United Nations, the plethora of flags, anthems, heads of state, and the like.[12] But Garvey, on his own account, would not have been satisfied with merely this, despite his call for the black man's Pope and Emperor. The colonies were released when the cost of Empire was becoming prohibitive in any case. Moreover, other forms of control, by way of economic domination and international arrangements institutionalized in the IMF and World Bank, could be concocted. Nigeria is oil-poor today and Jamaica is debt-rich.[13] Such contradictions continue to plague the black world, which has been given political freedom with one hand and deprived of it with another that continues to squeeze the economic life-blood out of the primary producers, whose products are compensated with arbitrary prices set in the North Atlantic.

South Africa is itself the obscene celebration of the international racism that is inherent in the world's economic arrangements and is mirrored within nations themselves, where a white, economically dominant class (if absentee, they support a native oligarchy) lords it over the black masses at the base. The white world, rich and technologically advanced, has too much at stake in South Africa to want to destroy apartheid in the way it sought to dismember Nazism and Fascism. Margaret Thatcher of Great Britain can afford to be obstinately difficult on the matter of not supporting economic sanctions against South Africa. She has fellow-travellers aplenty as support.

The situation in South Africa is just the grand expression of a world order which festers in its persistent racism, a phenomenon which has had its just confrontation when tried elsewhere from, say, Islam (dismissed by the West, one needs to observe carefully, as "fundamentalist" and "irrational" – all part of the mythology of the West's superior hold over intellect and science).[14]

Garvey's legacy of unrelenting combat against such an assumption is ignored at the peril of all concerned. And the evidence of the ACP–EEC understanding of the need to confront apartheid on all fronts, not simply the one of economic sanctions, is a step in the right direction.

The New Challenges

THERE IS NO DOUBT that the Garvey vision which is his legacy has come full circle to challenge us in the 1980s and at the end of the century. Many of the new challenges are surprisingly similar to or the same as the old ones in Garvey's time, since many things, though they have changed, have remained remarkably the same. Five such challenges come to mind. They by no means represent an exhaustive inventory of possibilities. They all integrate thought and action as Garvey would have had it and can be identified as:

(a) Continuing the assertion of Africa's cultural certitude and authenticity;

(b) Synthesizing that cultural authenticity with modern progress;

(c) Addressing developmental imperatives for the material improvement of African peoples all over the world, but especially within the framework of the nation-state;

(d) Mastering the know-how and know-why of communications technology and worldwide communications systems;

(e) Accessing power through the creative exercise of intellect and imagination.

(a) Continuing Cultural Assertion

There is a continuing need to focus the vision on African dignity, cultural certitude and authenticity in the face of continuing attempts to humiliate Africa. That humiliation may not be now expressed worldwide in the Jim Crowism of the United States, as was rampant during Garvey's time, but South Africa has gone further than any to institutionalize the affliction in contemporary times. Still, the ontology, epistemology, aesthetics, and other fundamentals of Western civilization remain predicated on notions of black inadequacies if not outright inferiority. How else does one explain black majorities operating as cultural minorities in polities that are stridently democratic? A popular BBC television series confidently entitled *The Triumph of the West: A Global View of History* spends but a couple of minutes of its 13 hours on trans-Atlantic slavery and its consequences; and while acknowledging the valid existence of Chinese, Japanese, Arab, and Indian civilizations other than that of Christendom, makes only passing reference to West African mask sculpture's influence on European artists. Language, religion, kinship patterns, artistic manifestations, and other cultural indices are perceived in terms of a Euro-centric (Western) mainstream waiting to be entered by lesser tributaries on their way to the open sea of universalism.

The cultural resistance strategy is as valid now as it was in Garvey's time, and the work of creative artists of the black world needs to continue in its uncompromising stance against the domination and indefensible notion of a master culture. In this, compromise must remain as a tactic and not be made to spell surrender.

(b) Synthesizing Cultural Authenticity and Modern Progress

The work of international festivals of arts of the black world should continue, if only because they have widespread support. They need updating, however, in order to make sense in terms of modern-day realities. They offer necessary moments of "communication with oneself", as Amadou Mahtar M'Bow, formerly of UNESCO, told the International Association of FESPAC in Libreville, Gabon, in June 1987. Indeed, as he further said, "any people which turns its back on culture loses what makes up its deep reality".[15]

But we need to be liberated from the self-indulgent notions of culture being a little bit of song and a step or two of dance. The African essence of "performing" must extend from the short-distance sprinting to the long-distance sustained race. And M'Bow's invitation to have arts festivals (international and regional) provide the framework for "joint reflection on the relations between artistic creation and technological research" is a direct response to the realities of the times we have upon us, living as we do in "an increasingly inter-dependent world, submitted to the constant challenge of accelerated scientific and technical progress, a definite bearer of great promises of freedom or increased well being, but also of threats of alienation and a certain uniformity taking place to the detriment of the identities of various peoples".[16]

African peoples now need to "efficiently master the necessary synthesis of cultural authenticity and modern progress". The vision is Garveyite to the core, even if the language is UNESCO-ese.

(c) Addressing Developmental Imperatives

The operative phrase is "modern progress". And though the European/Victorian idea of a linear progression to material betterment and spiritual upliftment has been put paid to by the experience of Europe itself, there are some basic indicators which suggest that the betterment of man in terms of his being increasingly able to wield command over his own destiny is still on the agenda for people of African ancestry worldwide. The impact of science and technology on contemporary human existence is central to this, and their role in the development of individual selves and the societies we are shaping must be our concern.

Marcus Garvey understood this like no one else. His emphasis on material self-development in the shaping of societies for full participation in the modern world, for command over a piece of the action in the international game of business and commerce, was an expression of his vision of Africa's functioning in the contemporary world not as surrogate, sibling or subordinate but as master of her own destiny. And his focus on knowledge as power and the need for Africans to educate themselves, to repossess the intellectual skills of the ancient Nilotic civilizations from which modern Africa sprang, was no idle indulgence. We need that vision now more than ever. Festivals, then, need not concentrate exclusively on what is established, proven, and incontrovertible, viz. black people's capacity to sing, dance, perform for the amusement of themselves and others. We have to remind ourselves that we can also think, are capable of inventing the know-why as well as grasping and applying the know-how; are capable of creating the science of which technology is the progeny.

Development imperatives for all of the African nation-states ("at home and abroad") must therefore be informed by a particular kind of knowledge which black people must themselves generate out of the realities of their ontology, epistemology, historical experience, and existential realities. The classic areas of the exercise are now known to be agriculture, food and nutrition; population and health (from the provision of potable water to the prevention of AIDS, which is subtly being projected worldwide as an "African" virus); education and human resource development; and information (that is, of the kind that employs the new powerful communications technologies).

These must now be on the agenda of any serious international initiative that will make sense of the myriad goings-on in the name of African solidarity. The front-line states need precisely such assistance for their internal development so as to decrease their economic dependency on white South Africa.

The cultural thrust at which African peoples are strong must find ways of integrating these seemingly basic needs and mundane concerns into any programme of survival and, more important, into the journey beyond survival by Blacks everywhere.

All of black Africa, as well as persons of African ancestry who reside in developed countries, constitute in reality the "South" in the North–South paradigm or must consider themselves "Third World", as against the OECD countries' First World. In very important ways they are marginalized in those developed countries, even when they serve the international bureaucracy in Brussels or Geneva or attain high positions as Assistant Secretaries of State in Washington, MPs in the British Parliament, or superstars in the entertainment world.

The inner reserves offered by black culture, however vaguely defined, sometimes help those of a mind to draw on it. But without a sense of territory, the force of a worldwide African culture does not have quite the impact that Islamic Iran or Jewish Israel has on the West. Not even the religious form that has emerged in the Orisha tradition, remarkably preserved across the Atlantic, can muster the impact. And neither Islam nor Christianity, which both claim the allegiance of millions of Africans, are, strictly speaking, African religions. All this probably explains the groping inner tensions of Rastafarianism in Jamaica and the Caribbean and of something like the secular "Negritude", which sought to define, articulate, delineate African "essences" as the irreducible kernel of a discrete ontology, epistemology and aesthetics.

The absence of a sense of territory may well be a serious constraint on many US Afro-American initiatives. Garvey understood this well and sought after a land on the African continent that would satisfy that most basic of human needs. Since his time, many black countries have become independent in Africa, but with legacies of conflict imposed on them by the wanton rape by Europe in the nineteenth century. They now spend their new energy sorting themselves out rather than shaping their new societies. The white world continues in its dominance while Kikuyus fight Luos, Ibos battle with Hausas and Hausas with Yorubas, Mr Mugabe spars with Mr Nkomo, Buthelezi with his progressive brothers in South Africa, and in the Caribbean chocolate-coloured middle strata blacks are in conflict with pot-black members of the ex-colonial underclass. The continuing dehumanization, in sundry forms, of the peoples of Africa wherever they be is a matter for concern. The Garveyite vision of the African's rehumanization on his own terms and by his own efforts is central to that classic vision.

It means, then, that the denial of human rights by power-hungry black rulers must be seen as a betrayal of that vision. And the international cry must come from Africans themselves in denunciation of what will clearly make black people less than whole. The continuing existence of millions in abject poverty and material destitution must be met not by a single concert raising millions of dollars (and salving the consciences of many), which will only be squandered for want of long-term planning and painstaking application of programmes and policies well thought out to rid Africa of hunger and famine.

The abuse of women, depriving our populations of the skills, insights, invaluable talents of half (in some places more than half) of our population cannot be in the interest of the rehumanization of the peoples of Africa. The understandable but unhelpful suspicion that keeps most of the African continent resistant to development strategies that can move it forward into the twenty-first century must disappear. The skills of First World Blacks should be mobilized to be shared with black Africa, not in the spirit of bringing "civilization" to the Dark Continent as black missionaries were encouraged to do earlier this century and some Afro-Americans themselves felt they were doing not so long ago. African elites themselves have to take some serious decisions about not wishing to be recolonized. Many of us have not done well in resisting seduction by the imperial West in our indulgence of luxurious ostentation even in the midst of poverty and famine. Worse still is the resolve to "make it" on the white man's agenda. This has serious implications for us all, since it declares premature closure on several tasks yet to be successfully tackled – tasks identified by Garvey in his time. The classic vision of self in terms of Africa's cultural certitude is therefore necessary in Garveyite terms, even while we "beat the (white) man at his own game". Schizophrenic? Maybe! Pathological? It need not be!

(d) Mastering Communications Technology

One important tool in all this is mastery over the fastest area of growth in the world today – that of communications technology. We all know the power of print: Garvey used it with his *Negro World* to internationalize black consciousness and to Africanize colonized sensibilities. Print continues to be one of the best ways of consolidating the vision among African peoples today, even if we have to do it in the tongues of former masters – English, French and Spanish, which were the international languages used by *The Negro World.* An international newspaper dealing with the problems and possibilities of the African peoples of the world may just find a market eager to consume.

But undoubtedly the most important and impactful aspects of the communications technology challenging the black world to action are the electronic media – satellites and all. The network of national television and radio stations throughout Africa, the Caribbean and the Americas needs to be fed with material created by African people about African people and against the background of the perceptions of such people. News of South Africa will continue to come from news agencies dominated by the North Atlantic, through the filter of white perceptions – liberal, radical and conservative. But such information filtered through the black sensibility, even of a conservative hue, would do the black world no harm.

The *Dallas*-ization of consciousness worldwide speaks to the power of the new communications technologies.[17] The Africanization of that consciousness must also be on the agenda. Independent countries of black Africa and the Caribbean need to be lobbied into responsibility, in the devising of their media policies, in the training of their young journalists and media workers, and in the production of material (i.e., programmes for audio, video and film), so that the people of Africa and the black diaspora can interpret themselves faithfully to themselves and to the rest of the world, which is currently afflicted with stereotype images of so-called lesser breeds. If the capacity for artistic achievement is now conceded, albeit with reservations, that for science and technological feats is actively doubted if not summarily denied.

(e) Accessing Power via Intellect and Imagination

That is why Garvey's own concern for the exercise of intellect and imagination in creative ways by African peoples in their own interest is one of the renewed challenges for the foreseeable future. These faculties are after all the monopoly of no one race, no one nation, no one civilization. Garvey was at pains to emphasize that the subjugation of Blacks was not the natural condition of the race and always invoked the history of the great African civilizations which flourished at a time when European civilization, in his own words, was yet to emerge out of barbarism.

Intellect and imagination are indeed given to all mankind to enable the members of the species to ask the right questions about themselves, about their relations one with another and with the environment around them. Their discoveries, if right, become the stock and capital of all mankind. We need now to ask ourselves the right questions of and about ourselves, and we need to ask whether the issues which today touch the hearts of Africans (Continental and diasporic) are being seriously addressed. Black scholars who are forced to seek recognition along the paths set by Adam Smith, Keynes or Marx may have to decide to muster more courage and find universality out of the specificity of the experience of their own societies. Those who may be attracted to do studies on Garvey may well be advised against bleeding the "blackness" out of Garveyism. Nor should they attempt to fit the particular experience of African descendants over the past half a millennium exclusively into seemingly more "acceptable" categories, such as class conflict, nineteenth-century nationalism, capitalism or socialism.[18]

The idea that black existence, however well fertilized by the phenomena of other civilizations, is of its own soil is something still to be grasped by many Caribbean social science scholars and political activists, admittedly long and deeply marinated in the Oxbridge ethos (even by proxy) and mid-Atlantic political culture. Add to this the contemporary bombardment of the notion of a pluralist dispensation in which all the ingredients of a pepperpot concoction are supposed to have equal value, despite the intrinsic potency of individual portions, and the poor Caribbean scholar becomes more often the harbinger of confusion and less the messenger of light.

Perhaps we have allowed ourselves to be blinded by the corrosive influence of a "triumphant civilization", which not only enslaved millions of African forebears but has had us consciously conditioned around to a world-view that places itself at the centre of the cosmos. The centuries of resistance have indeed provided Africa with strategies aplenty, and the textured diversity is a decided strong point of the race and its myriad cultural expressions all over the globe. But the diversity has come to spell fractiousness, and the underlying unities which carry the ancestral authority of ages are allowed to lie untapped.

We need power (nuclear and otherwise), but above all we need the power that inheres in the repossession of self to make sense of the power that manifests itself in mastery over science and technology. The need for potable water, good primary health care, food and nutrition, access to information for our use in determining our own destiny must be met by our efforts. And the capacity to do all such things is directly related to Africans' (at home and abroad) being able to make definitions about themselves on their own terms and being possessed of the capability to follow through with *action* on the basis of such definitions. The continuing commitment to this is primarily a function of the Garvey legacy.

NOTES AND REFERENCES

[1] Hill, Robert A., "General Introduction", *The Marcus Garvey and Universal Negro Improvement Association Papers,* Vol. 1 (UCLA Press, 1983), pp. xxxv-xc. Professor Hill's expertly documented section on "The Influence of Ireland" (pp. lxx-lxxviii) was not meant to detract from the originality of Garvey's thought and vision, as some would be tempted to conclude. The claim that the Irish revolutionary struggle assisted in "focusing Garvey's political perspective" is not an unreasonable one, since Garvey was a man-in-the-world, fully aware of all existing progressive initiatives for the improvement of humankind (hence his admiration of Lenin despite his distrust of Communists in America trying to delegitimize him). It is his worldly sophistication and breadth of vision that support Rupert Lewis's thesis of him as an "anti-colonial champion" (see Rupert Lewis, *Marcus Garvey: Anti-Colonial Champion* [London: Karia Press, 1987]). Irish influence did not lead to blind imitation any more than Russia's revolutionary initiative spawned purely Bolshevik clones among socialist-inclined people of African ancestry, whose historical experiences and existential realities as Blacks Garvey believed to be the only valid source of struggle for black dignity and liberation.

[2] See "The Black Moses", Marcus Garvey Centennial Supplement, *Carib News,* New York, week ending August 25, 1987; especially "Marcus Garvey's Teachings Alive in the 1980s" by Mark D. McMorris, p. 15.

[3] The "feeling" motivated the 10th anniversary conference organized by the Caribbean Cultural Centre, New York, under the direction of Marta Vega. The theme of the Conference (7-9 October 1987) was "Cumulative Impact of African International Movements: Culture, Education, Politics". The conference was held in the Dag Hammarskjold Auditorium, United Nations. Presenters included Pathe Diagne, President of the International Pan-African Festival of Arts and Culture (FESPAC); Abdias do Nascimento, President, Congress of Black Cultures of the Americas; Victoria Santa Cruz, former director of Ballet Folklórico Nacionál de Peru; Quince Duncan, sociologist and author (Costa Rica); and the present author. The month-long celebrations by the New York-based CCC was dedicated to the memory of Marcus Garvey.

[4] The Conference on Negritude, Ethnicity and Afro-Cultures in the Americas was sponsored by Florida International University and held on 26-28 February 1987 at FIU, Miami. In attendance were Aime Cesaire and Leopold Sadar Senghor, who, with the late León Damas (of French Guiana), are credited as founders of the Negritude movement which flourished out of France in the post-Garvey period of the 1940s and 1950s. The present author delivered a paper entitled "The Aesthetics of Negritude: A Metaphor for Liberation" (unpublished).

[5] The proposed conference promised to be a follow-up to the FIU conference (see Note 3 above). The venue has been shifted to Lincoln University, the alma mater of the African liberator Kwame Nkrumah, in Pennsylvania, USA. The World Congress of Black Intellectuals, as the conference is designated, will be hosted by Lincoln University and the city of Philadelphia on 3-9 June 1990 and hopes to "bring together two thousand delegates from all over the black world (scientists, scholars, artists, men and women of letters...)" around the theme "The Black World in the Third Millennium" (Letter of Announcement from Carlos Moore, International Co-ordinator). Marcus Garvey would have approved.

[6] Both Frantz Fanon and Marcus Garvey were icons of the Black Power movement of the 1960s in the United States and the Caribbean. Fanon's *The Wretched of the Earth* (London: McGibbon & Key,

1965) and *Black Skins, White Masks* (New York: Grove Press, 1967) were favourite texts among the faithful.

[7] See the writings of Marcus Garvey in *Philosophy and Opinions of Marcus Garvey,* Vols. I and II (New York: Atheneum, 1969), ed. Amy Jacques Garvey; *More Philosophy and Opinions* (London: Frank Cass, 1977), eds. Amy Jacques Garvey and E.U. Essien-Udom; *Garvey and Garveyism* (New York: MacMillan, 1970), by Amy Jacques Garvey. Also *The Marcus Garvey and Universal Negro Improvement Association Papers,* Vols. I-V.

[8] Tony Martin, *Race First – The Ideological and Organisational Struggles of Marcus Garvey and the Universal Negro Improvement Association* (Dover, Massachusetts: The Majority Press, 1986), pp. 15-17; also article in *Jamaica Journal,* Vol. 20, No. 3, August-October 1987, pp. 10-18. The plea for Caribbean "cultural sovereignty" has exercised the energies of a number of Caribbean opinion leaders and intellectuals – notably the late Prime Minister of Barbados Errol Barrow and the novelist George Lamming – in the wake of attempts by the United States to influence thought and action in the "Caribbean Basin". This is done overtly through technical assistance (tied aid) with mandatory study by recipients of scholarships in the United States and indirectly through burgeoning communications technology (satellite dishes and national television programmes). The Eurocentric bias of much of the offering reinforces the un-Garveyite tendencies to perpetuate the denigration of "things African" in the Caribbean ethos.

[10] See *Marcus Garvey: Life and Lessons (A Centennial Companion to The Marcus Garvey and Universal Negro Improvement Association Papers)*, eds. Robert Hill and Barbara Bair (UCLA Press, 1987), pp. 300-311 (Garvey's "lesson" on Commercial and Industrial Transactions).

[11] Popular entertainers oblige in providing this "image", and some have become superstars and wealthy in the process. The stereotype in the popular imagination has prompted some performing artists to express a desire to be identified as "artists" without any ethnic qualifier.

[12] Some forty or so countries of Continental African or with black diasporic populations are now independent, having been recently liberated from British, French or Dutch imperial rule, following on Haiti, which won its independence by armed resistance in the early nineteenth century, and Ethiopia, which had never been colonized except for the brief occupation by Italy in the 1930s.

[13] Both Nigeria and Jamaica are good examples of the plight of the developing world of which Garvey's world is a sizeable part. Their extreme dependence on the external economies of Western capitalist countries has guaranteed perpetual economic crisis, despite the existence of oil in countries like Nigeria.

[14] John Roberts, *Triumph of the West: A Global View of History* (television documentary, 13-part series by the British Broadcasting Corporation, England). See especially Episodes 6-11 and 13.

[15] Amadou Mahtar M'Bow, opening speech at Conference of Association Internationale du Festival Pan-Africain des Arts et Cultures (AIFESPAC), Libreville, Gabon, 9-11 June 1987, in *General Report of AIFESPAC Conference.*

[16] Ibid.

[17] The allusion is to the widespread popularity of US soap operas aired throughout the world. *Dallas,* the story of a wealthy oil family in Texas, is one of the favourites among Caribbean viewers. Garvey's reaction to the cultural penetration by "white culture" via this means is predictable.

[18] Contemporary Caribbean Marxism, as manifested in the Anglophone Caribbean, is yet to come to terms fully with Garveyism. Rupert Lewis and Maureen Warner-Lewis, in the volume of essays on Garveyism they edited and entitled *Garvey, Africa, Europe and the Americas,* introduced readers to Theodore Vincent's useful survey and insightful commentary on "The Evolution of the Split Between the Garvey Movement and the Organised Left in the United States 1917-1933" (pp. 165-199), and the contribution by Trevor Munroe, leader of the Communist Workers' Party of Jamaica, to the present volume indicates possible directions for the future. As to capitalism and Garvey, espe-

cially at this time in the Caribbean and North America, when "market forces" determinism informs much that is ideology and political action among governments in power, Tony Martin's reminder of Garvey's position on "unrestrained capitalism" is worth citing (see *Race First*, pp. 53-54). Not even George Padmore, despite his lingering reservations about Garvey, could resist the compliment, paid in his *Pan Africanism or Communism* (p. 82), that Garvey was the "greatest black prophet and visionary since Negro Emancipation". And W.E. Du Bois, a sworn enemy since the beginning of Garvey's career in the United States, made peace with Garveyism before he died (see Tony Martin, *op. cit.*, p. 333).

Select Bibliography

Akinyemi, A.B., *Foreign Policy and Federalism* (Nigeria: Ibadan University Press, 1974).

Alexander, Jack, "The Culture of Race in Middle Class Kingston", *American Ethnologist,* 4, 1977, pp. 413-435.

Alleyne, M.C., *Comparative Afro-America* (Ann Arbor: Karoma Publishers, 1980).

Anderson, Benedict, *Imagined Communities: Reflections on the Origins and Spread of Nationalism* (London, 1983).

Anderson, Jervis, *A. Phillip Randolph* (New York: Harcourt Brace Jovanovich, Inc., 1972).

Austin, Diane, *Urban Life in Kingston, Jamaica* (New York: Gordon and Breach, 1984).

Azikiwe, Nnamdi, *Zik* (London: Cambridge University Press, 1960).

Barnett, Ida Wells, *Crusade for Justice: The Autobiography of Ida B. Wells,* ed. Alfreda M. Duster (Chicago, 1970).

Baugh, Edward, "Vic Reid in His Own Words – An Interview", *Jamaica Journal,* Vol. 20, No. 4, November 1987.

Baxter, Ivy, *The Arts of an Island* (New Jersey: Scarecrow Press, 1970).

Beckford, George, *Persistent Poverty* (London: Oxford University Press, 1971).

Ben-Jochannan, Yosef, *The Black Man's North and East Africa* (Alkebu-Lan Books, JAMIA Consultants, 1982).

Best, Lloyd, "A Model of Pure Plantation Economy", *Social and Economic Studies,* September 1968.

Bosch, Juan, *De Cristóbal Colón a Fidel Castro* (Madrid, 1970).

Bradford, Helen, "Class Contradictions and Class Alliances", in *Resistance and Ideology in Settler Societies* in *Southern African Studies*, Vol. 4, ed. Tom Lodge (Johannesburg: Ravan Press, 1986).

Braithwaite, E.K., *The Development of Creole Society in Jamaica, 1770-1820* (Oxford: Clarendon Press, 1971).

Braithwaite, Lloyd, "Sociology and Demographic Research in the British Caribbean", *Social and Economic Studies,* Vol. 6, No. 4, 1957, pp. 523-571.

Brodber, Erna, "Marcus Garvey and the Politicization of Some Afro-Jamaicans in the 1920s and the 1930s", *Jamaica Journal,* Vol. 20, No. 3, August-October 1987, pp. 66-72.

Brotz, Howard (ed.), *Negro Social and Political Thought, 1850-1920* (New York, 1966).

Bruce, John Edward, "Dr Theophilus E.S. Scholes, M.D", in *The Voice of the Negro,* Vol. IV, No. 7, March 1907, pp. 114-115.

Burkett, Randall K., *Garveyism as a Religious Movement* (New Jersey and London: Scarecrow Press, 1978).

Cabral, Amilcar, *Revolution in Guinea* (New York: Monthly Review Press, 1969).

Campbell, Horace (ed.), *Pan Africanism: Documents of the Sixth Pan-African Congress* (Toronto: Afro Caribbean Press, 1975).

Rasta and Resistance: From Marcus Garvey to Walter Rodney (New Jersey: Africa World Press, 1987).

Campbell, Mavis, *The Dynamics of Change in a Slave Society* (Rutherford, New Jersey, 1976).

Cardoso, F.H., and Weffort, F., *América Latina: Ensayos de Interpretación Sociológico-Política* (Santiago: Editorial Universitaria, 1970).

Carnegie, James, *Some Aspects of Jamaica's Politics: 1918-1938* (Kingston: Institute of Jamaica, 1969).

Clarke, Colin, *Kingston, Jamaica: Urban Development and Social Change 1692-1962* (Berkeley: University of California Press, 1975).

Clarke, John Henrik (ed.), *Marcus Garvey and the Vision of Africa* (New York: Vintage Books, 1974).

Coleman, J.S., *Nigeria: Background to Nationalism* (Berkeley, 1960).

Cone, James H., *Black Theology and Black Power* (New York: The Seabury Press, 1969).

For My People: Black Theology and the Black Church (Maryknoll, New York: Orbis Books, 1984).

Crahan, M.E., and Knight, F.W. (eds.), *Africa and the Caribbean: The Legacies of a Link* (Baltimore: Johns Hopkins, 1979).

Cronon, E.D., *Black Moses – The Story of Marcus Garvey and the Universal Negro Improvement Association* (Madison: University of Wisconsin Press, 1955).

Cruise, Harold, *The Crisis of the Negro Intellectual* (London: W.H. Allen, 1969).

Curtin, Philip, *Two Jamaicas* (New York: Greenwood Press, 1970).

de Lisser, Herbert George, "The Jamaican Nobility, or The Story of Sir Mortimer and Lady Mat", *Planter's Punch*, 1925-26.

Twentieth Century Jamaica (Kingston: The Jamaica Times, 1913).

Dingwall, Rev. R., "Outlook for the Jamaican People in Jamaica's Jubilee", in Gordon, Rev. R., *et al.*, *What We Are and What We Hope to Become, by Five of Us* (London: S.W. Partridge & Co., 1888).

Diop, Cheikh Anta, *The African Origin of Civilization: Myth or Reality*, ed. Mercer Cook (Lawrence Hill and Co., 1974).

Draper, Theodore, *The Rediscovery of Black Nationalism* (New York, 1970).

Du Bois, W.E.B., "Marcus Garvey", *Crisis*, XXI (Dec. 1920), pp. 58-60.

Dusk of Dawn: An Essay Towards an Autobiography of a Race Concept (New York: Harcourt Brace, 1940).

The World and Africa (New York, 1964).

Eaton, George, *Alexander Bustamante and Modern Jamaica* (Kingston: Kingston Publishers Limited, 1975).

Edgar, Robert, "Garveyism in Africa", *Ufahamu*, Vol. VI, No. 3, 1976.

Edwards, Bryan, *An Historical Survey of the French Colony in the Island of St Domingo* (London, 1797).

Ehrenreich, B., and English, D., *For Her Own Good: 150 Years of Experts' Advice to Women* (Garden City, New York: Anchor Press/Doubleday, 1979).

Eisner, Gisela, *Jamaica 1830-1930: A Study in Economic Growth* (Connecticut: Greenwood Press, 1974).

Enloe, Cynthia H., *Ethnic Conflict and Political Development* (Boston: Little, Brown, 1973).

Fanon, Frantz, *Black Skins, White Masks* (New York: Grove Press, 1967).

The Wretched of the Earth (London: McGibbon & Key, 1965).

Foner, Eric, *Nothing But Freedom* (Louisiana, 1983).

Foner, Nancy, *Status and Power in Rural Jamaica* (New York: Teachers College Press, 1974).

Franklin, John Hope, *From Slavery to Freedom,* 4th ed. (New York: Alfred Knopf, 1974).

Frazier, E. Franklin, "Garvey: A Mass Leader", *The Nation,* 18 August 1926, pp. 147-148.

"The Garvey Movement", *Opportunity,* November 1926, pp. 346-348.

French, J., and Ford-Smith, H., "Women, Work and Organization in Jamaica 1900-1944", unpublished research study for the Institute of Social Studies, The Hague, Netherlands, 1985.

Furtado, Celso, *The Economic Development of Latin America* (Cambridge, London: Cambridge University Press, 1971).

Garvey, Amy Ashwood, "Marcus Garvey: Portrait of a Liberator" (typescript in possession of Lionel Yard, Brooklyn, New York).

Geiss, Immanuel, *The Pan-African Movement,* translated by Ann Keep (London: Methuen & Co. Ltd., 1974).

Genovese, E., *Roll, Jordan, Roll: The World the Slaves Made* (New York: Vintage Books, 1976).

Gordon, Derek, *Class, Status and Social Mobility in Jamaica* (Kingston: Institute of Social and Economic Research, 1987).

Gordon, Rev. Ernle, "Garvey and the Black Liberation Theory", *Sunday Gleaner,* 1 Feb. 1987.

Green, William, *British Slave Emancipation* (Oxford: Oxford University Press, 1976).

Hall, Douglas, *Free Jamaica* (London: Caribbean Universities Press, 1969).

Hamilton, Beverly, "Marcus Garvey: Cultural Activist", *Jamaica Journal,* Vol. 20, No. 3, August-October 1987.

Harland, Louis, *Booker T. Washington: The Making of a Black Leader, 1856-1901* (New York: Oxford University Press, 1972).

Hart, Ansell, "The Banana in Jamaica", *Social and Economic Studies,* Vol. 3, No. 2, Sept. 1954.

Hart, Richard, *Slaves Who Abolished Slavery* (Kingston: Institute of Social and Economic Research, 1980), 2 vols.

Henderson, John, *Jamaica* (London: Adam & Charles Black, 1906).

Henriques, Fernando, *Family and Colour in Jamaica* (London: Eyre and Spottiswoode, 1953).

Heuman, Gad, *Between Black and White* (Westport, Connecticut: Greenwood Press, 1981).

Higman, B.W., *Slave Population and Economy in Jamaica, 1807-34* (Cambridge: Cambridge University Press, 1976).

Hill, Errol, "Marcus Garvey and West Indian Drama", May 1971 (unpublished paper).

Hill, Robert A. (ed.), *The Marcus Garvey and Universal Negro Improvement Association Papers* (Berkeley: University of California Press, 1983-1985), 10 vol. projected.

Hill, Robert A., and Bair, Barbara (eds.), *Marcus Garvey: Life and Lessons (A Centennial Companion to The Marcus Garvey and Universal Negro Improvement Association Papers)* (Los Angeles: UCLA Press, 1987).

Hill, Robert A., and Priro, Gregory A., "Africa for the Africans: The Garvey Movement in South Africa 1920-1940", in Marks, Shula, and Trapido, Stanley (eds.), *The Politics of Race, Class and Nationalism in Twentieth Century South Africa* (London: Longman, 1987).

Hogg, D. *Jamaican Religion* (unpublished Ph.D dissertation, Yale University, 1955).

Holt, Felix, "Confessions of a Planter", *Jamaica Advocate,* 6 Sept. 1902.

Hooker, James R., *Black Revolutionary: George Padmore's Path From Communism to Pan-Africanism* (London, 1967).

Ibarra, Jorge, *La inmigración antillana: Desproletarización y desnacionalización de la clase obrera o aceleración de las contradiciónes sociales? Disagregación y marginalización de las luchas sociales o profesiera integración en la clase obrera?* (manuscript, La Habana, 1983).

Idong, A.J., *Internal Politics and Foreign Policy, 1960-1966* (Nigeria: Ibadan University Press, 1974).

Jacques-Garvey, Amy (ed.), *Philosophy and Opinions of Marcus Garvey* (New York: Atheneum, 1986), 2 vols.

Garvey and Garveyism (Kingston: A. Jacques Garvey, 1963).

Jacques-Garvey, Amy, and Essien-Udom, E.U. (eds.), *More Philosophy and Opinions of Marcus Garvey* (London: Frank Cass, 1987).

James, C.L.R., "Walter Rodney and the Question of Power", Race Today pamphlet, 1984.

James, George G.M., "Stolen Legacy" (San Francisco, 1982).

Jayawardena, Kumari, *Feminism and Nationalism in the Third World in the Nineteenth and Early Twentieth Century* (London: Zed, 1986).

Kalb, B., *The Congo Cables* (London: MacMillan, 1982).

Kaufmann, Michael, *Jamaica Under Manley* (London: Zed, 1985).

Kilson, M.L., and Rotberg, R.I. (eds.), *The African Diaspora: Interpretive Essays* (Cambridge: Cambridge University Press, 1976).

Kuper, Adam, *Changing Jamaica* (Kingston: Kingston Publishers, 1976; New York: Routledge and Kegan Paul, 1976).

Kwayana, Eusi, "Walter Rodney", Working Peoples Alliance pamphlet, 1986.

Lamming, George, "*In the Castle of My Skin*, Thirty Years After", *Anales del Caribe* (Havana), 3, 1983.

Langley, J. Ayodele, "Garveyism and African Nationalism", *Race* XI (11), 1969.

Pan-Africanism and Nationalism in West Africa, 1900-1945 (Oxford, 1973).

Laqueur, Walter, *A History of Zionism* (London: Weidenfeld and Nicholson, 1972).

Leakey, L.S.B., *The Progress and Evolution of Man in Africa* (Oxford: Oxford University Press, 1982).

Leslie, Charles, *A New and Exact Account of Jamaica* (Edinburgh: R. Fleming, 1739).

Lewis, Rupert, "Garvey's Forerunners: Love and Bedward", *Race & Class*, 28 (Winter 1987), pp. 29-40.

"Garvey's Significance in Jamaica's Historical Evolution", *Jamaica Journal*, August-October 1987.

"Robert Love: A Democrat in Colonial Jamaica", *Jamaica Journal,* 11 (August 1977), pp. 58-63.

Marcus Garvey: Anti-colonial Champion (London: Karia Press, 1987).

Lewis, Rupert, and Warner-Lewis, Maureen (eds.), *Garvey: Africa, Europe, the Americas* (Kingston: Institute of Social and Economic Research, 1986).

Lewis, Vaughan (ed.), *Size, Self-determination and International Relations: The Caribbean* (Kingston: Institute for Social and Economic Research, 1975).

Lindsay, Louis, "Colonialism and the Myth of Resource Insufficiency in Jamaica", in Lewis, Vaughan (ed.), *Size, Self-Determination and International Relations: The Caribbean* (Kingston: Institute of Economic and Social Research, 1975).

The Myth of Independence: Middle Class Politics and Non-mobilization in Jamaica (Kingston, Institute of Social and Economic Research, 1981).

Logan, Rayford (ed.), *What the Negro Wants* (Chapel Hill: University of North Carolina Press).

Long, Edward, *The History of Jamaica* (London: T. Lowndes, 1774), 2 vols.

Lowenthal, David, *West Indian Societies* (London: Oxford University Press, 1972).

Lumsden, Joyce, "Robert Love and Jamaican Politics" (Ph.D. thesis, University of the West Indies, 1988).

Madden, R.R. Madden, *A Twelvemonth's Residence in the West Indies* (Philadelphia: Carey, Lea and Blanchard, 1835).

Marks, Shula, and Trapido, Stanley (eds.), *The Politics of Race, Class and Nationalism in Twentieth Century South Africa* (London, 1987).

Marson, Una, "Pocomania" (Kingston: Institute of Jamaica, 1938), unpublished manuscript.

Martin, Tony, "International Aspects of the Garvey Movement", *Jamaica Journal,* Vol. 20, No. 3, August-October 1987.

Literary Garveyism (Dover, Massachusetts: The Majority Press, 1983).

Race First: *The Ideological and Organizational Struggles of Marcus Garvey and the Universal Negro Improvement Association* (Westport, Connecticut: Greenwood Press, 1976).

The Pan African Connection (Cambridge, Massachusetts: Schenkman Publishing Company, 1983).

(ed.), *Message to the People: The Course of African Philosophy* (Dover, Massachusetts: The Majority Press, 1986).

(ed.), *The Poetical Works of Marcus Garvey* (Dover, Mass.: The Majority Press, 1983), 2 vols.

Mathurin, Owen Charles, *Henry Sylvester Williams and the Origins of the Pan-African Movement, 1869-1911* (Westport, Connecticut, 1976).

McAdam, Doug, *Political Process and the Development of Black Insurgency, 1930-1970* (Chicago: University of Chicago Press, 1982).

McKay, Claude, *Harlem: Negro Metropolis* (New York: Harcourt Brace Jovanovich, 1968).

Songs of Jamaica (Florida, 1969).

McMorris, Mark D., "Marcus Garvey's Teachings Alive in the 1980s", in "The Black Moses", Marcus Garvey Centennial Supplement, *Carib News,* New York, week ending August 25, 1987.

Meier, August, *Negro Thought in America, 1880-1915: Racial Ideologies in the Age of Booker T. Washington* (Ann Arbor: University of Michigan Press, 1969).

Mills, Charles W., "Race and Class: Conflicting or Reconcilable Paradigms?", *Social and Economic Studies,* Vol. 36 No. 3. 1987, pp. 70-108.

Mills, J.J., *His Own Account of His Life and Times* (Kingston: Collins and Sangster, 1969).

Mintz, S.W., "Creating Culture in the Americas", *Columbia University Forum,* 13 (Spring 1970), pp. 4-11.

"The So-Called World System: Local Initiative and Local Response", *Dialectical Anthropology,* 2 (1977), pp. 253-270.

Mintz, S.W., and Hall, D.G., "The Origins of the Jamaican Internal Marketing System", *Yale University Publications in Anthropology,* No. 57 (1960).

Mintz, S.W., and Price, Richard, *An Anthropological Approach to the Afro-American Past: A Caribbean Perspective* (Philadelphia: ISHI, 1976).

Morris, Aldon, *The Origins of the Civil Rights Movement* (New York: The Free Press, 1984).

Moses, Wilson J., *The Golden Age of Black Nationalism, 1850-1925* (Hamden, Connecticut, 1978).

Munck, Ronaldo, *The Difficult Dialogue: Marxism and Nationalism* (London, 1986).

Munroe, Trevor, "The Marxist Left in Jamaica", ISER Working Paper No. 15, 1977.

Nettleford, Rex, "The Spirit of Garvey: Lessons of the Legacy", *Jamaica Journal,* Vol. 20, No. 3, Aug.-Oct. 1987, p. 3.

Caribbean Cultural Identity: The Case of Jamaica (Kingston: Institute of Jamaica, 1978).

Mirror, Mirror: Identity, Race and Protest in Jamaica (Collins and Sangster, 1970).

Newton, Velma, *The Silver Men: West Indian Labour Migration to Panama, 1850-1914* (Kingston: Institute for Social and Economic Research, 1984).

Nicholls, David, *From Dessalines to Duvalier: Race, Class and National Independence in Haiti* (Cambridge and London: Cambridge University Press, 1979).

Nkrumah, Kwame, *The Challenge of the Congo* (London: Pan Af Books, 1967).

O'Gorman, Pamela, "On Reggae and Rastafarianism – and a Garvey Prophecy", *Jamaica Journal,* Vol. 20, No. 3. Aug.-Oct. 1987.

Okonkwo, R.L., "The Garvey Movement in British West Africa", *Journal of African History,* Vol. 21, 1980.

Olusanya, G.O., "Notes on the Lagos Branch of the Universal Negro Improvement Association", *Journal of Business and Social Studies* (Lagos), I (1970), pp. 133-43.

"The Zikist Movement: A Study in Political Radicalism", *Journal of Modern African Studies,* No. 114, 1975.

Omi, Michael, and Winant, Howard, *Racial Formation in the United States: From the 1960s to the 1980s* (New York: Routledge & Kegan Paul, 1986).

Ottley, Roi, *New World A-Coming* (Cambridge, Mass.: The Riverside Press, 1943; rprt. New York: Arno Press and The New York Times, 1968).

Patterson, Orlando, *The Sociology of Slavery* (London: MacGibbon & Kee Ltd., 1967).

People's National Party, *Principles and Objectives* (Kingston, 1979).

Perez de la Rina, Juan, "La inmigración antillana", *Anuario de Estudios Cubanos 2: La Republica Neo-Colonial* (La Habana, 1973).

Pitman, F.W., "Slavery on British West India Plantations in the Eighteenth Century", *Journal of Negro History,* Vol. II (1926), pp. 585-668.

Post, Ken, *Arise Ye Starvelings* (The Hague: Martinus Nijhoff, 1978).

Strike the Iron: A Colony at War: Jamaica, 1939-1945 (The Hague, 1981), 2 vols.

Ramírez, Amador, *La Guerrita del 20 de mayo o de los Negros* (Palma Soriano, 1980), manuscript.

Reckord, M., "The Slave Rebellion of 1831", *Jamaica Journal,* 3 (June 1969), pp. 25-31.

Reddock, Rhoda "Women, Labour and Struggle in Twentieth Century Trinidad and Tobago 1898-1960", unpublished Ph.D. thesis, University of Amsterdam, 1984.

Redkey, Edwin S., *Black Exodus* (New Haven: Yale University Press, 1969).

Robotham, Don, "The Way of the Cockatoo", *Social and Economic Studies,* Vol. 34, No. 2, 1985.

Rodney, Walter, "The Imperialist Partition of Africa", *Monthly Review,* April 1970, 99, pp. 103-114.

"Towards the Sixth Pan-African Congress: Aspects of the Class Struggle in Africa, the Caribbean and America", in Campbell, Horace (ed.), *Pan Africanism: Documents of the Sixth Pan-African Congress* (Toronto: Afro Caribbean Press, 1975).

Rubin, Vera (ed.), *Comparative Perspectives on Slavery in New World Plantation Societies* (New York, 1977).

Satchell, Veront, "Rural Land Transactions in Jamaica, 1866-1900", M.Phil. thesis, UWI, Mona, 1986.

Scholes, T.E.S., *Glimpses of the Ages, or the "Superior" and "Inferior" Races So-Called, Discussed in the Light of Science and History* (London: John Long, 1905 and 1907), 2 vols.

The British Empire and Alliances, or Britain's Duty to Her Colonies and Subject Races (London: Elliott Stock, Paternoster Row, 1899).

Schuler, M., "Akan Slave Rebellions in the British Caribbean", *Savacou,* Vol. 1, No. 1 (June 1970) pp. 8-31.

Shepherd, V.A., "The Evolution and Expansion of the Pen-keeping Industry in Jamaica: An Introductory Note", paper presented at the Caribbean Societies Seminar, Institute of Commonwealth Studies, London, 9 February 1988.

"The Role of Pens in a Plantation Economy", paper presented to the American History Workshop, Faculty of History, University of Cambridge, May 1986.

Shepherd, V.A., Pens and Penkeepers in a Plantation Society: Aspects of Jamaican Social and Economic History, 1740-1845 (unpublished Ph.D dissertation, Faculty of History, University of Cambridge, 1988).

Simpson, G.E., *Black Religions in the New World* (New York: Columbia University Press, 1978).

Smith, M.G. *Corporations and Society* (London: Duckworth, 1974).

The Plural Society in the British West Indies (Berkeley and Los Angeles: University of California Press, 1965).

Culture, Race and Class in the Commonwealth Caribbean (Kingston: Department of Extra-Mural Studies, University of the West Indies, 1984).

Smith, R.T., "Culture and Social Structure in the Caribbean", *Comparative Studies in Society and History,* VI: 24-44 (1963).

"Family Structure and Plantation Systems in the New World", *Plantation Systems of the New World* Social Science Monograph No. VII (Washington D.C.: Pan American Union, 1959).

Kinship and Class in the West Indies (Cambridge: Cambridge University Press, 1988).

Stavenhagen, Rodolfo, "La Dinámica de las Relaciónes Interetnicas: Clases, Colonialismo y aculturación", in Cardoso, F.H., and Weffort, F. (eds.), *América Latina.*

Stein, Judith, *The World of Marcus Garvey: Race and Class in Modern Society* (Baton Rouge, Louisiana, 1986).

Stephens, Evelyne and John D., *Democratic Socialism in Jamaica* (London, 1986).

Stone, Carl, "Political Trends in Jamaica in the 1980s" (Department of Government, UWI, Mona), unpublished.

Class, State and Democracy in Jamaica, 1986 World Bank Monograph.

Democracy and Clientelism in Jamaica (New Brunswick, New Jersey: Transaction Books, 1980).

Electoral Behaviour and Public Opinion in Jamaica (Kingston, 1974).

The Political Opinions of the Jamaican People (Kingston, 1982).

Stone, Carl, and Brown, Aggrey (eds.), *Essays in Power and Change in Jamaica* (Kingston: Teachers Book Centre, 1977).

Stuckey, Sterling, *Slave Culture* (New York: Oxford University Press, 1987).

Thomas, Herbert, *The Story of a West Indian Policeman* (Kingston: Gleaner Co., 1927).

Thompson, Vincent B., *Africa and Unity: The Revolution of Pan-Africanism* (London: Longman, 1969).

Tolbert, Emory J., *The UNIA and Black Los Angeles* (Los Angeles, 1980).

US Department of Commerce, Bureau of the Census, *The Social and Economic Status of the Black Population in the United States: An Historical View, 1790-1978,* Special Studies Series, No. 80, 1979.

van den Berghe, Pierre L., *Race and Racism: A Comparative Perspective* (New York: John Wiley, 1967).

Wa Thiongo, Ngugi, *Decolonizing the Mind* (New Hampshire: Heinemann, 1986).

Washington, Booker T., *et al., The Negro Problem* (New York: Arno Press and The New York Times, 1969).

Williams, Eric, *Capitalism and Slavery* (Chapel Hill: University of North Carolina Press, 1944).

Wilmore, Gayraud S., *Black Religion and Black Radicalism* (New York: Anchor Books, 1973).

Wilmot, Swithin, "Race, Electoral Violence and Constitutional Reform in Jamaica, 1830-1854", *Journal of Caribbean History,* Vol. 17, 1982, pp. 1-13.

Wilson, Rev. C.A., *Men of Vision: Biographical Sketches of Men Who Have Made Their Mark* (Kingston: Gleaner Co., 1929).

Men With Backbone and Other Pleas for Progress (Kingston: Educational Supply Co., 1913).

Workers' Party of Jamaica, *Programme* (Kingston, 1978).

Index

A.M.E. Church 135
Abeng 253, 287, 290-291
Africa 41, 54, 160, 165, 171, 173, 190, 196
  South 23, 169, 173, 179, 182-183, 188, 313
African Blood Brotherhood 200
African Liberation Support Committee 169
African National Congress 173
African Orthodox Church 135, 138, 157
Ali, Dusé Mohammed 89, 203
American Negro Academy 136
Anderson, Marian 78
Apartheid 26, 182-183, 197, 313
Ashwood, Amy 67, 72, 77
Austin, Diane 279-280
Azikiwe, Nnamdi 191-192, 195

Back to Africa
  see Africa
Bailey, Amy 80-82
Barnett, Ida Wells 69
Bedward, Alexander 123, 129, 136
Bedward, Alexander, Alexander 130
Black business 219
Black Cross Nurses 70, 77-78
Black Madonna 75, 138-139
Black Man, The 149
Black Power 253, 290
Black Star Line 204-210, 223, 300-302
Blackman 149, 156, 159, 162, 231, 236
Blyden, Edward 59, 135, 190, 203
Boesak, Allan 139
Bogle, Paul 44, 280
Bonino, José Miguez 147
Braithwaite, Lloyd 266
Briggs, Cyril 200, 204
Brown, Sam 252
Bustamante, Alexander 124, 129, 302

Cabral, Amilcar 183
Carson, Roy 8, 110
Casimir, J.R. Ralph 145
Chilembwe, John 136, 176
Cipriani, Captain 235
Club Atenas 300-301
Colonialism 56, 168, 195, 233
  and economics 11, 57, 244
  and nationalism 172, 194
  see also Slavery
Communism 209
  see also Marxism
Cone, James H. 136, 161
Crummell, Alexander 135
Cupidon, Ernest 91

Davis, Henrietta Vinton 68, 78
de Lisser, H.G. 230
de Mena, Madame N.L.T. 80-81, 98
Delany, Martin 136
Dingwall, Rev. R. 50, 53
Douglass, Frederick 199
Du Bois, W.E.B. 202, 221-223, 280
Duncan, D.K. 253
Dunlap, Ethel Trew 72
Durham, Vivian 8, 111

Earle, Satira 79
Edelweiss Park 90-91, 93, 97-101, 106
Edwards, Bryan 230-231
Egypt 55, 139, 158, 172, 178, 193-194
Emigration 47, 49, 127, 251-254
Ethiopia 59, 137, 139, 158, 175, 177
Ethiopian Orthodox Church 129-130

Fanon, Frantz 181, 233, 311
Feminism
  see Women's movement
Fortune, T. Thomas 220, 222

Galloway, Lillian 69
Ganja 255, 257, 261

Garvey, Amy Ashwood
see Ashwood, Amy
Garvey, Amy Jacques
see Jacques, Amy
Garvey, Marcus
and business 78, 254, 257-258
and Catholicism 139
and Communism 70
and Cuba 299
and education 234
and Haiti 235
and labour 236, 240
and Methodism 146
and Pan-Africanism 19, 165, 168, 174-175, 177, 184, 186, 189-191, 203-204, 224, 238, 309
and the arts 85, 90-91, 95, 97, 99-100, 103-105
and the Bible 140-141, 145-146, 158, 174
and West Indian federation 235, 305
and women 67-71, 75-76, 79, 96
and Zionism 158-160
concept of God of 137, 145, 150, 156, 158, 161
see also Universal Negro Improvement Association
Ghana 178
Grajales, Mariana 300
Greenidge, Daisy 111
Guerra de los Negros 299
Gutierrez, Gustavo 141

Haiti 235, 311
Hall, Stuart 279
Harrison, Hubert 204
Hart, Daniel 40
Higglers 257
Huiswood, Otto 79, 96

Ikoli, Earnest 194
Indigenismo 19
International African Service Bureau 175
International Monetary Fund 256
Islam 313

Jacques, Amy 72, 77-78
Jamaica Labour Party 129, 250, 252-253, 256-258
Jamaica Workers and Labourers Association 236
Jim Crow 202-204, 314
Johnson, Millard 251
Jones, Claudia 71
Jordon, Edward 40

Kenya 179
Kid Harold 111
Kimbangoism 176
Knibb, Mary Morris 81
Kuper, Adam 265, 277
Kwayana, Eusi 182

Lamming, George 239
Leslie, Charles 24
Liberation theology 135-136, 139, 141-142, 156
Liberia 125, 127, 135, 174, 190, 194, 201
Liberty Hall 93, 98, 100
Love, J. Robert 44, 52-53, 60, 73, 75
Lumumba, Patrice 179
Lyon, Sammy 111
Lyons, George 42

M'Bow, Amadou 314
Maceo, Antonio 305
Manley, Michael 129, 253, 290
Manley, Norman 128
Marley, Bob 128, 182
Maroons 34
Marriott, Alvin 104, 111
Marryshow, T.A. 235
Marson, Una 80, 232
Marxism 169, 183, 243, 253, 278-279, 281, 286-287, 293, 295, 320
see also Communism
McFarlane, J.E. Clare 105
McGuire, Alexander 138, 146, 157-158
McKay, Claude 53, 59, 90
McKenzie, Cathryn 73
Menocal, Mario García 301
Mills, Charles 279
Morant Bay Rebellion 44
Morocco 179
Morúa Law 299
Moton, R.R. 206, 229
Mozambique 184

National Afro-American Council 220
National Afro-American League 220
National Association for the Advancement of Colored People 200, 207, 220, 222
National Congress of British West Africa 192

National Equal Rights League 220
National Negro Business League 206
Nationalism 19, 23, 130, 172, 181, 185, 194-195, 201-204, 206, 210, 216-217, 220, 222, 224, 238, 244, 250, 252, 254, 262, 264, 304
  see also Colonialism and nationalism
Negritude movement 175, 311, 316
Negro Churchman, The 138
Negro Factories Corporation 68
Negro World, The 90, 223
Niagara Conference 221
Nigeria 180, 189, 191, 194-197, 313
Nigerian Youth Movement 194-195
Nkrumah, Kwame 178, 184, 188, 193
Nyasaland 54

Organization of African Unity 168, 178-179, 182, 194, 196
Owen, Chandler 223

Padmore, George 187
Palmer, Edwin 44
Pan African Association 73
Pan-African Conference (1900) 202
Pan-African Congress 181
Pan-Africanism 19, 61, 165, 170, 173, 175, 179, 181, 183, 189, 202, 217, 220
  see also Garvey, Marcus, and Pan-Africanism
Pan-Caribbeanism 305
Panama 49
Pankhurst, Sylvia 77
Patterson, Iris 105, 111
People's Convention 60, 73
People's National Party 129, 250, 252-253, 256, 289-290
People's Political Party 79, 91, 251, 288
Prescott, Ruth 7, 111
Price, Charles 39, 42-43
Property qualifications 42

Race 11, 23-24, 196, 208, 244, 250, 263
  and class 6, 14, 36-38, 40, 56, 79, 249, 261, 265, 278-280, 283
  and conflict 14
  and economics 6, 11, 14, 243, 247, 258, 265, 283
  and education 249
  and nationalism 201, 216-217, 220, 230, 240, 279-280, 293
  and religion 35-36, 58
  and self-determination 232
  Slavery and 26
  see also Racism
Racism 12, 47, 52, 56, 76, 81, 160, 176, 186, 231-232, 238, 247, 261-262, 288-289, 294, 312
  and religion 58, 136
  see also Race
Randolph, A. Phillip 204, 219, 223
Rastafarianism 123, 129, 140, 170, 176, 181, 237, 252, 287, 316
Redkey, Edwin S. 135
Reggae 181
Reid, V.S. 231
Repatriation
  see Africa
Rodney, Walter 178

Same, Rev. Lotin 136
Savage, Augusta 72
Scarlett, Z. Munroe 110
Scholes, Theophilus E.S. 47
Seaga, Edward 252, 258
Selassie, Haile 123, 140, 175, 177
Sharpe, Sam 37
Shirley, Henry 42
Slavery
  Economics and 12, 31, 280
  Resistance to 14, 32-34
Smith, Harold ("Kid Harold") 111
Smith, M.G. 281
Socialism 184, 209
Solanke, Ladipo 192
South Africa
  see Africa, South
Spencer, Adina 79
Stewart, Cyril 111
Stokes, Rose Pastor 70
Stone, Carl 278-279
Struggle 290-291

Tacky 34
Thatcher, Margaret 313
Thomas, Herbert 51
Thompson, Dudley 252
Thorne, Albert 54, 88, 190
Trade unionism 209
Tribalism 25, 196
Trotter, William Monroe 220, 222
Turner, Henry McNeal 135, 222

UNIA
  see Universal Negro Improvement Association
United Fruit Company 302
Universal African Legion 70
Universal African Motor Corps 70
Universal Negro Catechism, The 148
Universal Negro Improvement Association
  19, 67-68, 70-71, 74, 77, 79, 89, 146, 156, 160, 162, 172-173, 191, 199, 201, 204-205, 207-210, 215, 223-224, 303-304, 311
  in Cuba 79
  in Dominica 145
  in Jamaica 79
  in Trinidad 79
  and women
    see Garvey, Marcus, and women

Vickars, Edward 39-41, 43

Walker, Madame C.J. 69
Washington, Booker T. 153, 203, 206, 218-220
West African Students Union 192
Wheatley, Phyllis 69
Williams, H. Sylvester 73
Williams, Ranny 97
Wilmore, Gayraud S. 135, 138
Wilson, C.A. 50, 53, 60
Wilson, Woodrow 223
Wint, D.T. 231
Women's Liberal Club 80-81
Women's movement 73, 80
  see also Garvey, Marcus, and women
Workers' Liberation League 290
Workers' Party of Jamaica 253, 286

Zayas, Alfredo 301

Rupert Lewis is a Senior Lecturer in the Department of Government at the University of the West Indies, Mona, Jamaica. A Garvey scholar of long standing, he is the co-editor, with Maureen Warner-Lewis, of **Garvey, Africa, Europe, the Americas** (1986) and the author of **Marcus Garvey, Anti-Colonial Champion** (1987).

Patrick Bryan is a Senior Lecturer in the Department of History at the University of the West Indies, Mona, Jamaica. His publications include studies of Haiti, the Dominican Republic, and Jamaica.